ADMIRAL HAWKE

Ruddock F. Mackay

ADMIRAL HAWKE

Published by Sapere Books.
20 Windermere Drive, Leeds, England, LS17 7UZ,
United Kingdom

saperebooks.com

First published by Oxford University Press, 1965.

ISBN: 978-1-80055-259-3.

To
Alison,
My Wife

TABLE OF CONTENTS

PREFACE

THE need for a new life of Admiral Hawke is apparent to anyone acquainted with two books: *The Navy in the War of 1739-48* by Admiral Sir Herbert Richmond; and *England in the Seven Nears War* by Sir Julian Corbett. Although published as long ago as 1920 and 1907 respectively they bring home the extent to which relevant material has become available since Burrows's *Life of Edward Lord Hawke* was published in 1883. On the one hand, special mention must be made of the Newcastle and Hardwicke Papers, together with all the work done on them by historians; and on the purely naval side, the scope for research at the Public Record Office and National Maritime Museum has been considerably augmented. All this might fail to prove that a new life of the Admiral was needed if he were not a person of obvious importance; but even a cursory examination of his record leaves no room for doubt on this score. It is sufficient to remember the crucial role of the Navy in British history and then to observe that Hawke's record as a winner of great decisive victories is probably unique. Both Hawke's victories — in 1747 and 1759 — fall into this rare category: they defeated the enemy's navy, in a major war, to an extent precluding reasonable hope of recovery. Whether or not even Nelson can be credited with a similar achievement will depend on the status accorded to the Battle of the Nile. Did it mark the point at which the enemy's navy was defeated beyond hope of recovery? It is sometimes forgotten, also, that the Seven Years' War was uniquely triumphant for Britain, and that, apart from the crowning victory at Quiberon Bay, Hawke's sustained blockade of

France was fundamental to the success of Pitt's enlightened grand-strategy. Considering the far-reaching consequences of British success in the Seven Years' War — especially for the long-term development of North America and India — it seems extraordinary that the life of Admiral Hawke has not received more attention.

Burrows's book was, of course, indispensable for writing a new biography of the Admiral — not least because some of the documents printed or used by that biographer have since disappeared. However, even on the side of Hawke's domestic life, Burrows does not seem to have had access to many of the private papers now made available by the Earl of Rosse.

The object, then, of writing this book has been to use the extant primary and secondary material to give a fuller appreciation and assessment of an outstandingly successful commander, who was also possessed of many sympathetic qualities. With regard to the selection of material, it might be as well to defend the inclusion of Hawke's experience as a squadron-commander in 1744-5. Although the operations are of minor importance in themselves, knowledge of them is necessary to an understanding of how, within a month of his rather fortuitous promotion to a junior Admiral's post, Hawke was able to take command of England's principal battle-fleet and carry through a difficult strategy to decisive triumph. In general, an attempt is made to clarify Hawke's standing as a strategist and tactician, and a re-appraisal is made of his hitherto suspect record in amphibious operations. The fresh examination of his relations with Pitt may also be of some general interest. Finally, it is hoped that this book will make some contribution towards scholarship in two spheres outside the limits of pure biography: eighteenth-century naval tactics and mid-century naval administration in time of peace. It is suggested that, owing especially to the contributions of Hawke and Boscawen, the usually received account of those tactics needs revision; and that the respective standing accorded to Anson, Hawke, and Sandwich as peacetime First Lords of the Admiralty requires modification.

It might be well to add a remark about corrections made, in the text or in footnotes, to various points contained in the aforenamed works by Richmond and Corbett. These corrections are made, not in any carping spirit, but rather as a token of admiration for these works. They provided much of the basis and motive power of this biography; but the fact that they tend inevitably to be regarded as authoritative makes it desirable to point out any errors that have come to light.

R.F.M.

Dartmouth

LIST OF ABBREVIATIONS

The following abbreviations have been used in footnotes:

H. — Hawke.
H.P.P. — Hawke family's private papers.
O.L. — Hawke's out-letters.
I.L. — Hawke's in-letters.
L.B. — Hawke's letter books.
O.B. — Hawke's order books.
Ad. — Admiralty.
S.P.Dom.(N.) — State Papers, Domestic, Naval.
P.R.O. 30/8 — Chatham Papers.
T. — Treasury.
N.M.M. — National Maritime Museum.
Add.MSS. — Additional Manuscripts.
N.R.S. — Navy Records Society.
Hist.MSS.Com. — Historical Manuscripts Commission.
D.N.B. — Dictionary of National Biography.

In footnotes, published books are usually indicated by the use of the author's or editor's name. In such cases, further details will be found in the List of Sources.

NOTE ON DATES

The years are given in New Style throughout; the dates of the month, before 1752, are in Old Style.

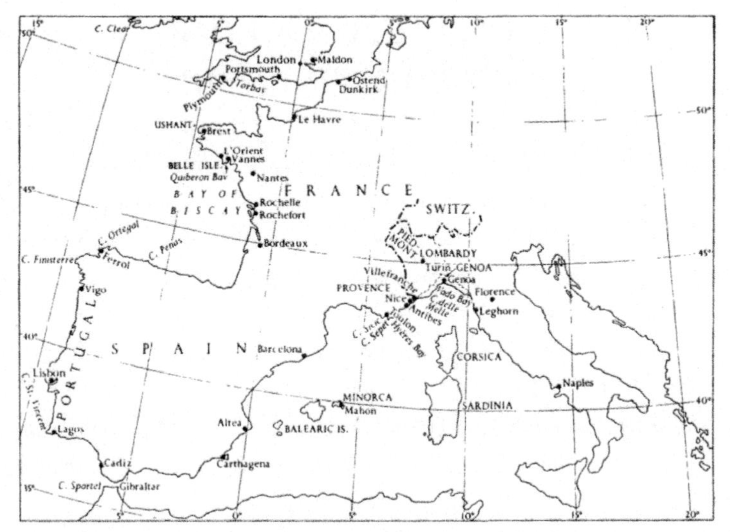

Places in Europe which are mentioned in the text.

CHAPTER I: A LONG APPRENTICESHIP

EVENING had already closed in when, on 8 February 1744, the British Mediterranean fleet came to an anchor in Hyères Bay, near Toulon. About a dozen miles away to the S.W. the twenty-eight ships of the combined Franco-Spanish fleet were already assembling. M. de Court, the French Commander-in-Chief, sought to drive Mathews's thirty ships away from the coast of Provence. Then, with the advantage of seaborne supplies and reinforcements, the French and Spanish troops would be able to advance eastwards along the coast against the Sardinian and Austrian forces in N.W. Italy.

Admiral Mathews was anxious. The light wind was with the enemy. De Court might seize his opportunity and attack while the British were still embayed in Hyères Road. Yet he might equally seek to draw them away from the coast. Mathews reminded himself that his principal duty was to support the Sardinians and Austrians. He also thought angrily of the slowness of his ships, foul-bottomed after their long spell at sea, and of the Admiralty's refusal to send out adequate reliefs. From the very time of his appointment in 1742, their Lordships had seemed determined to subject him to a maximum of annoyance by insisting, despite all his objections, that he should have Lestock as his Vice-Admiral. The Mediterranean service had proved complicated and troublesome enough without his having to endure the presence of such a man as second-in-command. Nor was Mathews's temper improved by his recurrent ailment, the gravel. Now that the French had clearly decided, at last, openly to enter the war against Britain, Mathews was absorbed in his strategic problem; and, as the gloom deepened around his flagship, the *Namur*, he did not welcome the news that Mr. Lestock was alongside in a boat and wished to converse with his Commander-in-Chief.

Mathews's nickname, 'Il Furibondo', was not inappropriate. Richard Lestock, Esq., Vice-Admiral of the White and a martyr to the gout, was equally quick to take offence. He had bitterly resented his earlier supercession by Mathews in the Mediterranean command. However, as he made his way up to Mathews's quarter-deck, his predominant motives may well have been purely patriotic; but, if this was so, evaporation of these motives soon followed.

Lestock inquired whether the Admiral had any orders to give him. Mathews felt it adequate to reply that he had no orders to give. He then terminated the interview by observing that it was a cold night; and his subsequent assertion that this remark was occasioned by concern for the Vice-Admiral's health was generally received with scepticism.

The humiliated Lestock, hunched up in the stern of his boat, bobbed away on the slow journey back to his ship; and in view of his conduct over the next few days, it is reasonable to assume that the idea of revenge was not absent from his meditations. It was clear enough that the situation of the fleet was critical; yet Mathews had declined to discuss with his Vice-Admiral any plans, general or tactical. He appeared to assume that the events of any battle which came about would be adequately covered by the General Printed Sailing and Fighting Instructions. If so, he was likely to be undeceived. The unforeseeable crises of any engagement would call for initiative on the part of individual commanders, and then the Admiral would wish that he had condescended to give some guidance on the kind of initiative likely to implement his intentions. Let him look, in the agony of an uncertain and crucial moment, for inspired comprehension on the part of his Vice-Admiral, and gladness would quicken the heart of Richard Lestock — it would indeed!

While the leading British admirals were thus occupied, there was one in particular of their captains whose thoughts were more exclusively concerned with the coming engagement. Edward Hawke had been in the active service of the Royal Navy for eighteen years and yet he had had no opportunity to show his quality as a fighting officer. This was not for want of inclination, though it should not be inferred that he was a bloodthirsty person. In his desire for a share of honour and prize-money, he held the attitudes of the average officer of his day. Where he might have been regarded as somewhat eccentric was in his suppression of profanity aboard ship, and in his unaffected piety.

Although still without experience of battle, Hawke was nevertheless a complete officer. In his lifetime, disease and shipwreck claimed many more lives than did fighting at sea, and Hawke, in combating these scourges, had found ample exercise for his careful foresight, courage, and intelligence. Now the more dramatic and rewarding test of battle was at hand. He was calm in the knowledge that he would not be found wanting.[1]

Edward Hawke was born in 1705. His father, whose Christian name was likewise Edward, was a barrister of Lincoln's Inn. His mother, Elizabeth, originated from the Yorkshire family of Bladen, who numbered amongst the gentry. Her father, like her husband, had been a barrister of Lincoln's Inn.

---

[1] Richmond, i and ii. Detailed refs, given later.

The baby Edward's father has left an impression of the manner of man he was, through having published 'A Poem upon the Amendments Made to the Law' in 1707. In his preface he wrote: 'Liberty is the most valuable treasure Human Nature can possess; an equal Blessing to the Prince and his People, rendering the one secure from any attempts of his exasperated Subjects, and the other happy under the Government of a reasonable Monarch.' In the poem, he explained, would be found a history of the vicissitudes of liberty in England. 'As for the poem itself, Mankind may censure it as they please; 'tis the first, and in all probability will be the last, I shall ever trouble them with.'

Edward Hawke the elder can fairly be credited with some part in the future Admiral's capacity for self-expression, his liberal inclinations, and, it would appear, his modesty.

However, in many ways, it was the baby Edward's uncle on his mother's side who was to prove his most important relation. Colonel Martin Bladen was born in 1680, became Comptroller of the Mint (1714-17) and then a Commissioner of Trade and Plantations (1717-46) — a position of moderate influence in that age of jobbery. Seeing that Edward Hawke senior died in 1718, Colonel Bladen can, remembering his subsequent help to the young Hawke, be credited with placing the lad as a Volunteer in the Royal Navy. This rank was roughly equivalent to that of the modern Cadet, though a Volunteer (despite the fact that he had to enter by the age of 16) was appointed by warrant, in the same way as a Boatswain or Gunner. To become a commissioned officer a youngster had to pass through either the rank of Midshipman or that of master's Mate; serve five years in seagoing ships; and, at the age of 20 or over, pass an examination for the rank of Lieutenant. Most officer-candidates in Hawke's lifetime went to sea at 13, as Captain's Servants, and later became Midshipmen.[2]

Therefore when, at the age of 15, Edward Hawke went aboard His Majesty's ship *Seahorse* (20)[3], as a Volunteer, he was beginning his sea service at an age when many of his contemporaries, having entered as Captain's Servants, were hardened old salts of two years' experience in ships. It was on 10 February 1720 that he mounted the sloop's gang-plank. She was being fitted out in wet dock at Deptford by Captain Thomas Durell. For the last few months Britain had been engaged in a largely Mediterranean war with Spain, and great must have been the disappointment of the newly joined Volunteer when, a fortnight after he had joined the Navy, it was announced that hostilities were to cease forthwith.

However, there was little time for sitting about and moping. The *Seahorse* had to be manned and made ready for sea, whether it were peace or war. On 29 February Captain Durell was complaining bitterly to Burchett, Secretary of the Admiralty, that he could find 'but few seamen willing to enter'. Burchett's helpful reply was to the effect that Durell was to use his best endeavours to obtain more men. Seeing that conditions of service in the Navy were much less attractive than those in the merchant service, the usual method of recruitment was to send out press gangs which would scour the ports for seamen. If the gang found a sailor, whether in the arms of a prostitute or elsewhere, the next step was to knock him over the head and convey him to the ship concerned. Midshipmen were often sent out in charge of these gangs, and

---

[2] Burrows, pp. 109-10. D.N.B.: Col. Martin Bladen. H.P.P., various. For length of sea service to qualify for Lieutenant's examination, see Ad. 107/3, *circa* f.153.

[3] Indicates number of guns borne.

there is every likelihood that the youthful Hawke helped to persuade seamen of the spiritual satisfaction to be derived from serving His Majesty, George I.

Burchett's advice did not provide Durell with an easy solution to his problems. On 11 March the latter reported, 'I can hardly make a boat's crew, for in my life I never knew such a scarcity of seamen. The number of press gangs, I believe, has hunted them all into the country.' He wanted orders to be given, through the Navy Board, for the Dockyards to fit the ship, while he used all his crew for a fulltime pursuit of more seamen. These methods bore fruit. By 8 April the *Seahorse* was in the Thames and nearly ready to sail. Durell could muster fifty men. However, frustration now suddenly appeared in a more dramatic form when, on the 9th, a merchant ship ran into the *Seahorse*, smashed her bowsprit and did structural damage. After a further spell in dock Mr. Hawke at last felt under his feet the spirited movement of a fighting ship, albeit a very small one. After completing his complement in the Downs — which involved seizing men from merchant vessels returning home — the Captain received information about his forthcoming service. He was to fit the ship in Portsmouth for a voyage to New England.[4]

By 21 June Durell was writing to Burchett about the order that he was to convey to his post 'the Governor of New York and his family, which I apprehend is pretty numerous'. He doubted the adequacy of his cabin accommodation. Burchett eventually replied that their Lordships of the Admiralty would have cabins built in the steerage for the Governor's family and retinue. In the middle of July, Hawke and the rest of the crew

[4] Ad. 6/12, f. 194: H.'s warrant as Volunteer. Ad. 107/3. Ad. 1/1694, 29 Feb. (and endorsement), 11 Mar., 8, 23 Apr., 22 May 1720.

threading their way through the Governor's progeny, the *Seahorse* set out on her voyage across the Atlantic.

Hawke thus learnt at an early age how a ship's company, consisting largely of hardened men who wished themselves elsewhere, was licked into shape. Durell was probably a good leader, since his log shows little record of punishments. As Captain he could order, on his own authority, up to twelve lashes with a cat-o'-nine-tails for the recalcitrant. For important offences, such as deliberate disobedience or desertion (which was, not unnaturally, a common crime), a court martial was necessary. Seeing that such courts not infrequently awarded 200 or even 300 lashes, and the recipients usually survived, a dozen lashes must have been considered a mere bagatelle in those robust times.

Shortly after the *Seahorse* had delivered the Governor and his family at New York, it looked as though the 15-year-old Hawke might see not only broad waters but a little fighting as well. Pirates from Martinique were proving a worry to British-American traders plying near Barbados, and particularly ships taking salt from the West Indies to Boston. This salt was of vital importance to the colonial fisheries. Therefore in December 1720 the *Seahorse*, now bearing 104 men, was on her way down to Barbados. Her transit was punctuated by a tempest, which blew out her mainmast. However, February 1721 found the little ship scouring the seas for pirates, but reports that the latter had shifted their domicile from Martinique, combined with further storm damage, caused Durell to put back to Barbados. He knew that a fleet of merchant ships bound for New England was awaiting escort home; so Hawke's first hope of combat proved abortive.

A four-year period of routine trade-protection followed. Refits were carried out in New England, usually at Boston.

Although the dangers of the sea were very much more imminent than the violence of the enemy, the *Seahorse* performed her useful task without serious mishap. Hawke gained experience in seamanship, in handling men and in the processes of refit and repair. He also changed his rank on two occasions. In February 1722 he became a Midshipman Ordinary and in April 1724 he was rated Midshipman.[5]

On 24 August 1724 Durell received Admiralty orders to return to England. The *Seahorse* was ready to sail in early October but violent gales caused damage and she had to put into Lisbon for repairs. On 30 January 1725 Hawke experienced a homecoming to Spithead — the first of many. Then he went with the ship round to Galleon's Reach in the Thames. Durell was clearly satisfied with Hawke's performance as a Midshipman, for he put him forward for the Lieutenant's examination, which he duly passed on 2 June 1725. Pepys had laid it down that Midshipmen must attain the age of 20 before they could take the examination, but young men with influential relatives were able to break this rule. It is significant that Hawke did not. Moreover, Colonel Bladen's support proved of only moderate efficacy over the next few years, for it was not until April 1729 that a Lieutenant's commission was made out for Hawke. Amongst those who managed to distinguish themselves in the eighteenth-century Navy, Anson and Boscawen illustrate the usefulness of more powerful 'interest' than that of a Commissioner of Trade and Plantations. When Anson had just turned 19 Sir John Norris wrote (on 17 May 1716) to the Admiralty Secretary that he intended 'to commission Mr. George Anson, who is cousin to my Lord Parker', Lord Chief Justice of England. As for

---

[5] Ad. 1/1694, 21 June, 12 July, 24 Dec. 1720, 17 Feb., 10 May 1721, ff. Ad. 107/3, f. 153.

Boscawen, he passed the Lieutenant's examination on 8 May 1732; and the fact that he had to wait only seventeen days before receiving his commission was not unconnected with his being the third son of the first Viscount Falmouth.[6]

On the day of his passing the Lieutenant's examination Hawke was entered aboard the *Kinsale*, of 40 guns, as an Able Seaman. There was nothing abnormal in this. Many of Hawke's contemporaries mixed service as A.B.s with their time as Midshipmen. While the ship cruised off the West Coast of Africa, visiting the trading stations at the mouth of the Gambia and on the shores of Sierra Leone, and then went across to the West Indies, Hawke tasted to the full what it meant to serve on the lower deck. On 2 January 1727 he was again advanced to Midshipman, by which time the ship had been on the pestilential West Indian station for six months. The *Kinsale* dropped anchor in Plymouth Sound on 24 May 1727 and on 18 June she was decommissioned at Woolwich. She remained laid up until the exigencies of war brought her back into service in January 1742.[7]

Between 1725 and 1729 Hawke may well have had regular recourse to the Psalmist's philosophical comment, 'For promotion cometh neither from the east nor from the west: nor yet from the south.' However, it did come at length from their Lordships of the Admiralty. The commission was dated 11 April 1729, and on the same day Hawke joined the *Portland* (50), under the command of Captain Rowzier, which was lying at Spithead. It was a tall, strongly built, good looking, cheerful

---

[6] ibid. The candidates' ages were not recorded on the certs, till Aug. 1733 (f. 221). Ad. 1/1694, 23 Sept., 23 Nov. 1724, 31 Jan., 9 Apr. 1725. D.N.B.: Anson and Boscawen.

[7] Ad. 36/1642; 36/1659: Kinsale, Ship's Bk. No. 224. Ad. 107/3, 230, for good example of mixture of time as Mid. and A.B. — John Wilson. Ad. 51/501.

yet diffident young officer who, at the age of 24, mounted the *Portland*'s gangway. He was destined to see a great deal of this ship over the next thirty years. In 1729 he had his meals with the other Lieutenants, the Master, Carpenter, Boatswain, Purser, and Chaplain in the Wardroom, which was in the after part of the upper gun-deck. The Captain's accommodation, which he was one day to occupy, was immediately overhead. Now, however, he was the 3rd and most junior Lieutenant, which entailed being Lieutenant-at-Arms, and his small cabin was probably to be found in the after part of the orlop deck — that is, on the deck below the lower gun-deck. This was a nauseous place with no portholes whatever, though Hawke had doubtless learnt to value a little privacy by this date.[8]

Captain Rowzier took the ship out of Spithead on 19 May 1729 for a month's cruise in the Downs. Off Beachy Head they stopped the merchantman *Whidah*, bound for Danzig, and in Hawke's brief words, 'We impressed four of her men and sent five of ours.' For not only were all seamen on shore liable to be waylaid by these press gangs, but even on the high seas well-remunerated freedom might in a twinkling be transformed into ill-rewarded servitude. In this case the *Whidah* appears to have benefited, numerically, from the exchange, but it is safe to assume that she proceeded on her way worse off as regards efficiency.

On the 17 June the *Portland* sailed back into Spithead. Under the appropriate heading of 'Remarkable Observations and Accidents' Hawke noted in his log: 'The Commissioner paid two months' pay.' The lateness of the pay, apart from its

[8] Ad. 6/14, f. 22; 51/709. N.M.M.: H.'s log as 3rd Lt. of *Portland*, 11 Apr.-24 Nov. 1729. H.'s appearance inferred from later portraits and H. Walpole's description in *Memoirs of the Reign of George II*, ed. Lord Holland, London, 1846; iii, 50.

inadequacy, was one of the scandals of the age. There was no redress until 1797, and even then a merchant seaman's pay remained about three times as big as that of his unfortunate naval contemporary.

Otherwise, this period in port is given colour by Hawke's observation of 20 November. The weather had been wild in the morning, but as it had moderated by the afternoon the ship's yawl was sent ashore for fresh meat. On the way back the yawl was 'by misfortune overset and the surgeon and four others drowned'.[9]

On 25 November Hawke came under the command of a new Captain, namely Peter Warren of the *Leopard* (50). Although the ship remained in Spithead till it was paid off on 22 December, this was to prove an important appointment for the young officer, whose road to fortune depended principally on his merit. For Peter Warren was destined to command the naval forces at the taking of Louisbourg in 1745 and to succeed to the command of the Channel Fleet in 1747, a juncture which was to present Hawke with a unique opportunity. It is clear that Hawke made a good impression on Warren during this month in port at the end of 1729. However, on the paying-off of the *Leopard*, Lieutenant Hawke remained on shore for a year and a half, during which time he was at least fortunate enough to receive half-pay (1 January 1730 to 18 May 1731).[10]

Direct evidence about Hawke's character during these early years is scanty. However, seeing that his later life reveals so consistent a pattern of qualities and attitudes, it can reasonably be inferred that as a young officer he was energetic and

---

[9] Log, *Portland*. See 7.

[10] Ad. 6/12, f. 42. N.M.M.: H.'s log as 3rd Lt. of *Leopard*, 25 Nov.-22 Dec. 1729. Ad. 25/25.

ambitious, though socially unobtrusive. This spell of half-pay would have been irksome to him, and it was doubtless with alacrity that he went back to sea as 4th Lieutenant of the *Edinburgh* (64) in 1731.

On 14 July Sir Charles Wager, who became First Lord of the Admiralty two years later, took twelve ships of the line out to the Mediterranean. Seeing that England had spent a fair proportion of the century in conflict with Spain, and, as late as 1726, had mounted damaging blockades against her, it might surprise the uninitiated to learn that Wager's mission was to help the Spanish to transport 6,000 troops from Barcelona to Leghorn. Underlying this enterprise was Robert Walpole's recent revival of the English alliance with the Austrian Empire and Holland. The conditions of the Anglo-Austrian alliance provided for settlement of the claims of Don Carlos (later Charles III of Spain) to the duchies of Tuscany and Parma. England, after all, was always interested in being able to use the privileges won from Spain at the Treaty of Utrecht (1713). Thus Hawke was given a chance to look over naval forces belonging to a country destined to cause him much irritation — albeit little straightforward resistance. He faithfully recorded how Wager dealt with the problem of territorial waters. On 25 July they were off the Portuguese coast, and shots were freely projected in order to stop French merchantmen and Portuguese warships, which were then invited to give an account of themselves.

After putting into Cadiz and Altea the squadron reached Barcelona, where Hawke observed some anachronistic craft — 'seven sail of Spanish galleys, with several transports loaded with soldiers for Leghorn'. After accompanying these transports to Leghorn, Hawke saw the Balearic Islands — scene of Byng's despair and his own frustration in 1756. From

16 to 19 November Wager's fleet visited Gibraltar; thence it headed for home. The Bay of Biscay fully lived up to its autumnal reputation. On one day, progress amounted to six miles. On another, ground was lost. It was not until 11 December that the squadron staggered into St. Helens; and the loss of sails and tackle suffered by the *Edinburgh* was reflected aboard the other ships.[11]

The year 1732 saw Hawke aboard the frigate *Scarborough* (24). Thomas Durell, under whom he had served as a Volunteer and Midshipman from 1720 to 1725, was Captain, and may have asked that Hawke should be his second-in-command. The *Scarborough* spent much of the year in Boston, Massachusetts, from whence she took the Governor on a visit to Falmouth. When he came on board, this dignitary was saluted with 13 guns, and, Hawke noted, 'at his going away with 15 guns'. Although one might conclude that enthusiasm rose to its height on his departure, such a zenith of explosive celebration was doubtless required by the General Orders and Instructions.

However, Hawke's time as a Lieutenant was coming to an end. After taking passage to Port Royal, Jamaica, he climbed aboard the *Kingston* (60). He took up the post of 1st Lieutenant, and seeing that Commodore Sir Chaloner Ogle was flying his broad pennant aboard her, Hawke might have hoped that further preferment was in the offing. This proved to be the case. It has been written that Hawke owed his promotion, first to Master and Commander and then to Post Captain, largely to the backing of Colonel Bladen; but his lifelong gratitude to Ogle, implied by a letter which he wrote to Ogle's widow in 1760 and also by his naming one of his sons after the

---

[11] Ad. 6/14, f. 77. Basil Williams, *The Whig Supremacy*, 1962; p. 192. N.M.M.: H.'s log as 4th Lt. of *Edinburgh*, 19 May-27 Dec. 1731.

Commodore, indicates that his promotion was a matter for Ogle. It may also be concluded that Ogle promoted him principally on merit. After three months aboard the *Kingston* on the Jamaican coast, Hawke, with a commission dated 13 April 1733, entered on his first command.[12]

To become Master and Commander of the sloop *Wolf*, of 10 guns, might not have been everyone's ambition. On 16 July 1732 Captain Richard Orchard died. Normally this melancholy event would have been recorded in the log of the sole Lieutenant under the heading of 'Remarkable Observations and Accidents'. However, in this case a scrawl against the date 16 July puts the matter succinctly enough: 'Capn. dead, Lieut, dead.'

The impression of mortality among commanding officers of the *Wolf* is heightened by a glance at the record for Captain Thomas Aikenhead, who succeeded Orchard and made way for Hawke. On 10 April 1733 his Lieutenant noted the manner of his passing thus: 'Moderate and fair weather. At 3 p.m. Captain Thomas Aikenhead departed this life.'

The *Wolf* was then lying in Port Royal, so Aikenhead was buried ashore with prudent celerity. From the time of Drake fever had been the scourge of British seamen serving in the West Indies, and was doubtless the usual cause of calamity aboard the *Wolf*. The Lieutenant duly welcomed his new Commander on 14 April 1733, when 'Captain Edward Hawke came aboard and took on him the charge of Master and Commander. He saluted the Commodore with 13 guns. He returned 11. Had a survey on our Purser.'[13]

---

[12] Ad. 6/14, f. 97,194. H.'s log as Lt. of *Scarborough*, 2 Feb.-26 Sept. 1732. cf. Burrows, p. 118. M.S. 108, H. to Lady Kingston, 9 Feb. 1760. H.'s log as 1st Lt. of *Kingston*, 24 Dec. 1732-12 Apr. 1733.

[13] Ad. 6/14, f. 194. N.M.M.: Lt.'s log, *Wolf*, 13 Apr.-3 May 1733.

On 4 May this Lieutenant handed over his duties to one Policarpus Taylor, thanks to whom Hawke's movements in the *Wolf* may be followed. This was a period of reversion to the usual unfriendly relations between Britain and Spain. Indeed, in the New World, enmity had remained the rule. The Spanish were officious in guarding their near-monopoly of West Indian and Central American trade, while the British traders persistently infringed the Spanish laws and the Treaty of Utrecht.

Before the end of May Hawke sailed with ten merchantmen under his not very powerful escort, scanning the horizon of those glinting waters for Spanish *guarda-costa* vessels. However, he saw his convoy safely through the zone of possible molestation and returned to Port Royal. In July and August he saw five more vessels out into the Atlantic and then put back to Port Royal for a refit. Ships' bottoms required frequent cleaning in those warm tropical waters.

The refit, partly carried out at Port Antonio, was not completed until October. During a further two and half months' cruising near Jamaica, the only moment of particular interest was an encounter with a French sloop which reported that 'the French and the Emperor had declared war with each other'. However, no news of British involvement followed.

Ogle took out his squadron, including the *Wolf*, for a week's cruise in February 1734. By the 27th of that month, they were at anchor in Port Antonio. The Commodore now proceeded to save Hawke from the fate to which commanders of the *Wolf* were accustomed. On 21 March, Lieutenant Policarpus Taylor recorded: 'Captain Hawke being removed into the *Flamborough*, Captain William Boutflower came on board.' That this removal was timely from Hawke's point of view is brought out by a letter which still lies in Taylor's log. It is from the Lords of the Admiralty to the Navy Board and dated 2 September 1735.

> Gentlemen,
>
> We do hereby desire and direct you to cause the wages due to Lieutenant Policarpus Taylor, for his service on board His Majesty's sloop the *Wolf* to be paid to him, if you have no other objection thereto than the want of a certificate from Captain Boutflower that he complied with his General Printed Instructions during the time he commanded her, which cannot be obtained by reason of the said Captain dying abroad.
>
> We are, Your affectionate friends
>
> Cha. Wager
> Tho. Clutterbuck
> H. Powlett.[14]

Hawke's appointment to the *Flamborough* took effect on 20 March 1734. At the age of 29 he had risen to Post Captain. This was as high a rank as an officer of middling ability, even though reinforced by influence, could normally hope to attain; but an excellent officer, lacking any influence, would be extremely fortunate to get as far. Hawke never forgot the vicissitudes of his own promotion, and, as an Admiral, he persistently pressed the claims of meritorious officers. As far as he himself was concerned, now that he was on the list of Post Captains, his name would inevitably come up for consideration for promotion to flag rank when he became sufficiently senior.

It is easy to imagine Hawke's satisfaction as he looked over the *Flamborough*. She was a frigate of 24 guns — 12 on each side of a single gun-deck. The quarter-deck, leading to the

---

[14] N.M.M.: Log of Lt. Policarpus Taylor, *Wolf*, 4 May 1733-4 Mar. 1734.

captain's cabin in the stern of the ship, covered the after part of the gun-deck. Her complement was about 200 men.[15]

During the seventeen months of this command, Hawke cruised near Jamaica, and went through the usual series of refits. Violent storms provided the only excitement. On one occasion, the *Flamborough* was at anchor when a tempest caught her. The vicious tossing of the ship, the shrieking of the wind and the tumultuous onslaught of the sea finally ceased. Hawke took stock of the tale of broken masts, tackle, and bowsprit. He had a jury foremast put up and rigged, and a spare mizen topmast became a fore topmast. These measures sufficed to get the sorry-looking *Flamborough* back to Port Royal. Although few commanders in the days of sail can more often have had to bring a ship through a storm, with heavy surf booming on a near-by lee shore, no ship in which Hawke sailed as Captain or Admiral was ever lost. There is no record that he even went aground. No one could have been better prepared for that supreme test of seamanship which, at a tremendous moment, it would lie with him to accept or reject as, with the main fleet of England, he raced to the entrance of Quiberon Bay.

Finally, the *Flamborough* was called home to Spithead and, after paying off the ship on 5 September 1735, Hawke went ashore on half-pay for a period of four years. There were 104 captains on the half-pay list: the 20 most senior received 10d. a day; then came 30 at 8d.; 40, including Hawke, at 6d.; and 14 at 5d. During the latter part of 1736, there was a reduction in these rates, and Hawke found himself on 5d. a day.[16]

Meanwhile the animosity between England and Spain continued to simmer. The Spanish always resented the concessions made to English trade by the Treaty of Utrecht,

---

[15] Ad. 6/14, f. 219. Namier, pp. 28, 33-4. Ad. 51/4190.
[16] ibid. Ad. 25/27.

which included the monopoly of supplying slaves to the Spanish West Indies; and the English retention of Gibraltar and Minorca was a perpetual irritant. Moreover, English traders persisted in smuggling and other illegal practices in the West Indies. The Spanish *guarda-costas*, for their part, constantly exceeded their brief and often attacked English shipping in an indiscriminate and indeed piratical manner. In 1738 an angry House of Commons was roused to warlike ardour by the recited grievances of one Captain Jenkins, whose ear, having been some years earlier separated from its owner's head by a Spanish coast-guard, was to give its name to the war that began in 1739.

While the brilliant but irascible Admiral Vernon was approaching the West Indies, about to make good his boast that he could take Porto Bello with six ships, Hawke, on 30 July 1739, was appointed to the *Portland*, then at Spithead. It must have been with gratification that he boarded her as Captain, this 50-gun ship, in which he had served as 'youngest Lieutenant' ten years earlier. But, when the time came to sail, he would leave a large part of his heart behind in England.[17]

On 3 October 1737 he had been married at the chapel of Somerset House to Catharine Brooke. He was then 32 years old; she was 17. They had before them nineteen years of marriage, before they were parted by Catharine's death. After that untimely event, Hawke set it down that she was 'the best wife, the best mother and the best of friends, for truth, engaging tenderness and good nature, the delight of all that knew her'. And one of her sons later recalled that 'the beauty of [her] person was excelled only by the accomplished elegance of her mind'. She was, by her own account, of a somewhat reserved disposition; but, despite the disparity of years between

---

[17] Richmond, i Chs. 1-3. Williams, op. cit., p. 197-8. Ad. 51/4294.

herself and her husband, her life with him was marked by complete candour and devotion. They based their marriage on the teaching of Mother Church; and there is no doubt that their lives were thereby infused with steadiness and dignity.[18]

They lived at first with — or near — Colonel Bladen at Aldborough Hatch in the Parish of Barking, a locality which was, one would guess, more fashionable than it is today. However, when Hawke went down to Portsmouth in July 1739 to take up his long-awaited command, he had to leave his young wife behind in Barking with two very small daughters. Whether from the all-too-prevalent smallpox or some other cause, one of them died on 13 September and was buried in Barking churchyard. Soon after the burial Catharine went down to Portsmouth to be with her husband.[19]

However, Hawke did not allow domestic misfortune to slacken his efforts on behalf of the sea service, and on 18 September he proposed in a letter to Burchett that the *Portland* should 'go once every year, in the hurricane season, to Boston in New England to clean, instead of going to Antigua'. It would take little extra time, would benefit the crew's health, and reduce expense. With a dislike of waste that was thoroughly characteristic — despite the fact that he had spent all his working life in an inherently wasteful Service — he urged that, while stores were cheaper at Boston than they were at Antigua, masts and yards could be bought for even less than in England.

Their Lordships approved the plan.[20]

---

[18] H.P.P. Certified copy of entry in Register of Marriages. At Church of St. Nicolas, N. Stoneham: tombstone, central aisle; monument. H.P.P., Letters from Cath. H. to H.

[19] Burrows, pp. 120-2. Ad. 51/4294.

[20] Ad. 1/1881, 18 Sept. 1739, and endorsement.

While all the bustle of fitting the *Portland* was in train, Hawke was doubtless relieved to receive a letter from Colonel Bladen, dated 2 October, in which he reassured him about Catharine's immediate future. She must have been low in spirits, what with the loss of her baby daughter and her husband's imminent departure. The Colonel wrote: 'If it may contribute anything to the satisfaction of your mind to know that during your absence all possible care shall be taken of my niece, be assured that, as well for her own sake as for yours, nothing shall be wanting that either my wife or I can do for her, and that we will endeavour to make her abode with us agreeable to her.'

But there was further sorrow in store for 'Kitty' and her 'Ned'.[21]

Hawke sailed from Spithead on 23 October but the weather was so bad and the winds so persistently contrary that he took twenty-four days to reach Madeira. However, his ship's company were still in sound health, and after effecting repairs he put to sea again on 21 November, arriving at Barbados on 13 December to begin his fourth stint on that deadly station. Edward Vernon, Vice-Admiral of the Blue, was Commander-in-Chief in the West Indies, and had successfully attacked Porto Bello on the very day that Hawke had sailed from Madeira. However, though the main West Indies squadron was based at Kingston, Jamaica, and Hawke was on detached duty protecting trade at Barbados, he was compensated for not sharing in Vernon's next success, at Chagres, through being equally dissociated from the subsequent disasters at Cartagena and Santiago de Cuba.[22]

[21] Burrows, p. 121.
[22] Ad. 1/1881, 16 Nov., 20 Dec. 1739. Richmond, i 46-8, 52; Chs. 6 & 12.

Between July and November, the *Portland*'s company enjoyed a reprieve from the deadly climate of their cruising station, owing to Hawke's programme for refitting at Boston. He told the Admiralty that he was taking special pains to prevent desertions, and appears to have succeeded in that object.

Some time during 1740 the news reached Hawke that his second little daughter had died. She was buried at Barking on 3 April. However, Catharine was able to take passage to join her husband at Barbados, probably in 1741. This adventurous move was doubtless prompted by the bereaved mother's need of consolation and distraction.[23]

In 1741 Hawke continued to convoy merchantmen to and from Barbados. In March he passed along the coast of Puerto Rico, one of the principal Spanish islands, and yet perceived never a Spaniard. Indeed, this cruising in tropical waters sounds agreeable enough, and might have been, if it had not been for the perennial problem of health.

By July the hurricane season was again approaching. Hawke planned to sail for Boston on the 12th. 'I have now about forty of my men ill,' he wrote to Corbett[24] on the 10th, 'and others falling sick every day, and these men would have no chance of recovering their health unless we went to the northward.' The *Scarborough* (24), under the command of Captain Lisle, had come out to assist Hawke; and the latter had ordered Lisle to refit at Antigua so that he would be quickly back on the Barbados station. Hawke terminated his letter of 10 July with a passage which shows that the Captain aged 36 was very much the same man as the future commander of fleets.

---

[23] Ad. 1/1881, 12, 15 Sept., 18 Oct., 28 Dec. 1740. Burrows, pp. 119, 122-3.

[24] Admiralty Secretary.

> My second Lieutenant, Mr. Richard Chadwick, having been very ill almost ever since he left England, with an ague and a fever, and very often been incapable of doing his duty for a considerable time together by reason of his low and weak condition, which has made me take the liberty, upon advice of the surgeons of this place, to give him leave to go home for his health, and I humbly hope that he will not incur their Lordships' displeasure by quitting his ship, as he is a very good officer and is both ready and willing at all times to do his duty, when he is well; but he is one that has been a long time in the West Indies, first and last, which has impaired his health very much. I beg pardon for this liberty and hope their Lordships will forgive what I have done, as it was with no other view but to preserve a good officer for His Majesty.

During his later career Hawke was sometimes notably indiscreet. Pitt, at the height of a splendid tirade, described him as 'no Minister'. But, although the first part of the above-quoted paragraph meanders somewhat and lacks a proper verb, the passage as a whole demonstrates no lack of tact. The range of vocabulary exceeds that of the average naval captain of the day. There is no lack of good sense, of willingness to take responsibility for breaking a rule, or of consideration for the welfare of a deserving individual. This, incidentally, is the only one of Hawke's dispatches from Barbados to be written in his own hand. It is evidence of the strength of his feeling about the case of Lieutenant Chadwick.[25]

The *Portland* reached Boston on 8 August. All went well, though sheathing the ship's bottom took time. They sailed for Barbados on Sunday, 8 November. There ensued a discomforting experience; and, on 15 December, Hawke described it for Corbett's benefit, thus: 'The Saturday

---

[25] Ad. 1/1882, 20 Apr., 10 July 1741. Add.MSS. 32913, f. 328.

following, there being a great sea from the S. and SSW., with a large swell from the Westward, and the wind blowing very hard, making two great hollow seas running in a different manner, occasioned the carrying away of all my masts; and the ship, notwithstanding she was very well caulked all over at Boston, made a great deal of water with her working.'

The masts had looked sound enough but it was found that the middle of the stumps had almost crumbled to powder through dry rot — a common complaint, as a contemporary minute of the Admiralty Board shows. Hawke, by now expert in the technique of rigging jury masts, took the usual energetic measures, and reached Barbados on 11 December. It had been a close thing to losing the ship altogether. 'But', wrote Hawke, 'in all the misfortune I lost not one man.'[26]

However, the merchants of Barbados saw little to be pleased about. They were in any case opposed to Hawke's taking the ship to Boston for refits, and had already protested to their Lordships against this practice on the ground that it gave encouragement to enemy privateers. In consequence, Admiralty orders had already been issued on 15 September directing Hawke to refit at Antigua in future.[27]

It proved impossible to obtain proper masts for the *Portland* but Hawke made do with small ones, and in February 1742 was escorting as many as forty-four sail to Las Tortugas where they loaded salt. At Barbados the merchants were obsessed with the notion of Spanish privateers infesting the surrounding waters; and, in June, Hawke, who had failed to sight any such raiders and was inclined to question their existence, reluctantly agreed to investigate a reported hide-out on the coast of Puerto Rico. He had the *Eltham* (40) and the frigate *Scarborough* with him;

---

[26] Ad. 1/1882, 15 Dec. 1741; 3/45, 1 Feb. 1742; 51/4294.
[27] Ad. 2/57, 15 Sept. 1741.

but the Spanish privateers, if they were really there, melted away at Hawke's approach. As he informed Corbett in his letter of 30 July 1742, he neither met nor saw anything 'but a poor little sloop with twelve Spaniards, come from Martinico'.[28]

Altogether, what with the mortal climate and the extreme elusiveness of the enemy, Hawke had seen about enough of the West Indies. Happily for him, their Lordships had already on 10 February ordered the *Advice* (50) to go out by way of Rio de Janeiro, pick up stores there, and go on to relieve the *Portland* at Barbados. (The *Advice* was to be furnished 'with a Sett of Fishing Gear'.)[29]

On returning to Barbados after his abortive search for Spanish privateers, Hawke found the *Advice* awaiting him with orders for his return to England. This was acceptable news indeed. Judging by letters from Colonel Bladen to his nephew, Catharine took passage in her husband's ship.[30]

The *Portland* was in poor condition and had to go to Antigua for refit before the crossing of the Atlantic could be undertaken. Groaning noises had emanated from her bows ever since she had come under Hawke's command; she let in water through her sides and decks so that the gunpowder was never dry; on the last cruise the pumps had been set to work every two hours; and the ship's company had maintained closer contact with their watery element than they normally anticipated. Some rigorous caulking was therefore to be done at Antigua. The ship reached English Harbour on 12 August 1742.

Hawke received a dismal impression of the conditions at Antigua, and, after his return to England in the New Year, he

---

[28] Ad. 1/1882, 22 Jan., 10 June, 30 July 1742.

[29] Ad. 3/45, 14, 15 Jan., 10 Feb. 1742.

[30] Ad. 1/1882, 30 July 1742. Burrows, pp. 122-3.

communicated his views to the Admiralty. The work on the *Portland* took from 12 August to 14 October, despite the fact that she was fully manned. The refit cost nine deaths and eleven desertions. Altogether, the place was most inconvenient. Hawke, having been directed to examine the feasibility of constructing a careening wharf at English Harbour, reported that it would have to be of stone, because wooden piles would be devoured by the worms in a twinkling. Seeing that there was no suitable stone on the island nor enough masons, their Lordships would have to judge whether it was worthwhile to send the men and material from England.

From Antigua he went back to Barbados to collect a convoy but was delayed because all the sugar was not loaded. At length he sailed for England with seven merchantmen on 1 December. Captain Peter Warren arrived at Barbados on the day that Hawke sailed, and there may have been a brief meeting between the two men. Hawke's homeward progress was shortlived. A sharp gale smashed one of the *Portland*'s yards, and she was back at Barbados on the 7th, by which time Warren's *Launceston* had departed. On the 12th, the *Portland* set out again for England with two merchantmen, but owing to further storms she lost company with the latter. By the time she reached the Chops of the Channel, the ship was leaking dangerously. On the morning of Sunday, 23 January 1743, the dark, jagged outline of Bolt Head could be discerned to the N.W., about fifteen miles away. Although ordered to proceed to Longreach in the Thames, Hawke felt that he had done well enough when the half-rotten, thoroughly saturated *Portland* dropped anchor at Spithead on the morning of the 25th.

Catharine's relief, as she set foot safely on dry land, can readily be imagined. She had not only experienced the violence of the sea, but had seen what it was for a ship's company to serve in the West Indies and die one by one even after leaving that fever-ridden station. The tale of officers lost during the *Portland*'s three-year commission indicates the chances of survival under the best conditions which the ship could offer. On 5 June 1740, Robert Hart, the Boatswain, died; on 3 July, George Fridge, the Surgeon; on 26 June 1741, Thomas Grundy, the Master; on 11 August, George Mitchell, the Gunner; on 31 January 1742, John Wilson, the Cook; on 5 September, James Rickman, the Purser; and on 22 November, Francis Colwell, Gunner. The fact that none of the commissioned (as distinct from warrant) officers died on board was probably due to their being relatively young.

After completing a modicum of repairs Hawke took the ship round to Longreach. On 17 March the log entry: 'This day we transported the ship into dock and the men were victualled aboard the Hulk', marked the end of a tiresome and not obviously rewarding service. But Hawke had the satisfaction of knowing that it had been conscientiously performed; and, moreover, after four spells of service in the West Indies — each time in a different capacity — he had survived! As for the future, the fact that his uncle was still living was to prove important.[31]

Colonel Bladen retained his position as a Commissioner of Trade and Plantations despite the fall of Walpole's Government in 1742 and continued to exercise influence on Hawke's behalf. He was friendly with Admiral Cavendish who was a member of the Admiralty Board of 1743. This Board was led by Lord Winchelsea, commonly described as the most inefficient First Lord of the century. However, Admiral Cavendish, who was removed from the Board by death a few months later, must have helped to secure for Hawke the

[31] Ad. 1/1882, n.d., but about 25 Jan. 1743; 51/4294.

command of the *Berwick*. As a ship of 70 guns, she was considerably more powerful than any of Hawke's previous ships, and, what was more she was being fitted for service with Mathews's large battlefleet in the Mediterranean.[32]

On 14 June 1743, Hawke, after a welcome break on shore, took command of the *Berwick* at Deptford. What with the near-by Greenwich Hospital in its unbegrimed splendour, surrounded by open greenery in place of today's hideous, sooty, industrial agglomeration, that reach of the Thames must then have been agreeable to the eye. Catharine was presumably installed in lodgings at Deptford. By August her third child had been conceived and this time the outcome was to prove happy. However, it may well have brought tears to the eyes of 'the best of friends' when, on 22 August, the *Berwick* began to glide away downstream from Longreach. From her own experience Catharine knew what was meant by the dangers of the sea. Her Ned's last departure was bound up in her memory with the death of her two little girls. Would he return this time? Would she survive her third childbirth? (a real hazard at that date). Would this child, if born quick, survive those first months which carried off so many babes, and be alive to greet its father if he came back?[33]

Hawke was not the sort of man to be insensitive to his wife's feelings but he was fortunate, perhaps, in the pressure of his day-to-day preoccupations. He had found it quite impossible to man the ship properly. After three years of war such seamen as had escaped the press gangs had perfected means of making themselves scarce. Two of the important warrant officers, the Boatswain and Carpenter, were far too old for their work and

---

[32] Burrows, pp. 122-3. Richmond, i, 180, 224-5; ii, 108-9. Charnock, iii, 219.
[33] Ad. 2/60, 15 June 1743; 51/106. *Burke's Peerage*, 1959.

had to be replaced. The Admiralty urged Hawke to send out a pressing-tender and to expedite a gang to London: but he could do neither for lack of men to fit the ship. The *Berwick* needed about 500 altogether. Even by taking on a few landsmen who volunteered, Hawke could muster only sixty-seven men on 25 June. The Admiralty waxed impatient; but altogether Hawke did well to be able to write on 20 July: 'We go on in fitting the ship as fast as possible, and have got on board our ground tier [of guns] and cables, and are now getting off our anchors and officers' stores. And she will be ready to fall down to Longreach by the middle of next week, when the tide will fall out right to carry her down.'[34]

He did indeed move down to Longreach on 25 July and in the course of a week received fifty-eight 'prest' men from the *Pomeroy*, a tender commanded by a standard figure in the nightmares of fugitive seamen — a Regulating Captain. Log entries made aboard the *Berwick* such as 'John Hall ran away', 'Isaac Samway fell overboard and was drowned', and 'Penticost Ireland hanged himself' show that the denizens of the lower deck were at least supplied with topics of conversation. Despite the efforts of the Regulating Captain, the ship remained almost desperately ill-manned. Nevertheless, as indicated above, on 22 August Hawke set sail for the Nore.

In July Hawke had at least received on board some Marines who were in his judgement 'very likely young fellows'; but, as he wrote to Corbett on 23 August, he could not enthuse about his crew as a whole. He had had to take a number of 'very little, puny, weakly fellows that have never been at sea'. He concluded, 'I beg their Lordships' pardon for mentioning this affair, but I thought it my duty to do it, for when a ship is so very badly manned, she can be of very little or no service.'

---

[34] L.B., 28, 29 June, 20 July 1743.

Yet this apparently self-evident statement about the *Berwick*'s fighting capacity was to be splendidly disproved. Hawke had left out of the reckoning the effect of his own leadership.[35]

On 24 September the *Berwick* set out from Spithead for the Mediterranean. In company was one other warship, the *Dorsetshire* (80), together with eight merchantmen. The *Dorsetshire*'s Captain, Burrish, was commodore of the convoy.

The health of the crew was Hawke's main preoccupation. Even before Gibraltar was reached reports of men dying began to reach the Captain's cabin. On 25 September, it was 'John McGregor, a Highlander' who succumbed; on 5 October 'at 3 p.m. I. Tankerpin died'; and on the 10th 'at 10 p.m. died Nicholas Knight'. From 16 to 19 October they lay in the exposed Bay of Gibraltar. Then, still under Burrish's command, they sailed for Hyères Bay, near Toulon, while fever and the scurvy continued to take their toll. The helplessness of the medical staff is eloquently brought out by the fact that on 29 October, 'at midnight, Mr. Pawlson Holderness, Surgeon's 1st Mate', was added to the number of the dead. On the 27th Hawke had written to Burrish:

> The Surgeon of His Majesty's ship the *Berwick* under my command, has this morning acquainted me that we have 123 working men ill. Out of that number, 84 have fevers. Six or eight of these are dangerously ill. The rest of them are mostly troubled with scurvy... We can no ways account for the men falling ill so fast, otherwise than that a great number of them are lately come from the East Indies, and others of them are raw men, picked up by the press gangs in London, and are poor puny fellows; and the ship being new and green is consequently damp, notwithstanding all my endeavours to keep her clean and dry.

---

[35] L.B., 28 July, 2, 22, 23 Aug. 1743. Ad. 51/106.

He therefore suggested that he should leave the convoy and put his sick on shore at Minorca.

Burrish demurred at first but on 6 November Hawke urgently pressed to go into near-by Port Mahon. Burrish reluctantly agreed. Then, for five agonizing days the *Berwick* was held up by unfavourable winds, while more men were dying and the ship's company as a whole was down to its last reserves of strength. On 12 November Hawke at last 'anchored in Mahon Harbour with the best bower in fathom water, and moored with the small bower'. At once, he 'sent to the Hospital 100 Seamen and 20 Marines'. By the 19th he had sent nearly another 100 men, and smaller numbers continued to go until the beginning of December.[36]

On 5 December the direction of flow was reversed when there 'came from the Hospital 21 Sick Men, employed in cleaning the hold'! This does not sound an enviable convalescent job but it presumably demanded less energy than work above decks. Gradually, the *Berwick*'s numbers were built up again, and on the 26th Hawke's clerk noted, 'Received from the Hospital 60 of our men and 18 supernumeraries. At 4, weighed and came to sail, and received on board 100 barrels of powder, 6 punchions of beef, 3 punchions of pork and 4 casks of pease.' Thus fortified, Hawke made for Hyères Bay where Mathews stood guard over the route from Toulon to Genoa. On the 29th the *Berwick* was off the French base, still nominally neutral at that date. It was not until 11 January 1744 that she finally joined the main fleet in Hyères Road. Her arrival brought Mathews's strength up to twenty-seven of the line.[37]

---

[36] Ad. 51/106. L.B., 27 Oct. 1743. Burrows, p. 136.
[37] Ad. 51/106.

The fleet was divided into the usual three divisions. Thomas Mathews, Admiral of the Blue, commanded the centre; the van came under Richard Lestock, Vice-Admiral of the White; and the rear under Will Rowley, Rear-Admiral of the Blue. The *Berwick* was placed in Rowley's division.

The general situation was that Admiral Mathews had to support the Austrians and the Sardinians in Northern Italy. He had already halted the progress of Spanish troops advancing northwards from Naples by interrupting their seaborne supplies. Now, a much larger Franco-Spanish army of 50,000 men was ready to move into Piedmont from Provence. Mathews had received many reports showing that the combined Franco-Spanish fleet would shortly come out of Toulon, presumably to clear him away from the Provençal coast and at the same time effect a declaration of war on England by France. This achieved, French transports and supply vessels would sustain, and indeed accelerate, the advance of the Spanish and French troops along the coast towards Genoa. As long as winter snows continued to block the Alpine passes, this was the only invasion route open to the enemy from the west. Provided that the King of Sardinia contrived to hold Villefranche, and Mathews could therefore use it as a base, Italy would be safe — at least till the end of the winter. However, apart from his uncertainty as to the intentions of the combined fleet at Toulon, Mathews was also worried by news reaching him at the beginning of February that the French had recently put to sea from their principal base at Brest. It was clearly possible that this force might join the Toulon fleet, catch Mathews at a numerical disadvantage and crush him.[38]

---

[38] Richmond, ii, 1-7. Ad. 1/3911.

To do Mathews justice, he had, since assuming his troubled command in 1742, displayed diplomatic and strategic qualities of a higher order than might have been expected of a man who had been court-martialed in the 1720's on a charge of trafficking with pirates, and, although convicted only of using His Majesty's ships for private trading, had been thrust into retirement and passed over for his flag. In the Mediterranean he had latterly risen to the situation in many respects; but on the side of leadership he remained open to serious criticism. From the moment of his arrival he was openly at odds with Lestock, his Vice-Admiral. Admittedly, the gouty Lestock might have proved a trial to any commander-in-chief. After a lapse of two centuries, his quivering signature at the foot of a dispatch seems about to explode with pent-up resentment and bad temper. But, apart from his deliberate failure to get on terms with Lestock, Mathews was to blame for not keeping his captains generally informed about the situation. There is no sign that he discussed tactical questions with them. Although he deserves credit for his statesmanlike approach to the complex strategic problems facing him, his treatment at his forthcoming, second court martial seems to have been deserved. Of course, the fact that he suffered from the gravel did little to mollify his temper, and obviously contributed to his failure as a leader.[39]

With the British lying at anchor in Hyères Bay, matters came to a head on 8 February. In the middle of the afternoon Hawke's lookouts could see the frigate *Winchelsea* approaching from the W. She was crowding sail and flying a red flag. This meant that the enemy fleet at Toulon was under sail. While all was bustle aboard the *Berwick* Hawke's telescope was trained on Mathews's *Namur*, and soon afterwards he saw the

---

[39] ibid., i, Ch. 11; ii, Ch. 1.

Admiral's 'public signal to unmoor'. However, evening fell before the fleet had made much progress. Meanwhile, the French ships had succeeded in getting to sea; but the Spanish had to anchor before they cleared the port.[40]

It was while the British fleet was thus uncomfortably placed — the wind being behind the enemy — that Lestock paid his abortive visit to Mathews.[41]

---

[40] Ad. 51/106.

[41] Richmond, ii, 9.

CHAPTER 2: OPPORTUNITY AT LAST — THE BATTLE OF TOULON

ON 9 February the wind was light and variable in direction but coming mostly from the W. While Mathews tried to extricate his ships and form a line of battle, Hawke, by 11 a.m., could make out several enemy ships already standing to the S. In the afternoon, according to Hawke's log, the British 'kept plying to windward in Hyères Bay in order to form the line of battle, the enemy's fleet then being in the offing, stretching to the southward'. What with tricky currents and the light wind veering to S.W., conditions were so difficult that the *Warwick* ran into the *Nassau* and then went aground but, as Hawke saw, she managed to get free. At 5 p.m. the *Berwick* 'anchored with the fleet' which was still in disorder.

At daybreak on the 10th the British were relieved to find that the wind was stronger, at W.N.W. This offered a better chance of working clear before the enemy converted Mathews's haven into a trap. Although the signal for line ahead was out, the wind began to die away again and all captains struggled towards the entrance, abandoning any serious attempt to get into the prescribed order. The enemy was standing towards them and the position looked most critical. At this juncture, Mathews had the good fortune to be joined by the *Boyne* and *Chichester* which had just arrived from England and had escaped wandering into de Court's fleet by sheer luck. But the danger remained that the leading British ships might be destroyed before their fellows could get up to help them. The *Berwick* had been unable to move ahead of the rearmost ships, and at noon, when he was still not clear of Porquerolles Island, Hawke could hardly see the enemy fleet for the clutter of British ships scattered all across his field of view. There appeared to be thirty-six sail of the enemy, about twelve miles away to the W.S.W. While a heavy swell rolled across from the W., the wind swung right round to come lightly from the E. This brought Mathews's ships out into the open sea and they began to form their line of battle, sailing on the port tack, with the flagships in the centre of their divisions. Rowley's division, including the *Berwick* became the van; and Lestock, who would have led on the starboard tack, found himself in the rear. The combined fleet was still to the westward of the British. Following the change of wind, de Court stood to the S., then turned away to the S.W. Both fleets wheeled into line abreast and, with the British following the enemy, they moved westwards at no great speed towards a position due S. of Toulon.

The allies had had time to form quite a straight line abreast, but Mathews, although he had hastened to turn into that formation to pursue them, did not wish to be drawn far to leeward and he brought to at 6.30 p.m. with his line still unformed. The rear division under Lestock and the van division under Rowley should have been due N. and S. respectively of Mathews's centre division, but at dusk they were both still well behind. When, at 6.30, Mathews signalled to his fleet to bring to, he left up the signal for the line abreast. His intention was that everyone should understand that, before they brought to, they should move up into their proper positions in the line abreast, but he failed to send any boats to see that this was in fact done. This omission was the chief cause of Mathews's tactical dilemma on the following day. It also gave Lestock an opportunity to take his private revenge, for, on the evening of the 10th he had been prompt to bring to as soon as Mathews's signal to that effect was seen, although he was about three miles to the N.E. (instead of N.) of the Commander-in-Chief at the time.

When the fateful 11 February dawned the weather was fine and a light breeze was blowing from E.N.E. to N.E. At 7 a.m. Hawke could see the enemy ships clearly through his glass as they lay about nine miles away to the westward in line of battle. In Hawke's life there were to be three days of the highest excitement, testing him as a man of decision and action. This was one of them.

When Mathews signalled to his Admirals in the van and rear to make more sail, Hawke may well have felt that things were going wrong. Mathews could be seen reducing sail so that the other divisions could come up level with his, but the wind was so slight that he had to sail ahead again to keep in touch with the enemy. By mid-morning the British line abreast was definitely closing on the enemy. De Court had now begun to head S. in a line ahead and at 10 a.m. Mathews conformed with his movement. Theoretically, the two lines ahead should have been parallel but while Rowley's division, with the *Berwick* in the second place after the Rear-Admiral's *Barfleur*, had come fairly well up, Lestock's rear division could be seen lagging a long way behind. During the two hours remaining before noon, Mathews waited for Rowley to sail sufficiently far ahead for the latter to be able to close on the French van ships without them having time to push ahead and overlap him. If, during the British approach the French did obtain an overlap, they would be able to tack to windward of Rowley and obtain a deadly concentration on his division. This manoeuvre, known as doubling, had been effectively used by the French in their victory over the British and Dutch at Beachy Head, fifty-four years earlier, and had remained a part of their tactical doctrine.

To Mathews's frustration, if not his surprise, the French proceeded to outsail Rowley's foul-bottomed ships. It was important not to be lured too far away from the coast; yet Cape Sicie, already about fifteen miles distant, was beginning to fade from view as the two lines ahead moved inexorably southward. Mathews's fretful impatience was expressed by the red flag for engaging twice fluttering up and down aboard the *Namur* when none of his ships was in a position to fire at the enemy. From time to time he swung round to direct furious glances in the direction of Lestock's division. He had already sent an officer in a boat to tell the Vice-Admiral to crowd all possible sail and it was obvious that he was very far from doing so. Although the *Berwick* was some distance further southward than the *Namur*, Hawke also noticed Lestock's division 'a pretty considerable distance astern'. It was generally understood throughout the fleet why this was so and morale did not benefit. At last, at about 1 p.m. Mathews decided that he could wait no longer. Although Lestock was miles behind and Rowley by no means as far ahead as he would have liked, Mathews swung the *Namur* hard over to starboard and headed straight for the enemy. Flying both the signal for the line ahead and that for battle, he plunged down towards the *Real Felipe*, the flagship of Don Jose de Navarro, who commanded the all-Spanish rear division of the combined fleet. Ordinarily, he would have pitted himself against de Court's *Terrible* but she was a long way too far ahead.

Rowley was quick to understand Mathews's extempore move and he at once bore down on de Court's flagship. He was closely followed by his seconds, the *Chichester* to port and the *Princess Caroline* to starboard. The *Berwick* kept beside the *Princess Caroline*. As she bore down on the enemy her bow heaved and dropped on the continuing western swell. Hawke singled out his probable opponent, the second ship astern of the *Terrible*. As the British sailed down-wind from the E., the French, in their defensive line ahead sailed on towards the S.[42]

On the *Berwick*'s starboard bow the cannon began to thunder as action was joined between the *Namur* and the *Real*. Then, on the port bow, Rowley's *Barfleur* engaged the *Terrible*. On Hawke's immediate left the *Princess Caroline* swung into position astern of the *Barfleur* and was soon exchanging broadsides with the ship behind the *Terrible*. Hawke was quickly in his place behind the *Princess Caroline* but the French ship on his starboard bow, the *Sérieux*, sheered away and sailed ahead. After her came the first of the Spaniards, the *Oriente*, but she also took evasive action. The enemy were well aware that Article 21 of the British Navy's General Printed Fighting Instructions read: 'None of the ships in the fleet shall pursue any small number of the enemy's ships until the main body be disabled or run.'

Foiled for the moment Hawke looked around for another opponent. By 1.30 p.m. the Spanish ship *Neptuno* (60) had come well up but was keeping somewhat to leeward, and Hawke set his foresail in order to bear down on her. He was intent on getting to grips this time, even if it meant leaving his strictly correct position in a line with the *Barfleur*. But he was the only captain of the van division to adopt this offensive attitude. Indeed, several of the other captains, far from edging down to leeward, were hanging back to windward of their Admiral. This demoralization was largely due to Mathews's defective leadership over a period of time, but, on this day of battle, Lestock's example was doing nothing to put an edge on other officers' spirits. In the centre division much the same was happening. A heroic exception in that part of the engagement was provided by one of Mathews's seconds,

---

[42] Ad. 51/106; 1/381, 11 Feb. 1744. Richmond, ii, Ch. i and App. I.

Captain Cornewall of the *Marlborough*. Unfortunately, this most promising officer lost his life in the action.

The Captain of the *Neptuno* eyed the *Berwick* as she moved down into his intended path. This was an unexpected phenomenon and he did not like it. He therefore made sail and slipped away to leeward, then went ahead, skirting the area of activity round the *Terrible*. Hawke would dearly have liked to follow him but he was prevented from doing so by Article 13 of the General Fighting Instructions. The effect of this was that no captain was to move out of his proper order in the line of battle. However, the incident made a strong impression on Hawke and, when eventually it came within his power to do so, he altered this Article for the benefit of the Western Squadron. But at the Battle of Toulon he could only wait for another enemy ship to sail up towards him.

At length, towards the middle of the afternoon, he saw a Spanish ship extricate herself from the fighting down near the *Namur*. She had lost her fore topmast, and had, Hawke wrote, 'got her main tack on board, with an intent (as I imagined) to get under the lee of the French. [She] made me continue bearing down till she came abreast of us, within less than musquet shot, then we brought to with the main topsail aback and engaged her.'

Hawke's decisive and thrilling intervention was seen from many of the other British ships. Aboard the *Princessa*, which had been hotly engaged with the Spaniard but failed to clinch matters, was Lieutenant Robert Harland — a future Admiral, who was to see another of Hawke's great moments. As he regretfully watched the Spanish ship (the *Poder* of 64 guns) apparently in the act of escaping, he saw the *Berwick* 'separate herself from the rest and run down to leeward, and engage her'. Likewise, James Moore, Master of the *Norfolk*, which lay between the *Princessa* and the *Namur*, watched the *Berwick* run down to the *Poder*. 'She engaged he [so] close on board,' he afterwards stated, 'that a stone might be thrown on board from one to the other.'

Various writers have disputed the question whether or not Hawke 'broke the line' at the Battle of Toulon. Some of the confusion has been due to the failure to recognize the existence of *two* Articles of the General Fighting Instructions which have a bearing on the matter. For example, Richmond, in his classic *The Navy in the War of 1739-48*, wrote: 'Hawke, like the others respected the line and was bound by the established rules'. Yet Richmond's account of the action includes sufficient detail to show that Hawke did leave the line in the sense indicated in the paragraph preceding this. In a nutshell, Hawke was restrained by Article 13, but not by Article 21 (both explained or quoted above). Moreover, the minutes of the subsequent court martial of Captain Pett, which include an interrogation of both Hawke and his 1st Lieutenant, imply that the tyranny of the 'line' has probably been overdone by writers on naval history. The latter have given the impression that the officers of the Navy understood it to be a heinous crime to leave the line, even by a yard, on their own initiative, because of the crippling Article 21; and that this interpretation was confirmed by the trials which followed the Battle of Toulon. A reading of the evidence leaves no doubt that the court which tried Pett was not perturbed by the obvious fact that Hawke had moved to leeward of the line to engage an enemy ship. What it was concerned about was that, when the signal for engaging was up, some captains hung back out of the line to windward, that is, farther away from the enemy than their Admiral. Significantly, Hawke later thought it necessary to change Article 13 only; not Article 21.

In the words of Lieutenant Tom of the *Norfolk*, 'The *Berwick* went down to leeward of the *Poder* and went close under her stern and went up again on his lee side, and hauled his wind upon her lee bow and there engaged her till her main mast fell.' This summary is paralleled by the account in Hawke's log. 'At ½ past 3, we shot away the Spanish ship's mizen jeers; soon after, the foremast below the parrell of the yard. At this time, having but little wind and a great swell occasioned our falling down on her lee bow, where we kept up a very smart fire with bar and grape shot, and plied her with our small arms.' Having the *Berwick* close on her lee bow, the *Poder* could not possibly escape. For three quarters of an hour the two antagonists hammered round-shot into each other at point blank range, the deadly wood-splinters flew and the multitude of smaller missiles buzzed about menacingly. At 4.15 the *Berwick*'s gunners gained a reward worth a cheer when the *Poder*'s mainmast tottered, hung for a breathless instant and then came crashing down. This was the end. Owing, in Hawke's opinion, to the *Poder*'s 'firing so very high', the *Berwick*'s casualties were still limited to only six men wounded, and, despite widespread damage to her masts, rigging, and sails, the British ship was full of fight. After the loss of his mainmast, with about 200 of his crew killed or wounded, the Captain of the *Poder* surrendered.

But this was the only triumphant moment in the whole battle. Elsewhere, while the *Namur*, *Marlborough*, *Barfleur*, *Princessa*, and one or two others had been closely engaged, Lestock, with the whole of the rear division, had deliberately held back, and several captains in the other divisions made little positive effort. To take an extreme case, one of these captains was Richard Norris, son of the Admiral of the Fleet. He commanded the *Essex* in third place astern of Mathews's *Namur*. According to the Master of the *Essex*, 'Captain Norris showed all the signs of the utmost fear and dejection.' With the idea of raising the crew's morale, the Master began singing 'The Famous Ninety Two' which presumably celebrated the British victory over the French at the Battle of Cape Barfleur. However, he received small encouragement from Norris who interjected, 'It will be over with us presently and we shall have no reason to sing.' Lugubriously he spent the afternoon as a safely-positioned witness of the fighting around the resolute Spanish Admiral in the *Real Felipe.* At 4 p.m. the British fireship *Ann* began to move slowly down on the *Real* to deliver the *coup de grâce.* The 1st Lieutenant of the *Essex*, Hugh Pallisser, (himself later to become a centre of controversy,) vigorously represented to Norris that if the *Essex* did not go down to cover the fireship it would be sunk by some Spanish ships coming up from astern of the *Real.* Norris inspiringly replied, 'We must not go down. If we do, we shall be sunk and tore to pieces.' The *Ann* was sunk a few yards short of her goal. After groaning his favourite phrase of the afternoon, 'I wish it was over', Norris vacated the quarter-deck and hid under the hammocks in the starboard gangway.[43]

At about the same time, Hawke was taking energetic steps to secure his prize. He ordered Lloyd, his 1st Lieutenant, with a party of seamen, to take possession of the *Poder* and send her Captain and some of her officers on board the *Berwick.* Once that had been accomplished Lloyd was to start ferrying the whole of the Spanish crew aboard the *Berwick* so that, if the enemy moved to recapture their ship, she could be sunk forthwith. This scheme was highly appropriate, for no British ships had moved down to Hawke's support, and if the large number of ships in the disengaged enemy van should tack, the

---

[43] Ad. 51/106; 1/5282 for courts martial of Sclater and Pett. Richmond, ii, Ch. 1. S.P.Dom.(N.) 42/28, 28 Jan.-5 Feb. 1745.

Berwick would stand in immediate danger of being engulfed. As Lloyd and his men pulled away towards the *Poder*, Hawke took stock of his ship. The main and mizen masts, though still standing, had been severely knocked about. Much of the standing and running rigging had been cut and most of the sails were in shreds. No sooner had Hawke glanced over these signs of reduced mobility than his attention was attracted by a most unwelcome development ahead.

At about 4.30 de Court hoisted the appropriate signal and the French centre and van went about. On the starboard tack they came slanting back towards the beleaguered *Real Felipe*. By now Hawke had drifted 'a great distance' from the British centre and was well to leeward of the rest of his own division. He was in imminent danger of being cut off and overwhelmed. At once he gave orders for getting the *Berwick* under way and shouted to Lloyd through a megaphone to come back from the *Poder*. During all this excitement the captain of the *Poder* and some of his officers were brought alongside the *Berwick*. In the 'great swell, the barge filled… and sank'. A Spanish officer was drowned.

In order to stand a chance of saving his ship, Hawke had to leave Lloyd and the prize-crew to make their own way back to the fleet. They had two yawls, and, with luck, would manage it. In fact Lloyd was already under way in one of the yawls, with prisoners aboard, and he did succeed in escaping the enemy. But the *Berwick*'s 4th Lieutenant and twenty-two men, who were engrossed in rigging jurymasts, did not get away in time and were captured by the French. (This Lieutenant lived to become Sir Edward Vernon, Admiral of the Blue.) However, two seamen, apparently on their own initiative, jumped into the remaining yawl in time to evade the enemy and found their way back to the fleet, after picking up 'the *Bedford*'s Lieutenants and People' who were mysteriously stranded in a launch.

Meanwhile, closehauled on the starboard tack, Hawke just managed to win his race against the leading French ships. Seeing that firing was still going on near Mathews and the Spanish Admiral, and that Rowley's division had followed the French move by tacking back towards the centre, Hawke headed for the fighting. Lestock having condescended to close up somewhat, Hawke saw his ships fire a few perfunctory long-range shots. By now it was about 5 p.m. Mathews wore the centre division and began to engage five Spanish ships which were coming up from astern of the *Real Felipe*. At 6 o'clock it was dark and the fleet brought to. The *Berwick* was then quite close to the *Namur*.[44]

Despite the exertions of the day Hawke could allow his men little respite. Aboard the *Berwick* lanterns bobbed about in the darkness as the crew fell to 'rigging, and splicing our rigging, mending our sails, making of wads, filling of powder, and putting the ship in a proper condition to engage in the morning'.

During the evening, Mathews shifted his flag from the damaged *Namur* to the *Russell*, and meditated the action which it would be appropriate to take against Mr. Lestock.

When dawn broke on 12 February there was a general expectation in the British fleet that the action would be renewed. In the first light, Sclater of the *Somerset* found that he was to leeward of the main body and not far from an isolated Spanish ship, the *Hercules*. Hawke was on the alert, and, as soon as he saw the *Somerset* open fire he began to move down to Sclater's assistance. However, the Spaniard withdrew with all possible celerity towards the allied fleet which was lying to

---

[44] Ad. 51/106. L.B., H. to Mathews, 24 Feb. 1744. Richmond, ii, 41.

about twelve miles to the westward. Sclater abandoned the pursuit. Hawke held on for a time, anxiously scanning the *Russell*'s masts in the hope of seeing the signal to chase. But, if Mathews was interested in the situation, he did not express himself in terms of signals and Hawke had no option but to haul his wind.

At 8 a.m. Hawke was gratified to see Lloyd coming alongside in one of the yawls. He reported that he and his international party had spent the night aboard the *Royal Oak*. There was another pleasant reunion when, at 11 a.m., the two men who had left the *Poder* in the other yawl found their way back to the *Berwick*. By this time Mathews was flying the signal for the line and the *Berwick* was back in her assigned position, two places astern of the *Barfleur*.[45]

The wind, still at E., was blowing more freshly and by 1 p.m. the British had closed the gap between the two fleets to nine miles. The allies then bore away before the wind and it was frustrating to see how easily they could outsail their pursuers. Mathews's approach at least compelled the French to abandon the *Poder*, and, shortly before dusk, Rowley acknowledge Hawke's feat of the previous day by ordering him to take possession of her. The wind had fallen away so Hawke sent Lloyd to pull to the *Poder* in a boat. Meanwhile, Mathews had perceived the *Poder* and had chosen a suitable captain to burn her. Out of all the captains available, his selection had fallen on that bulwark of the Royal Navy, Richard Norris! Norris approached in time to intercept Lloyd and made good use of the opportunity to put him in his place. While Lieutenant Pallisser (of the *Essex*) went off with a party to set fire to the *Poder*, Norris ordered Lloyd up onto his quarter-deck and told him that he was not to go aboard the Spaniard. Lloyd, finding

[45] Ad. 51/106. L.B., loc. cit. Richmond, ii, 42.

himself in a weak position, confined himself to a request that any trophies found aboard the *Poder* might be handed over to the *Berwick*, particularly seeing that a flag and other tokens from her had been lost when the *Berwick*'s barge sank on the previous afternoon. After there had been some coming and going between the *Essex* and the *Poder*, Norris firmly stated that there were no trophies left aboard the Spanish ship. Disconsolately, Lloyd and his men set off on their journey back to the *Berwick*. They emerged from the gloom complaining volubly that, as soon as they had drawn away from the *Essex*, Norris's long-boat had pulled away to the *Poder* to 'bring the plunder away'. The sentiments of the *Berwick*'s crew as they watched the flames begin to rise from their capture can readily be imagined. Those out of Hawke's earshot no doubt properly expressed their sentiments. By 9 p.m. the *Poder* was well and truly ablaze. Not long after, she blew up.

Hugh Pallisser, who appeared as a witness against Mathews in 1746, then stated that when he went aboard the *Poder* 'she had her bowsprit, foremast and mizenmast... She might have been saved had a sufficient number of hands been put on board her and a frigate ordered to attend and take care of her.'

In the early hours of the 13th it was reported to Mathews that the enemy's lights were growing dimmer. Although both fleets had brought to at nightfall, the allies had evidently decided to give Mathews the slip. With a strong N.E. wind blowing, the British Admiral at once made sail. When dawn broke no enemy ships could be seen from the *Berwick* but Lestock, with new-found enthusiasm, signalled that twenty-two sail were in sight. Mathews hoisted the chase and off went Lestock's division in pursuit. After a couple of hours Mathews signalled the recall. He had made up his mind to get back to the Riviera as soon as possible in order to safeguard the position in Italy. In fact, this appears to have been a serious mistake, because the combined fleet was becoming divided and disorganized and a determined pursuit would probably have led to a number of captures. As it was, Mathews's decision was made nugatory by the weather. After battling with strong gales from the E. and N.E. the British ended by falling back on Minorca.[46]

All in all, the Berwick's performance at the Battle of Toulon was a striking example of what an unprepossessing ship's company could achieve under an outstanding commander. His sound judgement, calm resolution, and moral courage resulted in activity of such effectiveness that, had his example been generally followed by the other captains, the battle must have ended as a decisive British victory in spite of the shortcomings of the senior admirals. Of course, for the lack of such a general response Mathews and Lestock must be held largely responsible. But against a background of such demoralization, the strength and independence of Hawke's character is struck in the clearest relief.

---

[46] Ad. 51/106; 1/5278, c.m. of Adm. Mathews; 1/4113, 16 Mar. 1744. L.B. loc. cit. Richmond, ii, 45-52, 120.

CHATTER 3: SQUADRON COMMANDER

ON 19 February, Jacob Hawkins, who had been badly wounded in the action of the 11th, died aboard the *Berwick*. By the 21st the ships were revictualling in Port Mahon and Hawke received from the Hospital twenty-one of the men he had left behind in December. The next day he sailed with the fleet, but, as if to cap Mathews's frustrations, a gale arose on the 26th. By evening the *Berwick*'s sails and rigging had suffered, and then, in the dark there was excitement when a near-by ship suddenly wore — perhaps involuntarily. She ran into the after part of the *Berwick* shattered her quarter-gallery, and carried away her ensign. The battered fleet made its way back to Mahon for repairs and, on the morning of the 29th, Hawke again dropped anchor off St. Philip's Castle.

Just before the fleet ran into the gale, Hawke had sent off to Mathews a protest about Norris's taking trophies from the *Poder*. 'This is really the true state of the case,' Hawke concluded, 'and what his own Officers know to be fact; and the reason why I am so particular in it is that my Officers and Ship's Company have applied to me to acquaint you with it.' It does not appear that Mathews took any remedial action in the matter but at least his attention was drawn to the *Berwick*'s achievement on the day of battle. As will be seen, Mathews's attitude to Hawke did become favourable, at least to some extent.

In Port Mahon Hawke busied himself with repairs and revictualling. Meanwhile Mathews inquired of Lestock why he had not participated more energetically in the Battle of Toulon.

An exchange of letters did little to lower the blood-pressure of either gentleman and, on 16 March, Mathews applied the closure to the correspondence by writing: '… for fear that His Majesty's service should suffer for the future by your misconduct, I therefore judge it my indispensable duty to order you home… I do hereby suspend you from all further authority in His Majesty's Fleet, till His Majesty's pleasure shall be known.'

Lestock's acknowledgement, complete with vibrant signature, was composed as follows:

> Sir,
>
> With pleasure I have received your order of suspension. I have taken down my flag, and am
>
> Your most obedient humble servant
>
> Richard Lestock.

On 24 March Hawke heard the guns of St. Philip's Castle saluting Lestock on his departure for England. His laconic log entry does not reveal his emotions but it is safe to conclude that his opinion of Mr. Lestock was not elevated.

After a scare that de Court might sail out of the Mediterranean to support a cross-Channel invasion of the British homeland, Mathews deduced from further reports of his movements on the Spanish coast and his failure to use a favourable wind for leaving the Mediterranean, that he intended to return to Toulon. It also seemed that French troops were ready to sail from Toulon for somewhere in Northern Italy. Mathews hastened to get back to his station on the Riviera but was delayed by the lack of stores and dockyard staff at Mahon.[47]

---

[47] Ad. 51/106; T/4113, loc. cit. Richmond, ii, 121.

Late on 30 March Hawke could again discern the outline of Cape Sicie. During the four days following, the *Berwick* like her fellows, was subjected to the miseries of another fierce gale. This time it was a westerly and it drove the British off station at the same time as it swept de Court into Toulon with fifteen sail. Blockade by sailing ships was always liable to be frustrated in this way, but Hawke could not have guessed how bitterly this lesson was to be written into his future experience. Mathews, of course, did not fail to complain to their Lordships of his ill-fortune, though it does not appear to have crossed his mind that he might have destroyed much of the same enemy force by a sustained pursuit after the Battle of Toulon.

Already the French and Spanish armies, in superior numbers, were in motion on the coast, heading for Genoa. In early April they took Villefranche after a costly assault, though a small number of Sardinians still held out in the two citadels. Mathews succeeded in bringing off a large number of Sardinian troops under the covering fire of some of his smaller ships. The Spanish, owing to the casualties which they had suffered and the prospect of continuous interruption from Mathews's squadron, began to doubt whether their offensive could be sustained. On the other hand, Mathews was conscious that his endurance was limited because a long-expected fleet of victuallers had failed to arrive. At last news reached him that they were at Lisbon, but if Mathews went with his whole force to fetch them, all would be lost in Italy. He did not want to send part of his force to escort them because the Franco-Spanish squadron in Toulon would then be superior to him. The lack of provisions and stores for the British Mediterranean fleet was, in fact, due to the Admiralty's imperfect strategy nearer home. A Western Squadron, cruising continuously off Brest, would have saved British communications with the

Mediterranean from the interruptions to which they had been subject, and safeguarded England against invasion at the same time, to say nothing of the effect on the commerce of the French.[48]

However, for the time being, the French and Spaniards were held in N.W. Italy. But the Austrians made new demands on Mathews because they were planning to advance against the southern Spanish army and occupy Naples. Before agreeing to make a detachment of ships to assist Lobkowitz, the Austrian general, Mathews decided to reconnoitre Toulon, and on 13 May he sailed from Vado Bay, near Genoa, with this object in view.

It was found that, amid general animation, twenty-one French and Spanish ships were being fitted for the sea. Also, the French and Spanish armies had begun to move ahead again; and the Republic of Genoa, hitherto neutral, was collecting troops, very possibly with the intention of falling on the Sardinians from the rear. This crisis clearly required the whole of Mathews's attention.

As in January he anchored the fleet in Hyères Bay and kept a small squadron — under Norris — cruising off Toulon. As if to bring out that some individuals are predictably unpredictable, Norris appears to have harried the enemy's coastal supply traffic with energy and daring! In June Mathews's strategy was crowned with abrupt, if transitory, success, when the Spanish army suddenly withdrew from the Riviera. It had been decided that a Franco-Spanish advance through the Alps offered better prospects.

Mathews persisted with the blockade of Toulon. If the enemy could unite the Spanish ships at Cartagena with the allied squadron already at Toulon, they would have 33 of the

---

[48] Ad. 51/106. Richmond, ii, 122-7.

line. Mathews, who had sent 4 ships of force to fetch the victuallers and 4 to Mahon for repairs, had 32 still with him. His strategy succeeded in keeping the enemy divided. Early in July he placed the main body of his fleet off Cape Sicie, just to the W. of Toulon; and off Cape Sepet, to the E., of the port, he positioned 7 of the line under the command of Captain Hawke. There were 2 linking ships. At this stage, the blockading force totalled 23 of the line, detachments having been made to help Lobkowitz, to prevent supplies from Spain and elsewhere reaching the enemy in Italy and to protect his own supply vessels going to and from Sardinia. But the enemy in Toulon, with 21 large ships, were completely immobilized for the time being.

On 8 July Mathews anchored the fleet in Hyères Bay. At 3 p.m. on the following day Hawke received further recognition from the Admiral when his signal was again hoisted aboard the *Namur*. After an interview with his Commander-in-Chief, Hawke weighed anchor at 5 p.m. with another squadron of seven ships. He stood close in to Cape Sepet and observed seventeen sail in Toulon. The guns of the forts on the Cape optimistically fired a few shots at long range but the balls splashed harmlessly into the sea.

From the 13th, Hawke with seven of the line cruised for a week off Cape Sicie in command of an inshore squadron, while Mathews with the main body was about four miles farther out to sea. The French made no significant move, although on the morning of the 20th there was brief excitement when Hawke's ships spotted four French galleys and chased them into Toulon. Otherwise, the main incidents were periodical examinations of the port which drew some fire from the forts and the capture of odd coasting vessels. On 23 July Mathews took all his ships back to Hyères Bay.[49]

At last, Il Furibondo's Mediterranean service, so heavily burdened with grievance and complaint, was drawing to a conclusion. On 8 August he sailed with the fleet for Villefranche, and on the 9th he signed a characteristic despatch, conveying to their Lordships his sentiments on relinquishing his command. The following sentence illustrates the tone of the whole: 'I will take leave to assure their Lordships of one thing, which is that I shall strike my flag with much greater pleasure and satisfaction than I hoisted it, which means I shall avoid any more of their Lordships' unjust censure.'[50]

When Mathews left the fleet on 21 August, he bequeathed the command-in-chief to the milder-tempered but less intelligent Rowley. The latter was given reason to suspect that the enemy squadrons from Toulon, Cartagena, and Cadiz might concentrate near Gibraltar. This would confront him with an adversary numbering over forty ships of the line. Seeing that he had only twenty-seven large ships, of which five had been ordered home by the Admiralty, that Commodore Osborn and the supply convoy were being blockaded in the Tagus, and that it was highly desirable to stop Spanish troops sailing from Barcelona to Naples, it is clear that Rowley had food for thought. Leaving Vado Bay on 3 September he reached Mahon with the fleet on the 13th.

In October Hawke sailed with the main body when Rowley escorted a large convoy of merchantmen right out of the Mediterranean and to a point well clear of Cadiz. Fortunately, the enemy, despite their numerical advantage, had evinced no inclination to develop an offensive strategy. Osborn was able to bring the victuallers through to Gibraltar whence Rowley

---

[49] Richmond, ii, 131-3, 137, 140. Ad. 51/106. L.B., 9 July 1744.
[50] Ad. 1/381, 9 Aug. 1744.

collected them and returned to the Mediterranean. But he failed to benefit from the improvement in his situation, for, on approaching the Balearic Islands, he detached Osborn with thirteen of the line and sent him on a wild-goose chase after the French Levant trade. This irrelevant policy did no appreciable harm to the enemy; instead it permitted them to send a squadron from Toulon to Cadiz, where it proved a persistent nuisance.[51]

As a consequence of these developments Hawke was given another independent assignment. From 13 November to 18 December, the *Berwick* like most of the other ships, lay refitting in Mahon Harbour. On the 18th, in the evening, she sailed with the *Royal Oak* (70), *Nassau* (70), the *Leopard* (50), in which Hawke had briefly served as one of Warren's Lieutenants, and the sloop *Sharif*. In obedience to his instructions, Hawke waited until five leagues clear of Cape Mola before opening Rowley's sealed orders. He then read that he was to seek out and destroy four French warships which had been reported off Cape St. Vincent. If he met the one or two British ships then likely to be in the Strait of Gibraltar, he was to take them under his command while engaged on this mission. He was to return to Mahon by 15 January 1745.[52]

Having reached St. Jeremy's Bay near Cape Spartel, he received advice that there were 19 French and Spanish ships already at Cadiz, 13 being of the line, and that 18 sail from Brest were expected to arrive there in the near future. These 18 ships would, it was thought, then proceed to Cartagena to combine with 14 Spanish ships at that port, and operate on the Italian coast. Seeing that his original quarry was reported as being at Cadiz, that his small force might be cut off from the

[51] Richmond, ii, 234-8; 141.

[52] Ad. 51/106; 1/382, 8 Dec. 1744. L.B., 8 Dec. 1744.

Mediterranean, and that Rowley, weakened to that extent, might be taken by surprise, Hawke decided to return to Mahon forthwith. As a strategist, he was always mindful of the importance of concentration of force, and it is interesting to see how he reacted to his first problem involving that principle. He reached Mahon on 10 January 1745.[53]

However, on the basis of the intelligence flowing to Minorca Rowley was already forming an almost opposite picture of the situation. Far from building up an overwhelming concentration in the Mediterranean, the French were evacuating that sea. The change in French policy foreshadowed either an attempt to invade the British homeland or a strong effort in America; but, as far as Rowley was concerned, the position was transformed for the better. Pending the arrival of new orders from England, Rowley decided to increase his support of the Austrians covering the Republic of Genoa. The Spanish had earlier resumed their advance along the Riviera, and John Birtles, the British Consul in Genoa, informed Rowley that the Republic seemed on the point of going over to the enemy. Moreover, a plea had been received from Arthur Villettes, the British Resident in Turin, who was concerned about the growing threat to Lombardy, for ships and bomb vessels to operate on the Genoan coast. Therefore, late in December, Rowley had sent off Captain Crookshanks with three sail. When Hawke reappeared at Mahon on 10 January, the Admiral at once determined to send him to Cape delle Melle, about fifty miles to the W. of Genoa. He gave him the *Berwick*, *Royal Oak*, *Nassau*, *Leopard*, and *Lowestoft* (28). On reaching his station, he was to take Crookshanks's force, consisting of the three 50-gun ships *Dartmouth*, *Chatham*, and *Antelope*, under his command, and send Crookshanks to Mahon with the latest

[53] Ad. 1/382, 11 Jan. 1745. L.B., 19, 31 Dec. 1744.

intelligence. Hawke was to harry the Spanish army, to intercept its supplies, and destroy its magazines.[54]

The Mediterranean may symbolize smooth blue water and brilliant sunshine but in winter it does not necessarily resemble its stereotype. After leaving Mahon on 12 January Hawke's squadron struggled with high seas and contrary winds, and it was not until the 22nd that the miserable outline of Cape delle Melle could be identified. Hawke penned a letter to Birtles, informing him of the new squadron's arrival, but the weather was such that the ship carrying the message took a week to traverse the fifty miles to Genoa.

Hawke appears to have made the acquaintance of Birtles, a lightweight character, on a previous occasion, and he showed a happy touch in adapting accordingly the tone and style of his letters to the Consul. When writing on 22 January he asked for news of the enemy troops, 'also whether you expect them to pay you a visit at Genoa or not, which, if you should, if you have a mind to leave that place with the rest of the English Merchants, and to bring away your effects, if you'll send me word what time you shall be ready to come away, I will send a ship to the place you shall appoint.'

On the 31st he despatched Captain Crookshanks with the latest intelligence from Birtles and from the 'very sensible and very artful' Arthur Villettes, together with a letter to Rowley from himself. Hawke, in Vado Bay, rounded off his dispatch in the following manner:

> I beg, Sir, I may have the honour to assure you that I shall endeavour to the utmost of my power to obey your orders, but if I may presume to take the liberty to offer my opinion, it will be next kin to an impossibility to attempt anything against

[54] Richmond, ii, 238-40. Ad. 1/382, loc. cit. L.B., 11 Jan. 1745.

> the enemy along this shore, the weather being so very bad; having had nothing else since we came upon the coast (until we came in here) but fresh gales of wind, and continuous rains, mists and fogs. However, this will not hinder me from doing everything I am able for His Majesty's service, as far as is consistent with the safety of the ships. The very instant that they have completed their wood and water, I shall go from hence for my station, where I shall keep cruising, and every now and then send a ship into Genoa to the consul for intelligence, as Mr. Villettes desires.[55]

James Young of the *Chatham*, who had been with Crookshanks, now came for the first time under Hawke's command. There was to be a long and cordial association between the two men. Young had been promoted to Post Captain in 1743. In 1759 he was to fly a commodore's broad pennant and command a division at the Battle of Quiberon Bay. Now, on 5 February 1745, Hawke ordered him to scour the coast from Antibes to Nice, attack any vessels of the enemy found in the latter port — provided that he did not hazard his ship — and otherwise to observe what was happening in the various harbours. Young duly carried out his observation, but was unable to make an attack on Nice.

Not long afterwards, another personal connexion began when the *Feversham* (40) came under Hawke's command. On board, she had Midshipman the Honourable Samuel Barrington, who participated as a Captain in Hawke's campaigns during the Seven Years' War, and was himself a prominent Admiral of the American War of Independence.

Meantime, John Birtles had little faith in the Genoese pretensions to neutrality and wanted Hawke to keep a ship

---

[55] L.B., 22, 31 Jan. 1745. Lewis W. S., Vol. 20. pp. 277, 283, for Birtles. Erskine, p. 57, for Villettes.

permanently in the port, thus guaranteeing a means of hasty retreat. This Hawke refused to do, on the grounds that the ship might be immobilized, whether by contrary winds or the sudden intervention of the Republic of Genoa. Instead, he continued to send a ship into the port every three or four days if the weather was favourable. On 12 February he remarked in a letter to Birtles that his squadron had been meeting Dutch ships in some number carrying food to Genoa. This suggested that the Genoese, in accordance with some secret agreement, were accumulating supplies for the use of the Spanish army. Hawke had informed Rowley on the subject and hoped soon to receive orders to intercept such vessels, 'else', he remarked to Birtles, 'you may chance to have corn in too great a plenty on your hands'.[56]

Throughout February Hawke persisted with his blockade, buffeted by choppy seas and frustrated by slippery neutrals. Rowley ordered him not to touch Genoese shipping unless word came from Villettes to do so. He was to be ready to evacuate Horace Mann (British Resident at Leghorn and sounding-board for Horace Walpole) if need arose, and give assistance to the Regency of Florence. This was because a threat had developed from the southern Spanish army under de Gages. However, as far as Hawke was concerned, the weather remained the dominant factor. During the first half of the month hard easterlies thrust him well away towards Corsica; then, with conditions still difficult, he worked his way back to the Riviera.

On 1 March Crookshanks returned to the squadron with a welcome communication from Rowley. On the 5th Hawke wrote in reply:

---

[56] L.B., 1, 5, 9, 10, 12 Feb. 1745. N.R.S.: Barrington Papers, i, 4, &c.

> I am not all sorry that you are so good as to say you will relieve me soon, for we have scarcely had anything else but a constant series of bad weather since we have been upon this station, which has rendered us incapable of doing anything material for the Service. However, until it shall be your pleasure to do so, I am perfectly well satisfied, and shall always be, in executing your commands, if I can only be so happy as to execute them agreeable to your pleasure.
>
> My brother officers make great complaints to me of the badness of their sails and rigging. To speak truth, though most of the ships' sails were new that were bent to their yards when we came out, yet we have split them over and over again, and reeved so much rope that we have now no more to reeve, which has been partly owing to the sails and rope being very bad, as well as to the weather.

Hawke thanked Rowley for saying that he would send him back to England in one of the older ships.

> I have wrote to my friends to acquaint them with it. And I beg you'll please to permit me to tell you that wherever fortune shall carry me, I shall always retain the most grateful sense of the favours you have been pleased to show me, ever since I had the honour of being under your command.[57]

It certainly appeared that Hawke now had behind him a commander-in-chief who would do justice to his merits. Although it was Mathews who first appointed him to command a squadron, he could be discounted as a patron, both because of his lack of credit with the Admiralty and his preoccupation with his own grievances. But Rowley had always shown full appreciation of Hawke's revealing initiative at the Battle of Toulon. Most unfortunately from Hawke's point of

[57] L.B., 23 Feb.-5 Mar. 1745.

view, Rowley was also to put himself on the wrong side of the Admiralty. Early in February he had handled an investigation into the conduct of Richard Norris at the aforesaid battle in an extremely partial manner. Probably out of regard for Norris's much-respected father, Rowley prevented justice from taking effect against him. Norris was allowed to leave the fleet and discreetly disappeared by way of Gibraltar. However, the minutes of this court of inquiry in due course reached their Lordships, and they were, to their credit, highly displeased. It is not irrelevant to note that Winchelsea's Board had been replaced by that headed by the Duke of Bedford and included Rear-Admiral George Anson. Their Lordships requested the Duke of Newcastle — then a Secretary of State, but later, as First Lord of the Treasury, to prove something of a stumbling-block to Hawke — to order the Governor of Gibraltar to see Richard Norris put 'into custody and sent home in close confinement in the first man of war bound for England'; and, on 29 May, they recommended to the Cabinet that Rowley should be 'forthwith recalled from the command of His Majesty's Fleet in the Mediterranean.' Thus was removed from the scene the most influential advocate of the 40-year-old Hawke. When, in the not very distant future, seniority brought him into the zone for promotion to a flag, his case was much more hazardous than it should have been.[58]

However, Hawke's experience in the Mediterranean as a commander of squadrons was undoubtedly of the first importance in fitting him for the supreme responsibility which was suddenly and unexpectedly thrust upon him in 1747. Already, by March 1745, he had commanded an inshore squadron during a close blockade of Toulon; he had cruised beyond Gibraltar for an enemy force whose movements were

[58] S.P.Dom.(N) 42/28, 16 Apr., 29 May 1745. Richmond, ii, 252.

inaccurately known and where it was his function to collect and assess intelligence; and he had conducted a loose form of blockade near Genoa, studied the relevance of sea power to the movement of armies, and appreciated the problems raised by neutrals.

Although Hawke does not seem to have rated highly the amount of success which he achieved off the Riviera, the French and Spanish appear, on the contrary, to have found the persistent cruising of the British ships extremely embarrassing. One French historian wrote: 'The English fleet continued to cruise in the Gulf of Genoa and on the Spanish coast. Its ships, sometimes in one body, at others in separate squadrons, appeared from time to time in full view of our ports or those of the Republic of Genoa and inspired amongst their inhabitants a terror fully justified by their acts of violence.'[59]

Early in March Commodore Osborn appeared on the Italian station, and after taking Hawke under his command he had nine of the line. He withdrew towards Mahon by way of Toulon, and on the 20th sent the *Berwick* and *Stirling Castle* to go in close and observe the French port. The activity there was certainly on a small scale compared with what Hawke had seen the previous July. Now, there were only four ships ready for sea. After a brief spell in Mahon at the end of March, Hawke sailed with Rowley's fleet of twenty-six of the line on 2 April and for the rest of the month took part in a blockade of Cartagena. During May Rowley moved down the Spanish coast towards Gibraltar. He put in there at the beginning of June, by which time there was a good deal of sickness aboard the *Berwick*. At home, a new policy had been evolved to counter the possibility of a cross-Channel invasion. The Mediterranean fleet was being reduced in favour of the Channel Fleet, and

[59] L.B., 12 Feb. 1745, ff. Pajol, iii, 86.

Rowley decided to dispense with one of his three squadrons, namely that off Cartagena. This left his Riviera force dangerously exposed; but, if he was gambling on the enemy's inertia, his guess was justified by events. With twenty of the line, he sailed for Cadiz, hoping to waylay fifteen large ships which had come out from that port. He was also interested in the chance of a Spanish treasure fleet wandering into his clutches. Sir John Laughton, commenting on this strategy, has pointedly described Rowley as a man 'of slender ability except in the matter of looking after his own interest'. As far as Hawke was concerned, a consequence of Rowley's sweep was that, on 26 June, he was ordered to look into Cadiz. The next day found him scanning the heavily fortified outlines of the port. Directing his glass below the forts he could make out, at a distance of about four miles from the *Berwick* 'thirty-two sail of square-rigged vessels, most of them ships'. As he was on his way back to Rowley, who was cruising off Cape Spartel, Hawke learnt of the brilliant action just fought by the *Jersey* (50), which had forced the powerful *Saint Esprit* (74) and a convoy of five vessels to return to Cadiz.[60]

Finally, on 1 August, Rowley moved Hawke out of the *Berwick*. Although in retrospect Hawke must have realized that his appointment to this ship had saved his professional career, he can hardly have left her with unmixed regret. It had required constant effort and attention to keep so unprepossessing a crew battle-ready over a period of two years. It was doubtless with relief that he took over command of the *Neptune*, Lestock's former flagship, which was to go back to England. He set off on the homeward voyage with four other naval

[60] L.B., 3, 10, 17, 20, 24 Mar., 20, 21 May, 26, 27 June 1745. Ad. 1/382, 1 Apr., 1 May, 2 June 1745. Richmond, ii, 243-5, 247 n-2. D.N.B.: Rowley.

vessels under his orders, called at Lisbon to collect several British merchantmen and headed for Portsmouth. The winds proved persistently unhelpful and, with his convoy almost out of water, Hawke was glad to make Plymouth on 20 September.

He found England in an unsettled condition. Prince Charles Edward had triumphantly entered Edinburgh on the 17th and menacing concentrations of French troops had been built up at Ostend and Dunkirk. It transpired that on 31 August the Admiralty had issued an order for Hawke to attend the forthcoming court martial of Admiral Mathews — a trial arising from a recommendation of the House of Commons that Mathews, Lestock, and several of their captains should be arraigned. Mathews had asked for Hawke as a witness for his defence. The series of trials was to begin on 23 September; so, as soon as their Lordships heard that Hawke had reached Plymouth on the 20th, they ordered him to hand over charge of the *Neptune* to the 1st Lieutenant and go overland to Chatham where the trials were to be held.

Seeing that Colonel Bladen was still living, Hawke was probably reunited with Catharine in London on about 29 September. The high rate of infant mortality, common to all peoples up to that date, had not robbed them of their third-born child. The warmth of Hawke's joy on first seeing little Martin, his 18-month-old son, can readily be inferred from the former's home-loving, affectionate nature. Martin, who had been born on 29 April 1744, had been given the second name of Bladen, after his great-uncle. The love between Hawke and Martin was to endure, steady and unbroken, through the coming years of sadness and of triumph.[61]

---

[61] Ad. 1/382, 1 Aug. 1745; 1/1885, 20, 27 Sept. 1745. Hist.MSS.Com., *Du Cane MSS.*, Adm. Medley's Papers, 31 Aug. 1745. Clowes, iii, 103.

CHAPTER 4: THE COURTS MARTIAL

ALTHOUGH so speedily summoned to attend the courts martial at Chatham, Hawke had to bear the frustration of sitting for day after day without being called to give evidence. In the course of the first two days, the lieutenants of the *Dorsetshire* (which had not fully supported the *Marlborough* at the Battle of Toulon) were examined and acquitted. Then Burrish, the Captain of the same ship, under whose orders the *Berwick* had gone out to the Mediterranean in 1743, came before the court. After a trial lasting from 25 September until 9 October, the court, under the presidency of Hawke's former patron, Admiral Sir Chaloner Ogle, sentenced Burrish to be 'cashiered, and for ever rendered incapable of being an Officer in His Majesty's Navy'. Hawke had not been called at all, for the obvious reason that the *Berwick* had been well out of view of the *Dorsetshire* during the battle.

The Government originally intended to have the minutes of all the trials published, and those concerning Burrish and his lieutenants did appear in 1746. However, the original plan seems to have been abandoned. The minutes in respect of Captains Edmund Williams and John Ambrose, who were tried after Burrish, also came out in 1746, but at that point publication appears to have ceased. This helps to explain the public ignorance of Hawke's conduct at the Battle of Toulon. Ironically, it was well brought out in the trials of Captains Sclater and Pett, which followed those of Williams and Ambrose, that the performance of the *Berwick* had been quite outstanding.

On the fourth day of Pett's trial, 25 November 1745, Hawke was at last heard in evidence. He gave a modest account of what he had seen of the battle, which was almost entirely restricted to his own sphere of action. The activity or inactivity of other British ships had clearly not struck him as relevant to his own duty. Seeing that he had not bothered particularly to watch what Pett's *Princessa* was doing, his part in the court's proceedings came to an end when Ogle enquired, 'Captain Pett, have you any questions to ask?' and Pett replied, 'No, as Captain Hawke knows so little of me, I have no questions to ask.'[62]

Sclater's trial began on 17 December. Hawke was ordered to attend, but was not called in evidence. Apart from the probability that he had nothing to contribute, he was in any case unfit to travel for much of the month. On 9 December he had reported to the Admiralty from Marlborough Street that a 'violent cold and cough' had kept him indoors for a week and was not improving. These colds and coughs were a recurrent ailment with him, though he seems to have kept free of them when at sea.[63]

By this time Bonnie Prince Charlie's revolt was being contained, and the masterly dispositions of the hot-tempered Admiral Vernon had frustrated any French hopes of crossing the Channel when, on the 26th, their Lordships wrote to the said Admiral, 'In regard to your so often mentioned desire of laying down your command… we signify hereby our content

---

[62] *Minutes of the Proceedings of a Court Martial assembled on the 23rd September*, printed and published by Charles Fearne, Judge Advocate of the Fleet, 1746. *Copies of all the Minutes and Proceedings taken… upon the several tryals of Capt. George Burrish, Capt. Edmund Williams, Capt. John Ambrose* [and the Lts. of the *Dorsetshire*], 1746. Ad. 1/5282.
[63] ibid. Ad. 2/492, 22 Oct. 1745; 1/1885, 9 Dec. 1745.

thereto.' Prince Charles was finally defeated at Culloden on 16 April 1746.

The following month there was a general expectation of severe treatment being prescribed when Richard Lestock was brought before the court, which now had Rear-Admiral Perry Mayne as president. To the astonishment of posterity — and, obviously, to the inconsolable chagrin of Admiral Thomas Mathews — Lestock was acquitted on all seven of the charges brought against him by his former Commander-in-Chief. Seeing that the (unpublished) minutes leave no room for doubt that Lestock had been far from doing his best at the Battle of Toulon, and that twenty-six witnesses, including five captains, testified to this effect, the view that the Whig Government exerted undue influence on the court on favour of the Whig Lestock is not without plausibility.

On 5 June, amid the bitter preparations for his own trial, Mathews wrote from Hammersmith again asking Corbett to include Hawke amongst his witnesses. Hawke and his family were then at Lymington in Hampshire — later the place where Catharine's premature death occurred. Hawke appears to have attended this last trial which began on the 16th, although once again he did not give evidence. It was not until 22 October that Mathews was adjudged to be cashiered, because he had been 'a principal cause of the miscarriage' off Toulon.[64]

Hawke must have found the overall result of the trials instructive if not completely edifying. The principal villain, Lestock, was not only cleared of all the charges brought against him but was soon afterwards appointed to command the naval escort of St. Clair's remarkably inglorious expedition against l'Orient. Mathews, who had at least tried to fight, had been

---

[64] Ad. 1/5278, 5279; 1/381, 5 June 1746; 1/1886, 9 June 1746. Clowes, iii, 104-6. Richmond, ii, 54-7, 260-71.

pushed out of the Service for his pains — though it can only be admitted that he had been an unsatisfactory Commander-in-Chief, despite his grasp of strategy. Otherwise, the principal charge brought, not unreasonably, against the various captains was that they had not fought hard enough; and consequently Burrish was permanently cashiered, Edmund Williams was found unfit to be employed at sea, Ambrose was cashiered during the King's pleasure (and later restored to the list of captains), Dilkes was placed on half-pay; both Pett and Sclater, who had been charged by Lestock, were acquitted; and Temple West, Thomas Cooper, and James Lloyd, who had intelligently kept to windward of the enemy's van in order to discourage doubling, were cashiered only temporarily. Two other captains would have been tried if they had been available. Captain Frogmore had died while still away on service, and, as previously related, Richard Norris had decided to explore foreign pastures for the good of his health.[65]

For the rest of 1746 Hawke remained unemployed. Catharine was expecting another child, and it was probably at this time that the Hawkes first lived at the rented property at Swaythling, not far north of Southampton, where the children were mainly brought up. Hawke himself seems to have regarded it as the family home although he never owned it.

A second son was safely delivered in December and was named Edward.[66]

---

[65] Clowes, loc. cit. Richmond, iii, 24, 27-34.

[66] Ad. i/1886, 24 Apr. 1747.

CHAPTER 5: PROMOTION OF A STRATEGIST

IF Hawke's temperament had resembled that of Admiral Mathews he might have felt, at the end of 1746, that all the world had conspired to suppress knowledge of his Mediterranean services. Yet, unbeknown to him, the first of patrons in that age of patronage had almost certainly read the minutes of the trials of Pett and Sclater and drawn his own conclusions. George II had been born a Hanoverian in 1683 and in Hanover his heart had remained. But he was also the last of the Kings of England to draw a sword and lead his troops into battle. On 27 June 1743, at Dettingen, he had rejected advice to place himself in safety from the advancing French with the words, 'What do you think I came here for? To be a poltroon?' So there is nothing improbable in the traditional story that, because of his behaviour at the Battle of Toulon, Hawke became the King's favourite Captain.

However, New Year's Day 1747 found Hawke still a Captain, nearly 42 years of age, and ashore on half-pay. Moreover, Colonel Bladen had died in 1746, leaving his nephew apparently without any patron whatever. In January 1747 there was much talk in the coffee houses about a forthcoming promotion, probably of six captains, to the rank of rear-admiral; and according to one retailer of the gossip, Hawke's chances were generally rated below those of Knowles, Forbes, and Boscawen. The three latter were junior to him on the list of captains, but, as this John le Keux observed to his friend Admiral Medley, all three of them were 'honourables and good men'. This, in the eighteenth century, was an ideal combination of qualities, and Hawke stood in real danger of being squeezed out.[67]

April 1747 saw Hawke at Plymouth. The *Mars* (64) having been captured from the French the previous year by Captain Philip Saumarez of the *Nottingham* (one of Anson's protégés), Hawke was given command of her and was to collect a team of officers, petty officers, and foremast men while she was being fitted for sea.[68]

When summer came the promotions were hatched. If Hawke was looking to the peers of the realm for kindly support, he looked in vain. Though Anson, a baron since the Battle of Cape Finisterre in May, had emerged as the dominant member of the Admiralty Board and wanted the promotions to go to the best officers, he does not seem to have established a system for collecting reports on officers. Instead, he relied a good deal on first-hand knowledge. As a result Hawke, despite the Battle of Toulon and the valuable months in command of squadrons, would have been consigned to oblivion if the maker of peers had not intervened. The King had not forgotten his Captain. The story runs that when the Duke of Bedford presented to the Monarch the list of captains, showing those recommended by the Admiralty for promotion and superannuation respectively, the King at once exclaimed that 'he would not have Hawke yellowed!' The upshot was that although, as the Admiralty wished, the promotion was extended down the list to include the Honourable Edward Boscawen — and, above him, those other 'honourables and good men', Knowles and Forbes — Edward Hawke obtained

[67] Williams, i, 107. (Williams, i and Williams, ii refer to 'Pitt' — see Sources.) Hist.MSS.Com., *Du Cane MSS*, Adm. Medley's Papers, p. 163.

[68] Ad. 1/1886, 24 Apr., 12, 29 May 1747.

full benefit of his hard-earned seniority. On 15 July he became a Rear-Admiral of the White.

It probably should be mentioned here that the ranks of admiral were subdivided according to squadron. The Squadrons of the Fleet (taken as a whole) were, in order of seniority, the Red, the White, and the Blue. Thus, the most junior rank of admiral was that of Rear-Admiral of the Blue. The highest rank being reserved for one admiral only, there was no such designation as Admiral of the Red. The holder of the rank was 'the Admiral of the Fleet'. As for the expression 'yellowed', this referred in jocular fashion to Anson's scheme whereby worthy captains who were not wanted as active admirals could be superannuated as rear-admirals without squadron — or, as the saying had it, Admirals of the 'Yellow' Squadron.

On 21 July Hawke hoisted his flag aboard the *Gloucester*, Captain Philip Durell, and took command of the port and dockyard at Plymouth. The extent to which he was unknown to Anson's following is brought out by Augustus Keppel's inquiry of Philip Saumarez, then docking the *Nottingham* at Plymouth: 'What do you think of all these promotions? How do you like Admiral H.? Does he carry it high or low?' There is no record of Saumarez's reply; but it can be taken for granted that Hawke accepted his advancement with unblemished modesty.

Hawke now came across Captain George Brydges Rodney, probably for the first time. That young officer of 28 years, although he had not made the voyage round the world, did not lack social and political connexions; and, besides being on good terms with the Anson group, he also commanded the *Eagle* (60) at an age when Hawke commanded the *Wolf* (10). The first interchange of correspondence between the two men was devoid of that quality imagined by some to attach to admirals, namely mystique. On 25 July Hawke ordered a survey to be made on Rodney's rotten cheese.[69]

A feature of Hawke's command at Plymouth, which brings out the spirit in which the war was being fought, was the treatment of enemy prisoners. Of the 2,965 for which Hawke was responsible, 471 were allowed to move about on parole.[70]

However, as far as his future career was concerned, by far the most important event of the Admiral's command at the port was his acquisition of a secretary, one John Hay. No other instance comes to mind to show that Hawke was not a good judge of character, but he certainly made a considerable error on this occasion. His recognition of his mistake did come in the end but it was astonishingly belated. Captain Augustus Hervey, who came across Hay in 1756, described him as 'a damned interested Scotch secretary, a fellow without a grain of understanding who had been bred up to business in a shop'. Hervey and his *bête noire*, Anson, were at least in perfect agreement in their view of the mischievous character of John Hay and of the undue influence which he exercised over Hawke. Horace Walpole also remarked on this curiosity, though he may have been following the opinion of his friend Hervey. Hay's success in ingratiating himself with Hawke was probably due to the latter's dislike of letter-writing and paper-work. Hay was clever enough to take a good deal of this off the Admiral's shoulders. Undoubtedly, he possessed a good literary style and a capacity for clear self-expression. Although Hawke in his holograph letters — many of them written

---

[69] Namier, pp. 33-4. D.N.B.: Hawke. Keppel, i, 104. Erskine, pp. xxi, 79, 301. Clowes, iii, 344, 565. O.B., 25 July 1747. Burrows, p. 106. Ad. 1/88, 21 July 1747.
[70] Ad. 1/88, 28 July 1747.

without Hay hovering over his shoulder — demonstrated that he could, when inclined, write clearly and well, it remains true that his official dispatches acquired more polish after his appointment of a secretary. For example, on 4 August he wrote to Corbett in his own hand that he would have Captain Rodney's Gunner tried 'as soon as possible, provided the ship dont go to sea before the witnesses can be examined'. No such homely expressions appear in the long series of dispatches written out by clerks after 12 October 1747, although the 'dont' is typical enough of Hawke's domestic correspondence. Up to October, Hawke wrote the original version of most of the dispatches.

Therefore, some of the reputation which Hawke subsequently acquired as a writer of dispatches properly belongs to the execrable Hay. The subject will again be taken up, at an appropriate moment.[71]

Hawke would not have found his role at Plymouth particularly congenial. He was eager to exercise command at sea, but he could hardly have imagined the magnitude of the opportunity which, at the beginning of August, was suddenly presented to him.

Following the ideas of Vernon, Anson had established the policy of keeping a strong Western Squadron constantly cruising in the Bay of Biscay. This was becoming the cornerstone of British naval strategy. From the autumn of 1746 until the spring of 1747, Anson had commanded this squadron, which was in fact the main battle-fleet, and in May his policy had borne fruit. His strong force overwhelmed an

---

[71] O.B., 23 July 1747, ff., for Hay's initials on orders. Erskine, pp. 217, 220, 301. Add.MSS. 35359, f. 410, for Anson's opinion of Hay. Walpole, *Memoirs of George II*, 1846, iii, 50. Ad. 1/88, 4 Aug. 1747. Other holographs: 20 Aug., 5, 6, 12, Oct. See H.P.P. for examples of H.'s natural style.

inadequate French squadron which was covering a convoy, at what has become known as the First Battle of Cape Finisterre. Anson was raised to the peerage in recognition of this, the first important naval success against the French since Rooke's strategic victory off Malaga in 1704, and for the rest of the war he directed policy at the Admiralty. He bequeathed the command of the Western Squadron to Vice-Admiral Sir Peter Warren who had played a prominent part at the recent battle.

By early August the Admiralty had hopes of a second major success for the Western Squadron. According to intelligence reports, a large convoy and escort were making ready to sail from France; and, on 3 August, Keppel, who had recently been a prisoner of war in that country, wrote to their Lordships: 'The intelligence I got in France I have not mentioned to the Board, as I could not be certain of it, for I heard it in France, where there is seldom any truth spoken on such occasions. However, their talk was that fourteen sail were nearly ready, eleven of which were at Brest, and three at Rochefort, in order to convoy their trade to the East and West Indies and Canada.'[72]

It was at this juncture that Warren, suffering badly from the dreaded and all-too-common scurvy, appeared at Plymouth in the *Yarmouth*. On 3 August, he wrote to Corbett that he must have 'a little respite in port' and medical advice. Believing that, as he told Anson in a personal letter of the same date, there was 'no immediate service of great importance', he suggested that Hawke should be appointed as his second-in-command and take charge of the squadron until he had recovered his health. Hawke, he added, would 'not be displeased' with such an appointment. If the Lords approved, Hawke could sail with the *Monmouth* (64), *Windsor* (60), *Eagle* (60), and *Amazon* (20) to join the remnant of the squadron (the *Prince Frederick* (64),

[72] Keppel, i, 101.

Centurion (54), and *Augusta* (60)) which was still cruising in the Bay of Biscay. Warren brought out his opinion of the newly promoted Admiral by writing (to Anson) of 'Mr. Hawke, with whom I should like very well to serve, and, I dare say, he with me'.[73]

Until 7 August, Hawke was kept in suspense, waiting for the Admiralty's decision. He was 'prepared to go at a moment's notice'. However, Warren's dispatch of the 3rd had caused considerable perturbation amongst their Lordships. Anson wrote to Warren that he was anxious about putting the squadron 'under so young an officer'! This querulous response can only be explained by the supposition that Anson's knowledge of Hawke's record and character was virtually nil.

After hearing from Anson, Warren was 'uneasy' about the situation, but assumed that there was no reasonable alternative to giving charge of the squadron to Hawke and had all his instructions ready before, on 7 August, the Lords' confirmation arrived at Plymouth. Hawke, accompanied by his Flag Captain, John Moore, and his secretary, John Hay, hurried aboard the *Windsor* and hoisted his flag. In his haste and enthusiasm he left many of his clothes and belongings on shore in the charge of Lieutenant James Hobbs who was serving under his patronage. Warren had already sent out Rodney with the *Eagle* and *Amazon* to join the squadron; so when, on 10 August, the *Windsor*'s sails began to fill and she slid down past Drake's Island, she had in company only the *Monmouth* and the dogger *Hunter*.[74]

---

[73] Ad. 1/88, 3 Aug. 1747. Ad.MSS. 15957, f. 205-7; also f. 211 for Warren to Anson, 7 Aug.

[74] ibid., f. 211. I.L., 30 Oct. 1747. Ad. 1/88, Warren to Clevland, 7 Aug.; H. to Clevland, 10 Aug. 1747.

The Captain of the *Monmouth*, who became a close friend of Hawke's before the end of this remarkable cruise, was an outstanding character by the name of Henry Harrison. He had been promoted to Lieutenant in 1706, when Hawke was a one-year-old baby and the date of Boscawen's birth was six years ahead. During the War of the Spanish Succession he performed several outstanding feats of daring and, when on service against privateers, improvised an early version of a 'Q' ship to the surprise and discomforture of his quarry. In 1711 his merit was recognized by Admiral Sir John Leake who gave him a temporary command. But it was all to no avail. Harrison possessed no 'interest' and he reverted to Lieutenant. When the War of Jenkins's Ear broke out, it may have failed to restore the organ in question to its original position, but it did bring belated justice to Harrison who was promoted to Post Captain on 27 February 1740. By 1747 he must have passed the age of 60, but he was yet to achieve great things — for he sailed that summer under the command of one whose fighting qualities were immeasurably enhanced by his ability as a strategist.[75]

Warren's instructions to Hawke, dated 8 August, were as follows:

> Pursuant to an order from the Right Honourable the Lords Commissioners of the Admiralty bearing the date the 5th instant, directing you should serve in the Squadron under my command;
>
> You are hereby required and directed accordingly to put yourself under my command, and follow all such orders as you shall from time to time receive from me for His Majesty's service, sending me weekly accounts of the state and condition of the Squadron, and acquainting me with your

[75] Charnock, v, 24-32.

> proceedings, as often as opportunity offers, for their Lordships' information.

It was thus made clear that Hawke was to report to Warren, not to the Board. This was later to cause some embarrassment.

On a separate paper, Warren instructed Hawke as to his conduct. The ships already on station in the Bay of Biscay were hoping to intercept four French East Indiamen and two warships. After joining them, Hawke was to aim at 'destroying the commerce of the enemy, outward and homeward bound,... suppressing their privateers, and annoying their commerce as much as possible'. Warren's own instructions — like those of Anson before him — left him a wide exercise of discretion, and Warren put Hawke in the same position, free to adapt his movements according to the information he obtained. The rendezvous (for reinforcements, ships bearing messages, etc.) was 'between the latitudes of Belle Isle and Ushant, from ten to thirty or forty leagues to the westward'. Hawke was at liberty to establish a new rendezvous if need arose, provided that he left a frigate or sloop on the old one. Finally:

> You are to continue at sea as long as your provisions and water will last, or as you shall judge necessary for His Majesty's service, according to what intelligence you shall get of the enemy, and then to return into port with all or part of your squadron, proceeding with all those above the 4th rate to Portsmouth, and sending such of the rest as you think fit into Plymouth, and to leave orders with those which you shall keep at sea or send thither after your coming into port to cruise diligently on such station as you shall judge best.[76]

[76] L.B., 8 Aug. 1747.

It should perhaps be explained that 4th rates were the smallest ships deemed fit to stand in the line of battle. They carried 50 or 60 guns, and at about this time the Admiralty began to exclude the 50s from the lists of ships of the line because they were much smaller than the least powerful line-ships of the French navy. Otherwise, 1st rates carried 100 guns, 2nd rates had less than 100 but more than 74, and 3rd rates bore 64 to 74. During Hawke's cruise, his largest ship was a 3rd rate of 66 guns.

As soon as 12 August, Hawke found and took under his command the *Prince Frederick*, *Augusta*, and *Centurion*, which had meanwhile been joined by the *Gloucester* (50).[77] He made sure of being able to communicate with any ship likely to join him by issuing a set of ships' signals for the whole of the Western Squadron, comprising forty-two sail. Thus, the signal for the *Monmouth* was a red pennant at the mizen topmast head; that for the *Eagle* a white pennant at the main topsail yardarm. Richmond thought that Hawke also issued a set of the famous Additional Fighting Instructions during this cruise, but he was almost certainly mistaken in this. The copy to be found in Hawke's Letter Books forms part of the material passed on to Hawke by Warren, and the captains of the squadron clearly had their copies of 'the General Printed Sailing and Fighting Instructions, with the Additional Signals thereunto annexed' before Hawke went to sea in August. Hawke referred to the Instructions by the title just quoted when he issued his first order to the squadron, the set of ships' signals of 12 August. As there is no sign that the Additional Signals, including a full set of Additional Fighting Instructions, existed before 1746, it is now possible to date the original issue a little more accurately than heretofore. By far the most probable time was during

---

[77] Ad. 1/88, 20 Aug. 1747 (H. to Warren).

Anson's cruise which began in the autumn of 1746 and ended in the spring of 1747. This is an appropriate moment at which to summarize the state of British naval tactics at the period of Hawke's cruise of 1747.

Naval manoeuvres and tactics were primarily governed by the General Printed Sailing and Fighting Instructions. The Additional Fighting Instructions, issued through Anson's influence as part of the Additional Signals, were designed to supplement the General Printed Instructions but not to alter their basic character, and for this reason only a limited importance should be attached to them. As has already been indicated in the account of the Battle of Toulon, two of the key articles of the General Fighting Instructions were those which forbad captains to leave the line in pursuit of an adversary, and ordered that each ship was to remain in its prescribed position in the line. These articles imparted a defensive flavour to British tactics, although, as Hawke had shown at the Battle of Toulon, it was not certain that Article 21 was completely defensive in intention. The actual wording was: 'None of the ships in the fleet shall pursue any small number of the enemy's ships until the main body be disabled or run.' Seeing that Article 13 read: 'As soon as the Admiral shall hoist a red flag on the flagstaff at the fore topmast-head, every ship in the fleet is to use their utmost endeavour to engage the enemy, in the order the admiral has prescribed unto them', it seems that the meaning of 'pursue' in Article 21 was doubtful. Hawke always assumed that as long as an enemy ship was still part of its main body, its British opponent was not using its 'utmost endeavour to engage the enemy' unless it pressed in to very close quarters. It therefore seemed to him that the only impediment in the Instructions to really aggressive tactics was represented by the last phrase of Article 13, 'in the order which the Admiral has prescribed unto them', which had bothered him at the Battle of Toulon. It will be seen later that, when he was fully established as a fleet commander, Hawke radically altered the phrase in question. The fact that Boscawen issued an Additional Instruction to much the same aggressive effect, about two years after Hawke's alteration, suggests that, in so far as the Fighting Instructions were blamed for the indecisive character of actions fought by admirals such as Byng, it was not the Instructions which were at fault. It was primarily the admiral. If he possessed spirit, understanding, imagination, and self-confidence, he saw to it that his fleet was supplied with aggressive instructions. If he was defeatist in temperament and mediocre in ability, like Byng, he was only too glad to leave unaltered a set of instructions susceptible of a thoroughly defensive interpretation. The fact that the Admiralty issued the same printed General Instructions from the time of Rooke till the American Independence War did tend to favour lack of enterprise; but Hawke showed in 1744 that a defensive interpretation was not unavoidable — and the members of the court martial of 1745 seemed to agree with him.[78]

By 13 August Hawke's squadron was off Belle Isle and a French sloop was captured. Following the usual procedure, the prisoners were taken aboard different British ships and the

---

[78] O.B., 12 Aug. 1747, copied from list in L.B., f. 55. This list was received by H. from Warren. For the Additional Ins. already issued before H. took command, see L.B. f. 41-55. Richmond, iii, 263. Ad. 1/5282 for cts. m. of 1745. N.M.M.: Duff Papers: also Papers of Michael Clements. There are sufficient amendments to the General Printed Ins. here to invalidate Corbett's concept of 'The Permanent Instructions', cf., N.R.S., *Fighting Instructions*, p. 195 ff. Not surprisingly, the alterations made to the printed Instructions by Hawke, and — through an Additional Instruction — by Boscawen (*Fighting Instructions*, p, 224), are more important than those made by other commanders-in-chief.

results of their interrogation compared. It emerged that seven merchantmen had been sailing by twos and threes from l'Orient since 5 August.

Nothing further of note occurred until, on 19 August, two vessels hove into view. They were immobile. Soon it could be seen that they were both damaged. If they had been fighting, they were ill-matched opponents. In fact, they had been fighting, and the large-ship, of 500 tons and 28 guns, had been captured by the little one which mounted 10 guns! The latter was the sloop *Viper* which had sailed from Plymouth a few days ahead of Hawke and the other was a French, South-Pacific trader. Hawke reported to Warren that Hay, the *Viper*'s commander, 'was killed after he had engaged her with the greatest bravery imaginable for two and a half hours, although she was so greatly superior to him'. Hay's Lieutenant maintained the attack and after another half hour the trader surrendered. Hawke sent the *Viper* and her prize to Plymouth under the escort of the scurvy-stricken *Prince Frederick* and also the dogger *Hunter* which was foul-bottomed. He was thus left with only five of the line and no frigate or sloop. In his letter to Warren of the 20th he therefore asked for reinforcements and for a frigate. As soon as the latter arrived he would send it to examine Rochefort — which in fact proved later to be l'Etanduère's point of departure. Hawke's final paragraph is worth noticing: 'I flatter myself you will do me the justice to believe that I have nothing so much at heart as the faithful discharge of my duty, and in such manner as will give satisfaction both to the Lords of the Admiralty and yourself. This shall ever be my utmost ambition, and no lucre of profit or other views shall induce me to act otherwise.' In this cynical, platitude-weary age, it is tempting to dismiss Hawke's words as a perfunctory formula. But this would be a fundamental error.

At the date when they were written such sentiments were far from platitudinous. They comprise a statement of attitude by a man who may be fairly regarded as the first great professional officer of the naval service, and who conceived of duty as something to be kept distinct from politics or the hope of monetary reward. This is not to argue that Hawke was uninterested in prize money; but he set an example in showing that such personal considerations were to be subordinated to patriotic duty.[79]

The following day, the 21st, brought with it another interesting encounter. The *Amazon* (24) which had been sent off (before Hawke's arrival on station) to look into Brest, now appeared, as did the familiar *Portland* (50) and another frigate, the *Grand Turk* (20). Between 1 and 20 August, Hawke's ships, including the latest arrivals, had collected information from fifty-one different vessels. He inferred that the French were collecting warships at Brest which were to ensure a safe passage for the merchantmen at La Rochelle and Bordeaux. This appraisal was accurate. As a result of Anson's persistent open blockades, the French were experiencing acute economic distress and had determined to fight a way through for their important West Indian trade.

Altogether the situation did not look bright from the point of view of the French and the usual ineptitude of their Ministry of Marine did not improve matters. The West Indies were France's most important area of colonial trade but this trade was now at a standstill. The Ministry therefore determined to send out to the West Indies a huge convoy of merchant vessels (ultimately numbering 252). Initially, it was seriously proposed to let this convoy sail with an escort of one ship of the line and a few frigates. However, Captain Conflans — destined to meet

[79] Ad. 1/88, loc. cit.

Hawke on a certain day in 1759 — wrote to Maurepas, the Navy Minister, advising him that this was not an ideal arrangement. It would be better to send out l'Etanduère's Brest squadron in strength, or alternatively to defer the sailing of the merchantmen till late in the year. As will be seen, the latter suggestion would probably have succeeded. In any case, Conflans, referring appropriately to the 'triste exemple' of la Jonquière's convoy the previous May, advised that only small numbers of merchantmen should be sent out one at a time. The result of Conflans's intervention was that l'Etanduère with eight of the line and a 60-gun East Indiaman were provided as escort, but the rest of the former's suggestions were rejected. This proved a fatal compromise. The naval squadron represented an important part of the French sea service, but was not strong enough to safeguard the convoy unless at the cost of sacrificing itself. Such a sacrifice might achieve its immediate purpose, but only at the expense of French sea-power and the future movement of French trade, let alone any hope of defeating Britain by invasion or blockade.[80]

After assessing the situation on 21 August, Hawke, with six of the line and two frigates, most of them with foul bottoms, sent off a dispatch to Warren by the *Amazon*. He asked urgently for some clean ships to join him 'with the utmost expedition'.

The *Amazon* put into Plymouth on the 23rd. Warren, now at Portsmouth, soon had the dispatch; and the news it contained was productive of excitement at the Board of Admiralty. On the 29th, Clevland, the Assistant Secretary, wrote to Anson that Sir Peter Warren 'is under a great dilemma, judging it necessary to go to sea at this critical juncture himself and fearing his health will not admit of it'. The degree of

[80] ibid., 21 Aug. 1747. Lacour-Gayet, pp. 172-3. Chevalier, i, 256.

confidence reposed in Hawke by Admiralty opinion is reflected in Clevland's agitated suggestion that Anson himself should rush off to sea to take charge of the squadron. In any case their Lordships were irritated by the fact that Hawke's first two dispatches had been addressed to Warren instead of to themselves, and they inquired of both Admirals the reasons for this irregular proceeding. They told Warren 'to reinforce Admiral Hawke effectually and speedily' and implied a hope that he could somehow get away to sea himself.

Although by no means recovered from his bout of scurvy, Warren made a valiant effort to get to sea. On 30 August he wrote to Clevland: 'As their Lordships have done me much greater honour than I can ever have the vanity to think I deserve, I am determined to sail tomorrow morning at daylight with [the *St. George*, *Hampton Court*, *Devonshire*, one sloop, and two fireships], and to detach one of them as soon as I get out to Plymouth to order the ships there to join me off Plymouth Sound, and will proceed without a moment's loss of time to join Mr. Hawke.' As to Hawke's not reporting direct to the Board, he 'has orders to transmit all the intelligence he can procure to me, for their Lordships' information, and I presume he thought me in town, but I will direct him by the first opportunity to send such immediately to their Lordships'.[81]

The just and generous Warren was frustrated by the weather, as Keppel reported to Anson on 7 September: 'It is with the greatest concern that, for these five days, we have seen Sir Peter Warren tumbling about with the tide, and was not got out of our sight; it will vex him extremely, and make him low-spirited, I fear. I saw him the day before he sailed. His spirits

[81] Ad. 1/88, 21 Aug. and Warren to Clevland, 30 Aug. 1747 (2). Add. MSS. 15956, Clevland to Anson, 29 Aug. 1747.

were then good, and his zeal great. I wish him success, and well out of the Channel.'

Out in the Bay, Hawke was in constant expectation of Warren's arrival, but, having been given wide discretion, he began to develop the kind of relentless strategy which was to leave its mark on the history of two major wars. He sorted out and assessed the intelligence, and related it to the facts and possibilities of geography, the season and the weather. Simple probabilities emerged, and he held these clear in his mind. While keeping the enemy as far as possible in ignorance of his true position, he patiently worked for an interception, and maintained his strength fully concentrated, ready to strike a single, stunning blow.

Until 27 August he cruised on the initial rendezvous to the W. of Belle Isle and Ushant. Reports indicated that the enemy were not on the point of sailing, doubtless because they knew of the presence of the British squadron. Hawke therefore adopted a form of deception. He wrote to Warren on 7 September:

> The 30th we made Cape Ortegal, and stood well in with the land, under an easy sail, in order to give the people on shore reason to believe we were cruising off there. This I thought a proper method to prevent the enemy's avoiding us... By the intelligence you will receive herewith, it seems to me pretty clear that there is a large fleet of merchant vessels and ships making up at Rochelle, bound to the West Indies. I should think the most effectual method to intercept them would be by cruising with a squadron (if we can't have two) between the latitudes of 48.00° and 44.00° N., at a tolerable distance to the westward. By taking this measure, if they should gain intelligence of us, they could never well know how to avoid us.[82]

On 5 September he arrived back off Belle Isle and stood in desperate need of a reinforcement of clean ships. The *Centurion* and *Augusta* had been out for three months and 'were very foul, and in want of water and provisions'. This left one 64, one 60, three 50s, and a frigate — not a very impressive Western Squadron. Great was the Admiral's relief on the 10th when Captain Watson appeared with four 60s and a 40-gun frigate. Watson handed over to Hawke an Admiralty letter dated 28 August which did not contain much sweet encouragement. Why had the Lords not been kept properly informed about the movements of the squadron? However, Hawke does not seem to have been unduly perturbed over the matter and it was not until 5 October that he wrote a dignified explanation along the lines of that offered by Warren.[83]

Meanwhile the Admiralty had been trying — fortunately in vain — to interfere with Hawke's conduct of operations. Warren had been attempting to get onto his station in early September, but, to his bitter disappointment, the scurvy forced him to return ashore. Broken-hearted, he asked for permission to resign the command which he had been so proud to receive. Their Lordships decided to appoint Hawke to the operational command, not of the Western Squadron as a whole, but of a squadron of listed ships. He was issued with two sets of instructions, both dated on 8 September. The first set was like that given to Warren and passed on to Hawke by him. As has been indicated, this allowed the Admiral considerable freedom of conduct. But the second set was an entirely different matter. The principal clause read as follows: 'Whereas we have by our order of this day appointed you to command a squadron of His Majesty's ships to be employed in the Soundings and seas

---

[82] Keppel, i, 110. Ad. 1/88, 7 Sept. 1747.
[83] Ad. 1/88, 5 Oct. 1747.

adjacent, we do in addition thereto hereby require and direct you to cruise with the said squadron or the major part thereof between Ushant and Cape Finisterre, keeping twenty leagues to the westward of each cape, and to make the land of the former every fourteen days.' An escape clause was inserted towards the end of the instructions but, seeing that Hawke would have to give unassailable reasons for departing from the policy laid down, these instructions certainly restricted his freedom of action. More important, it will be seen that the recommended type of cruising would have been most unlikely to bring about an interception.

Richmond has been the only historian to devote much attention to the instructions of 8 September and to show their importance; but he was mistaken in thinking that Hawke received them from Captain Fox, who joined the squadron with a reinforcement on 26 September. The last of Fox's ships to sail from England moved down from Spithead to St. Helens on 8 September, and all of them had got clear of 'the Ledge' by p.m. on the 9th, so there was not time for the instructions of the 8th to reach them. In any case, when Hawke wrote to Warren as late as 11 October he was obviously unaware of the existence of the instructions in question. Exactly when he did receive them remains a small mystery. The first and only sign of his having them is an order which he issued to his captains on 15 October to inform them that they were under his command on a more permanent basis than before, according to 'an order from the Lords Commissioners of the Admiralty dated 8 September 1747'. By 15 October the instructions had ceased to be an embarrassment. The decisive battle of the First Maritime War had been fought.[84]

---

[84] Richmond, iii, 101-3. Cf. Burrows, p. 178. Richmond was probably misled by this into believing that H. had received the instructions by

Captain Watson's reinforcement of 10 September brought the squadron's strength up to nine of the line and two frigates. As he now had 'a tolerable force', Hawke decided to move 'into the latitude of 45.00° N., off Cape Ortegal, so as to lie in the fair track for intercepting the enemy, should they sail from Basque Roads to the westward. He left the frigate *Amazon* on the station off Belle Isle with a scaled rendezvous of the new station in latitude 45.00° N., whither they arrived on the 12th. There he remained (about 100 miles N. of Cape Ortegal) until 19 September. 'Not having heard anything of Sir Peter Warren, and believing he might have pushed on to Cape Finisterre' he made sail for that Cape. The winds faded away almost completely. At times the ships were stationary. However, Cape Finisterre was at last sighted on 26 September, and to the general satisfaction they were joined by Captain Fox with seven of the line and six smaller vessels. Seeing that the *Devonshire* (66) had been sent out with Fox because she was more suitable as a flagship than the *Windsor*, Hawke went aboard the former, taking Moore and Hay with him. He then settled down to a close study of the intelligence and dispatches. His main objects were to clarify the aim of his operations and to keep his force concentrated. On 5 October he wrote to Corbett, having sorted out the various bits of information as follows.

> By what I am able to judge from them all, I think the principal point to be followed is: to use our utmost endeavours to intercept the convoy bound out from Rochelle. For this purpose I have taken upon me to keep the *Windsor*, *Portland*, *Monmouth*, *Falkland*, and *Gloucester* some time longer, having supplied them with water and some species of provisions out of other ships. It is true it might occasion all of us going to

---

Fox's hand. L.B., 8 Sept. 1747. Ad. 51/261; 51/538. O.L., 11 Oct. 1747. O.B., 15 Oct. 1747.

> port sooner than we might else have done, but as it is of material consequence to the nation that we should be full a match for the enemy in case of meeting with them, I am in hopes what I have done will meet their Lordships' approbation.

In particular, Hawke had rejected a suggestion of Warren's that, as some Spanish galleons were expected to return home before the end of the year, Hawke might consider detaching some of his ships to cruise for them. He did not refer to Warren's idea in his dispatch of the 5th; but in a letter written on the following day to that Admiral, he remarked: 'As it's uncertain when they will come home, and likewise impossible for me to divide my force, in the present necessitous condition of the ships under my command, I must lay aside all thoughts of them during this cruise, which cannot be of long continuance. And indeed if I may presume to give my opinion, I should think 60 or 70 leagues to the westward of Cadiz would be the best station to look out for them, in which case a squadron must go out from England directly thither.'

On his way down to join Hawke, Fox had sent a couple of frigates to see what was afoot in the Basque Roads, off Rochelle and Rochefort. One of the frigates became seriously involved with a French privateer. Meanwhile Hawke was waiting impatiently at Cape Finisterre because the reconnaissance in question was of vital importance. On 3 October the second frigate, commanded by Captain Pat Baird, found the squadron, and Hawke was relieved to learn that the enemy ships were still in port. Hawke now calculated that the most likely point for interception lay between 45.00° and 47.00° N. in the meridian of Cape Ortegal. The winds had been blowing between N. and E. and the squadron would have to do some arduous tacking to reach its station in good time.

Also, the supply position was difficult. Water was short and, to make things worse, much beer had been jettisoned because it was 'stinking, sour and unfit to drink, occasioned by its being badly brewed and the casks not cleaned'.[85]

Hawke had committed himself to an all-or-nothing policy. As long as he remained at sea at all, he would be in sufficient strength to ensure that, given the sound but aggressive tactical direction which he was ready to supply, a crushing victory would be obtained. Now everything depended on the French sailing before shortage of beer and water forced the whole British squadron to go into port, and, equally, on Hawke's ability to station his ships in the right place at the right time. The period 7 to 13 October proved to be crucial. By the morning of the 7th Hawke had tacked up to the 45th parallel and was more than 100 miles W. of the meridian of Cape Finisterre. From there he worked ahead on a north-easterly course and on 9 October he reached 47.00° N. Having thus attained the northern limit of his new station, he spent a day sailing to the S.E., the wind being at S.W. By noon on the 10th the squadron was in the meridian of Cape Finisterre. Because the winds had been almost constantly between S.E. and S.W. since the 8th, he decided to shift his average position to a point somewhat N. of his previously chosen limit of 47.00°. This was decisive. Success in interception and then in battle depended on a whole series of good decisions; but of them all the decision to spend the days 12 to 14 October somewhat to the N. of latitude 47.00° was absolutely essential if the whole effort of the cruise was not to be wasted. In some naval campaigns, supply or health have in retrospect appeared to be decisive factors. In some naval battles, the efficiency and morale of the

---

[85] Ad. 1/88, 5 Oct. 1747; 51/261, O.L., 6 Oct. 1747. O.B., 1 Oct. 1747.

men on one side and the lack of those qualities on the other — both conditions resulting largely from the long-term policies of the respective governments — may appear to determine the result almost irrespectively of the merits of the victorious admiral. If ever there was a good example of victory depending on the deliberations and tactical leadership of one man, this Second Finisterre campaign was one. No particular innovations on the supply or medical side were involved. The fighting spirit of the French service was about equal to that of the British, as was seen in Anson's battle and would be seen in that which was at hand. Success or failure depended primarily on the interplay of the decisions of the British and French commanders.[86]

On 11 October Hawke communicated his thoughts to Warren, believing that the latter was still his Commander-in-Chief.

> I was in hopes, when I had the honour of writing to you last, that I should have been able to have kept out the *Monmouth*, *Windsor*, *Falkland*, *Gloucester*, and *Portland* some time longer. But water being so scarce, I am afraid it won't be in my power to detain them so long as I could wish. Therefore, to make the best of it, I have resolved to let them go in by one and two at a time, that the enemy may not get intelligence of a number being returned into port at once; and by taking this step I hope we shall be able to stay out some time longer than we could otherwise have done.
>
> I have now with me two frigates only, the *Hector* and *Shoreham*, neither fit to be sent anywhere; the first being very weak, leaky and going badly (the time of her contract being just completed), and the latter is very foul, that she hardly goes through the water at all. If you shall send any clean ships

[86] Ad. 1/88, 5,12 Oct. and H. to Warren, 6, 11 Oct. 1747; 51/261.

out, I believe you will find it proper to send a number together, and to assign them such a station as you shall think best. For, as it's the middle of October, blowing weather is naturally to be expected, which will render their joining me, if I shall be out, or any other, during their cruise, very uncertain. The winds having been set in westerly [S.W. to be precise] for some days past, I am apt to think the French fleet will not attempt sailing now, if they have not passed; and that I believe they could not have done, unless they pushed out well to the northward.

The 8th of this month Captain Haddock of the *Advice* happened to fall in with our squadron, from seeing the West India Fleet into the Channel. He told me that six days ago he had spoke with a privateer which had met a Dutch vessel four days from Rochelle, who informed him that, when he came from thence, there were eight sail of ships of war and near two hundred sail of merchant ships and vessels, but knew nothing when they were to sail. Captain Haddock likewise spoke with the *Tigress*, privateer, belonging to Bristol, who had a French Martinicoman in company with him. The Captain of the *Tigress* told him that he took that ship in the latitude of 47.00° N., and west longitude from London 9.00°, and that she came out in company with three more, and had left two hundred sail with two frigates behind, who, he said, were not to sail till March. I am in hopes the latter part of this is not true, and that these will prove to be the forerunners of the rest, as they may have lost company with them. Our present situation, if Fortune will stand our friend, seems to be very well calculated for intercepting both the outward and homeward bound trade of the enemy…

I shall contribute everything in my power to keep the ships out with me, as long as possible, and will stay out myself while I can keep any number together, and when I do go in, shall take care to leave out some number under the command of Captain Mostyn (if he joins me) or Cotes, if we can find water enough for them. I have only to add that I hope this will find

> you growing better every day. It will give me infinite pleasure to hear that you have recovered your health again.[87]

The above letter is, incidentally, a good example of Hawke's own style, unpolished by Hay. Despite the claims to the contrary which Hay was one day to make, his influence on Hawke's dispatches was probably not profound.

On the 12th Hawke wrote a dispatch to the Admiralty which was expressed in a more formal manner and amounted to a summary of that to Warren. However, it shows that Hawke had still not received the Admiralty's potentially disastrous instructions of 8 September. He sent the *Falkland* home with the two dispatches. This left him with the following ships and Captains in his line of battle. Seeing that the Captains were, in Keppel's not unreasonable opinion, 'the best in the Service', their ultimate rank has been inserted after their names, as a matter of interest.

LINE OF BATTLE

The *Kent* to lead with the starboard and the *Princess Louisa* with the larboard tacks on board.

Kent, 64, Thomas Fox, Superannuated Rear-Admiral

Eagle, 60, George B. Rodney Admiral of the White; Vice-Admiral of Great Britain

Defiance, 60, John Bentley, Vice-Admiral of the White

Portland, 50, Charles Steevens, Rear-Admiral of the Red

Nottingham, 60, Philip Saumarez, Captain (Killed, 14 Oct.)

Edinburgh, 64, Thomas Cotes, Vice-Admiral of the Red

Devonshire, 66, (Edward Hawke, Rear-Admiral of the White), John Moore, Admiral of the Blue

Yarmouth, 64, Charles Saunders, Admiral of the Blue

Windsor, 60, Thomas Hanway, Captain; retired as Commissioner at Chatham

[87] Ad. 1/88, 11 Oct. 1747.

Gloucester, 50, Philip Durell, Vice-Admiral of the Blue
Tilbury, 60, Robert Harland, Admiral of the Blue
Lyon, 60, Arthur Scott, Captain
Monmouth, 64, Henry Harrison, Vice-Admiral of the Red
Princess Louisa, 60, Charles Watson, Vice-Adimiral of the White

N.B. As I may often have occasion to detach ships from the squadron, you are to observe what ships are absent at any time, that when the signal may be made for the line of battle, you may close and form the line with the ships that remain in company.

Hawke referred to the signals for particular ships, and added, 'For all other signals, I refer you to the general printed Sailing and Fighting Instructions, with the Additional Signals therunto annexed, and to such other signals and instructions as you shall receive from me.'

When dawn broke on 14 October, the sluggish frigates *Hector* (44), Captain Thomas Stanhope, and *Shoreham* (24), Captain Cosby, were still with the squadron, as was the *Vulcan* fireship, commanded by John Lockhart.[88]

It was a great day.

[88] Ad. 1/88, 12 Oct. 1747. O.B., 27 Sept. 1747.

CHAPTER 6: THE SECOND BATTLE OF CAPE FINISTERRE

ON 14 October, sixty-four days after he had last set foot on shore, Hawke was cruising about 140 miles to the W. of Ushant and he was, as planned, almost due N. of the distant Cape Finisterre.

The squadron had been spread out to widen the area of effective search and was heading W. by S., with a moderate wind at S.S.E. At 7 a.m. a signal went up aboard the *Edinburgh* which was then in the lead. There were seven sail to the S.W! Hawke must have felt a leap of the spirit as he began to make out a growing number of sails in that quarter and knew that the fulfilment of his efforts was at hand.

At once he ordered that the signal be made for his squadron to chase. For an hour they sailed at all speed, regardless of order, to close the gap. By 8 a.m. Hawke was in the presence of a vast concourse of ships and vessels, and for a time it was impossible to tell what was the strength of the enemy in terms of warships. Therefore at 10 a.m. he replaced the chase signal with that for the line of battle. If the French proved stronger than expected he might have to fight a defensive battle, and he had to remember that their ships would be cleaner and faster than his.

The British squadron, with the wind at S.S.E., formed upon the port tack and headed S.W. in the direction of a group of enemy warships. As prescribed by the orders attached to the Line of Battle, Charles Watson worked the *Princess Louisa* towards the leading position. Soon afterwards he signalled that the enemy had eleven ships of the line. At 10.30 Fox of the

Kent, who was tacking in from his cruising station towards his place at the rear of the line, hailed the Admiral to the effect that the French had 'twelve large ships'. In fact l'Etanduère had only eight ships of the line and a 64-gun Indiaman, the *Content*. As the British drew nearer the French commander signalled to the convoy to flee and sent the *Content* as an escort.

This left him with

Intrépide, 74
Terrible, 74
Trident, 64
Tonnant, 80 *Chef d'Escadre* (equivalent of rear-admiral)
Monarque, 74
Severn, 50
Fougueux, 64
Neptune, 70

Although outnumbered, these ships were not only more heavily armed than the British but were much more strongly constructed and bore bigger complements.

The frigate *Castor* remained at the head of the French line till 1.30 p.m. when she bore away after the convoy.

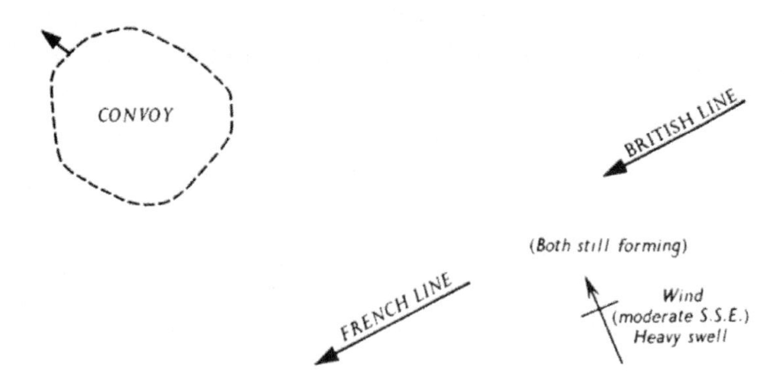

11 a.m. The British close on the French escort, while the convoy escapes.

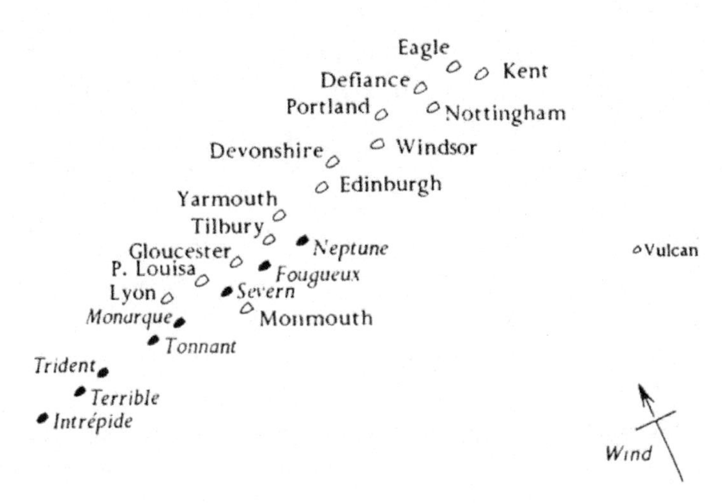

Noon. First phase of action developing.

While the British were forming their line the French warships showed no sign of running away. By 10.40 Hawke could see that they were forming a line of battle and sailing slowly to the S.W., close to the wind, while the convoy ran to the N.W. under a crowd of sail. He wished to bring on an engagement as quickly as possible, in order to deal with the escort and still stand a chance of catching some of the merchantmen. The obvious method of closing rapidly on the French line was to hoist the chase again. This would leave it to every captain to sail as fast as he could, regardless of his place in the line of battle, and the subsequent action would be fought on an individualistic basis. However, the General Fighting Instructions provided for the chase only if the enemy fleet *ran*, and not if they were simply in inferior numbers. The effect of the General and the Additional Instructions taken together was that, on finding the enemy prepared to fight in line, Hawke should have pitted his eight strongest ships against them, ship for ship, and signalled to the other six to fall back into a *corps de réserve.* This tactic would have taken a long time to bring into effect, and, in view of the superior strength of the individual French ships, could even have engineered a reverse for the British squadron. In this situation, therefore, the outcome depended entirely on the character and judgement of the commanding admiral. One feels that Byng, for example, would have followed the letter of the law and congratulated himself on producing an indecisive result. But Hawke rose to the occasion. He hauled down the signal for the line and replaced it with the chase.

At about 11.30 Hawke could see that Scott in the *Lyon* and Watson in the *Princess Louisa* had closed to within gunshot, and he ordered the red flag for engaging to be hoisted.

The French ships were moving more freely through the water than the foul English ones and, though they refrained from setting all their sails, in order to remain in a position covering the convoy, it took a good hour for all Hawke's ships to come up into the action. Because of the period spent in trying to form the line, the British tended to join the battle in the order assigned to them in that formation.

The general pattern of the battle was that the fighting flowed along the French line from rear to van — from N.E. towards the S.W. While almost every British captain hastened initially to engage the nearest French ship, some commanders then passed quickly ahead to guard against the possibility of the leading enemy ships escaping. Mahan and various French writers have indicated that the British squadron deliberately divided into two sections in order to catch the French column in a double fire; but this was not the case. Most British captains were so busy working up against the wind that they were content to engage the enemy from to leeward. Once in action, they generally sailed ahead to make room for those following, but there were several variations on this theme.

It was at 11.30 then, that Scott, having outsailed Watson and Harrison, saw the red flag flutter up to the *Devonshire*'s fore topmast head and his guns roared in response. His target was the powerful *Neptune* of 70 guns, massively built compared with the 60-gun *Lyon* and towering above her. Scott hurried on down the lee side of the French line and by 11.45 he was engaging the next ship, the *Fougueux* (64). Although not much superior to the *Lyon* in gunpower, she, too, was a formidable opponent on account of the strength of her sides and her much larger crew. By now Watson had drawn abreast of the *Neptune* and was fighting her 'within pistol shot'. The *Louisa*, like the *Lyon*, was only of 60 guns, but her task was lightened when, almost at once, Henry Harrison delivered a broadside from to windward of the *Neptune*. That splendid veteran needed no instructions to tell him the virtues of an overwhelming concentration of firepower and he had worked hard to get up into the wind to double the French rear. He and Watson made a devastating team as together they swept down the French line, catching ship after ship in a double fire. By noon the *Severn*, the weakest link in the French line, was feeling the stroke of this manoeuvre.

Hawke may well have reflected, as the *Devonshire* drew up towards the fighting, that so far there was not much resemblance between the unhesitating onslaught of his ships and the general performance of those led into battle by Thomas Mathews.

Philip Durell was probably next into action with his little 50-gun *Gloucester*. Like Scott and Watson ahead of him he battled on down the lee side of the French line. Right on his heels, at about noon, Harland in the *Tilbury* (60), Saunders in the *Yarmouth* (64), and Cotes in the *Edinburgh* (64), swept up to the hard-pressed rear of the enemy. After firing a few shots at the *Fougueux*, Saunders fastened onto the *Severn* which had fallen away to leeward of her fellows. This is where Hawke came into action, so Saunders left the *Severn* to him while he sailed ahead for the *Fougueux* which had continued to move forward beyond the *Severn*.

Hawke mentioned the surrender of the *Severn* in his dispatch: 'The enemy having the weather-gauge of us, and a smart and constant fire being kept on both sides, the smoke prevented my seeing the number of the enemy or what happened on either side for some time. In passing the first ships we could get near, we received many fires at a distance, till we came close to the *Severn* of 50 guns which we soon silenced and left to be taken up by the frigates astern.' And Saunders recorded: 'The *Devonshire*, getting ahead of the ship she was engaged with, endeavouring to take her, brought the ship into the wind which obliged them to tack; and the French ship struck her colours to the *Devonshire* who wore round and made sail up to the enemy.' The *Severn* had originally been a British ship, captured in 1746 by Captain Conflans. Although she was comparatively small she carried a complement of 550, similar to that of the *Devonshire*, the most powerful ship in the British squadron. The *Severn* had about 100 casualties.

While Hawke was setting about the *Severn*, Cotes (*Edinburgh*) intelligently passed through the rear French ships to get to windward and, between 1 and 1.30, exchanged fire with l'Etanduère's ship, the redoutable *Tonnant* (80). The *Tonnant* brought the *Edinburgh*'s fore topmast crashing down onto her upper deck and sailed contemptuously ahead. Cotes could only wait for another French ship to come up from astern; one soon did. The *Monarque* (74), like the other French ships to the rear of the *Tonnant*, had been engaged at the outset by Scott, Watson, and Harrison and, as will be related, by a number of others. She was considerably the worse for wear by the time she came forward to meet the *Edinburgh*.

Hanway's *Windsor* (60) had opened fire, like the *Yarmouth* and *Edinburgh*, at about 12.15. Having had a tilt at all four ships of the enemy rear, she had just moved ahead from the *Monarque* when the latter found the *Edinburgh* waiting for her. The *Portland* (50), under the command of Charles Steevens, must have been close on the heels of the *Windsor*. She exchanged broadsides with the *Monarque* at 12.30 and then went bravely up to the *Tonnant*. A dramatic incident followed. The diminutive *Portland* had a moment of glory when she 'received and fired a broadside at the *Tonnant* which carried away her mizen topmast with the *chef d'escadre* flag upon it'.

Of the British ships of the line, the *Nottingham*, *Defiance*, *Eagle*, and *Kent* were the last to reach the scene of action. The *Nottingham*, Captain Saumarez, reached the *Monarque* before 1 p.m. and was still firing at her as she went forward to the *Edinburgh*. Towards 12.30 John Bentley had fetched the rearmost French ship, the *Neptune*, and fought her 'within musket-shot'. Then, seeing the *Eagle* and *Kent* coming up behind him, he sailed his ship, the *Defiance* (60), ahead to the *Fougueux*. He was 'some time closely engaged' with her, but left her to be finished off by the *Yarmouth* (Saunders) which had, as related above, consigned the *Severn* to the mercies of the *Devonshire*.

The Captain of the *Eagle* (60), George Brydges Rodney, made a statement at the court martial of Captain Fox, which was held after the battle. This provides intriguing comment on some of the events occurring at this stage. (Rodney had been with Fox on the latter's successful cruise against French commerce earlier in the year, and seems to have conceived a dislike of him.) At about 12.20 Rodney was close enough to the fighting to decide on his line of conduct. In his own words:

> I took notice to my First Lieutenant that I intended to attack the sternmost of the enemy's ships, and thought it would be prudent if both the *Kent* and *Eagle* stuck close to the said ship till she struck. The *Kent*, who was then before our weather beam, backed her mizen topsail and let us shoot ahead of her. Shortly after, we began the engagement... After being engaged some time with the *Neptune* on our larboard side, we were attacked by another of the enemy's ships on the starboard side, which put us between two fires, and obliged us to divide our men, in order to fight both sides at the same time. [The other French ship was the *Fougueux*. Having been immobilized by Saunders, she happened to be lying near the path of the *Neptune* and *Eagle* as, struggling desperately, they moved slowly ahead together.]
>
> During our being thus hard pressed, the *Kent* did not come between the *Eagle* and either of the enemy's ships, in order to save us from a double fire. After my exchanging a few broadsides with the ship on my starboard side, she, being much disabled, dropped astern and left us engaged with the *Neptune* only. A short time after, one of my officers on the poop told me that the *Hector* was engaged with the said ship that fell astern of me which I saw plainly from my stern windows. Some short time after that I was informed that the said enemy's ship had struck to the *Hector*. I immediately looked through the stern...
>
> Our engagement with the *Neptune* still continued but, about 2 in the afternoon, an unlucky shot carrying away the steering wheel, our masts and sails being very much shattered, so as to render the ship ungovernable, we unfortunately fell twice

> aboard the *Devonshire*, who was on our lee quarter, coming up to our assistance.

Hawke's dispatch gives his view of the incident. He had left the *Severn* to be collected by the *Shoreham*.

> Then, perceiving the *Eagle* and *Edinburgh* (who had lost her fore topmast) engaged, we kept our wind as close as possible in order to assist them. This attempt of ours was frustrated by the *Eagle*'s falling twice on board us, having had her wheel shot to pieces, and all the men at it killed, and all her braces and bowlines gone.

Rodney pursued his tale as follows:

> This accident prevented my observing anything for a considerable time, as I was employed in putting the ship again in a proper condition for battle. However, to the best of my memory, between 3 and 4 in the afternoon, I observed the *Kent*, who did not seem damaged, steering for the French Admiral's ship. I then remarked to some of my officers that I hoped the *Kent* would stick close by her, and regain the honour I thought she had lost at the beginning of the battle. But, to my great surprise, I saw the *Kent* bore round up, discharge[d] some of her guns, then sheered to leeward and ahead withall, till quite clear of that ship's fire.

The story of Fox's part in the battle is filled with his errors of judgement and bad luck. On approaching the *Neptune* at about 12.30 he was undoubtedly wrong to slow down and make room for the *Eagle* to precede him on the French ship's lee side. In any case, according to the evidence given at his court martial, he could probably have gone to windward of the *Neptune* — an ideal manoeuvre, as Rodney perceived at the time. He might, however, have joined the battle soon after

Rodney, if an upper-deck gun's crew had not found some rigging in their way, namely a cross-jack-brace and bowline, and simply unreeved the whole contraption. This Gordian knot approach resulted in the mizen topsail remaining aback and holding up the ship's progress for ten minutes longer than Fox had intended. This delay gave a bad impression. From a number of ships the *Kent* was seen to be hanging back, and Hawke, who was then engaged with the *Severn* hoisted the *Kent*'s signal. Under the circumstances, this would normally be construed to mean, as it did, that the *Kent* was to get into action. Fox had originally been induced to back his mizen topsail by those 'two damned bad fellows', his Master and 1st Lieutenant. But there was no excuse for a Captain who could not properly exercise his own judgement. The different atmosphere on Rodney's quarter-deck is sufficiently indicated by his above-quoted statement — for example: 'I took notice to my 1st Lieutenant that I intended to attack the sternmost of the enemy's ships'!

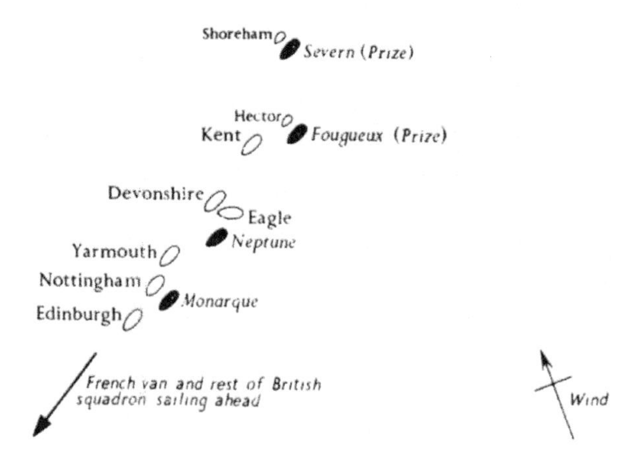

2 p.m. French rear being eliminated.

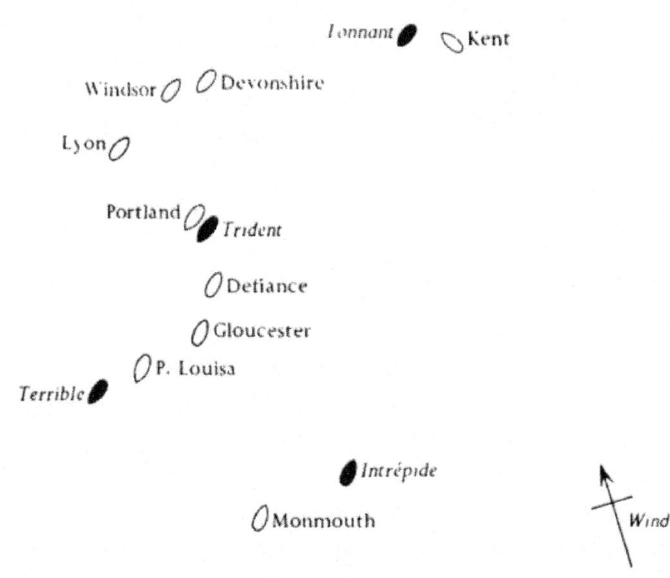

4.15 p.m. Final phase. *Intrépide* heading back towards Tonnant.

At about 1 p.m. Fox wore ship and raked the *Neptune* with a few guns, probably at a fair distance. Then, on the starboard tack, he passed back to windward of the *Fougueux* which had by now fallen astern of the embattled *Eagle* and *Neptune.* Completing a circular manoeuvre, he wore a second time, raked her and came round onto the port tack, opposite the *Fougueux*'s leeward side. The *Hector* (40) came up, also to leeward of the *Fougueux*. Fox moved ahead to give her room to engage the French ship. Seeing that the *Hector* was only a frigate, it was somewhat odd to leave her the more direct berth for engaging the *Fougueux*. However, Stanhope drew up to the

French ship and, when she hauled down her colours at 1.40, he was able to claim that she had struck to the *Hector*.

By 2 p.m. the *Monarque* (74) and the *Neptune* (70) were therefore the only ships still resisting out of the four originally constituting the French rear. It was at this time that the *Monarque* came up to the waiting *Edinburgh*. Clinging grimly to the *Monarque* was Saumarez in the *Nottingham*, who had been fighting her for more than an hour. Saunders of the *Yarmouth*, after leaving the crippled *Fougueux*, had also been firing at the *Monarque*, then somewhat ahead of him and to windward. But, seeing that the *Neptune* had shaken off the *Eagle* and *Devonshire* and was again coming ahead, Saunders turned his full attention to her. This was decisive. The *Yarmouth* 'shot away her mizen mast and disabled her in such a manner as she lay muzzled'.

It was already some time since the *Neptune* had lost her Captain, but her 1st Lieutenant, Kerlérec, continued to resist beyond the requirements of duty. According to Lacour-Gayet, the *Neptune* had seven officers and 300 men actually killed out of a complement of 650. At 3.15 the shattered *Neptune*, slippery with blood, surrendered to the *Yarmouth*.

Meanwhile, the Captain of the *Monarque* had also been killed. That ship had struck her colours to the *Nottingham* and *Edinburgh* at 3 p.m. Aboard the *Monarque* as a *garde-marine* (officer cadet) was Suffren, later recognized as the greatest French admiral of the century. He afterwards gave it as his opinion that, from the point of view of the French resistance, the action was 'one of the most glorious battles ever to be fought at sea'. There was certainly no lack of fighting spirit in the French Navy at that time, but the seagoing personnel were at the mercy of an uncomprehending government, a futile Navy Minister, and a defensive strategic and tactical doctrine. For example, with regard to tactics, the Marquis de l'Etanduère should almost certainly have abandoned his formal line ahead as soon as Hawke hoisted the chase for the second time. As Monk had demonstrated at the Four Days' Battle in 1666, it was very difficult for a superior fleet to secure a concentration of force on ships retreating in a line abreast. Admittedly, against an admiral so aggressively inclined as Hawke, the situation was bound to prove costly to l'Etanduère, however he reacted; but his actual formation was the worst possible. His ships were bound to be overwhelmed by superior concentrations of gunfire as the British swarmed up to them.

One officer who obtained an exceptionally fine (historically useful) general view of the battle was the 25-year-old John Lockhart, commanding the diminutive *Vulcan*, fireship. He had managed to work up to windward of the fighting. That he found no opportunity of bringing his somewhat anachronistic vessel into action was certainly due to no lack of zeal. Hawke formed a high opinion of him which was brilliantly justified during the Seven Years' War, and, on the unhappy Fox's suspension from command of the *Kent*, Hawke appointed Lockhart temporarily in his place. The Admiralty, however, would not confirm him.

With the surrender of the *Neptune* at 3.15 the resistance of the French rear was brought to an end. It remains to deal with the fortunes of the four ships in the enemy's van.

As noted above, the *Tonnant* had been brought to action before 1.30. By 2 p.m. all the French van, except for the *Intrépide* (74), had been heavily engaged, but it was probably not until after 3 p.m. that this powerful ship was made to fight. This merely serves to emphasize the extent to which the French were handicapped by their *Chef d'Escadre*'s adherence to a formal line. There was no virtue whatever in having the *Intrépide* sailing along at the head of the line without a care in the world, while her fellows astern were being systematically overwhelmed. Rodney discovered how uncomfortable it was to spend even a few minutes sandwiched between the *Neptune* and the *Fougueux*. If the eight French ships had sailed in pairs they would have been an awkward proposition. If they had been in a line abreast they would have been more awkward still. But, to their acute discomfort, they were not thus arranged. By 2 p.m. the *Tonnant*, *Trident* (64), and *Terrible* (74) had all, like their brethren of the rear in the earlier stages, been subjected to attack by superior numbers of British ships. The *Lyon*, *Princess Louisa*, *Monmouth*, *Gloucester*, *Tilbury*, *Portland*, and *Windsor* had all reached this sector of the battle.

At about 2 p.m. the *Defiance* also reached the *Tonnant* and engaged her for half an hour. By the same time Hawke was hoping to close with the French Admiral. He had just managed to get clear of the *Eagle*. The two collisions with her 'drove us to leeward, and prevented our attacking *le Monarque* of 74 and the *Tonnant* of 80 guns within any distance to do execution. However, we attempted both, especially the latter. While we were engaged with her, the breechings of all our lower-deck guns broke and the guns flew fore and aft, which obliged us to shoot ahead, for our upper and quarterdeck guns could not reach her. Captain Harland in the *Tilbury*, observing that she fired single guns at us in order to dismast us, stood on the other tack between her and the *Devonshire* and gave her a very smart fire.'

By now it must have been after 3 o'clock.

Not very far astern of the *Tonnant*, the *Monarque* had just surrendered, as has been said. Elated by the *Nottingham*'s success, Lieutenant Man 'went onto the quarter-deck to wish Captain Saumarez joy' and was in time to see the *Kent* threading her way past the motionless prizes and their captors.

'As soon as the *Kent* came pretty near us', Man afterwards told Fox's court martial, 'our people gave them three cheers which she returned.' Sir Peter Warren, the president of the court, was perplexed to hear of this enthusiasm for the *Kent.* He asked Man: 'Were the three cheers given by your people to the *Kent*, do you imagine, done as a mark of joy for the *Monarque*'s having struck to you, or do you know what they meant by them?' Man replied: 'Thinking they were going to engage the French Admiral, as they cried out, "Now for the French Admiral".'

At about this time (3.30) the *Lyon* had at last reached the *Intrépide* (74). In pretty poor shape, the British ship then wore, which manoeuvre brought her back towards the *Devonshire.* Shortly after, Harrison brought the *Monmouth* up close under the lee of the almost unscathed *Intrépide*, and compelled her to tack. The French writers indicate that the *Intrépide*'s Captain, in a flash of tactical insight, conceived the idea of swinging back to the centre to free his hard-pressed Admiral. This may be. But Harrison recorded that the *Monmouth*'s guns were the origin of this inspiration. At the time when the *Intrépide* did her about-turn, she was probably six miles ahead of the *Tonnant.*

Watson's *Princess Louisa* had fallen away from the struggle in the van at about 2.30, with damage aloft. Having completed running repairs, she worked back into the battle at 4 o'clock. The *Terrible* (74) was now leading the remnant of the French squadron and she held dourly to her south-westerly course. Watson tacked to get ahead of her and gave her a broadside from to windward as he came back on the starboard tack. In the words of his log, he 'then stood and wore after him; he being now the headmost of the enemy's ships and none of ours engaging him, I thought it proper to stop him. At 5 got close upon her weather quarter.'

At 4.15 Durell's *Gloucester* was somewhere to windward of the *Terrible* but she wore towards the following *Trident* (64). Bentley seems to have followed a similar policy of keeping the *Defiance* constantly manoeuvring near the *Terrible* and *Trident*. The methods of Watson, Steevens, Saunders, Saumarez, Cotes, and Rodney, who tended to stick to an opponent till she struck seem to have been more effective than the roaming habits of Scott, Durell, Harland, and Bentley. Hawke himself provided probably the best example of the fight-to-the-kill method. Three out of the six French ships taken made their surrender to the *Devonshire*.

When the *Kent* was last mentioned she was being watched by Saumarez, Man and others aboard the *Nottingham* as, towards 4 p.m., she closed up on the *Tonnant*. Aboard the *Devonshire* Captain Moore was also studying the *Kent*, but without evincing any sign of the enthusiasm expressed by the *Nottingham*'s crew. He afterwards stated: 'I stood for near a quarter of an hour in the Balcony, expecting to see the *Kent* make sail and engage the *Tonnant*, but his not doing so made me take the liberty of calling Admiral Hawke to me, and asked him whether the *Kent* was doing the duty of a man of war. He gave his opinion she was not.'

Thereupon, the *Kent*'s pennant was hoisted for the second time since the start of the engagement. It was not seen by Fox who was, as it happened, moving ahead to the *Tonnant* in any case, albeit not very quickly. Hawke considered that the *Kent* was making sail and had her signal taken down again.

Moore, however, was still not satisfied and returned to his place of vantage on the balcony. His account of Fox's next manoeuvre agrees well with that given by Lieutenant Man of the *Nottingham* and his consequent emotions, one would guess, were in sympathy with those expressed a little later by Captain

Saumarez. The *Kent* reached the port quarter of the *Tonnant*, bore to starboard across her stern and raked her, and then, at a fairly respectful distance, swung into a parallel station to engage her from to leeward. Moore may well have been disconcerted to see the Tonnant's main topmast come down. However, the *Kent* did not remain to bask in her glory but almost at once edged away to leeward and sailed ahead out of range. Thereupon Captain Saumarez, who was watching with Lieutenant Man, ejaculated, 'My God! What is she about to shoot ahead!'

It happened that Hawke was then considering whether to hoist the red and white flag for engaging more closely, because, what with the end of fighting in the rear and the roaming tactics of some of the captains, there were several British ships out of the action. The *Kent*'s pennant had been put away but Hawke agreed with Moore that if the red and white flag went up the *Kent* should understand that she was to go back to the *Tonnant*. Lockhart saw the signal hoisted at 4.30 and it was also seen as far back as the *Yarmouth*. Aboard the *Kent* a typical discussion now took place on the quarterdeck where the worried Fox said that he ought to go back to the *Tonnant*, but advice to the contrary was volubly expressed by Ryall, his 1st Lieutenant and Townshend, his Master. The latter pair insisted that the signal meant the *Kent* was to follow the *Devonshire* which was then heading towards the *Trident*. Fox weakly permitted their interpretation to prevail even after the *Kent*'s pennant flew out for a third time.

Meanwhile, Saunders and Rodney unhesitatingly responded to the red and white flag by making what sail they could to close on the *Tonnant*.

By the time that Hawke's 'new breechings were all seized' and his guns ready for action it was getting on for 5 p.m. and he was drawing near the *Trident.* Steevens of the *Portland,* after bringing down l'Etanduère's flag, had exchanged fire with the *Terrible.* He then fell back to the *Trident,* a more suitable opponent for his armament of fifty guns. Steevens had been fighting the *Trident* for two and a half hours before the *Devonshire* came up. From time to time he had been assisted by other British ships, and both the *Portland* and *Gloucester* claimed that the *Trident* struck to them. However, shortly before the arrival on the scene of the *Devonshire,* the *Trident*'s colours had again been hoisted. In characteristic fashion Hawke pressed straight in alongside her and at 5 p.m. her colours came down and stayed down.

The Second Battle of Cape Finisterre was clearly drawing to a close; yet its last hours match in interest those which had preceded them.

While Hawke was preparing to forge ahead and clinch matters with the *Terrible* which was still fighting the *Louisa* and, latterly, the *Defiance,* the *Intrépide* came down on the opposite tack to pass between the *Kent* (still trailing along behind the *Devonshire*) and the *Tonnant.* The battered *Tonnant* was then engaged with the *Tilbury* which was to windward. Captain Hanway of the *Windsor* was following Hawke and was well placed to describe what ensued. 'I saw the *Intrépide* bearing down to the French Admiral, and, I believe, passed so near as to hail her, as the French Admiral immediately wore after her and kept before the wind under her foresail and part of her mainsail — the only sail she appeared to me to have to set.'

It was now about 5.30. The light was fading. Whether Hawke actually saw the two French ships as, a mile or two astern of him, they broke away to the N., is uncertain. He had already hoisted the pennants of the *Kent, Lyon,* and *Tilbury* together with the signal to tack, meaning those ships to attack the

Tonnant. But the light was now so poor that none of the three ships saw the signal. It was at this point that three other British ships responded to the situation in the most splendid manner. Rodney's terse log-entries give the gist of what happened. '½ past 5 [the *Tonnant*] bore away — the other was ahead — and engaged by four of our ships. At 6 we bore away after the above ships of the enemy. [Rodney asked Saumarez for assistance which he gave at once. They were joined by Saunders.] At 7 at night began to engage and continued for about an hour and a half.'

Near the beginning of this action, Saumarez was killed. Thus was cut off what should have been as distinguished a career as that of Saunders or Rodney.

Finally, wrote Saunders: 'We lost sight of them. Our masts and rigging all shot to pieces.'

The merit of these three outstanding captains resides in the fact that, though their ships together were hardly a match for the two powerful French ones, they unhesitatingly bore away after the enemy without being specifically ordered to do so. Several captains in the van were content merely to observe the departure of the *Tonnant* and the *Intrépide* though their ships had hardly borne so great a share in the previous part of the action as the *Yarmouth*, *Nottingham*, and *Eagle*. This no doubt goes some way towards explaining the subsequent bitterness of Rodney towards Captain Fox.

Meanwhile, away to the S., the action in the van had been brought to a conclusion. As, at about 6 o'clock, Hawke drew up to the 74-gun *Terrible*, the wan light faded away. For a further hour and a half flashes of red and orange leapt in the darkness as broadside answered broadside. Watson was continuing the struggle. The *Devonshire* closed to 'within musket shot'; and the *Terrible* (de Court's flagship in 1744) struck to the British admiral at about 7.30.

At Fox's court martial Hanway gave an excellent idea of how Hawke conducted himself at the moment of triumph. Hanway had made his way by boat to the *Devonshire* to ask whether the Admiral had any further orders for him.

> When I came on board the *Devonshire* I found Admiral Hawke in the Gunroom, dressing by the Surgeon, he having been very severely blown up by gunpowder. I acquainted him with the circumstances of my own ship, and the position of the several ships that were nearest to him, and informed the Admiral that just as I was coming aboard I heard several guns fired to leeward, which I believed had been from some of our ships who had renewed the action with the French Admiral. Admiral Hawke seemed surprised that the *Kent* was not one of those ships, and directed me to send immediately to Captain Fox to let him know that he should take any ships he could find in any condition to proceed with him, and go immediately to the assistance of any of His Majesty's ships then engaged; but if he found those ships had struck, then to give assistance to any of our disabled ships, or the enemy's that had struck, and might want it.

So humanity after victory has not been a purely Nelsonic prerogative.

The end of the battle is neatly summarized in Hawke's dispatch.

> Having observed that six of the enemy's ships had struck, and it being very dark and our own ships dispersed, I thought it best to bring to for the night; and seeing a great firing a long way astern of me, I was in hopes to have seen more of the enemy's ships taken in the morning; but instead of that I received the melancholy account of Captain Saumarez being

> killed, and that the *Tonnant* had escaped in the night by the assistance of the *Intrépide* which, by having the wind of our ships, had received no damage that I could perceive.

Despite the fatigues of the battle, Hawke's ships rang with activity throughout the night, as emergency repairs were made.

On the next day, 15 October, the Admiral had to determine what action was appropriate with regard both to the escaped French warships and the convoy. He called a council of his senior captains — a proceeding open to criticism if used before a possible engagement but sound enough under those circumstances. However, before the council could begin its deliberations there was another difficulty to settle.

Of the nine captains called to the council, eight 'refused to rank' with Fox, the most senior of the captains. Most persuasive in producing this stand were Watson, Cotes, Moore, and Rodney, although, as became clear during the subsequent trial, only Moore and Rodney had seen much of the *Kent* during the action. Hanway and Stanhope seem to have contributed to the angry talk, while Saunders and Steevens characteristically said little. Hawke found that he had no option but to exclude Fox from the council, informing him that he would ask for a court martial in order to give him an opportunity to clear his name. Fox subsequently complained of the vindictiveness of the other captains, who charged him with cowardice without making any inquiry into the reasons for the behaviour of the *Kent*. At the trial he bitterly observed, 'The business of minding that duty which was incumbent on me in my command prevented my minutely observing what others did in theirs.' It is indeed possible that, if full investigation had been made into the performance of every captain, one or two more might have been found to approach the degree of incompetence displayed by Fox.

John Hay recorded the outcome of the council of war.

> Then they came to the following resolution:
>
> 1. That four ships, the least of them of 60 guns, could only be sufficient to go in quest of the two French ships, the *Tonnant* of 80 guns and the *Intrépide* of 74, which had escaped from the action in the evening of the 14th.
> 2. That none of the ships under their command were at present in a condition to be sent on that service.
> 3. That by the time a sufficient number of them could be got ready, it would be impracticable to come up with the enemy ships.

With regard to the merchantmen, Hawke's dispatch made it clear what was done.

> As to the French convoy's escaping, it was not possible for me to detach any ships after them at first or during the action except the frigates and that, I thought, would have been imprudent as I observed several large ships of war among them; and to confirm me in that opinion I have since learned that they had the *Content* of sixty-four guns, and many frigates from thirty-six guns downwards. However, I took a step which seemed to me the most probable to intercept them, for, as soon as I could man and victual the *Weazel* sloop, I detached her with an express to Commodore Legge.

Legge, who had been Commander-in-Chief at the Leeward Islands, died before the *Weazel* arrived. However, Legge's effective methods were continued by Captain George Pocock and, partly owing to the arrival of the *Weazel* and partly to advice received from the Admiralty, he rounded up forty of the French vessels. After leaving l'Etanduère, the merchantmen had scattered widely. Altogether, Pocock captured 900 French seamen, and immobilized more than 100 merchant vessels at

Martinique. Therefore, although l'Etanduère succeeded in saving his convoy from immediate destruction, France reaped little advantage from this fact.

Back at the scene of the battle, Hawke had to lie to for a matter of two days, rigging the prizes with jury masts. Out of six French ships of the line, two had their foremasts; otherwise there were no masts standing at all. Hawke admitted that his own ships had also 'suffered greatly'. As far as manpower was concerned, 4,000 seamen had been eliminated from the French Navy through death or capture. The British had 170 killed and 577 wounded, distributed through the ships as follows:

Ship: *Lyon*, Guns: 60, Captain: Scott, Killed: 20, Wounded: 79.
Ship: *Yarmouth*, Guns: 64, Captain: Saunders, Killed: 22, Wounded: 70.
Ship: *Monmouth*, Guns: 64, Captain: Harrison, Killed: 22, Wounded: 68.
Ship: *P. Louisa*, Guns: 60, Captain: Watson, Killed: 18, Wounded: 60.
Ship: *Eagle*, Guns: 60, Captain: Rodney, Killed: 16, Wounded: 52.
Ship: *Devonshire*, Guns: 66, Captain: Hawke; Moore, Killed: 12, Wounded: 52.
Ship: *Defiance*, Guns: 60, Captain: Bentley, Killed: 11, Wounded: 42.
Ship: *Nottingham*, Guns: 60, Captain: Saumarez, Killed: 13, Wounded: 39.
Ship: *Windsor*, Guns: 60, Captain: Hanway, Killed: 8, Wounded: 41.
Ship: *Gloucester*, Guns: 50, Captain: Durrell, Killed: 8, Wounded: 17.
Ship: *Edinburgh*, Guns: 64, Captain: Cotes, Killed: 5, Wounded: 19.
Ship: *Portland*, Guns: 50, Captain: Steevens, Killed: 7, Wounded: 14.

Ship: *Tilbury*, Guns: 60, Captain: Harland, Killed: 6, Wounded: 15.
Ship: *Kent*, Guns: 64, Captain: Fox, Killed: 1, Wounded: 10.
Ship: *Hector*, Guns: 40, Captain: Stanhope, Killed: 1, Wounded: 1.

Hawke particularly praised Moore in his dispatch of 17 October and sent him in the *Hector* to deliver it, with its tidings of victory, to their Lordships of the Admiralty. This dispatch was widely published and its manner of expression much admired. Hay later wrote something to the effect that he had written it, and complained that Hawke's only contribution had been to 'spoil' it by insisting on some alteration 'at the request of Admiral Harrison and Sir John Moore'. The dispatch was indeed clearly written and judging by the other evidence, was almost completely accurate as far as it went. However, it devoted undue space to the part played by the *Devonshire*, mentioned Harland rather more favourably than he deserved, and omitted any reference to Saunders and Steevens or to their ships. Altogether, the captains were not very pleased about the dispatch. In so far as Hay claimed to have written it (and it appears to be in his style) he merits a good share of the accruing praise and blame. It is only fair to exonerate Harrison from taking undue advantage of his friendship with the Admiral, because, although he had played a distinguished part in the battle, there was no reference to him in the letter. Finally, it may be accepted that, by 17 October 1747, Hay had insinuated himself into a position of influence with Hawke which was to prove harmful to the latter and the Admiral was greatly to blame for allowing this to happen.

The Admiralty did not formally read Hawke's dispatch till 30 October, but the news which it contained was generally known by the 26th. Of particular interest is a letter from Keppel to Anson, dated 26 October.

> I congratulate your Lordship on the success of the English navy, and have great joy myself in hearing how nobly all my friends behaved. Surely there was never more spirit shewed except by the Captain of the *Kent*, from whom, indeed, I never expected much. The French must now be quite ruined. Poor Saumarez died like what he was, alongside of *le Tonnant*, much regretted by the whole squadron. I need not say more of him as your Lordship knew him so well. I inquired particularly after Rodney and Charles Saunders, and by accounts no one outdid the latter. The *Yarmouth* lay by one of their very large ships, was laid on the careen for some minutes, and, what is more surprising, she had a gun dismounted, which dropped down the powder scuttle and stopped their communication to it, so that for a long time they were useless in a manner.

The French ship, onto which the *Yarmouth* had been run, was probably the *Neptune*, On 27 October the Duke of Newcastle wrote to felicitate the Duke of Cumberland 'upon the great news we received yesterday. The marine of France will, I hope, by these two last affairs have received an almost fatal blow. Sir Peter Warren told me this morning that the King had more French ships in his ports than remained now in the ports of France; that we could beat them with their own ships; and that he desired to carry the challenge.'

It was true that the French Navy was weakened beyond reasonable hope of recovery by Hawke's victory at the Second Battle of Cape Finisterre. The reason why he has not received credit for winning one of the decisive battles of naval history is that the British Government was not in a position to exploit the victory to the full. France was predominant on land and the United Provinces were in a desperate plight. Also, at home,

Britain was in serious financial difficulties. The stalemate was expressed in the terms of the peace-treaty; but the triumph of the Royal Navy cannot be denied. Its dominance was clinched by Hawke who had proved himself a formidable commander in battle and an extremely sound and tenacious strategist.

The Admiral was not unmindful of how much Warren had done to help him towards his great opportunity. Although he had by now learnt of Warren's resignation from the chief command, he sent him the following note, dated 17 October, by Captain Moore: 'If I had not met with the misfortune of having my right hand burnt with powder, I should not have made use of amanuensis, but given you myself a full detail of our action on the 14th. For though your bad state of health has obliged you to resign the command of the Squadron, yet the many and great obligations I lie under induce me to send enclosed the material part of my letter to the Lords of the Admiralty. Wishing you a speedy recovery...'

At Versailles the news of the battle did not arouse much general enthusiasm. But an exception was provided by the Young Pretender, whose tactless reactions were not unconnected with his expulsion from France under a clause of the Treaty of Aix-la-Chapelle which was signed in the following year. Until then Prince Charles appears to have enjoyed his stay at the French Court. According to a French writer, he had 'wrought more havoc in the hearts of the ladies at Versailles than he had amid the heather of Scotland. One day, in the presence of Mme. d'Aiguillon, who was then competing with the Princesses of Guéméné and Talmont for the Pretender's affections, Charles Edward dwelt with evident pride on the reports of the recent successes of Admirals Anson and Hawke. When Montesquieu respectfully pointed out to him that he was rejoicing in the defeats of his own supporters, the Pretender replied, "That's true, but it's my country's fleet!'" No doubt Hawke would have considered this a proper remark to be made by an Englishman abroad.[89]

[89] Principal sources for the 2nd Battle of C. Finisterre: Ad. 1/5291, c.m. of Capt. Fox; 1/88, 15, 17 Oct., 4 Nov. 1747; 51/261, *Devonshire*; 51/282, *Defiance*; 51/306, *Edinburgh*; 51/326, *Eagle*; 51/415, *Gloucester*; 51/501, *Kent*; 51/538, *Lyon*; 51/613, *Monmouth*; 51/739, P. *Louisa*; 51/995, *Tilbury*; 51/1084, *Windsor*; 51/1089, *Yarmouth*; 51/3940, *Portland*. No Captain's log for *Nottingham*, but see statements of Lts. Man and Loggie at c.m. See Ad. 1/799 for casualties. O.L., 17 Oct. 1747. Lacour-Gayet, pp. 173-4. Chevalier, i, 253-5. Salmon, pp. 55-60. Keppel, i, 113-14. Also, for end of above chapter: Add.MSS. 32712, Newcastle to Cumberland, 27 Oct. 1747; Germinv, i, 71. For a general account of the battle, cf. Richmond, iii, 104-11.

CHAPTER 7: AWARD OF HONOURS AND A WINTER CRUISE

WHILE the news of his victory was being spread about in England, Hawke considered whether it was possible further to prolong his cruise. The fact that he spent a fortnight on station after fighting the battle is, if the shortage of his supplies be remembered, a sufficient testimony to his devotion to duty. Having then decided that the limit of endurance had been reached he wrote to the Admiralty suggesting that Captain Mostyn, who had recently joined him in the *Hampton Court*, might soon be sent out again with any other available ships to cruise off Ushant. To facilitate such a move, he included the *Hampton Court* with those ships ordered to refit in Plymouth. With the rest, he bore his six large prizes into Portsmouth Harbour, dropping anchor at 1.30 p.m. on 29 October.[90]

Catharine Hawke now received some recompense for her years of waiting and anxiety. She went down to Portsmouth and shared in her husband's glory. No doubt, the 3-year-old Martin and the 10-month-old Edward went with her. Amid the spate of congratulations she was by no means forgotten. 'Pray give my compliments to Mrs. Hawke whom I wish all joy on this occasion', wrote Rear-Admiral Chambers who, in August, had succeeded Hawke as commanding officer at Plymouth.[91]

As far as Hawke personally was concerned, the first days after his homecoming were entirely gratifying. Anson went down to Portsmouth to greet the victors. The Admiralty, after

---

[90] Ad. 1/88, n.d. and O.L. 28 Oct. 1747; Ad. 51/261.
[91] I.L., 30 Oct. 1747.

all their anxious doubts about Hawke's competence to command a major squadron, let alone organize a campaign, were now prepared to accept his plan for sending ships out to cruise under Mostyn and left it to him to determine their disposition. Corbett's letter of 30 October paid full tribute to his 'great victory'. 'Their Lordships', wrote the Secretary, 'direct me to congratulate you in their name for the great service you have done your country in defeating so great a force of the enemy and taking so many of their capital ships, wherein you have shown a conduct that has very much distinguished your character and fully answered the expectations of their Lordships.' If 'answered' had been replaced by 'enormously exceeded' the wording would have approached nearer to accuracy.

Whatever Hawke may have thought about this side of the matter, he was undoubtedly moved to read that his success had given 'great satisfaction' to the King. Hawke never forgot that he owed his flag to George II's intervention, and his devotion to him acquired the stature of a moral principle.[92]

Unfortunately, Hawke, through signing without due attention a letter of 1 November, committed the kind of tactless act for which he was from time to time responsible. On this occasion he ruffled the susceptibilities of Corbett, the ageing Admiralty Secretary, by acknowledging his letter of congratulation in a postscript to a dispatch to his assistant, Clevland. This dispatch was in answer to a letter from Clevland, which had reached Hawke at the same time as Corbett's and concerned the disposition of the ships. Although the fighting of the campaign was doubtless of more importance than making formal acknowledgement of the

---

[92] Ad. 1/88, 4 Nov.; 2/506, 30 Oct. 1747. I.L., 30 Oct. 1747. N.M.M.: MS. 108, H. to Lady Kingston, 9 Feb. 1760.

Board's praise, it must have stung Corbett quite sharply to read, at the foot of the dispatch addressed to his junior, 'Pray my compliments to Mr. Corbett and I beg he and you will accept my hearty thanks for your kind letters'! One is tempted to suspect that Hay contributed to this blunder, for Hawke could reasonably have left the writing of such a letter to him.

Corbett did not fail to point out 'the slight' laid upon his office. The Admiral sent an answer by express on 4 November and included the following apology: 'I am heartily sorry that I should have given you occasion to complain of my disregard to your office, and hope you'll readily pardon it, when I tell you that it was entirely owing to the negligence of my clerk.'[93]

Still, Hawke had signed the dispatch as it stood and was ultimately responsible. Such mistakes could prove costly.

It may indeed be no coincidence that, shortly after this incident, Hawke failed to secure promotion to Captain for Lieutenant Cornelius Smelt, his 1st Lieutenant aboard the *Devonshire* in the recent battle, and for John Lockhart, provisional Captain of the *Kent*, both of them officers of whose merit he had 'very strong proof'. This considerable set-back may well be explained by the above-mentioned blunder, although jealousy on Anson's part can not be ruled out. Smelt, incidentally, had been one of the lieutenants of the *Dorsetshire*, acquitted by the court martial of 1745.[94]

Among the congratulatory correspondence received by Hawke after his return to Spithead was a letter from Lieutenant James Hobbs. This points to the personal isolation out of which Hawke had risen to distinction. Hobbs, who was earlier mentioned as serving under Hawke at Plymouth, wrote:

---

[93] Ad. 1/88, 1, 4 Nov. 1747. I.L., 2 Nov. 1747.

[94] Ad. 1/88, 1 Nov. 1747. Unfavourable comment on Anson's character is collected in Erskine, p. 79, etc.

> Sir, I hope you'll please to think of me having no friends to rely on but yourself, and if this glorious affair has given you an opportunity of providing for the few friends which was out with you, I hope you'll be kind enough to apply to their Lordships for me in time, before they shall put any more upon you, for Lord Anson has a great many hanging on him… If you want your chest, or anything else you left here, please to let me know and I shall take care to forward them. I am sorry the maid carried away the key of your chest, otherwise I could have got your clothes aired.

Hobbs, who had been promoted to lieutenant in 1741, later served as Hawke's Flag Captain aboard the *Ramillies* in the Seven Years' War, but was then sent out to the West Indies and never had much opportunity to distinguish himself. He was remembered by the Admiral in 1767 when he was appointed Captain at Greenwich Hospital.[95]

Between 8 and 23 November Hawke was up in London. The King's award to the Admiral of a Knighthood of the Bath was announced, but, because he soon afterwards went back to sea, Hawke was not installed until as late 11 December 1753.

No medals were struck to commemorate the Second Battle of Cape Finisterre although it was the outstanding victory of British arms during the war. In fact, over the whole period of 1700 to 1794 very few medals were given to the Navy. Anson himself was given one to commemorate the First Battle of Cape Finisterre; but there were no general issues, and occasional presentations were made to officers only — for example, after the capture of Louisbourg.[96]

---

[95] I.L., 30 Oct. 1747. Charnock, vi, 169.

[96] O.L., 7 Nov. 1747. Burrows, p. 199. W. H. Long, *Medals of the British Navy*, 1895, for eighteenth-century medals.

Before going to London in November Hawke had ordered Mostyn to put to sea with six of the line and three smaller vessels. While in town, Hawke was told by the Admiralty that Mostyn had been driven back into Plymouth by bad weather but was to be directed to sail again at once. On 23 November Hawke hurried back to Portsmouth to deal with the matter and to hasten the refitting of the main squadron. During his absence, some of the captains, who had shown little conformity with the stereotype of the silent naval officer in the case of Fox, had been equally voluble in denouncing the wording of Hawke's dispatch about the recent battle. As has been said, there was some ground for this criticism. On 26 November Sir Peter Warren, who had arrived at Portsmouth to preside at the court martial of Captain Fox, wrote to Anson: 'I have set all matters right with the gentlemen of Sir Edward's squadron who were a good deal dissatisfied at some expressions in his account of the action.'[97]

The refit proved a long-drawn-out business. The fact that the use of the docks was dependent on whether the tides were spring or neap was as usual a source of delay.

Now that Mostyn had gone back to sea, Hawke's friend Harrison was the senior officer refitting at Plymouth. After the grumbling that had been going on at Portsmouth Hawke must have found it agreeable to read the following letter from the old warrior, dated 13 December:

> I congratulate you on the honours His Majesty has been pleased to confer on you, and heartily wish you health and long life to enjoy it.

[97] O.L., 7, 20, 23, 24 Nov. 1747. I.L., 22 Nov. 1747. O.B., 8 Nov. 1747. Add.MSS. 15957, Warren to Anson, 26 Nov. 1747. Salmon, pp. 56-7.

> My son Tom, who you was so kind to appoint Second of the *Windsor*, has been in London, passed his Examination, and received a commission for 3rd Lieutenant of the *Nottingham*, and is returned on board. He joins me in our best compliments and grateful acknowledgements of your favour…
>
> I wish you a happy conclusion of the troublesome Court Martial, and should esteem it a favour if you'll please to let me know how it is determined.[98]

On the whole, this must have been the happiest time in Hawke's life. His wife, at 27, was enjoying the good health of youth; he had two little sons to whom he was devoted; his Knighthood was supplemented by a seat in Parliament; and his financial circumstances were about to be enhanced by a lion's share of the prize money deriving from the six captured French ships of the line.

Seeing that Hawke was one of Portsmouth's two Members of Parliament for a matter of 29 years, it is appropriate to explain the significance of his election. The seat was in the hands of the local Corporation. Until 1774 the Corporation was willing to accept the Admiralty nominees as Members, because the Navy was the most important customer in the port. These Admiralty members were expected by the King's Ministers to vote for their measures as a matter of course in the House of Commons; while the Burgesses of Corporation, for their part, assumed that influence would be exerted on behalf of their personal interests. Portsmouth Corporation remained compliant to the desires of the Admiralty and Government until, round about 1774, Sir John Carter's party formed an opposition. In the early years, at least, Hawke made

[98] I.L., returns from Portsmouth and Plymouth Dockyards, early Dec. Mostyn to H., & Harrison to H., 13 Dec. 1747.

no attempt to resist the 'establishment'. Like other prominent naval officers he valued his seat as an enhancement of his stature and influence. Nevertheless, when questions of patronage arose, he tended, like Anson, to stand against the promotion to naval posts of unqualified persons.[99]

The Admiral had little leisure in which to share his hour of triumph with his Lady. Besides the continual prodding, supervision and correspondence connected with refitting the ships for the next cruise, Hawke, as complainant, had to attend the court martial of Captain Fox, which dragged on from 25 November to 21 December. At no stage had Hawke shown himself keen to bring charges against Fox. He gave no evidence himself and asked only a few questions in order to clarify minor points. On his side, Fox evinced deep respect for the Admiral: 'I cannot help saying,' he declared, 'that I have so great a reverence for Admiral Hawke's honour that I should rely on the truth of any instrument to which his name is signed, as much as if 'twas on his oath.' On the whole, this tribute was deserved; but it is also significant that Fox was here trying to strengthen his case by making use of a slight inaccuracy in Hawke's dispatch of 17 October! Reverence for Hawke's obvious honesty of intention was commonly experienced by those who had any dealings with him, but the fact that his name appeared at the foot of an official letter (especially if it happened to be written by Hay), was far from being a guarantee of its absolute accuracy.

The extent to which Hay had established himself in Hawke's confidence is implied by the fact that it was he who wrote an

---

[99] Keppel, i, 122. S.P.Dom.(N.) 42/33, 15 Dec. 1747. Namier, esp. pp. 29-36, 137-8. Lake Allen, *History of Portsmouth*, 1817, pp. 104-8. Murrell and East, pp. 409-10. N.R.S., *Naval Misc.*, iv, 171. H. could presumably have been 'despised' only because of his lack of enthusiasm in satisfying private importunity.

answer to Harrison's friendly letter of 13 December. On the 21st, he wrote: 'This day Mr. Fox makes his last defence and they talk of passing sentence before night. In my opinion they will take the middle way, and pass one neither too mild nor too severe.'

Augustus Keppel sat as a member of the court martial and his letters to Anson of the 16th and 22nd include interesting comment on the trial and its outcome.

> The length of this trial is so different from the idea your Lordship seemed to have of it, that I reckon you are surprised how we have contrived to protract and lengthen it out as we have. However, latterly we have been as concise as possible. I suppose you know at your Board how it has so far gone. Things are differently represented on both sides; but, upon the whole, poor Fox is hardly treated by the squadron, and to me he seems to have been in the hands of his first lieutenant and master — two d—d bad fellows, I verily believe. As it is not over, I can't inform your Lordship further.

> We have at length ended this long and troublesome trial. You will know the sentence, I conclude, before you receive this, and know likewise the reason of its being so favourable. Poor man! I firmly think him no coward, but an unsettled, silly man, with a confused mind, but a good heart, I really believe... I reckon we are abused by the world for not shooting Fox, and he, poor man! fancies, I believe, that he should have been acquitted. What his first lieutenant deserves, I can't determine; but he must be a sad dog, and so must his master have been.

Fox was dismissed from active service but his name found its way onto the list of 'yellow' Admirals on half-pay.[100]

---

[100] Ad. 1/5291. Erskine, p. 221. Even H.'s critics admitted his

As Christmas Day approached, bad weather held up the refitting at Portsmouth and lashed Mostyn's squadron as it cruised to the W. of Ushant. Two damaged ships sought refuge at Plymouth, but brought in with them two captured privateers, one French and one Spanish. Hawke was now reaping the financial rewards of high command. His share of prizes taken by his ships was probably one eighth of their value, seeing that he did not have to divide the flag share with any other admiral at that time.

Shortage of masts, a recurrent problem throughout the century, was bothering the dockyard superintendent and he remarked to Hawke on the sharp rise in their price since the previous year. He was anxiously awaiting arrival of a consignment from Riga.

Hawke was disconcerted to find that no reply came from the Admiralty following his strong recommendation that Smelt should be made Captain of the *Devonshire*. On 22 December he wrote: 'I hope their Lordships will be so good as to grant me the following officers — Mr. Smelt, if it's agreeable, to command her, and Lieutenant Bladen, late of the *Edinburgh*, to be first, Mr. James Hobbs of the *Mars* second, Mr. Samuel Spencer third, and Mr. Hackman of the *Hector* fourth.' Jack Bladen was a nephew of the late Colonel Bladen, who went out to the West Indies with Hawke in 1739 and was promoted to Lieutenant as a result of that service. Spencer had been a junior Lieutenant aboard the *Devonshire* at the recent battle and he went on to become a Captain in 1757. William Hackman had also fought at Second Finisterre.[101]

The most interesting intelligence of the enemy which had been passed on to Hawke was that fourteen French East

---

honesty. O.L., 21 Dec. 1747. Keppel, i, 120, 123-4.
[101] I.L., 13, 23, 24 Dec. 1747. O.L., 22 Dec. 1747.

Indiamen were expected to sail soon from l'Orient. On 29 December the Admiralty, in view of the winds setting in easterly, thought that the French would take the opportunity of sailing and ordered Hawke to put to sea forthwith. He was to take the *Kent*, which had suffered little damage in the battle, and any other ships that were ready 'or near ready'. Collecting from Plymouth some ships reported by Harrison as fit for sea, he was to go at once to the Belle Isle area and send vessels to investigate at Brest and l'Orient.

Hawke moved with the required degree of precipitation; but for the first time an undertone of irritation began to show through his letters to the Admiralty, which, while it is extremely mild compared with the incendiary outbursts of Admiral Mathews, illustrates the dignified but defensive attitude adopted by Hawke towards their Lordships from this time onwards.

> Having reason from their Lordships' silence to apprehend that they do no approve of my having Mr. Smelt to be my Captain in the *Devonshire*, I am to beg they will be pleased to grant me Captain Thomas Sturton to bring her out to me.
>
> Though it puts me to a good deal of inconvenience, having made no preparations to go to sea in any other ship than the *Devonshire*, yet as the service requires it I shall use my utmost endeavours to collect what ships I can and proceed to sea with the utmost expedition.

Hawke was undoubtedly sensitive where his personal honour and reputation were concerned, as he was to demonstrate on a number of occasions. It is therefore something to be remembered to his credit that he helped to establish a convention of restraint in the wording of official correspondence which contrasts with the fulminations of Mathews and Vernon. On the debit side, this moderation dried out of dispatches some of the colourful quality which they might have otherwise possessed; but from the point of view of the effective carrying out of the country's naval policies the gain was clearly immense.

Installed as Captain of the *Kent* instead of the less-favoured Lockhart was Francis Holburne, with whom Hawke now began a long association. On the whole, the connexion did more good to Holburne than it did to Hawke. Holburne appears to have spent a fair proportion of his naval service in an aggrieved state of mind, and Boscawen, writing of him in 1755, was not at all enthusiastic on the subject: 'He is a Scot, you know I don't think much of that nation for upper leather, nor was he ever thought much of in our service. He is sick and has contrived to insinuate himself into the good graces of Lord Anson… You see by this I don't like him, nor ever did, having known him from my first entering the service.'

However, 'Mr. Holbum' was probably of considerable competence as an officer. He was almost an exact contemporary of Hawke's, having been made a Lieutenant a year earlier (Dec. 1727), a Post Captain six years later (Feb. 1740); and, as an Admiral of the White, he ultimately became a member of Hawke's Board of Admiralty.[102]

On 8 January 1748, the *Kent* (64), *Anson* (60), and *Centurion* (50) unmoored. No other ships could be made ready at Portsmouth. A squadron of the United Provinces' Navy had recently arrived, but, through being unready for service, it had proved as useless to the British ally as had other Dutch squadrons earlier in the war. From Hawke's point of view, a crowning exasperation was provided by an Admiralty order

[102] L.B., 29 Dec. 1747. O.L., 30 Dec. 1747. For Holburn's character: Add.MSS. 35359 f. 410; N.R.S., *Naval Misc.*, iv, 189, 194; Aspinall-Oglander, p. 237.

that the ship's company of the *Anson* should be paid. This directive might appear admirable in intent but in practice it was more like a match to a powder-keg. Most of the *Anson*'s crew had gone into captivity with Keppel, when, in June 1747, he pursued an enemy vessel with excessive zeal and finished up aground on the French coast. Although they had now been back in England for some months, they had never been paid the wages due from their time in the *Maidstone*. The result of paying them at the moment of rushing them off to sea was not difficult to anticipate, and the event was succinctly described in Hawke's dispatch dated at St. Helens on 9 January: 'Last night, the *Anson*'s ship's company being in great disorder by their having been paid the day before, obliged me to come to an anchor at this place.' As Keppel had remarked to Anson in a letter of the previous day: 'We are now in a great hurry for sailing, and I in a sad pickle with my whole ship's company drunk — not a man quartered or watched.'[103]

With a squadron built up to nine of the line (albeit including two 50s) and four frigates, Hawke finally cleared the Channel, after calling at Plymouth, on 16 January. Among his captains were several who would often serve with him in the future — Holburne, Keppel, Geary, Peter Denis, Barrington. Geary did not stay out long. As could be expected at that season, the weather was tempestuous, and all the *Culloden*'s masts were swept overboard. By then the *Gloucester* had gone into Plymouth just in time to avoid foundering. However, all was not misery at sea, for, on 31 January, Hawke sent off Harland with the *Nottingham* and *Portland* in chase of a large French ship. The result was not reported to the Admiral for some time but it turned out to be the capture of no less a vessel than the

---

[103] I.L., 5 Jan. 1748. L.B., 6 Jan. 1748. Ad. 1/88, 8, 9 Jan. 1748. Keppel, i, 130.

Magnanime (74), in command of which Howe achieved much distinction during the next war. This was a proud addition to the six of the line brought into Portsmouth after the Second Battle of Cape Finisterre. Meanwhile, the fierce westerly winds made it impossible for the frigates which Hawke had sent to observe l'Orient and Brest to report back to the Admiral.

On 22 January Warren had been restored to the command of the Western Squadron. He sailed on 5 February with three British ships and the Dutch squadron of six vessels, and headed for Hawke's rendezvous off Belle Isle. On the 9th he received advice that a Spanish squadron at Cadiz was stronger than that which, under Captain Cotes, had been posted to watch the port. Meeting Hawke on the 10th, he therefore ordered him to proceed to Cotes's station with the *Kent*, *Yarmouth*, *Defiance*, *Anson*, and *Tavistock* (50), and take over the command there.

But he failed to make contact with Cotes. The latter in the *Edinburgh*, with the *Eagle* (which was still commanded by Rodney), *Windsor*, *Princess Louisa*, and a sloop, finally encountered a large outward-bound Spanish convoy on 7 March. The enemy escort proved to consist of no less than nine ships of the line but Cotes boldly cut off five merchantmen and the Spanish, astonishingly, failed to make a counter-attack. With his prizes, Cotes sailed into Lisbon.[104]

Hawke continued to cruise on the prescribed station between Cape St. Vincent and Cape Cantin, until shortage of water and provisions, together with scurvy and fevers, forced him to put into Lagos on 28 March. In accordance with his orders he then went up to Lisbon to collect the homeward-bound trade, and

---

[104] Ad. 1/88, 3 Feb., 10 Apr. 1748. L.B., 25 Jan. 1748. Richmond, iii, 227, 229, 231. (He has wrong date for Cotes's action. See Ad. 51/1084.)

on 4 April he discovered Cotes's ships at that port. The frustration felt by the Admiral's squadron is conveyed in Keppel's letter of 12 April to Anson.

> Fortune has been kind to the Spaniards, and not so to the squadron the *Anson* has been in. Mr. Cotes and his squadron have seen that which might have made us all happy, had we been lucky enough to have joined; but bad fortune always attends the squadron I am in: I am its evil genius. If care and fatigue could have procured us a sight of these Spaniards, we, of Sir Edward Hawke's division, I think, have deserved it; but instead of seeing even one sail of the enemy, we have had but nine sights of any ship whatever, which made nine chases in twelve weeks, all which we spoke to, but they were not of the nation we were in search of.[105]

Warren had been cruising W. of Belle Isle in the hope of intercepting the long-expected French convoy from Martinique. This vast array of enemy vessels in fact remained penned-in at the island until the end of the war, immobilized for a whole year by the relentless pressure of British sea-power. However, intimations reached Warren of an enemy plan to concentrate a force, mainly French and including armed transports, at Corunna or Ferrol, with a view to recapturing Louisbourg. He therefore concentrated his squadron off Cape Finisterre but in early April he had to return to Spithead for refreshment and repairs. It was reported that the enemy ships, known to be at Brest, Rochefort, and Marseilles, had still not sailed for their point of concentration at Ferrol, so orders were sent to Hawke to cruise to the N. of Cape Finisterre. He reached this station before the end of April with the *Kent*,

---

[105] Ad. 1/88, 10 Apr. 1748. Keppel, i, 132-3.

Anson, and *Tavistock*. It was there that he was found by Warren on 12 May.

This happened to be the occasion of the last promotion of flag officers during the war. It was only ten months since Hawke had barely achieved flag rank on the active list. In the course of the brief period which had elapsed since then, he had experienced the quiet routine of the command at Plymouth; the responsibility and strain of operational command at a crucial moment; the excitement of battle; the glory of success; the acclaim of the public and the rebuffs of the Admiralty; the hardships of seven months out of nine spent at sea, with a winter included for good measure. Now, by the promotion of 10 May, he rose to Vice-Admiral of the Blue. Warren, though also promoted, was now only one step ahead of him as a Vice-Admiral of the White. Anson kept his distance as an Admiral of the Blue. Boscawen, who moved up to Rear-Admiral of the White, was nevertheless falling farther behind Hawke whom he had nearly eclipsed in July 1747. Osborn, whose first commission was dated twelve years earlier than Hawke's, became, like Warren, a Vice-Admiral of the White. Perhaps another of these promotions is worth noting — that of the Honourable John Byng (born in 1704, Lieutenant in 1724 and Rear-Admiral of the Blue in 1745) to Vice-Admiral of the Red. Thus, in so short a space of time, Hawke had risen from obscurity to rank amongst the senior Admirals then in active service.

Hawke continued to cruise with Warren until the fifteen ships of the squadron returned home together. Early in May a truce had been arranged between the British and French governments, so Warren's measures to prevent an enemy concentration at Ferrol proved unnecessary. But, on 19 May, he received an order to continue hostilities against Spain. He conferred with Hawke and his captains, reinforced Cotes who was again off Cadiz, with five ships; and with the remaining ten he instituted a blockade of the Canaries. Thus the final stages of Hawke's long cruise proved unexpectedly protracted. At last it was all over. The squadron dropped anchor at Spithead on 24 July. During the final weeks they had been cruising on one of the principal Spanish trade-routes without sighting a single vessel of the enemy. Such was the effect on Spanish commerce of the Admiralty's well-conceived strategy.[106]

[106] Richmond, iii, 229, 230-4. Ad. 1/88, 3, 16, 25, 26 May 1748. S.P.Dom.(N.) 42/33, 18 May, 23 July 1748. L.B., 7 June 1748.

CHAPTER 8: THE ADMIRAL IN TIME OF PEACE

WITHIN a week of the squadron's return to Portsmouth Warren wrote to Corbett: 'I shall with great pleasure give Sir Edward Hawke their Lordships' order to take upon him the command of His Majesty's ships and vessels at Spithead and in Portsmouth Harbour as soon as I have struck my flag.' The generous-hearted Warren was, at every stage, delighted with Hawke's success. On the next day, 30 July, Hawke received from the Admiralty the Lords' order to take over the most important peacetime command which the Service could offer.

On the strength of this and of prize-money accruing from his two cruises as an Admiral, Hawke began to set himself up as a man of property. At the end of 1748, probably, he acquired a London house in Gerard Street; and, by the winter, Catharine was engaged in the exciting pursuit of choosing silver fit for the table of persons of high repute.

The table itself cost £65 16s. 4d. and the charge for 'engraving the arms and a fine border' was £8 8s. 0d. As a motto for his arms Hawke had chosen the appropriate word 'Strike'. The crest was engraved on the silver, and the final cost of the set was £337 17s. 10d. — a tidy sum, at a time when the pay of an Able Seaman was about 9d. a day. For his 'inexpressibly dear' Catharine the Admiral purchased a splendid adornment in the form of 'a pair of large cluster brilliant 3 drop ear-rings'. Henry Hurst, the jeweller, received £235 for them on 22 March 1749.

The money of 1749 may be converted approximately to its present-day value if it is multiplied by 6½. That is, the food and consumer goods of little-changing character, which might have been bought in 1749 for the £235 paid for ear-rings, would cost about £1,500 today.

It may be inferred from Hawke's purchases of books that he habitually did a fair amount of reading when not actually involved in service at sea. On 28 April for example, Thomas Cooke acknowledged receipt of £2 2s. 0d. 'for one set, on royal paper, of my edition and translation of Plautus's Comedies'. Later in the year Hawke purchased another set of the same edition 'on small paper' for £1 1s. 0d.[107]

Meanwhile he had been kept quite busy with his naval duties. From the first day of his command at Portsmouth he was responsible for arranging a court martial — a duty which never appealed to him. On this occasion one Captain Eaton of the *Old Noll*, privateer, charged several of his men with mutiny. In a dispatch of 16 August 1748, Hawke reported to Clevland that the trial had been held aboard his flagship, the *Fougueux* — one of his prizes of 1747. The upshot was that 'one was acquitted, ten ordered to be whipped and sent in any of His Majesty's ships on a foreign voyage, and the other seven sentenced to die. As the crime of the latter was chiefly owing to ignorance and thoughtlessness, I hope', wrote Hawke, 'their Lordships will give me leave to beg that they would intercede for mercy to be shewn them.' Seeing that the King was then abroad, the Lords, accepting Hawke's recommendation, referred the matter to the Lords Justices of the Kingdom. Meanwhile a misunderstanding had occurred over the ten men 'to be

---

[107] Ad. 1/88, Warren to Corbett, 29 July 1748. L.B., 26, 20 July 1748. H.P.P., bills addressed Gerard St., Feb.-Apr. 1749. For 'inexpressibly dear', see petition of Robert Tomlinson [1768-9]. *Economica*, Nov. 1956. 'Seven Centuries of the Prices of Consumables,' by E. H. Phelps Brown and Sheila V. Hopkins, p. 299. The figure 6% is inferred from the chart.

whipped'. The Lords had intended to delay their punishment also, but Hawke took it that Clevland meant only the death sentences to be postponed, especially seeing that commanders-in-chief were normally expected to have floggings carried out on their own responsibility. An interchange of letters, with messengers crossing each other between Portsmouth and Whitehall, heightened the confusion, before it was finally resolved — but only after the unfortunate ten had received a gratuitous whipping! However, on 22 August Hawke was brought to write: 'Besides my being convinced that I had sufficient authority to cause that part of the sentence to be put into execution, I had the strong motive, Humanity, to hasten it. The men had been confined about ten months, were naked, overrun with vermin, and in every respect objects of pity and compassion. Upon the whole, if I have erred, I beg their Lordships will do me the justice to believe it was without design.'

In due course a pardon, dated 26 August, was received at Portsmouth. In accordance with standard practice the wretched prisoners had to be kept in ignorance of their reprieve, and on 31 August they were brought out, as they thought, to be executed. Attitudes to punishment have changed so much that it is difficult today not to read a touch of irony into Hawke's account of the event. But it is highly improbable that any such irony was intended by the Admiral. 'The ceremony was carried through with the same solemnity as if they had really been to die. They were all very penitent, behaved with great decency and resignation, and seemed truly sensible of their Lordships' goodness when their pardon was read.'

However, when it was conveyed to the prisoners that their Lordships had found time to ponder the question of their rehabilitation, these feelings of gratitude may have undergone some modification. The *Prince Henry*, about to sail for the Guinea Coast under Captain Jaspar, had been selected as most likely to restore them to rude health and heighten their appreciation of what the lower deck had to offer. The popularity of this particular cruise has already been demonstrated. Aboard the *Dover* (50), 109 men had been informed of their imminent transfer to the *Prince Henry* and, as Hawke reported to Clevland: 'A number of them immediately jumped into the vessel that was to receive them, and carried her off, with the lieutenant who endeavoured to prevent them; and only 49 remained.'[108]

Hawke now felt himself sufficiently well-established to resist the time-wasting aspects of bureaucracy, as may be gleaned from the following correspondence. On 8 September, Clevland wrote: 'Not having received a letter from you these last two posts, I am commanded by my Lords Commissioners of the Admiralty to observe to you that it hath been usual for the officers appointed to command in chief at any of the Ports to correspond with their Lordships by every post.'

This argument from convention failed to impress Hawke, who replied on the 10th: 'I have received your letter of the 8th instant, in answer to which I am to acquaint their Lordships that my not writing by the two posts you mention was owing to my having nothing relative to the Service to communicate to them.'

The subject was dropped.[109]

At this time Hawke clearly believed that Anson was well disposed towards him, for, on 15 September, he wrote to him

---

[108] I.L., 30 July 1748. L.B., 30 July 1748. O.L. and Ad. 1/917, 13, 16, 22, 31 Aug. 1748.
[109] I.L., 8 Sept. 1748. O.L., 10 Sept. 1748.

personally to ask for assistance in connexion with the valuing of the *Terrible*, *Monarque*, *Neptune*, *Trident*, *Fougueux*, and *Severn*. A provisional estimate had already been given which, in Hawke's opinion, 'much undervalued' the prizes. Now, the Navy Board was seeking further to reduce the figure, as a result of a report from the Officers of the Yard whom they had instructed to survey the ships 'with all the strictness possible to find out their defects.' Anson's reply has been lost but Hawke's letter of acknowledgement, written in his own hand on 28 September, shows that Anson, who had apparently done his best to help, had not achieved anything. 'Still', wrote Hawke, 'we are nevertheless to return to your Lordship a great many thanks for espousing our part with so much friendship… My wife joins with me in desiring our compliments may be acceptable to yourself and Lady Anson.' Anson had recently married Elizabeth Yorke, the daughter of Hardwicke, the Lord Chancellor, with whom he was 'united in friendship and politics'.

The value to the Navy of the prizes taken by Hawke is brought out if they are compared with the ships taken by Anson at the First Battle of Cape Finisterre. By 1751 only the *Invincible* (74) out of the assortment of vessels captured by Anson was still on the lists; whereas, of the six ships of the line taken by Hawke, the *Terrible* (74), *Monarque* (74), *Trident* (64), and *Fougueux* (64) were still worthy of retention. To these might be added the *Magnanime* which, as has been mentioned, was taken by Hawke's squadron in 1748.[110]

It was not long before Hawke was given to understand what the Corporation of Portsmouth required of its two Members of Parliament. Of the two the senior was Admiral Isaac

---

[110] Add.MSS. 15956, f. 46; 9338 for list of Navy in 1751. Montagu MSS. 25446, f. 59. Aspinall-Oglander, p. 71.

Townsend, but he seems to have been considered less influential than Hawke at this time, because it was to the latter that an approach was made over a matter of seamen being paid in Portsmouth. Where ships had previously been decommissioned at that port it was decreed by the Admiralty that only the seamen themselves, or their wives or widows, could receive the money due by attending at Portsmouth. Moreover, 'the opportunity would be brief. The effect of this was that the honest townsfolk who had already cashed the pay-tickets of many of the seamen, usually at a scandalous discount, would have to make the journey to London to convert the tickets into money, as would any seamen who missed the payment at Portsmouth. If, on the other hand, all the money were disbursed at Portsmouth, the local tradesmen would benefit. 'As I am circumstanced with regard to this Corporation', wrote Hawke on 23 October, 'I could not avoid giving attention to a case wherein their interest seems so much concerned. But if, in this, I should ask a thing without precedent or incompatible with the Public Good, I hope their Lordships will forgive me.' Judging by Clevland's brief endorsement, their Lordships forgave him readily enough but felt no inclination to alter the arrangements which had already been made.[111]

After a period of leave in London, extending from 28 November 1748 until 22 June 1749, Hawke returned to his command. He forthwith issued instructions for the guardships in the port which give a good idea of life aboard these vessels, comprising in peacetime the country's most immediately available naval force.

Eight ships of the line were then employed as guardships at Portsmouth. Their function was to provide a squadron which

[111] O.L., 23 Oct. 1748. Murrell and East, pp. 409-10.

could be quickly made operational, and meanwhile they safeguarded the port, dockyard, and such ships as were completely laid up 'in ordinary'. A 3rd rate of 64 guns may be regarded as typical. When employed as a guardship she bore 140 officers and men, against a wartime complement of 480. It would be possible to get such a guardship under sail but difficult to man many of her guns. The normal routine was for a scout boat to sally forth from the guardships twice every night to take a close look at the ships in ordinary, which had small care-and-maintenance crews aboard them. Hawke ordered the inspection to be made at varying times so that the watch would be kept alert aboard the ships in the ordinary; also that all candles and fires were to be put out by 8 p.m. 'except for the candle necessary for the watch which is always to be kept in a lanthorn proper for that purpose'. If an emergency occurred the alarm was to be sounded 'by ringing of bells and making of false fires'. During the day the men from the guardships were to be busy with 'Works of the Deck, Ropeyard and the Moorings in the Harbour' and, if they were sent away from their ships, were to be in the charge of 'a discreet Midshipman'.[112]

Early in July Hawke shifted his flag to Anson's prize, the *Invincible*. Another mutiny, this time aboard the *Chesterfield* (40), had to be dealt with by court martial and an unusual feature was that two Lieutenants of Marines figured amongst those condemned to death. On 8 July Hawke saw fit to write to Corbett: 'Compassion excites me to address their Lordships in behalf of that unfortunate person, Lt. Morgan, now under sentence of death. He was but little acquainted with sea service, is extremely weak and ignorant. Besides, he has a wife and several small children, whose bread depends solely on him. It is

---

[112] O.L., 22 June, 27 Nov. 1749. O.B., 22 June 1749.

true, his crime was heinous, but I would fain hope that the above considerations might induce their Lordships to intercede with His Majesty graciously to spare his life.'

Clevland noted that there were 'no comments from the Lords about the Lt. of Marines', so it remained incumbent on Hawke to issue orders for the execution. It is obvious, not only from what he wrote about Lieutenant Morgan but also from his life as a whole, that this duty caused him acute distress.

But the law took its course. At 8 a.m. on 14 July, Lieutenants Couchman and Morgan were brought onto the quarter-deck of the *Chesterfield*, the ship aboard which their crime had been committed. Confronting them they found a file of musketeers provided by the guardships. From the *Invincible* came the report of a gun, and a white and yellow striped flag could be seen on its way up to the flagship's topmasthead. This was the signal for mustering the crews of the guardships. When they had all assembled on deck the captains read out a notice of the crime and sentence. The muskets barked aboard the *Chesterfield* and the ordeal of the lieutenants was at an end.

Later in the month Hawke ordered arrangements to be made for the ex-carpenter and three ratings of the *Chesterfield* to be hanged. Apparently even warrant officers did not qualify for death by shooting which was reserved for commissioned officers.[113]

By 27 July Hawke had again shifted his flag, this time aboard one of his own prizes, the *Monarque.* Shortly after, he went on sick leave and stayed at home until 4 October. His 'indisposition' was probably one of the feverish colds which, from time to time, immobilized him completely. However, during this period of illness he dragged himself back to

[113] O.L., 28 June, 8, 11 July 1749. I.L., 10 July 1749. Ad. 1/918, 1 Sept., 7 Oct. 1749, 28 Apr. 1752.

Portsmouth to receive Hasselaer, 'the Head of the maritime affairs in Holland'. This was to meet the wishes of the youthful Lord Sandwich, amongst others — that nobleman having become First Lord of the Admiralty earlier in the year in succession to the Duke of Bedford. He and Anson, who were mindful of Holland's sluggishness as an ally in the recent war, had Corbett write to Hawke on 29 August: 'Lords Sandwich and Anson hath it much at heart to inform this gentleman in whatever he shall desire to know, as a means to put the ships of the States General in a condition to act with us more to the purpose than they have hitherto done, when need shall require.'

After his return to duty at Portsmouth, Hawke issued in November an order to the captains of the guardships about the wearing of uniform, which is of interest because uniform had been first instituted, for combatant officers of the Navy, during the previous year. 'You are', he commanded, 'to appear, on all proper occasions in your proper uniform; in particular, never to sit at a court martial in any other habit.' The other 'Officers and Gentlemen on the Quarter-deck' were to wear uniform whenever on duty and none, Hawke enjoined, 'are to walk the said quarter-deck unless they strictly comply' with the order.

During the following year, 1750, Hawke's third son, Chaloner, was born. He was named after the Admiral's old patron, Sir Chaloner Ogle, who died before the year's end.[114]

As regards Hawke's naval duties the year was uneventful, though he may have been somewhat intrigued by a dispute which arose between the Captain and Purser aboard the *Fly* sloop. The latter complained 'of being greatly oppressed in the performance of his duty' by the Captain of the ship. Lord Anson himself conducted an investigation into the matter and

---

[114] I.L., 28, 29 Aug. 1749. O.B., 14 Nov. 1749. *Burke's Peerage*, 1959.

the Lords sent a copy of his report to Hawke, who was to arrange for the said Captain to be court-martialed.

Anson discovered that the trouble had begun over the Purser's pet monkey. Until then, perfect amity had prevailed between Smith, the Purser, and Wyatt, his Captain, the latter having frequently honoured Smith by inviting him to dine at his table. But 5 September 1749 had proved to be a fatal day. The valiant Captain happened to be indisposed, and the hullabaloo of three monkeys chattering outside his cabin door did nothing to assist his repose. He peremptorily ordered them to be carried up to the foretop and left there until further notice. News of this event apparently reached the Purser shortly after darkness had fallen. He bustled up, collected his monkey and groped his way back towards the quarter-deck, intending to place it in the security of his cabin. A sentry intervened, the monkey took fright, and in an instant the animal became a squealing flurry of arms and legs. Wyatt hurtled out into the gloom, demanding in passionate tones 'what rascal, scoundrel, or villain had dared to insult him… To his great astonishment, Mr. Smith faced him immediately with the monkey on his shoulder'. Wyatt, with no thought of the R.S.P.C.A. to counsel restraint, forthwith bellowed orders for flinging the animal overboard. Smith expostulated, but Wyatt was not to be denied. As Anson put it: 'At last, one of the officers wrested it from him and threw it into the sea, and the Captain returned to his cabin, after telling the Purser he must not expect any further favours or indulgences from him or words to that effect.' The Captain remained true to his intention. While the ship was in the Mediterranean, the Purser more than once came aboard 'disguised with liquor', and Wyatt, taking a tougher attitude than in the pre-monkey days, stopped his leave almost completely.

In the end, the case seems to have fizzled out without a court martial being held.[115]

An event of more consequence was the reduction of the complements of the guardships by the Admiralty's instructions of 20 July 1750. As a result, Hawke ordered the captains to discharge from the Service twenty of the 'most useless men' borne aboard each ship. 'As it is requisite,' he continued, 'your ship should be kept in as good a condition as possible, you are to take care to entertain none but Able Seamen before the mast.'

In the autumn the Admiralty instructed him to come up to town and assume command of the ships in the Thames and Medway, so that, as a sufficiently senior officer, he might preside at the court martial of Vice-Admiral Griffin. The latter had been accused by his own captains of failing to do his duty by engaging a French squadron on the India Station in 1748, and at the head of these captains was Lord Harry Powlett, later pejoratively known in the Service as 'Captain Sternpost'. Seeing that Hawke was connected with the incident from which the nickname was derived, the matter will be taken up in due course. Meanwhile, Powlett had succeeded for a long time in delaying Griffin's trial on a plea of ill-health, and the Admiral in question bitterly complained that this was a mere manoeuvre, intended to force him, through pressure of mounting expense, to release a number of his material witnesses. The outcome was a limited victory for Powlett. Although Hawke's court acquitted Griffin on the capital charge of cowardice, it found him guilty of errors of judgement and sentenced him to be suspended from the flag list. However, Griffin busied himself in mobilizing political support and

[115] L.B., 11 May, enclosing copies of Anson to Corbett, 16 April 1750.

ultimately turned the tables on Powlett by getting himself restored to the list of admirals on half-pay.[116]

After the court rose Hawke rejoined his family at Swaythling. Two days before Christmas he wrote to Clevland: 'I had the ill luck to get a great cold at Mr. Griffin's court martial, which has since laid me up, in so much that I have not been able to stir out of doors since I got home, or otherwise I should have been at Portsmouth at the beginning of last week. But I shall not fail being there, before I set out hence for London.' Sandwich had given him leave to take his 'family to town against the meeting of the Parliament'.

During Griffin's trial Hawke had recourse to a Dr. Wilmot who wrote no less than six prescriptions in order to combat the Admiral's indisposition.[117]

It was not until May 1751 that Hawke again hoisted his flag at Portsmouth. Soon after he had to investigate a complaint by one Richard Mason, Carpenter of the *Savage* sloop, against his Captain, Thomas Foley. The Captain admitted calling Mason 'Rascal', but he explained, with ample corroboration from his officers, that the Carpenter was 'a very idle, drunken fellow'; and added, as if apologetically, 'I have also refused his wife admittance on board, on account of her getting drunk and appearing naked before the sloop's company.' On balance, the Admiral felt that the Captain's choice of epithet did little violence to the claims of justice.[118]

On 28 August Clevland wrote privately to say that Pelham, the chief Minister, and Anson (who had recently displaced Sandwich as First Lord of the Admiralty) were interested in the

---

[116] I.L., 15 Nov. 1750. D.N.B.: Griffin. For Powlett's character, cf. *Naval Misc.*, iv, 231-2. Richmond, iii, 216.

[117] Ad. 1/918, 23 Dec. 1750. H.P.P., Dr. Wilmot's prescriptions, 7-13 Dec. 1750. Namier, p. 32.

[118] I.L., 10 July 1751. O.L., 13 July 1751.

possibility of Hawke becoming Mayor of Portsmouth. The election for this office was held annually on 29 September. Seeing that Hawke was already an Alderman, and that his three sons, aged 7, 4, and 1 respectively, had been deemed of sufficiently mature wisdom to be elected Burgesses the previous May, it may have appeared that the Admiral did not lack 'interest' with the Corporation. However, Hawke told Clevland that, in fact, he had 'no personal interest in the place'. In 1750 it had been his turn in the normal way to become Mayor but he had decided to stand down. The leading figure in the Corporation was William Rickman who had been three times Mayor and, as far as the election of 1751 was concerned, had declared his support for John Leeke. On account of the intimation that the Government would like to see him elected, Hawke had sounded Rickman. The latter had protested his firm attachment to the King, Lord Anson, the Navy, and 'the case of the Administration', but without committing himself to a change of policy with regard to the election. In Hawke's opinion, Rickman's party required only the offer of a little inducement to bring it to support the Admiralty's wishes in Portsmouth. He was ready to act as an intermediary if necessary but evinced no keenness to become Mayor himself. In the upshot, Rickman's man, John Leeke, was duly elected and one can only presume that, for the time being, a *modus vivendi* was re-established between the Admiralty and the Portsmouth Corporation.[119]

On the whole, the Navy retained a steady grip on Portsmouth until just before Hawke came to the end of his long term as one of its Members in 1776. He himself never

---

[119] H.P.P., H. to Clevland, 1 Sept. 1751.Murrell and East, pp. 25-6 (Mayors); 409-10 (M.P.s); 295 (Burgesses of 18 May 1751). Lake Allen, op. cit., pp. 104-8 (political struggle).

became Mayor but he continued to follow the political developments at the port, even after his personal connexion with it had lapsed.[120]

From the time that he achieved high command in the Navy, Hawke was frequently brought into touch with people offering inventions to the Service and, following the example of Anson's Board of Admiralty, he seems to have been always ready to give any invention a fair trial. That autumn, following the Board's instructions, he saw tested a device supposed to improve gunnery, namely a 'spring lynch stock', designed by one Arthur Edgecombe of Portsmouth. Taking advantage of the presence aboard the *Kent*, which was now the flagship, of eight captains, assembled for a court martial, he had the invention used in their presence. The result was general agreement that 'it could be of little or no service in general action. But,' Hawke added characteristically, 'as the poor man has been at great pains in the invention, and as he has a large family, I hope their Lordships will give me leave to recommend him to their favour.'

In October he had to take up with the Admiralty a recurrent irritation, namely the despatch of orders from their Lordships direct to ships in his command, instead of adherence to the normal practice of sending the orders through the commander-in-chief. Apart from implying a degree of insult, this irregularity tended to engineer confusion. For the moment the matter was amicably settled. 'I send this to acquaint you', Clevland wrote on 21 October, 'that for the future the said orders shall be conveyed through your hands.'[121]

Hawke spent Christmas at Swaythling. On 23 December his baby daughter, named Catharine after her mother, was

---

[120] H.P.P., G. Goodenough to H., 25 Jan. 1777.
[121] O.L., 17 Oct. 1751. I.L., 21 Oct. 1751.

baptized at the serenely beautiful parish church of St. Nicolas. The poor little mite had a sad life ahead of her. She would have no mother to preside over her fifth birthday and, having reached maturity, she was to be permanently afflicted by a crippling, undiagnosed ailment. With a steady devotion, her father did all he could for her welfare.

As if Providence were already preparing a compensation for the blow which would descend on the Admiral and his four young children with the death of Lady Hawke, a young woman called Sally Birt came to live with them at about this time. The Birts were friends of the Hawkes, and from the first Sally lived as a member of the family, although she appears to have come to assist Lady Hawke with the children. Therefore, she was concerned with their upbringing for a matter of five years, before she was called on to fill the breach which so tragically opened up.[122]

Hawke resumed his command, but in the spring of 1752 he was again taken ill and had to write to Clevland: 'I have lately been troubled with a violent cold and cough, by which I am reduced to a very weak and bad state of health, and as I have often been in this way, my physician tells me I have no chance to get thoroughly well of my disorder, nor to my being liable to continual complaints of this kind for the future, unless I go to Bristol to drink the waters of that place.'

He therefore requested two months' leave as 'a case of absolute necessity'.

The leave was granted. Hawke did not return to Portsmouth until 3 July, when he hoisted his flag aboard the *Monarque*.[123]

---

[122] H.P.P., bill for furniture delivered to Miss Birt by Wm. Linnell, 30 Jan. 1752.

[123] Ad. 1/918, 28 Apr., 3 July 1752. O.B., 3 Nov. 1752.

In November his command was virtually eliminated. He received orders to pay off seven of the eight guardships. On the 12th he struck his flag; and until 12 February 1755, he remained on half-pay, except for two brief intermissions during which he presided at courts martial.[124]

Note should be taken of the wider significance of laying up these guardships. For long the view that Anson was the only great First Lord during the eighteenth century has attracted steady support. That he was a sound strategist who took a sensible interest in tactics and many other aspects of naval life is beyond dispute. However, other First Lords of this period have come in for censure, not because they failed in the activities in which Anson succeeded, but because they failed to produce a Navy adequate to the emergencies which it was called on to face. Sandwich, to take the outstanding example, became firmly established as a symbol of calamity because his Navy was not strong enough to cope with the war of 1778-81. If he knew that not enough money was being spent on the Service, why, it is asked censoriously, did he not resign?

If one is hoping to form a reasonable judgement on the First Lords of the eighteenth century from the point of view just mentioned, it would seem advisable to take a look at the official records of expenditure on the Navy. Such inspection produces something of a shock. The Treasury records, echoed by those of the Admiralty, show that, of all those who graced the office of First Lord between 1738 and 1790 inclusive, Anson was the least successful in extracting money from the Government for the use of the Navy during the years of peace. On this count the most successful First Lord was Sandwich.

---

[124] O.B., loc. cit. H.P.P., 'Hawke MSS., 1702-1800', f. 76. Ad. 1/918, 12 Nov. 1752, 4 Jan. 1754.

Further discussion of this important matter must await the time when Hawke's own administration is reached.[125]

Although not yet by any means outstandingly rich among admirals, Hawke was nevertheless very comfortably situated. A note dated 21 November provides a reminder of this. It concerns payment of £1,072 10s. 0d. for some Government Annuities bearing interest at 3½ per cent. These appear to have been the equivalent of today's dated government securities and were redeemable at Christmas 1757. Applying the yardstick mentioned earlier in this chapter, one could calculate that the investment was worth about £6,500 in present-day money. As for his half-pay, £1 5s. 0d. a day as a Vice-Admiral of the Blue in 1752 somewhat outshone 5d. a day as a Captain in 1739.

In the spring of 1753 Hawke was living at a house in George Street, Hanover Square, having apparently disposed of his property in Gerard Street. At this time his wife was expecting a fifth child — seventh, in terms of children born — and later in the year it was delivered at Swaythling. It was not long for this world. In the middle aisle of the Church of St. Nicolas there is a tombstone which bears the following inscription: 'Under this stone lies William, the son of Sir Edward and Lady Hawke, who died Sep 14th 1753, aged 4 days.'

At the beginning of 1754 Hawke was offered the command on the India Station. 'It is a sensible mortification to me', he replied on 21 January, 'that I am prevented from accepting it by my present state of health, which confines me to my house, and renders me incapable of undertaking so great a voyage. I hope that their Lordships will believe, when in my power, I am always ready to obey their commands.'[126]

---

[125] T. 38/638 and Ad. 7/567.

[126] H.P.P., annuities. Ad. 25/43; 1/918, 10 Apr. 1753, 21 Jan. 1754.

Towards the end of the year Hawke went up to his house at George Street, leaving Catharine, Chaloner, and baby Kitty at Swaythling, together with Sally Birt. There are only four letters written by Catharine to her husband which are known to exist today, and three of them belong to the time of this separation. They are dated 2, 7, and 9 December. Catharine had been worrying about Martin, who was then 10 years of age and away at Eton, and also about Edward, aged 8 and also away at school, because the small-pox was prevalent in London.

> May I beg that Martin may be fetched home precisely on Thursday next, and poor dear Ned the day he breaks up, and my Ned set out with them the next day for Swaythling, for I am sure one day here will do you more good than five in London…
>
> I am afraid by yours that you are worse than you will own. For God's sake don't conceal anything from me, but if you are anything ill, let me come and nurse you. I am now quite strong and well, and able to travel to you without anybody with me. Therefore make no ceremony of sending for me, who is in every sense
>
> Yours
>
> Cath: Hawke
>
> [P.S.] The children are both well and my arm mends, but even if it was ever so bad, it should not, nor could not, prevent my coming to do you service. Mark — self interest. For I can [not] serve myself more essentially than in serving you and my babes.

Catharine must have heard from Hawke that he was in fact not well, for 9 December found her writing in her round, open hand that she would come up to town and look after her husband and the boys there. Her businesslike statement to this effect having been completed, the tone of the letter changes abruptly, as if in a premonition of death, to one of prayer: 'God of His great and infinite mercy preserve you and my dear children, and grant me the blessing that, whenever He is pleased to close my eyes, I may have you with me in perfect health; and that after my decease the four little ones may turn out virtuous and good, so as to be a comfort to you, who I pray may be an aged parent before you leave them.'

Thus wrote Catharine, Lady Hawke, at the age of 34. Two years later the chilly hand of death would lie upon her. Of her three sons, two would indeed turn out virtuous and good, as far as the inner truth is indicated by appearances; her daughter from the time of her young womanhood would be incapacitated by her mysterious malady; and her third surviving son would prove a wild young man, possessed of redeeming features, and come to an untimely end. As for herself, when her eyes closed for the last time, her Ned was far away in the Western Mediterranean, engaged on a hopeless mission with only his courage to sustain him in his private grief.[127]

[127] H.P.P., 4 letters from Lady H. to H.

CHAPTER 9: HOSTILITIES, THOUGH UNDECLARED

BY 1754 it became clear that another major clash between Britain and France could not be long delayed. It was in North America that the two powers came most sharply into conflict.

It is, of course, incorrect to think of the French colony in Canada in terms of the extended and developed state which today stretches from the Atlantic to the Pacific. The French had effectively occupied only the area round the St. Lawrence. Elsewhere, on the southern flank of the thirteen British colonies, they had a settlement in Louisiana — and that was all. Seeing that the British colonists were almost twenty times as numerous as the French, the fort-building activities of the latter, designed to pen the British to the East of the Alleghany and Ohio Rivers, seem in retrospect to have been foolishly provocative. However, the disunity of the British colonies together with the fact that the population of France itself was about double that of Britain, provided encouragement for the French. Moreover, the total strength of the French army exceeded that of the British to an extent beyond that suggested by the disparity of the populations, so dispatch of a sufficient number of troops from France to North America before the war began offered a prospect of ultimate victory. Britain's essential task was to reassert command of the Atlantic to prevent the passage of French troops and supplies, not only when hostilities had actually been declared but as soon as the French Government's intentions had been sufficiently indicated. Such command of the Atlantic would, of course, safeguard the British homeland against invasion by the formidable French army, at the same time as ensuring victory in Canada.

On 6 March 1754 Henry Pelham died; and the main direction of British policy fell into the hands of his brother, the Duke of Newcastle. William Pitt assessed accurately enough the Duke's fitness for such responsibility by remarking that while he did not lack ability as a Secretary of State, as chief Minister he would have to rely on Hardwicke's 'wisdom, temper, and authority'. Without Hardwicke, he would be 'feeble'.

Before long the news reached England that an inadequate force of Virginians under Colonel George Washington had been defeated and captured by the French in the Alleghany Valley. In January 1755 the British Government sent out General Braddock with a reinforcement to strengthen the colonial forces. At the same time it seemed important to avoid any appearance of aggression on the British part because, if open war supervened, Holland would be entitled not to enter the conflict on the side of Great Britain. With Austria slipping away from her former alliance with Britain towards alignment with France, Newcastle adopted a defensive strategy.

The French reaction to the departure of Braddock's reinforcement of 800 men was, however, the assembling of 3,000 regular troops. Eighteen naval vessels were made ready to carry them to Canada. In January 1755 while these developments were taking place, Newcastle held a meeting of the Cabinet Council to decide what was to be done next. This Inner Cabinet which resembled a modern War Cabinet was a feature of eighteenth-century government both in peace and war. On this occasion Newcastle heard the advice of Hardwicke, the Lord Chancellor; Granville, the Lord President; Holderness and Sir Thomas Robinson, the Principal Secretaries of State; Anson, the First Lord of the Admiralty; and Sir John Ligonier, the Lieutenant-General of the Ordnance, representing the Duke of Cumberland, who was Commander-in-Chief of the Army. It was decided to deploy sufficient naval strength to prevent the French reinforcement from reaching Canada.[128]

On 5 February Clevland wrote to Hawke (who had been advanced to Vice-Admiral of the White on 6 January) to ask whether his health would permit him to serve. The Admiral was still at George Street where, as has been related, he had been unwell during the previous December. There is no evidence as to the speed of his recovery. However, he answered Clevland's question in the affirmative and, by Admiralty Order of the 6th, he was appointed Commander-in-Chief at Portsmouth. According to Boscawen, Hawke 'was very ill' when he left London, so it is clear that it was only by an exertion of will that the latter was able to answer this call to duty. On the 12th his flag was hoisted aboard the *Terrible* (74), one of the prizes of the Second Battle of Cape Finisterre.[129]

During the years 1752-4, the number of men on the Navy's establishment had sunk as low as 10,000. After noticing in the previous chapter the respective records of Anson and Sandwich with regard to naval expenditure, one is not surprised to find that the figure of 10,000 compares unfavourably with the lowest ebb of the decade preceding the War of American Revolution. Hawke had an establishment of 16,000 and under Sandwich the number never sank below 18,000.[130]

---

[128] Tunstall, pp. 110-12. Nicolas, i, 207 for N. American populations. Corbett, i, 14-15, 20, 24-5, 31-6.

[129] H.P.P., Clevland to H., 5 Feb. 1755. L.B., 6 Feb. 1755. O.L., 12 Feb. 1755. N.R.S., *Naval Misc.*, iv, 172.

[130] Clowes, iii, 5, 327. H. W. Richmond, *Statesmen and Seapower*, 1946,

Under these circumstances, manning was bound to be Hawke's most pressing problem. The first step was to send tenders to scour the Channel and the small ports along the coast; but in order to man even the tenders, it was necessary for the ships which had begun to make ready at Portsmouth to be denuded of men. The result was that there were not enough seamen left aboard these ships to provide a proper watch and soldiers had to be posted as sentries. However, the press gangs went to work with their customary energy and before long batches of their captives were flowing into Portsmouth. But their arrival, while promising eventual solution of the manning problem, created new troubles for the Commander-in-Chief. 'Five men sent by the Mayor of Sandwich on board the *Arundel*', wrote Hawke, 'I find very unfit for the Service, besides having the itch [scabies] and labouring under other distempers.' In order to check infection he had to send such people to the hospital.[131]

The inhumanity of this system of manning is illustrated by the Admiralty's rejection of a plea by Hawke on 22 February that men brought into Portsmouth, *en route* for ships at Plymouth, who had 'neither clothes nor bedding', should be 'supplied with bedding and slops in the ships they shall be put on board of' at Portsmouth. This proposal presumably made difficulties for the Navy Board. But no determined attempt appears to have been made to find a solution to the problem.[132]

By the beginning of March some ships had acquired skeleton crews, so Hawke distributed orders that gunnery training, as prescribed in the regulations, was to commence forthwith. 'The whole ship's company and supernumeraries, in turns'

---

p. 124.

[131] L.B., 8 Feb. 1755. O.L., 14, 21 Feb. 1755.

[132] O.L., 22 Feb. 1755. I. L., 24 Feb. 1755.

were to be drilled in firing the 'great guns and small arms'. The order ended, 'And this you are not to fail doing on all proper occasions, as you will answer to the contrary.'[133]

However, the Admiral found that his tenders were not catching enough men and that this was due to elementary geographical considerations. The principal source of supply was to be the homeward-bound merchantmen approaching the Channel from the W. But seeing that there was need for seamen at Plymouth, and this port was strategically placed to the W. of Portsmouth, the tenders from Plymouth were not allowing much to pass through the net. Indeed, after receiving attention from the tenders from Plymouth the masters of merchant vessels had to display seamanship of the highest order to coax their denuded ships into the nearest port. As far as Hawke was concerned there was scant alternative to keeping his volunteers at sea in the tenders and leaving the rigging and fitting of his ships largely to landsmen. Moreover, such men as had been impressed tended to filter away through desertion, and the army had to be asked to help check the outflow. Some soldiers, who had succeeded in dragging deserters back to the fold, had applied for a reward, and Hawke asked the Admiralty whether any was allowed. 'Their Lordships', Clevland averred on 10 March, 'are very sensible of the difficulty you lie under in fitting out the ships… They have already ordered you 600 men from the Nore… Their Lordships have ordered the Navy Board to direct the Clerk of the Cheque at Portsmouth to pay to the soldiers for each deserter they take up a reward of 20s., and to charge the same against the men's growing wages.'[134]

The constables of the Borough of Portsmouth were already aware that they were entitled to a reward for performance of

---

[133] O.B., 5 Mar. 1755.
[134] O.L., 8 Mar. 1755.

this kind of service, as two of them, namely William Bedford and William Walker, made clear in a protest addressed to Clevland on 9 March. They had succeeded in tracking down a man who had been taken on board the *Monarque* on 14 February but had subsequently made his escape, 'one Peter Willis, a seaman, he being skulking about in a House of Ill Fame and disguised with liquor'. After completing the Hogarthian scene by guiding the reluctant Willis aboard the *Monarque*, the constables were aggrieved when the Captain refused to give them 'a receipt, as of custom, to carry to the Clerk of the Cheque'. Ultimately Hawke ordered the Captain to issue a receipt.[135]

On 11 March the Admiral received instructions from the Admiralty to administer a reprimand to Lieutenant Charles Middleton for showing insufficient zeal in command of a pressing tender. Middleton had informed their Lordships that he intended to return to Portsmouth with a haul of twenty-three men, when his tender would carry 100. On the 15th the future Lord Barham (who was to become Comptroller of the Navy and finally First Lord of the Admiralty) came into port with thirty-two captives. Before long he was giving an account of himself to his Commander-in-Chief and appears to have made an eloquent and convincing defence. 'Upon a strict examination', reported Hawke, 'I cannot find that he has been negligent in his duty.' On 29 March the Admiralty came back with a report from Commissioner Hughes of Portsmouth that the tender in question 'was capable of carrying more than 100 men' and that Middleton was to set his sights accordingly. In early April the Lieutenant was doubtless quite pleased when a general recall was issued for all tenders out from ships completing for sea.[136]

---

[135] I.L., 10 Mar. 1755. O.L., 12 Mar. 1755.

As far as Hawke was concerned, the men coming in from Deal, Dover, and other eastern ports continued to be 'rather a nuisance than otherwise, for want of size, years and strength'. The Lords therefore sent orders 'to the Senior Captain in the Downs not to encumber the ships with useless men'. Meanwhile, Hawke had no option but to send numbers of 'very sickly' men to Haslar Hospital 'in order to save their lives'; and inevitably his attention was progressively taken up by problems developing at that institution.

When completed in 1761 Haslar Hospital was ranged on three sides of a quadrangle and was notable for being the largest building made of brick in England; but in 1755 only the first wing was standing. This had been opened in 1754 and contained eight wards, thus permitting contagious cases to be kept apart. The foundations had been laid in 1746, and while the original wing was being constructed, a number of sheds already housing naval patients clustered around it. By 1755 it appears that these sheds were being used for convalescents. The water came from an open, unlined well; and the water was hard. Its flavour was not improved by the fact that the pumping machine was worked by four horses, whose tramping encouraged the sides of the well to fall in. Considering that the desire to desert could safely be ascribed to the average patient, it is not surprising to find that, during the latter half of March, Hawke was repeatedly asking the Admiralty to arrange for a military guard to be posted at Haslar. 'For', wrote the Admiral, 'till it arrives, the benefits expected to arise from that Hospital are in great measure frustrated by the desertion and straggling of the men, and their having opportunities of selling their clothing for spirituous liquors, which greatly retard their cures.' On 30 March Hawke paid a personal visit to the Hospital,

---

[136] I.L., 11, 29 Mar. 1755. O.L., 13, 16 Mar. 1755.

standing on its mud-girt peninsula, and the next day was largely devoted to communicating with their Lordships on the subject:

> As there is but one man to serve as porter at the gate, light the fires, and many other offices, I found the gates had not been properly attended, and idle people with liquor had thereby access, and the sick people free egress and regress. To remedy which I ordered the porter to attend the gates only and do no other duty. If their Lordships approve of it, I think there is an absolute necessity for another porter and two labourers to pump water, light fires, and clean and sweep about the rooms, even after the twelve invalids are placed there; for it would require at least nineteen sentries, constantly on duty, to guard the hospital properly, I found also, thirty-two men fit to return to their ships and several incurables, whom I ordered to be discharged to make room for others.

Because more 'cradles' were urgently needed, he had had them taken ashore from the transports serving the garrisons of Gibraltar and Minorca. He had told the Contractor for the Hospital to purchase more bedding locally instead of waiting for it to be supplied through the normal channels. Finally, he had ordered that a commissioned officer and a surgeon should visit the Hospital three times every week.[137]

The Lords ordered the Commissioners for the Sick and Hurt to supply 'immediately' articles of furniture requested by Hawke, and asked the Secretary at War to make up the guard to twenty men. Meanwhile, two days after his visit to Haslar, the Admiral was able to write, 'The Agent has rectified what I found amiss'.[138]

---

[137] O.L., 20, 22, 29, 30, 31 Mar. 1755. I.L., 21, 26 Mar. 1755. Lloyd and Coulter, pp. 207-12.
[138] I.L., 1, 2 Apr. 1755.

On 24 March Hawke had hoisted his flag aboard the *St. George* of 90 guns and 1,655 tons. In her he was to make his next two cruises. His Captain was John Storr (who finally rose to Rear-Admiral in 1779); the 1st Lieutenant was James Hobbs; also a Lieutenant was Samuel Spencer who, like Hobbs, had been appointed to the *Devonshire* in December 1747 at Hawke's request; and, among the Volunteers were John Birt, a brother of Sally Birt, and Robert Tomlinson, who had been recommended in the first instance to Lady Hawke, and was to be connected with the Hawke family for a long time to come.[139]

Meanwhile, as a result of the Inner Cabinet's deliberations, Boscawen had been chosen to cruise with seven of the line off Louisbourg, and, on meeting the French reinforcement, to capture it. Hawke was to provide the squadron from the ships which he was making ready at Portsmouth but, as the need for secrecy was extreme, neither the Navy Board nor the Victualling Board had been informed about the project. Hawke was to obtain Boscawen's supplies direct from Commissioner Hughes and the Agent Victualler at Portsmouth. Despite these precautions, the French may have suspected that something was afoot, for, on 14 April, Hawke was reporting that two French vessels had come in as far as St. Helens 'and pretended to be drove in by stress of weather'. To their Lordships' satisfaction he 'immediately ordered them off the coast'.[140]

During this strenuous time the Admiral probably had no chance to see his family at all. To permit of some amelioration in this respect he hired some accommodation in Portsmouth,

[139] O.L., 24 Mar. 1755. H. P.P., Tomlinson's petition and his letter to H. of 5 Nov. 1776. cf. N.R.S., *Tomlinson Papers*, pp. vii, viii.

[140] Corbett, i, 43. I. L., 31 Mar. 1755, but this copy not written till 25 Apr. L.B., 31 Mar. 1755, but this copy not written till May. O.L., 21 Apr. 1755.

and on 15 April he took a few hours off in order to welcome Catharine on her arrival.[141]

Finally, after a spate of frantic activity, Boscawen sailed on 21 April with ten ships on his mission of preventive war. Seeing that he had, no doubt, carried away with him a large proportion of the number of fit seamen, Hawke may have felt more than a little overburdened when he received the Lords' instructions of the 23rd to have seventeen of the line ready 'to proceed to sea at a moment's warning' under his own command. The men were to be conjured up from somewhere, somehow.[142]

When account is taken of the difficulty of overland transport at that date, of the limited means of preserving foodstuffs, and of human frailty, it is not surprising to find that this abrupt expansion of the fleet exposed shortcomings in the Navy's supply services. Of the food and stores supplied for the sick, Hawke wrote:

> The sugar is extremely black, coarse, and ready to run into molasses, and the fruit in general mouldy and so masked and clotted that it is scarce possible to determine the species it was of. The sago, or rather what was put up for it, full of dust and musty. The cinnamon very coarse and having neither spicy taste nor flavour. The sheets so patched and darned that it is impossible to make a roller a yard long out of them, and several short of the number allowed. Instead of shallots and garlick, stipulated by contract, there is in each box a few ounces of chocolate, no way adequate as to usefulness to the articles it is given in lieu of. I must therefore request that their Lordships would give direction to enquire into the same.

---

[141] N.R.S., *Naval Misc.*, iv, 172. O.L., 3, 21 Apr. 1755.
[142] L.B., 23 Apr. 1755.

Clevland responded that the Navy Board had been ordered to appear before their Lordships, 'that an immediate stop may be put to such proceedings, and such measures taken with the Contractor as his infamous conduct deserves'.[143]

Anson's Admiralty was certainly exerting itself to get things done and raise efficiency. Also, scandalous though the system of impressment was by present-day standards, the Board tried to administer it conscientiously, and regularly ordered investigation of petitions against wrongful impressment. Only professional seamen were properly liable to serve, and normally there were some categories of these which were exempt. Where a complainant was found to have been illegally impressed, he was promptly released — provided that he was still in a home port! On account of petitions addressed to the Admiralty, Hawke had to look into a dozen or so cases every month. To take one example, 'The Petition of Samuel Woodward of Maldon in Essex', which was sent to the Admiral by Clevland on 25 April, 'most humbly showeth that about three weeks ago your petitioner was impressed in the town of Maldon and carried on board His Majesty's ship the *Prince*, where he is detained to the unspeakable grief of his inconsolable wife (big with child), and the rest of his family; that he is a Freeholder of the county of Essex and had never been to sea'. Charles Saunders, then commanding the *Prince*, stated that Woodward had been impressed, not at Maldon, but at Colchester. In any case, he had been turned over — not inappropriately — to the *Terrible* on 22 April. As far as one can see, Hawke rejected Woodward's petition and his wife remained unconsoled.[144]

---

143 O.L., 27 Apr. 1755. I.L., 28 Apr. 1755.

144 I.L., 25, 28 Apr. 1755. Other petitions Feb.-July.

Meanwhile, numbers of the pressed men continued to be lost through desertion. On 28 April Hawke wrote: 'As most of the deserters from the squadron here pass through Godalming and Guildford, I submit it to their Lordships whether an order from the Secretary at War to the commanding officers of the troops quartered there, to stop all seamen travelling upwards, would not prove greatly beneficial to the Service.'[145]

At this juncture a crisis was fast developing on the international plane.

The British Government was concerned over the possibility that the escort of the French reinforcement for Louisbourg might turn out to be too strong for Boscawen's squadron, consisting of ten ships of the line. Consequently, on 28 April the Lords ordered Hawke to advance the readiness of four of the ships at Portsmouth. ('We recommend to you to do this in preference to everything else.') By 8 May the Admiralty had heard that la Motte had sailed from Brest with no less than nineteen of the line. It was indeed doubtful how many of these carried their full armament — some, at least, were transporting troops — but the possibility remained that Boscawen would attack, without declaration of war, and be disastrously repulsed. Hawke was immediately told that Francis Holburne, his Captain aboard the *Kent* in early 1748, was to be the Commodore of the reinforcing squadron.

On 11 May Holburne, just promoted to Rear-Admiral, sailed with as many as six of the line.[146]

---

[145] O.L., 28 Apr. 1755.

[146] Corbett, i, 47. L.B., 28 Apr. 1755. I.L., 8 May 1755. O.L., 9, 11 May 1755. Corbett, i, 48, asserts that Holburne was promoted 'to give Hawke a capable flag-officer in the Channel Fleet'. This is contradicted by I.L., 8 May 1755 and O.L., 9 May 1755. Before being promoted R/A, Holburne had already been appointed as commander of Boscawen's reinforcement.

At this time George II was in Hanover, trying to negotiate treaties to safeguard his principality which was liable to be overrun when war came between Britain and France. He was making no progress with Austria, which, with its eye on the possibility of recovering Silesia from Prussia, was sliding away into alignment with France. It can be imagined that the monarch, who was not the most placid of individuals, would not welcome news that Britain had committed a flagrant act of aggression, and would not become more friendly to his British Ministers if the act in any case produced a sharp reverse.

Having manned and put to sea sixteen of the line, Hawke strove to complete his own squadron. The Admiralty, desperate for men, had sent the Admiral an order, dated 6 May, to 'cause all seamen and seafaring men whatsoever to be pressed without regard to any protections, excepting all Masters of ships and vessels, and their First Mates, Boatswains and Carpenters of such as are of 100 tons or upwards, and also excepting the men belonging to outward bound ships and vessels, which shall either have broke ground or shall be cleared at the Custom House, laden, and ready to sail'. Indiscriminately, the press gangs raked in everyone who came approximately within these widened limits; and soon Hawke had to set up under Rear-Admiral Temple West an organization for combing through all the crews at Portsmouth, ship by ship, and tossing out of the Service all the unfit men who had been caught in the net. On 21 May matters were further complicated for Hawke when the protections were brought back into force.[147]

Probably the most spectacular incident arising from this spate of impressment involved Lieutenant Robert Sax who was sent out in command of a tender by Captain Rodney, now in

---

[147] L.B., 6 May 1755. I.L., 20 May 1755. O.L., 22 May 1755.

the *Prince George* (80). From the merchantman *Britannia*, sailing peacefully up Channel on her way home from Leghorn, Sax's menacing vessel was seen to emerge from the vestiges of the night at dawn on 1 June. Instantly, the crew of the merchantman seized control from their officers, and exerted themselves to outsail Sax. The gallant Lieutenant had, however, not been chosen because he lacked spirit for his job. Later in the day, Rodney found himself assembling, for the enlightenment of his Admiral, an account of what ensued.

> Mr. Sax, after acquainting the men several times that the Channel was full of tenders, and that it was impossible for them to escape being pressed, could not prevail upon them to submit. They answered with three cheers and fired a shot at him, on which Mr. Sax boarded them with the tender.
>
> [As the master of the *Britannia* put it: 'They ranged up under our larboard quarter to enter their men, but our people, acting upon the defensive with handspikes, spits, etc., laying about the ship, but no arms, I acquainted the officer our guns were all powdered but not shotted... Our people resisting their entering the ship, the Tender fired a volley of small arms, which killed three of our people upon the spot.']
>
> Mr. Sax assures me [continued Rodney] he gave positive orders to his men not to fire... I should be glad to receive your directions how I am to proceed in this affair and what is to be done with the men that were killed, as I find they are still on board the ship.

Seeing that the shooting had occurred at sea, it was not legally a matter for the authorities on shore, but for Hawke as Commander-in-Chief of the area concerned. There was probably no admiral in the Service more humane than Hawke but he saw no virtue in publicizing the irreparable. Therefore, on 2 June, he prescribed for Rodney a course of action which was simple, practicable and to the point. 'You are... to cause the utmost dispatch to be used by the Surgeons... in finishing their examination of the three men killed... Then you are... to put on board [the *Britannia*] men sufficient in number and quality to navigate her in safety to her moorings in the River Thames, directing them as soon as they get without St. Helens to throw the dead bodies overboard.'[148]

Hawke reported the matter fully to the Admiralty and was soon ordered to assemble a court martial on Sax and his trigger-fondling men. But the Admiral had caught another of his prostrating colds and obtained permission to place the proceedings in West's hands. In the upshot, Hawke sailed with his squadron before the trial could be held, so the affair was turned over to Admiral Osborn who succeeded Hawke in the command at Plymouth. The court martial finally held that Sax and his men had been justified in firing their muskets.[149]

On 23 June Hawke wrote to the Admiralty recommending his 1st Lieutenant, James Hobbs ('a very diligent, good officer') for the command of one of the many small vessels about to be commissioned. 'It is', the Admiral stated, 'the first favour of the kind that I have ever asked, and shall be very much obliged to their Lordships if they will be so good as to grant my request.' The Lords replied that they would, 'upon a proper occasion'; and, in fact, they soon did. The incident illuminates a remark made a few years later by Lord Hardwicke to the effect that Hawke was 'diffident'. Ultimately, Hawke's memorial at North Stoneham was to bear the words: 'A prince unsolicited conferred on him dignities which he disdained to ask.' And the not-very-friendly Horace Walpole thought of him as 'a man void of ostentation or ambition'. So it is fair to say that

---

[148] I.L., 1 June 1755. O.B., 2 June 1755. Hutchinson, pp. 229-31.

[149] O.L., 3, 13, 14 June 1755. I.L., 6, 13, 16, 17 June 1755.

modesty, a rare quality among naval officers at that time, was one of Hawke's outstanding characteristics. This modesty stemmed from his devoted Christianity; but a natural sensitivity, associated with a strongly held conception of personal honour, also contributed to it.[150]

By mid-July Hawke was almost ready to put to sea with sixteen of the line, but the King's Ministers were severely agitated by the problem of what instructions to give him. It was known that Boscawen, owing to fog, had been able to intercept only a small part of la Motte's fleet. For an Admiral who had been sitting on the Board of Admiralty up to the time of his going to sea, he had shown poor judgement of political consequences by attacking at all in such weather. He risked involving England in a major war at the same time as estranging her potential allies, while his gains were limited to three captured ships. The Government therefore hesitated to order Hawke to sweep up the French trade sailing in from India and the West Indies.

On 15 July the Admiralty told Hawke to be ready to sail at 48 hours' notice. Then, on the 17th, orders were sent for him to put to sea at once. Yet not till the 21st did Newcastle, Hardwicke, Cumberland, Granville, Anson, Robinson, and Fox decide what instructions to give him![151]

The instructions, dated the 22nd, were to the effect that, because of French aggression in North America it was necessary to protect His Majesty's interest both in that theatre and on the high seas. Therefore Hawke, with sixteen of the line, was to intercept the French naval squadron under du Guay, which had recently sailed from Brest for the Spanish coast. The Comte du Guay had only nine sail and was

[150] O.L., 23 June 1755. I.L., 24 June 1755.
[151] Corbett, i, 57-8.

apparently on a training cruise. The self-same gentleman, incidentally, had been afforded hospitality by Hawke in 1747 after surrendering the *Terrible* to the *Devonshire*.[152]

In the interim Hawke was endeavouring to get his ships out of port and along the coast to Torbay. On the 20th a fresh gale from the W.S.W. was holding him at Spithead. In his dispatch of that date he had reason to make specific reference to his secretary: 'Captain Lloyd of the *Newcastle* acquainted me last night that the Purser of the said ship having been detected in some things not so decent to name had run away and left her in want of necessaries. That she might not be detained on that account, I appointed Mr. John Hay, my Secretary, to act as Purser of her, and shall be greatly obliged to their Lordships if they will be so good as to grant him a warrant accordingly.'[153]

On 23 July the Admiral reported from St. Helens that he had received his Secret Instructions, summarized above, and on the afternoon of the 24th he put to sea.[154]

He divided his line of battle into two divisions, the first of nine ships, being under his own command and the other, of seven, under Temple West, Rear-Admiral of the Red. The captains in his own division included some who had served under him before. Henry Harrison, now aged about 70, still commanded the *Monmouth*; and at this stage he was generally known in the Service as 'Harry of Monmouth'. Other veterans of the Second Battle of Cape Finisterre were Steevens and Saunders. Otherwise, there was John Storr, Hawke's Captain in the *St. George*; Peter Denis, who had been round the world with Anson; John Lloyd, who had been Hawke's 1st Lieutenant aboard the *Berwick* at the Battle of Toulon, and for whom

[152] Burrows, pp. 234-6. Corbett, i, 68-9. Lacour-Gayet, p. 238.
[153] Ad. 1/89, 20 July 1755.
[154] ibid., 23 July 1755.

Hawke had specially asked on this occasion; the Honourable Captain Hamilton; Charles Catford; and George Cokburne, soon to be Comptroller of the Navy. In West's division, captains who had commanded ships at Hawke's battle of 1747 were Rodney and Hanway. West himself, as mentioned in connexion with the courts martial of 1745-6, had commanded a ship in Mathews's van at the Battle of Toulon and had displayed outstanding initiative and judgement, for which he had been temporarily cashiered. Finally, it is worth noting that Lord Harry Powlett, the manoeuvring prosecutor of Admiral Griffin, had particularly asked to go out with Hawke's squadron. He found himself in West's division as Captain of the *Barfleur*.[155]

In Chapter 5, reference was made to Hawke's eventual transformation of the vital Article 13 of the General Fighting Instructions. However, in 1755 he had not yet determined to make this change. Before leaving port he had issued copies of the General Printed Sailing and Fighting Instructions in which Article 13 did bear a handwritten alteration, but it was only a minor one, to the same effect as that made by Mathews before the Battle of Toulon. The Article, with the insertion underlined by the present writer, now read: 'As soon as the Admiral shall hoist a red flag on the flag-staff at the main topmasthead, and fire a gun, every ship in the Fleet is to use their utmost endeavour to engage the enemy in the order the Admiral has prescribed unto them, <u>and on no account to fire before the Admiral shall make the signal.</u>'

Also, the printed version had had 'fore topmasthead'. (The position for the red flag was changed where it would otherwise have been hoisted on the same mast as the Admiral's own flag.

[155] O.B., 21 July 1755. Charnock, v, 34.

As a Vice-Admiral, Hawke wore his flag at the fore topmasthead.)[156]

On 28 July Hawke lay off Plymouth Sound, completing his supply of beer and malt spirits. The same day he set out on a sweep down the Bay of Biscay towards Cape Finisterre. It took eight days to reach that Cape and nothing was heard of du Guay.

As the squadron had sailed without a full complement of officers, the Admiral made some temporary appointments, including that of Mr. John Birt as 4th Lieutenant of the *Captain* (64).[157]

When writing about Hawke's movements, firstly down to Cape Finisterre and then to a more northerly rendezvous between 45° and 47°, Corbett seems to have exaggerated the Admiral's cunning and foresight. He argued that Hawke ordered his cruise in such a way that he would be reported to du Guay as being off Cape Finisterre. On emerging from Cadiz the French *chef d'escadre* would therefore sweep well out to the W. and then head back for Brest by the mid-Biscay trade route. Hawke had employed a stratagem of this kind in 1747; but in 1755 his initial movements, first to Cape Finisterre and then up towards Ushant, were simply in accordance with his instructions. Not until 23 August did he decide to wait in the mid-Biscay position. At that point, however, he certainly did take into account the probability that du Guay had heard of his being off Cape Finisterre.[158]

While he was off Cape Finisterre Hawke in fact anticipated that du Guay, if he had indeed been ordered to return to Brest

---

[156] Add.MSS. 40073 for Gen. Printed Ins. issued to Capt. Murray of the *Trident*, 19 July 1755. cf. *lighting Ins.*, p. 190 n.
[157] Ad. 1/89, 28 July, 6 Aug. 1755. O.B., 30 July 1755.
[158] Corbett, i, 69. O.L., 6, 30 (2) Aug., 30 Sept. 1755.

rather than to go to America or elsewhere, would head due N. approximately through the position now occupied by the British squadron. Therefore when, on 6 August, he headed away for Ushant as he had been ordered to do, he left the sloop *Savage* on the Finisterre station. The vessel was commanded by the Lockhart who had impressed him in 1747. If Lockhart sighted 'a squadron or any ship or ships of war belonging to the French', he was to note their number, strength, and course — also the winds. Then he was to open the Admiral's sealed rendezvous and find him.[159]

When the squadron was still off Cape Finisterre, Lord Harry Powlett made the disquieting discovery that water was seeping through the sides of the veteran *Barfleur*. Hawke ordered that a survey should be made as soon as the weather was fine, and this proved to be the case on 9 August. Evidently the Carpenters who examined the ship considered that she was in no danger. However, Powlett was soon complaining 'that the second and third pintles of the rudder' were very loose and, although the Carpenters were no more impressed by this defect than the other, Lord Harry — as will appear — maintained a strong interest in it.[160]

Back in England there was animated discussion amongst the political *cognoscenti* about the instructions which the Cabinet had given to Hawke. At Kew, the supple intriguer Bubb Dodington inquired of the Princess Dowager 'if she could account for Lord Anson and the Duke of Cumberland concurring in tying Hawke's hands' by allowing him to take action against warships only. In Dodington's words, 'She said she could not, for the Duke had strongly declared (though not to her, who had not

---

[159] O.L., 30 Aug. 1755. O.B., 6 Aug. 1755.

[160] O.B., 6, 9, 10 Aug. 1755. O.L., 6 Aug. 1755.

much conversation with him) for a *naval* war... She added nobody knew what to do — no two people were together.'[161]

However, on the very day that Dodington noted this conversation in his diary, namely 6 August, the leading Ministers and the other Lords Justices placed their signatures beneath a set of Additional Secret Instructions for Hawke. 'You are to endeavour to seize and take, by every means in your power, all French ships and vessels, as well men of war and privateers as merchantmen, that you shall meet, sending them into some convenient port in His Majesty's dominions, together with their effects, to be there kept without embezzlement till His Majesty's pleasure shall be known concerning them.'

Hawke, remembering the frenzied pillaging aboard the ships taken by him in 1747, may have felt a little sceptical about the possibility of preventing 'embezzlement'. Of what had happened aboard those prizes, the Admiral had written, 'Their common men rob and plunder their own ships and officers. The latter confusedly throw their own things together. Neither is there any restraining our own people, egged on by their resentment, from plundering when they first enter them, and destroying papers and everything else which appears useless to them.'[162]

The new instructions, carried in the *Essex* by Hawke's old acquaintance Robert Harland, reached the squadron on 23 August. If it had not been for contrary winds, Hawke, after reaching latitude 47° on the 16th, would have headed back towards Cape Finisterre, in accordance with his original instructions. As it was, he had been carried to the E. of his

---

[161] G. B. Dodington, *Diary*, cd. H. P. Wyndham, Dublin, 1784, p. 240.
[162] H.P.P., Additional Secret Instructions of 6 Aug, 1755, O.L., 22 Dec. 1747.

rendezvous in hazy weather. On the day that the *Essex* joined, Lockhart appeared in the *Savage* with the news that du Guay had sailed from Cadiz on 1 August. He could give no information as to his course.[163]

It seemed to Hawke that du Guay had either gone out to America 'or to cruise to the Westward and Southward for the protection of their homeward bound trade'. To cater for the latter eventuality, he decided to cruise with his main squadron forty leagues W. of Ushant, between 47° and 48° N. He at once ordered Henry Harrison to take the *Monmouth* and *York* and see what intelligence he could collect between Belle Isle and Rochefort. During an eight-day cruise, he was to seize any French ships he saw, to 'see that no plunder or embezzlement be made of them, and their crews be treated with all possible civility'. John Lloyd in the *Newcastle* was to cruise off Cape Finisterre for fourteen days and take any warships he could 'cope with'. Then, leaving Denis in the *Medway* to spend fourteen days on the rendezvous and watch out for an expected reinforcement of four of the line, the Admiral headed N. with the rest of his squadron.[164]

Supplies were beginning to run short although the squadron had been out for only a month, and on 25 August all officers and men were put on a half allowance of beer and brandy. Earlier in the cruise Hawke had had to complain to the Admiralty of the poor quality of the beer supplied from Plymouth — a nuisance which was to plague his squadrons through a great part of the war.[165]

Water deteriorated more rapidly than beer. The latter was often severely rationed on cruises, like those undertaken by

[163] O.L., 30 Aug. 1755 (2).
[164] ibid., loc. cit. O.B., 23, 24 Aug. 1755.
[165] O.B., 25 Aug. 1755.

Hawke in the Seven Years' War. One effect of these conditions was to produce a minor scourge of eighteenth-century seamen — not noticed as much as it might have been — popularly known as the 'gravel'. Alimentary calculi, to give the crystals their medical name, form as deposits in the kidneys, in cases where the patient has formed a habit of not drinking enough. Amid considerable discomfort, he may pass the stones through to the bladder and thence they may emerge with the urine. It has already been observed that the failure of Mathews's leadership at the Battle of Toulon can be partly attributed to this ailment. As far as Hawke was concerned, the conditions of his summer cruise of 1755 were preparing slowly but inexorably the basis of years of intermittent misery in the future and this must have applied to many others in the squadron. As far as can be ascertained, the Admiral did not have to seek medical advice on the subject until June 1763.[166]

In early September several prizes, described by Rodney as being 'of considerable value', were sent into English ports. By the 7th the squadron was in latitude 47° 26 N. and thirty-two leagues W. of Ushant, having spent a few days being blown off station to the S. by a gale which elicited from Rodney the comment, 'Nothing in nature is so disagreeable as hard weather at sea.' However, on the 8th Harrison returned with a French supply vessel which had been heading for Louisbourg, and Hawke was comforted to learn that du Guay had not returned to port by the beginning of September. He thought now that the French admiral's destination was certainly Rochefort or Brest.[167]

On the 9th the frigate *Ambuscade* joined with a letter from the Admiralty communicating a stern rebuke to Lord Harry

[166] H.P.P., prescriptions of 1763-4. cf. Lloyd and Coulter, p. 115.
[167] P.R.O. 30/20/6, 8 Sept. 1755. O.L., 7, 8 Sept. 1755.

Powlett for depositing twenty-one men aboard a beer hoy for conveyance to the Hospital, just before the departure of the squadron from Portsmouth. Even though they had doubtless given every outward sign of being at the point of death, the men had at once sprung into vigorous life and profited by this God-given opportunity to desert, so it probably did not surprise Hawke to read that their Lordships deemed such proceedings detrimental to their 'utmost efforts' to man the Fleet. However, it was impracticable to convey the reprimand to Lord Harry, because, during the recent gales, that commander had decided that, whatever the Carpenters thought about the pintles of his rudder, he took a serious view of them; and therefore, without so much as a wave of a handkerchief, he had headed for home. Because of this incident he became widely known as 'Captain Sternpost' and he did not have long to wait before he was afforded an opportunity to enrich his experience of courts martial — this time as the accused.

By the middle of September Hawke saw that his cruise could not continue much longer. Fever was running through the ships' companies.

In the naval medical service, the stage had been reached at which Surgeons could distinguish between some of the kinds of fever. In 1750, Dr. John Huxham, who was connected with the Navy, published an *Essay on Fevers*, giving symptoms of intermittent fever (malaria), slow nervous fevers (perhaps enteric), and pestilential fever (typhus). At the same date the expression yellow fever was first used, although this illness had been distinguished from malaria some years earlier. In general, 'fevers', in the context of naval service in cool climates, meant typhus; while yellow fever predominated on the dreaded West Indies Station and on the coast of Africa. When, on 14 September, Hawke wrote: 'I find the ships' companies falling down so fast in fevers that I am afraid I shall not be able to keep out long', the affliction in question may be assumed to be typhus. What this meant in terms of life on board is well conveyed by the following account of the normal course of the fever, supplied by William Turnbull in 1806:

> The skin acquires a dry and parched feel, the tongue becomes hard and furred, and the secretion of saliva as it were suspended. The confusion of head, and tendency to stupor, increase, accompanied with more or less delirium, which, being at first transient, becomes gradually more continued. The state of the bowels and urine is irregular, but as the disease proceeds, diarrhoea comes on. Symptoms of putrescency now make their appearance, consisting in small livid spots, like flea-bites, dispersed over the skin. The stupor of the head becomes more permanent; great anxiety prevails about the precordia, and frequent sighing takes place; haemorrhage also arises from the different parts, especially from the gums and intestines, being in the latter case conjoined with diarrhoea; and hiccup soon succeeds, to terminate in death.

After 1750 naval surgeons, including the outstanding James Lind, emphasized the importance of hygiene in preventing typhus, but the century ended without anyone discovering that the disease was communicated by lice and rats. It has been noticed that in 1743 Hawke was attentive to cleanliness on board ship. During the Seven Years' War medical science could recommend no better way of dealing with typhus, which was the principal scourge of the Channel fleet. That Hawke continued to insist on cleanliness is fairly indicated by the excellent health of his squadrons later in the war, notably in 1759. Attention will also be paid in due course to Lind's contribution, through the control of scurvy.[168]

On 13 September conflicting reports were received of du Guay's whereabouts, some being to the effect that his ships had gone into Brest and Rochefort on 6 September, others that he had crossed the Atlantic. Meanwhile, Hawke's ships were collecting numbers of French prizes. Captain Denis of the *Medway* (60) brought in the *Arc en Ciel* (64). The *York*, from off Rochefort, and the *Newcastle*, from off Cape Finisterre, each rejoined with four French vessels in company.

If one reads the satisfied comments enunciated, for example, by Corbett, on the soundness of this British policy of sweeping up commerce before an official declaration of war, one is not completely surprised, on turning to the French writers, to find some irritation expressed at the attitude to the subject of some English histories — 'ouvrages où éclate à chaque page la joie d'être Anglais, et par conséquent d'appartenir au premier nation du monde'![169]

It was not till 23 September that Hawke received confirmation that three French ships of the line and three frigates had reached Brest and du Guay's other three large ships had arrived at Rochefort. Writing to Clevland on the 27th, he commented that it would have been very difficult for the French admiral to have got in unobserved unless with 'the hard gale of wind the beginning of the month. Be it as it will, I used every probable means in my power to intercept him, as long as the squadron was in a condition to keep the sea.'

Soon after this, the amount of sickness in the squadron forced him to go into port. Having sent Temple West and half of the ships into Plymouth to clean, he anchored at Spithead

[168] O.L., 14 Sept. 1755. I.L., 13 Aug. 1755, recd. 9 Sept. Lloyd and Coulter, pp. 330, 338-41; 114, 116-18.
[169] Ad. 1/89, 14 Sept. 1755. Germiny, 'Avant-Propos'.

with the *St. George*, *Prince*, *Newcastle*, and *Prince George* on the morning of 29 September.[170]

Their Lordships did not welcome the news of Hawke's return with marked enthusiasm. Earlier they had received intelligence that la Motte, having fulfilled his purpose of reinforcing Louisbourg, was soon expected to bring his ships home. This news was sent out to Hawke. Therefore, on hearing that the latter had come into port and not left any ships out, the Lords expressed their disappointment in somewhat censorious tones. Hawke was always sensitive to criticism of his professional efficiency and zeal. On receiving Clevland's letter on 1 October he lost no time in taking up the pen and expressing himself to the Secretary as follows:

> I have received your letter of the 30th and am extremely sorry to find that their Lordships think that any of the ships of my squadron could have stayed out longer. I hope they will be of another opinion when they reflect that most of the men had been pressed after long voyages, cooped up in tenders and ships at Spithead for many months, and the water in general long kept in new casks, which occasioned great sickness, beside the number of French prisoners and the men spared to navigate them into port. For my part, I should not have come in had it been possible for me to continue longer out.

He then summarized his strategy against du Guay, meeting the

---

[170] Ad. 1/89, 27, 29 Sept. 1755. cf. Corbett, i, 72: 'Till the last week in December Hawke continued to battle with the weather and disease till his foul and stricken ships would stand no more, and he ran for Plymouth.' For 'December, read September; and for 'Plymouth', read Portsmouth. Also the statement 'Scarcely was his back turned when de la Motte appeared on the ground he had left' overlooks the fact that Hawke was still out when la Motte reached Brest. (See p. 134, n. 47.)

Admiralty's criticism of his change of rendezvous on 23 August from between 45° and 47° to between 47° and 48°. He had anticipated that du Guay would steer clear of his own earlier cruising station off Cape Finisterre. As far as the question of keeping some ships at sea was concerned, he had sent four ships of the squadron in to clean and had asked for others to be made ready to come out; but, for reasons beyond his own control, he had not received any reinforcements which were fit to stay out beyond the end of his cruise. His final paragraph expressed how deeply he felt about what he took as an affront to his personal honour. 'Upon the whole, I am conscious of having used my utmost endeavours to answer the end of my being sent out, and of never once losing sight of the principal object of my cruise. If their Lordships should be of another opinion, I am ready to resign my command to anyone else in whose abilities they may have more confidence.'[171]

Having thus unburdened himself he waited fretfully for a reply. None came.

By 6 October he could no longer restrain himself and wrote again to Clevland. He thought that, when the Lords complained of his return to port as being premature, they could not have attended to his dispatch of 27 September in which he had given his reasons for coming in. Altogether, he had done his best. 'How then', he asked, 'can I be easy under the superadded neglect and tacit disapprobation of their Lordships, in not thinking me worthy of an answer to mine of 1st October?'[172]

In order to ensure privacy Hawke had written this last letter, like that of the 1st, in his own hand, and no copies of these, or

---

[171] Ad. 2/514, 30 Sept. 1755; 1/89, 1 Oct. 1755 (holo.).
[172] Ad. 1/89, 6 Oct. 1755.

of the Admiralty's rebuke of 30 September, found their way into his Letter Books.

At last a letter from Clevland, dated 7 October, set the Admiral's mind at rest; although it implied without much appearance of justice that the latter had been making a fuss about nothing. 'Upon Friday the 3rd inst. and not before, I read your letter of the 1st which I had no opportunity of communicating to my Lords Commissioners of the Admiralty till this day, being the first time they have met since its receipt, and am commanded by them to acquaint you that on the further perusal of my letter to you of the 30th past, they cannot conceive any part of it which conveys an idea of their being dissatisfied with your conduct, nor was it their intention.'

Hawke made the best of the matter. 'I beg leave', he replied on the 9th, 'to return my hearty thanks to their Lordships for the trouble they have taken to explain themselves.' However, his sensitivity on the subject of his personal honour, while refreshing to dwellers in a world peopled by such creatures as 'organization men', was to bring damaging humiliation upon him before the lapse of many years.[173]

Incidentally, Clevland's letter of the 7th took on an ironical flavour from an item of information contained in it — namely that the Lords had just received intelligence of la Motte's arrival at Brest on 23 September. Seeing that Hawke had clung to his station for several days beyond that date, he might have expected some sort of commendation. But officialdom then showed itself no more generous with its apologies than it commonly does today.[174]

---

[173] Ad. 2/514, 7 Oct. 1755. O.L., 9 Oct. 1755.

[174] Ad. 2/514, loc. cit. Lacour-Gayet, p. 240. La Motte reached Brest on 21 Sept.

On 14 October Hawke went off on leave and can hardly have been pleased when he had to quit his family in order to attend Powlett's court martial, beginning on 20 October, in the role of prosecutor. While at sea, he had simply observed that Powlett had disappeared; and it had been the Lords of the Admiralty who had followed up the matter. The case lasted until 22 October. James Hobbs, who had just been promoted to Master and Commander, figured prominently in the proceedings because he had been Day Officer when Powlett's *Barfleur* had last been seen from the flagship. Hobbs showed that he was a punctilious officer in so far as he had, in the role of 1st Lieutenant, kept a good check on the Master's log, which turned out to be an important source of evidence, especially with regard to signals. Apparently this log was actually written by the Master's Mates, who were senior ratings, and when the nautical day terminated at noon the log was always checked by the Master. Characteristically, Hawke, although he was prosecutor, was much less zealous in cross-questioning the witnesses than were the president, Vice-Admiral Osborn, and the other members of the court, amongst whom was Rodney. Finally, Hawke heard Powlett acquitted of desertion but censured for bad judgement in his unsuccessful efforts to rejoin the squadron.

Hawke now asked for an extension of leave and this was granted. It may be taken as a sign of the Admiral's lack of intimacy with the Board that Clevland did not apparently know how to spell 'Swaythling'. The Lords said that Hawke could stay 'till Tuesday next at Swethland'. The close relationship between Clevland and the Boscawens, from at least 1748 onwards, is in marked contrast — though it must be remembered that Boscawen was appointed as a member of the Board in 1748.[175]

After rehoisting his flag aboard the *St. George* on 29 October Hawke sent to the Admiralty a list of the lieutenants he would like to have in the flagship. Among the six one may note Tinker, to be 1st Lieutenant, who bore the familiar Christian names of John Bladen; William Hotham, to be 4th, who had obtained a commission in January, would become a Post Captain as early as August 1757, and later a Baron and well-known Admiral of the Nelson period; and William Locker, who was recommended for confirmation of his acting rank and appointment as 6th Lieutenant of the *St. George* — Locker, whom Nelson, at the height of his renown, was to address as 'my dear friend' and to whom he would write: 'Nothing can alter [my] gratitude and attachment to you. I have been your scholar. It is you who taught me to board a French man of war by your conduct when in the *Experiment.* It is you who always said, "lay a Frenchman close, and you will beat him", and my only merit in my profession is being a good scholar. Our friendship will never end but with my life…'

Nelson served under Locker in 1777 after receiving his first commission. It will be seen that Locker was given an insight into Hawke's character and methods of command at a later stage of the Seven Years' War, and there is some plausibility in the view that Hawke exercised a formative influence on Nelson by way of Locker.

Although five out of the six lieutenants were duly appointed, Locker was, for the time being, rejected by the Admiralty, on the ground that the Admiral's list included two newly-made lieutenants. Hawke was invited to nominate another lieutenant.[176]

---

[175] O.L., 9, 23 Oct. 1755. I.L., 17, 24 Oct. 1755. Ad. 1/5295 for Powlett's c.m. N.R.S., *Naval Misc.*, iv, 177, 181 and Aspinall-Oglander, pp. 94, 102, 104, etc., for Clevland and the Boscawens.
[176] O.L., 30 Oct. 1755. Locker, 'William Locker', p. 32. Marcus, pp. 30-1.

On 10 November Hawke received from the Admiralty a summons to go up to London. Meanwhile, Vice-Admiral John Byng was cruising with the Western Squadron. By the time of his return to port on 21 November, he and Hawke between them had collected something approaching 300 French merchantmen; and France had also lost 6,000 officers and seamen, and 1,500 soldiers. Even now, war had not been declared; but the French Government was not inactive.[177]

At the Admiralty, Anson was building up a strategic picture which was destined to bring joy to the heart of Marshall Belleisle, now very influential at the French Court. Having learnt of mounting preparations at Toulon, apparently directed against Minorca, Anson remarked to Hardwicke on 6 December: 'I think it would be a dangerous measure to part with your naval strength from this country, which cannot be recalled if wanted, when I am strongly of the opinion that whenever the French intend anything in earnest their attack will be against this country.'

This attitude, though superficially unobjectionable, was precisely that foreseen by Marshall Belleisle. Early in 1756 he proceeded to mass a large army on the Channel coast, while persisting with the smaller-scale activity at Toulon. If the latter attracted enough British warships to the Mediterranean the invasion of England might prove feasible; but if, as was more likely, emphasis was placed on the naval defence of Great Britain, Minorca could be taken by a swift descent.[178]

The fundamental difficulty confronting Anson, and the British Government as a whole, was that the very marked running-down of the Navy from 1750 to 1754 made it impossible to cope confidently with every threat. The

---

[177] Clowes, iii, 142. O.L., 10 Nov. 1755. Lacour-Gayet, pp. 241-2.
[178] Add.MSS. 35359, f. 384. Corbett, i, 87-91.

comparative failure of Boscawen's expedition, including his loss of 2,000 men through fevers and scurvy, had not eased the overall problem. Dodington, who became Treasurer of the Navy on 22 December 1755, left an interesting record of a conversation which he had with Newcastle on 6 May 1756, by which time it was known that a French army had landed on Minorca, and that la Galissonnière's squadron might be stronger than Byng's.

> I said, as we were alone, that 'twas astonishing that Byng was not there a month ago. Newcastle blamed manning difficulties, and the need to ensure the superiority of the squadron cruising off Brest.
>
> I asked, 'Why were you not ready? Why have you not more ships and more men?'
>
> He replied that he had not the direction of the sea, and His Grace laid a great deal of blame there. And without naming Lord Anson, showed himself extremely dissatisfied with him.

Seeing that His Grace persisted in trying to persuade Anson to give naval appointments to useless persons in the interests of the Government's parliamentary majority, his aspersions on the First Lord, who adamantly rejected such suggestions, might be suspected of issuing from malice rather than equity. But, if it has been fair for historians to point out resignation as the proper course for Sandwich to follow when, in his opinion, insufficient funds were being found for the Navy, it is hard to understand why Anson has not received more vehement criticism. He stayed on as First Lord while the Navy was run right down; whereas, during Sandwich's term of office from 1771 to the beginning of hostilities in America, naval preparations certainly continued at a higher level than had normally been known in time of peace. If Anson is to be excused on this count, Sandwich must be praised.[179]

At the end of 1755 Hawke spent a last Christmas in the company of his deeply loved wife. The family was gathered at George Street and it must have been a happy occasion for the Admiral. In January he was weighed down by one of his feverish colds; and, in that uncertain dawn of medical science, he was promptly bled by his doctor. He managed to survive this treatment but, not unnaturally, he was invalided for a time. When he finally left home to return to Portsmouth in February two of the children had fallen seriously ill, and he had to leave a harassed Catharine to watch over them.[180]

When Hawke reached Portsmouth on 16 February 1756, he found in charge an old acquaintance who had established himself as a *bête noire* of Boscawen — namely, Francis Holburne. Although at about this time Boscawen made it clear to his wife that he held no great opinion of the said 'Holbum', ('I don't like him, nor ever did'; 'nor was he ever thought much of in our service',) the latter had just made an intelligent suggestion to the Admiral which was to carry relevance for Hawke's later operations. On reaching Portsmouth Hawke was shown the correspondence which now included an answer. Holburne had recommended that French pilots, well acquainted with the coast of France, should be recruited. Their Lordships said that they would have inquiries made in the Channel Islands.[181]

No sooner had Hawke hoisted his flag aboard the *St. George* than Henry Osborn arrived to take command at the port. At the promotion of 6 January 1755, this capable commander, who was Hawke's senior in age by as much as 19 years, had

---

[179] T. 38/638. N.R.S., *Naval Misc.*, iv, 196. Clowes, iii, 141. Dodington, *Diary*, pp. 379-81.
[180] Ad. 1/89, 12, 22 Jan. 1756. H.P.P., Lady H. to H., 23 Feb. 1756.
[181] N.R.S., *Naval Misc.*, iv, 189, 194.

become a Vice-Admiral of the Red, thus maintaining a slender superiority over Hawke who had then moved up to Vice-Admiral of the White. After a week or so, Osborn circumscribed the sphere of his authority by leaving Hawke in undisputed command of the squadron allocated to him. Although there are indications that Osborn was of an obnoxiously haughty disposition, Hawke does not seem ever to have clashed with him. It will be remembered that Hawke came under him as a Captain when Osborn was a Commodore with Rowley's fleet in the Mediterranean in 1745. However, to illustrate a common reaction to Osborn, we can read what Boscawen wrote to his wife on the subject in April 1756. '… In short, he is a damned stupid fellow, and puzzles me very much. Don't imagine by this that I have had the least dispute with him, we have been very civil. He has invited me to dine with him, I refused because he dines at four, his Lady is elegant and fine, and cannot submit to anything but London hours.'

Osborn has been chiefly remembered for his effective blockade of the French Mediterranean squadron in 1757-8.

Seeing that the French at Brest were known to be preparing twelve of the line to sail under Conflans, and that others were lying at Rochefort, Hawke was very much occupied by the work of making his squadron ready for sea.[182] In the midst of all the bustle, he received a letter from Catharine — the last of the four which are still extant. It was dated 23 February and had been written at George Street.

> I am not angry, my dear Ned, tho' I can't help complaining of your silence. Does it proceed from my not being a tongue-pad, and therefore from thence you conclude I am easy in

[182] I.L., O.L., and O.B., 16-25 Feb. 1756. Corbett, i, 98, 103. Clowes, iii, 565. For Osborn's ability, age and character: Erskine, p. 270, 277; Charnock, iv, 202-3; N.R.S., *Naval Misc.*, iv, 198.

your absence? If so, I can't prevent your thoughts, for it is my nature when unhappy to feel more than I can express. How have I this day watched the post, but, to my unspeakable disappointment, not one line from you to relieve me a moment from the distress I am in for my children. They tell me they are both out of danger. If I was not a fool, I ought to believe them, for my own sake; but while I see 'em both with a languishment in their countenances, I can't help fearing the worst.

However, do you make yourself easy with the assurances they give me, and if it does not interfere greatly with your own thoughts or business, let her hear from you who has ever been without art,

Most faithfully and truly yours
Cath: Hawke

P.S. Osborn, your senior officer, is at Portsmouth, which makes me the more wonder at not hearing from you. But what must be must be.[183]

From the fact that this letter was so carefully kept by the Admiral, it may be inferred that she did not have to wait long for a reply. On the very day that Catharine was writing to him, Hawke probably had the family at George Street in mind as he penned a letter to Clevland, asking that, in view of a promise given by Lord Anson, young John Birt, Sally's brother, should be sent his commission. Birt had been acting as 4th Lieutenant of the *Captain* since his appointment to that post by Hawke on 30 July 1755. To Hawke's surprise, an answer came to the effect that Birt had not yet passed his Lieutenant's examination. The explanation was that, since going to the *Captain*, he had been so keen to continue serving in her that he had not applied 'for leave to go to town, lest he should be left behind'. Seeing that the *Captain* was not ready for sea, Birt

[183] H.P.P., Lady H. to H., 23 Feb. 1756.

went up to London in March and was commissioned on the 20th.[184]

During the month of February the Admiralty's attention was mainly taken up with the cross-Channel invasion threat, and Hawke was to cruise in the Bay of Biscay as soon as possible. By the 28th the latter had managed to get a squadron ready to sail. However, successive days produced in turn no wind, a wild westerly, and then impenetrable fog. On the fourth day, 3 March, he reported: 'The weather continues so foggy and thick that even boats can hardly pass and repass.' The extent to which sailing fleets could become weatherbound, especially in winter, is illustrated by the fact that it was not until 12 March that conditions permitted the squadron to sail.[185]

As commander of his second division, Hawke had been given Savage Mostyn, a close friend of Boscawen, who seems by then to have lived down a reputation for shyness of battle acquired in 1745. The whole squadron consisted of the very adequate force of fourteen of the line and the Captains were all people worthy of remark. Jack Brett, who was offered promotion that year on 4 June (together with Charles Saunders and others) but turned it down; Robert Duff, prominent on Hawke's great campaign of 1759 and later a Vice-Admiral; Thomas Stanhope, who had commanded the frigate *Hector* at the Second Battle of Cape Finisterre and would be knighted for his part at the Battle of Lagos; Francis Geary, 'a stupid fellow' but 'a good officer' according to Boscawen, who commanded the Channel fleet loyally though without distinction during the American Independence War; Richard

---

[184] O.L., 23, 25 Feb., 9 Mar. 1756. *The Commissioned Sea Officers of the Royal Navy, 1660-1815*. Compiled under auspices of Admiralty and N.M.M. (1954).
[185] Corbett, i, 97-8. O.L., 28 Feb., 3, 12 Mar. 1756.

Howe, who had through influence become a Post-Captain in 1746 at the age of 20 but of whose calibre Hawke was to form the highest opinion; John Byron, with a record behind him of fantastic adventure in South America and spectacular failure as a battle-commander in store for him; Hugh Pigot, who later enjoyed the curious distinction of superseding Rodney after the Battle of the Saints — though Boscawen thought him 'a very good sort of man'; Alexander, Lord Colville, who recovered Newfoundland from Ternay in 1762; Witteronge Taylor, Hawke's Flag Captain in 1758-9, who went down with the ill-fated *Ramillies* in 1760; and Richard Tyrrell, who obtained a flag at the end of the war. The other Captains, Storr, Denis, Lloyd, and Steevens have been noticed in connexion with Hawke's cruise of the previous year. They all became Admirals.[186]

With this very competent array of captains, Hawke escorted a convoy out to a safe position, 150 leagues W. of Ushant, and went on down to Cape Ortegal which he sighted on 19 March. He sent off the frigate *Seaford* to ascertain 'the exact number of ships in Rochefort Road'. The squadron was then subjected to a terrific hammering from bad weather, and blown well away from the Cape to which the *Seaford* had been ordered to return. However, a French brig from Rochefort was intercepted and it appeared that six warships at that port were being made ready to sail up to Brest. The crew of the brig possibly considered that the interception was providential from their point of view. The vessel 'was bound to Louisbourg with flour but was so leaky that Captain Howe was obliged to take the crew out and leave her to sink'. Hawke decided to send the *Newcastle* down to Cape Ortegal for a period of ten days. With the rest of the squadron he headed for Brest.[187]

---

[186] N.R.S., *Naval Misc.*, iv, 226, 243 for Brett; 232, Geary; 239, etc., for Mostyn; 248, Pigot. Clowes, iii, 277-8.

By 6 April the *Swan* sloop was off St. Matthew's Point, looking right into Brest; and soon after she and the *Rochester* (50), Captain Duff, performed the improbable feat of turning back into port three French ships of the line and a frigate. But, unbeknown to Hawke, a small squadron, bearing a particularly distinguished party, had already slipped out and was on its way to Canada. The party included Montcalm, Lévis, and Bougainville.[188]

Hawke now decided to concentrate on blockading Brest, seeing that he lacked sufficient strength to seal off Rochefort as well. Nevertheless, on hearing that a convoy had sailed on the 2nd from Bordeaux for Martinique, and taking into account the westerly winds which had prevailed since then, he dispatched the and *Rochester* on a quick sweep to Cape Ortegal and back. Soon after their departure, he learnt from intercepted vessels, including a sloop brought in by the *Newcastle*, that small batches of French troops were going out to Canada in merchantmen. Therefore, judging that nothing would venture out of Brest for a few days, he decided on 11 April to sweep to the southward with his main force and return speedily to his blockading station. Aboard the *Orford* (70), Captain Steevens, sickness had reached the stage where she had to be sent home.[189]

The squadron searched as far S. as the latitude of Bordeaux, in the meridian of Cape Peñas. Then, having enjoyed no great success, the Admiral resumed his watch over Brest on 16 April. 'That night', he reported, 'I was joined by the *York* and the *Rochester* who had fallen in with Admiral Byng and his squadron

---

[187] O.L., 24 Mar. 1756.
[188] O.L., 9 Apr. 1756. Corbett, i, 102.
[189] O.L., 9, 11 Apr. 1756.

off Cape Ortegal. But it blowed so hard that the boats could not go on board him.'[190]

The uninspired Byng had Been sent out with ten ships of the line to join Commodore Edgecumbe who was already in the Mediterranean with three of the line and four frigates. His principal duty, if he found that the French had attacked Minorca, was to do everything possible for the relief of the island. The said Byng was to waste little time in proving conclusively how utterly misguided was his selection for this command. When Hawke heard that Byng had been sighted *en route* for Gibraltar, he little suspected that in two months' time he would be hurrying in the same direction, with orders in his pocket to supercede that Admiral — his superior in rank — and to send him home under arrest.[191]

Meanwhile, as winter merged into spring, Hawke persevered with his blockade. Despite a suggestion from the Admiralty that he should station part of his squadron off Rochefort, he insisted on keeping an effective concentration off Brest. Through cruising at that season, ships had to be sent in for urgent repairs, and sickness was by now rife throughout the squadron. From the length of the cruise, one would guess that scurvy was much less prevalent than typhus. As the authors of the third volume of *Medicine and the Navy* have neatly put it: 'Typhus was the inevitable concomitant of cold, undernourishment, overcrowding, dirt, and misery.' Hawke doubtless did his best to encourage elimination of dirt, but the other factors were beyond his control.

He determined that, as soon as Holburne arrived with some promised reinforcements, he 'would make as long stretches to

---

[190] O.L., 18 Apr. 1756.

[191] Corbett, i, 100-1. Erskine, pp. 203-18.

the southward as possible', but then return off Brest with his whole strength.

On 18 April Holburne duly hove in sight with his flag flying in Hawke's old prize, the *Terrible*. He was accompanied by the equally familiar *Monmouth*, still commanded by Henry Harrison, though in another six weeks he would hoist aboard her one of the best-earned Rear-Admiral's flags in British history and take charge of the port of Plymouth. Other new arrivals were the *Essex*, *Eagle*, and *Torbay*. The last-named was commanded by Augustus Keppel. 'There is no better seaman than Keppel', wrote Boscawen to his wife that July, 'few so good, and not a better officer.' The litigious Hugh Pallisser, last noticed giving evidence against Mathews at the latter's court martial, was now Captain of the *Eagle*. Hawke may have had time to gain an impression of Pallisser's undoubted professional competence, for he later appointed him to the chief post on the Navy Board — namely, that of Comptroller.[192]

After the arrival of this reinforcement Hawke continued for three weeks to put his declared policy into effect. Finally, on 6 May, two months after the beginning of the cruise, the sails of an approaching squadron could be discerned. This was Boscawen with ten of the line, and that Admiral has left us with a glimpse of the scene in a postscript written to his wife at 8 a.m.: 'I am dressed in uniform frock and hat, and all in order to wait on Sir Edward Hawke, who I see ranged in line of battle to receive me. The signal has been made that we are friends, and I find that not one of my squadron have been in the least on their guard about them… I suppose the said Sir Edward will not stay much longer.'[193]

---

[192] O.L., 18 Apr. 1756 (2). Lloyd and Coulter, p. 338. N.R.S., *Naval Misc.*, iv, 243.
[193] O.L., 27 Apr. 1756. N.R.S., *Naval Misc.*, iv, 203.

After 'maturely deliberating with Vice-Admiral Boscawen on the intelligence he had procured', Hawke left out with him eight of the line and a frigate from his own squadron. With the rest, he reached Spithead on 8 May. He sent to the Admiralty an announcement of his arrival which terminated: 'As the ships arrived with me are to be cleaned and refitted, I hope their Lordships will indulge me with as long a leave of absence as they can.'

Leave was granted. For a month he remained undisturbed with Catharine and, no doubt, the 6-year-old Chaloner and little 4-year-old Kitty, with Sally Birt in attendance. Then a summons arrived urgently requiring his presence at Portsmouth.[194]

[194] O.L., 8 May 1756. Ad. 2/1331, 8 June 1756.

CHAPTER 10: COURAGE ON A FORLORN MISSION

BY the end of May, Byng's dispatches from Gibraltar had provided the Admiralty with disturbing evidence of his irresolution, not to speak of the extreme pusillanimity of General Fowke, the Governor of Gibraltar, who refused to reinforce the troops taking passage in the squadron. This disobedience, in the face of clearly worded orders, was based on the profound consideration that such a move would weaken his own garrison. The fact that the garrison of St. Philip's Castle was facing an enemy seven times its number, and that there was no sign of an imminent attack on Gibraltar, was a matter of minor consequence to General Fowke. Byng, however, at least reached the state of sailing towards Minorca, though in no very confident state of mind. In due course, the outcome was reported to the Duke of Newcastle through his admirable intelligence service. An informant at Versailles wrote on 1 June: 'There was an action the 20th past between the two fleets near Minorca. I have seen many relations of it, but not one tolerable. Nor have I heard any reason why Admiral Byng should choose to retire; for he had the wind of us, and his fleet suffered less than ours.'

That Byng had left Minorca to its fate was only too true. As long as the British garrison continued to hold Richelieu's army at bay, Byng had only to blockade the island and there was a fair prospect of forcing the French troops to surrender.[195]

---

[195] Add.MSS. 32865, f. 159, 167. Corbett, i, 127.

During the first days of June there was a buzz of anxious discussion in the Cabinet. Although the Government was responsible for the fact that the Navy had proved too weak to dominate all the main theatres of war, its members felt, not unreasonably, that Byng had failed to make determined use of what had been given him; for his squadron was at least roughly equal in strength to that of his opponent, la Galissonnière. Therefore, harbouring decidedly unfriendly sentiments towards Byng, the King's Ministers agreed that he should be replaced by the Admiral most likely to retrieve the situation, namely Hawke. On 8 June, his Secret Orders were signed by Anson and the other Lords of the Admiralty. He was to go to Gibraltar in the *Antelope* (50), supersede Byng, and send him and his second-in-command, Rear-Admiral Temple West, back to England in the *Antelope*, under arrest; and, not surprisingly, General Fowke was to keep the latter gentlemen company. Then, if he found that the garrison at Port Mahon was still holding out, Hawke was to relieve it and to attack any near-by French shipping; but, if the island had fallen, he was to defeat la Galissonnière (in the event of his remaining in the vicinity), and in any case to blockade the island. In addition, he was to afford protection to British trade. His ships were to be cleaned at Gibraltar — which was much less suitable than Port Mahon for such a purpose.[196]

On 9 June Hawke was at Portsmouth. In view of Temple West's recall, a rear-admiral had to go out as second-in-command. The choice fell on Charles Saunders and, in order to reach his seniority on the list of captains, it was necessary to have quite a large promotion of flag officers. It is commonly assumed that Anson pushed for Saunders's appointment, but it is perhaps of interest that this is denied by Boscawen, who was

[196] Corbett, i, 129-30. Ad. 2/1331, loc. cit.

still a Lord of the Admiralty at the time. According to the latter, 'Clevland and Lord Anson both say Saunders's promotion is by the King's orders — to be sure he had no prompter.' If so, George II gave the Navy two out of the five most successful operational commanders of his reign. Hawke, Boscawen, Saunders, Anson, and Pocock — this seems near the mark as a list of the first five seagoing Admirals of that triumphant period. Amongst the promotion on 4 June, there was one in particular which aroused Boscawen's exasperation. 'Had Lord H. Powlett the least word to say for himself? He has been in three scrapes this year, two of them are most certainly strong objections to him.' One of these cases had involved a list of false names on the *Barfleur*'s books, and it had fallen to Hawke to initiate an inquiry into it before he sailed from Portsmouth in March 1756. The blame was laid to rest on Powlett's clerk. One has heard the assertion that, even in the eighteenth century, the Navy was a democratic service. In this case, the democratic principle operated only to the extent that Powlett was never entrusted, as an Admiral, with an active command. Although unemployable he steadily ascended the ladder of flag officers, and finally, on 31 March 1775, he attained the land-bound but not unremunerative glory of an Admiral of the White. Only the solitary eminence of the Admiral of the Fleet was denied to him by a grateful country. However, it is pleasant to notice, before passing on from this remarkable promotion of 4 June, that the long-neglected merit of Henry Harrison received an appropriate reward.[197]

---

[197] Ad. 1/383, 9 June 1756. Corbett, i, 130, for Anson asking for Saunders's promotion. N. R.S., *Naval Misc.*, iv, 229, for Boscawen's contradiction of this, ibid., pp. 231-2 for Powlett. I.L., 20 Feb. 1756. O. L., 23 Feb. 1756. O.B., 23 Feb. 1756.

The party collecting aboard the *Antelope* included Lord Tyrawley (to replace General Fowke); also James Hobbs, whom Hawke took with him to be Captain of the *Ramillies*. All the officers of that unlucky flagship, as well as those of Temple West's *Buckingham*, were to be replaced by order of the Admiralty. Inevitably, John Hay accompanied what was known as the 'little cargo of courage'. Hawke also took out the lieutenants and some of the petty officers and foremast men from the *St. George*.[198]

After being weatherbound for a few days the *Antelope* made her way out of the Channel and thence southwards into the Bay of Biscay. On 19 June, Boscawen, who was still cruising with the Western Squadron, wrote to his wife, 'There is now a large ship in sight.' Taking up the pen again at 5 a.m. on the following day, he added:

> Our disgrace in the Mediterranean has so filled my spirits that I could not sleep all night. What shall we come to? Sir Edward Hawke was chased yesterday by some of my squadron and sent me the whole news, as did Lord Tyrawley, and the French and English Gazettes containing the accounts. [He was glad that he had not been at home during the past month.] I should have gone to Minorca to have retrieved if possible, but the back game is hard work. If courage will do it, that won't be wanting.[199]

Boscawen's letters, which are such an excellent source of candid opinions of people and events, are unfortunately not extant for the period after 1756. However, for Hawke's difficult Minorcan campaign, the *Journal* of Augustus Hervey to some extent supplies the want of an unofficial source, provided

---

[198] Corbett, i, 130. O.B., 3 July 1756.

[199] Ad. 1/383, 11 June 1756. N.R.S., *Naval Misc.*, iv, 225-7.

that it is handled with appropriate mistrust. Hervey wrote it from notes or journals which he compiled at the time of the events related in the *Journal*, and regarding facts such as times of sailing or the composition of various squadrons, he was quite reliable. But the *Journal* was not written until about 1767 and, being apparently intended for the entertainment of some unspecified individual — could it have been Lord Sandwich? — it is packed with vehemently partisan and deliberately malicious opinions on such matters as motivation and character.[200]

Hawke's party arrived at Gibraltar on 2 July to find Byng's squadron refitting. The new Commander-in-Chief lost no time in putting his orders into execution with as much courtesy as the extraordinary circumstances permitted. According to Hervey, who was then Captain of the *Hampton Court* and was firmly committed to Byng's cause because that Admiral had previously put him in the way of some urgently needed prize-money, Hawke condemned the behaviour of Henry Fox, Lord Anson, and the Duke of Newcastle in circulating reports at home calculated to defame Byng and dissociate themselves from the disastrous turn of events in the Mediterranean. It was true enough that such discreditable activities were in train in England. Hawke may well have felt concern at having been appointed to the Mediterranean by dignitaries who were more concerned to protect their own interests than to ensure justice for their seagoing commanders.[201]

However, there was one person with the fleet at Gibraltar who found the situation entirely to his liking and that was John Hay. The *Ramillies'* lieutenants had all been superseded on 4

---

[200] Erskine, p. xxxiv.

[201] ibid., p. 217. Ad. 1/383, 4 July 1756. Add.MSS. 32886, f. 210-14. Tunstall, pp. 156-7. cf. Tunstall, *Admiral Byng*, 1928, pp. 166, 208-9.

July. 'The next day', wrote the indignant Hervey, 'I felt the stroke of this attention to Mr. Byng, for they took eighty of my best seamen away from the *Hampton Court* to put in other ships. This was a poor, mean, dirty spite, and could scarce have first entered into the head of anything but a dirty secretary, whom Sir Edward was ever cursed with.' Still, it is worth noting that here Hervey must be faulted, even on a point of fact. According to Hawke's Order Book the *Hampton Court* was to discharge 'thirty good and able foremast men into His Majesty's ship *Prince George*', not 'eighty'. Also, the order directed that two ships besides the *Hampton Court* were each to send thirty good men to the *Prince George* (Saunders's flagship), and that they were to receive a like number from her in exchange. But Hay's officiousness is not in doubt.[202]

Hawke was making very strenuous efforts to get the squadron to sea. To the Admiralty, he stated that the latest intelligence about Minorca had reached Gibraltar on 16 June. 'St. Philip's, it was said, then held out, and I flatter myself does so still, and that I shall certainly find the French squadron before it.'

Corbett, apparently basing his ideas on Hawke's dispatches, asserted that the Admiral refused to proceed to Minorca until the damaged *Intrepid* was ready. This, Corbett argued, went some way towards extenuating the 'formalism and tactical bigotry' for which Byng had often been condemned. 'Of all the men of that time', wrote Corbett, 'Hawke is held to be the personification of dash, of readiness for daring risk, of impatience of formalism in war. Yet at that high crisis, when every hour was precious, four whole days were spent "in exercising the fleet in lines of battle". On the 14th the *Intrepid*

---

[202] Erskine, p. 217. O.B., 5 July 1756. H.P.P., Hay to H., 17 Feb. 1777 and H. to Martin H., 19 Feb. 1777.

joined, and not till then did he push for Minorca.' This is good literature and contains some appropriate remarks about Hawke; but inspection of that Admiral's dispatch of 8 July discovers the statements: 'I cannot yet be certain whether I shall be able to carry the *Intrepid* with me. If she can not be got ready by Saturday [10th] I will sail at all events.'

Rather curiously, a similar phrase about exercising the fleet in lines of battle is to be found in Hervey's *Journal* but it is not in Hawke's dispatches.[203]

Hervey was no partisan of Hawke, but to say that he mentioned fleet exercises is by no means to concede that Hawke was wasting time or was waiting for the *Intrepid*. On the contrary, Hervey considered that Hawke was foolish to be in such breakneck haste to reach Minorca, 'tho' it was evident they would be too late to do any business'. It is therefore difficult to find any reason for doubting Hawke's statement that he was held up by light, contrary winds rather than by any reluctance to go without the *Intrepid*. According to Hervey: 'The 10th July we all sailed about noon and had a regiment from Gibraltar. We were sixteen sail of the line and five frigates. I was in Rear-Admiral Saunders' division and one of his seconds. We kept making up for Minorca with little winds contrary, and exercising the fleet in lines of battle.'

Meanwhile, Hawke had left orders for the *Intrepid* to sail for Minorca as soon as possible. That she caught up with squadron on the 14th can only have been due to an accident of the winds.[204]

---

[203] Ad. 1/383, 4, 8 July; 15, 29 July 1756 for negative evidence. Corbett, i, 131. Erskine, p. 217.

[204] Ad. 1/383, 8, 15 July 1756. Corbett, i, 131. Erskine, p. 217, 219. O.B., 10 July 1756.

Early on 15 July any doubts about the continuing resistance at Mahon were laid to rest. Some transports appeared and it was found that they were carrying part of the garrison, 'which', wrote Hawke, 'capitulated on honourable terms the 27th ulto… I shall make the best of my way off Mahon, and use my utmost endeavours to find the French squadron, and keep as strict a look-out upon Minorca as I can'. He had been saddled with the distasteful and rather impracticable duty of inquiring into the conduct of the captains who had participated in Byng's battle, but he sensibly avoided arousing bad feeling to no effect by simply writing to Clevland: 'Byng… made no public complaint to me of bad behaviour in any of the captains.' Hervey recorded his impressions of the squadron's return to Minorca.

> The 19th we were off Minorca and saw the French colours on St. Philip's and a number of men on the fortifications. They fired a shot at one of the men-of-war as she was wearing off. We found the French fleet were gone, and I was anxious to know what would become of all our blustering, and what this mighty fleet was to perform, which, had it been sent earlier, would have given the finishing stroke to France. We heard there were about 5,000 troops left on the island. I thought we might easily have forced the harbour, had we had troops. In short, we satisfied ourselves with cruising off and on this harbour to no purpose in the world, to our eternal shame and the reproach of those who gave the orders, till all our men fell sick with despair and scurvy, and when we were sure that nothing could be obtained by it.[205]

By intercepting a small vessel near Mahon on 1 August, Hervey discovered 'that the French used the Minorcines very

[205] Ad. 1/383, 15 July 1756. Erskine, p. 219.

ill, which', he added, not uncharacteristically, 'I was very glad of, as the treacherous dogs deserved it for their behaviour to us.'

Hervey, apparently intending to show that Hawke lacked the capacity displayed by Byng, consistently slanted all his journal-entries to depreciate Hawke, except where that Admiral was fitfully and inexplicably blessed with sufficient wit to appreciate the merits and sagacity of Captain Hervey. Making allowance for a certain lack of objectivity in the comments of 'my dear Augustus', one may thank him for leaving behind him the only surviving account of Hawke preparing his captains for battle:

> The 2nd was an idle day. The 3rd at daylight there was a signal for Flag Officers, and soon after for all Captains, when the Admiral told us that he had intelligence by a Dane that the French fleet lay with their topsail sheets hauled home at Toulon and were determined to come out and fight us. Then he made us a fine speech that he was determined to run close up to them, and that the honour of our country required we should do our very utmost to destroy these ships and he did not doubt that we should, with a great deal of all this sort of stuff. For my part I told Mr. Saunders that I was certain this was all artifice of the French in sending us this sort of intelligence to keep us useless here, where we were effectually destroying ourselves, that the French could have no view or interest in coming out to fight us merely for blows... He was of my opinion, but yet thought it right not to speak it openly and discourage people.

It is clear that, having weighed his own experience at the Battles of Toulon and Cape Finisterre together with what he had gleaned about Byng's formalistic brush with la Galissonnière, Hawke was meditating the aggressive article with which he transformed the General Fighting Instructions issued by him in 1757. Secondly, his exhortation to the captains was badly needed. Judging by Hervey's remarks, it was not greeted by the fever of enthusiasm attributed to Nelson's 'Band of Brothers' on like occasions; but Nelson inherited his 'Brothers' from Jervis, who was one of the greatest fleet-trainers in history, and Hawke inherited his captains from Byng. Finally, when it came to judging that the French might sally forth to fight, doubt is cast upon both Hervey's omniscience and his imputation of stupidity to Hawke by the revelation from French sources that la Galissonnière spent August strenuously preparing a new squadron for sea. By the end of the month, he had sixteen of the line, six frigates, and two fireships ready to come out and fight Hawke. He was delayed by an illness which within the following two months, proved mortal.[206]

Probably with much better reason, Hervey unburdened himself with heat on the subject of John Hay. Everyone, he said, was getting 'tired of this inactive, dispiriting work… especially as our men fell down sick every day in the fleet, and that we all knew Sir Edward Hawke was totally governed by a damned interested Scotch secretary, a fellow without a grain of understanding who had been bred up to business in a shop and had the impudence to show his ascendancy over the Admiral to the whole fleet'. Elsewhere, Hervey noted that: 'Mr. Saunders seemed very uneasy at our situation; he told me he looked on Sir Edward as a very honest man, but thought he was lost from this expedition wherein we made so silly and useless a figure.'[207]

Hawke himself wrote on 10 August: 'All the intelligence I have received since my last confirms the account of the French

---

[206] Erskine, pp. 220, 325. Lacour-Gayet, pp. 273-4.
[207] Erskine, pp. 220-1.

squadron's intending to come out. I should look upon it as a great happiness to meet. But come or not come, I shall stay here as long as I possibly can.'

During September, with the whole of his squadron on two-thirds rations and la Galissonnière never making an appearance, Hawke himself became extremely weary. The enemy's reduction of the island's garrison to 5,000 men had ensured that the blockade would prove inconclusive. The Admiral's frustration broke through to the surface when, on 12 September, he wrote to their Lordships: 'I have now been near ten weeks out, and own I am sensibly mortified at not having heard from England.' The weather had been hot. Many men had the fever. Captain Catford, commanding one of the ships of the line, had died on the 8th. As to the ships, the Admiralty's orders of 8 June had required him to refit at a Sardinian port or at Gibraltar, as convenient. 'What port in Sardinia can be convenient?' he inquired. He was left with Gibraltar, where he could not clean anything above a 60 because, especially with winter approaching, the anchorage was too exposed. (Yet his force comprised twelve ships of more than 60 guns.)

A few days later the *Prince* (90) and *Colchester* (50) arrived as reinforcements and delivered a number of Admiralty letters and orders, written in July. One of these orders was for a number of captains and lieutenants (including Augustus Hervey) to go back to England to give evidence at Byng's trial.

On 2 October Hawke returned to Gibraltar with his 'exhausted and sickly' squadron. He now made a number of temporary promotions in view of the forthcoming departure of the recalled officers. John Birt, for example, who had gone out to the Mediterranean with Byng as 4th Lieutenant of the *Captain*, moved up to 3rd Lieutenant and by 27 October he was acting 1st. William Locker, who had been refused a commission the previous October but had been taken out by Hawke in the *Antelope*, had already been made acting Lieutenant of the *Experiment* (20). It was in July 1757 that he led a boarding party onto a powerful privateer in the gallant manner that made such an impression on Nelson.

On 15 October, Hervey, who had been busy jotting down fuel for criticism of Hawke's handling of the fleet — 'in trifles as well as essentials 'twas all alike, nothing fixed, nothing could be determined' — received from the Admiral an order which did not strike him as evidence of poor judgement. 'Sir Edward Hawke shewed me a favour in telling me he would give me his packets for England, that when I arrived I might immediately go to Town with them, wherein he said he had desired I might be sent out to him again as he wished to have me with him, and that he had done this to show he distinguished me from the rest.'

Although there is no mention of this in Hawke's dispatches it seems likely that he did send some such recommendation addressed to Lord Anson personally. Hervey was certainly an effective operational commander and Hawke was to make full use of him on a future occasion. However, Hervey's *Journal* strongly suggests that here is an example, to parallel the case of Hay, of the Admiral's being imposed upon by a two-faced individual.[208]

At Gibraltar Hawke's policy was to refit the ships as far as facilities permitted, while keeping a close watch on the Gut for any French ships trying to get out of the Mediterranean. This was, of course, sound strategy, because the French threat to

---

[208] Ad. 1/383, 10 Aug., 12, 23 Sept., 15 Oct. 1756. Erskine, pp. xxvi, 223, 227-8. Ad. 2/1331, 8 June 1756. Locker, 'Wm. Locker', pp. 8-9.

invade Britain might be renewed and it was essential to prevent a concentration of enemy ships at Brest.

The somewhat desperate dispatch which Hawke had written off Minorca on 12 September reached the Admiralty on 25 October and resulted in orders, dated the 28th, being issued for his return to England. In view of what he had said about the impracticability of refitting the large ships at Gibraltar, he was to bring all of them home with him, leaving only a small squadron with Rear-Admiral Saunders. In his letter accompanying the order, Clevland reported that the Lords were 'extremely well satisfied' with all Hawke's doings, and that he personally wished him 'health and a pleasant voyage to England'.[209]

It was on the next day, 29 October, that Catharine died at Lymington. She had been under the care of a physician there but no record of the cause of her death survives.

Today one may enter the Church of St. Nicolas near Swaythling, walk down the central aisle and uncover the black stone 'placed by Sir Edward Hawke, Knight of the Bath' over the remains of 'the best wife, the best mother, and the best of friends'.

On 7 November Jane Rodney — herself destined for a premature death — told her husband, the future Admiral, of 'poor Lady Hawke' being carried to her place of burial. 'I wonder', she added, 'whose care the poor children are left to. 'Tis to be hoped not wholly to servants. I am sure my heart aches for them.'

Martin was then aged 12, Edward 9, Chaloner 6, and little Catharine 4. It was a very great mercy that Sally Birt was there to look after them. She had been a member of the family as long as Chaloner and Kitty could remember, and to them all

[209] Ad. 1/383, 15 Oct.; 2/518, 28 Oct.; 2/77, 28 Oct. 1756.

she faithfully devoted her youth. She retained the affection and confidence of the young Hawkes till the end of their lives — for she outlived them all, except perhaps Martin. She was still corresponding voluminously with Martin's wife in 1801. Martin himself died in 1805.[210]

Oblivious of the crushing tragedy which had befallen him, Hawke had received and distributed some printed orders from home, dated 2 October, 'forbidding the commanders of His Majesty's ships to obstruct the trade and navigation of any Spanish vessels'. The Admiral had been exasperated by a number of disputes with various Spanish authorities because of the assistance which they had, in breach of their neutrality, been giving to the French throughout the area of his command. He was thus driven to remark in his dispatch of 27 November: 'None of them [i.e. Spanish vessels] within the limits of my command have ever met with the least molestation, while they act with regard to our enemies with a shameful partiality, and distress our trade as much as if we were at actual war with them.'[211]

Leaving Saunders with five small ships of the line and a polacre (of which he had made William Hotham the acting captain), Hawke sailed from Gibraltar with the squadron on 9 December. Even if he was still unaware of Catharine's death, it was hardly 'a pleasant voyage'. Instead, a stormy passage, 'with very hard gales and a high sea', had to be endured. Finally, on 14 January 1757, the *Ramillies* dropped anchor at Spithead. Hawke wrote that day: 'When I was ordered to the Mediterranean, I had just returned from a long cruise to the Westward. Since my embarking at Portsmouth, I have never

[210] P.R.O. 30/20/20, Mrs. Rodney to Capt. G. B. Rodney, 7 Nov. 1756. H.P.P. tor Miss Birt's letters.

[211] Ad. 2/518, 2 Oct. 1756; 1/383, 27 Nov. and enclosure.

slept one night out of the ship, or scarce ever set my foot on shore, all which have so impaired my health that I must beg the favour of their Lordships to indulge me with leave to be on shore some time for the re-establishment of it.'

As Boscawen had predicted, the 'back game' had been 'hard work'. Courage had done its best. The forlorn mission was at an end.[212]

[212] Ad. 1/383, 14 Jan. 1757.

CHAPTER 11: ROCHEFORT, BUT NOT THE BOARD

AFTER going in January to his London home, Hawke no doubt did all he could to comfort his family. During February he had correspondence with the Admiralty about the temporary appointments of officers which he had made in the Mediterranean, and he objected strenuously to a second refusal of a commission to William Locker. 'If my health will permit, I intend waiting on their Lordships tomorrow', he wrote on the 6th. However, the Admiralty refused to budge on the subject; but no written record of their reasons is to be found.[213]

During the course of the month John Byng was convicted by his court martial, principally on the ground that he had failed to do his utmost against the enemy. This was undoubtedly true, at least in some sense. Unfortunately, this caused him to fall under the recently fortified 12th Article of War, and the court was left with no alternative but to sentence him to death. Outside the government circles which were determined to have his blood, it was generally thought that the King should be advised to exercise mercy. Hervey's *Journal* provides comment on the situation, including an uncomplimentary reference to Hawke.

> The 3rd February I was recommissioned for the *Hampton Court*, and to go out to the Mediterranean again passenger to her, as Admiral Osborn was to go commander-in-chief there, it was reported. In the meantime I was entirely taken up printing things for Mr. Byng's case, and stirring up his friends.

[213] Ad. 1/383, 6 Feb. 1757.

> Lord Bath told me he thought it was impossible they could execute such a sentence. Sir Edward Hawke, who was come home, told me the morning I was with him (the 5th) that he would go live in a cottage rather than serve to meet such treatment, and that Mr. West had been very false in all this, and rose on Mr. Byng's ruin. This indeed was but too true, but Sir Edward was as double in all his boastings, and was ever so about it.[214]

Temple West certainly does not appear to have suffered through his association with Byng. Soon after the court martial he was promoted to Vice-Admiral and, on the formation of the Ministry of 26 June 1757, he was made a Lord of the Admiralty.

This appointment was a minor item in a ministerial settlement which ended a period of confusion, and an understanding of Hawke's position from this time onwards requires a summary of these political developments.

The previous autumn, Newcastle's Government, widely denounced for mishandling the war, had collapsed. The King had reluctantly appointed the popularly acclaimed Pitt as Secretary of State and *de facto* leading Minister. However, the Government was soon in difficulties through lack of parliamentary support. On 26 December 1756 — while Hawke was returning home through wintry storms — Henry Fox gave his friend Sir Charles Williams an epistolary picture of the chief Minister's behaviour. 'Pitt is single, imperious, proud, enthusiastic. Trusting in Bute, Leicester House, and the belief that the Duke of Newcastle and I shall not join against him, and above all in the confidence he has in his superiority over

---

[214] Tunstall, *Admiral Byng*, op. cit., for general picture. Corbett, i, 133. Erskine, pp. 236-7.

all mankind, he comes — or, having the gout, sends Legge and Grenville to talk miserably to a majority set against them.'

In the New Year Pitt proceeded to irritate George II, who could in any case hardly endure the sight of him, by trying to persuade the King to grant a reprieve to Byng. The upshot was that Byng was duly executed aboard the *Monarque* on 14 March 1757; and His Majesty cast about for some way of excluding the Great Commoner from the royal closet. A suitable occasion soon presented itself. The Duke of Cumberland wished to command in person the allied army defending Hanover. However, he refused to serve unless Pitt were first dismissed. This provided his father with what he considered a sufficient pretext and he gladly rid himself of his eloquent Minister on 6 April.[215]

For a period of nearly three months Britain was virtually without a Government. There were hardly any effective departmental heads. A Board of Admiralty existed, but seeing that its chief member was that proven author of confusion, Daniel, Earl of Winchelsea, morale in the Fleet was probably some distance below its zenith.

Under these conditions it was always probable that the resilient Duke of Newcastle would re-emerge in a prominent role; and it became unmistakably clear that the nation required the firm, directing hand of Pitt. After a period of animated haggling it was agreed that the Duke should again become First Lord of the Treasury and that Pitt should be Secretary of State for the Southern Department. It was understood that Lord Holderness, who was Secretary for the Northern Department, would be little more than an assistant to Pitt, and that the latter would run the war while Newcastle devoted himself to his favourite occupation — the management of Parliament.

---

[215] Stowe MS. 263. Tunstall, pp. 162-80.

As part of the deal, Anson was restored as First Lord of the Admiralty. Boscawen, the sole survivor of the clean-out of the previous autumn, still retained his seat on the Board. Anson wished to see Hawke appointed as one of the Lords but his influence was still at a low ebb because of the loss of Minorca. Pitt had only a few months before cast doubt on Anson's ability to command a cock-boat on the Thames, and, in June 1757, the rehabilitation of the Admiral's reputation was incomplete. As noticed already, it was Temple West who was appointed to the Board instead of Hawke. This was not because anyone imagined that his professional standing was in any way comparable with that of Hawke, but because he was closely linked with the Grenvilles who were Pitt's brothers-in-law and had returned to power with that Minister. The group led by Newcastle, Anson, and (in the background) Hardwicke was not favourably disposed towards West.[216]

After a short interval, and doubtless to his own surprise, Hawke was for a second time put forward as a candidate for the Board. In the spring West had been sent out to blockade Louisbourg but had had to return to England owing to ill health. It was as a result of his death at Tonbridge on 10 August that an occasion arose whereby Hawke was afforded a much closer insight into the process of making government appointments in the age of Newcastle than he would otherwise have had. However, before tracing these machinations which perfectly illustrate the Duke's methods and character, it is necessary to turn to Hawke's acceptance, five days before the death of Admiral West, of a very important command.[217]

---

[216] Tunstall, pp. 180-5. Williams, i, 319. Add.MSS. 15956, Hardwicke to Anson, 18 June 1757; 32873, f. 60; 35359, f. 399.
[217] Clowes, iii, 170. Add.MSS. 35359, f. 339.

Having at last achieved power on a secure basis, Pitt lost no time in imposing his masterly strategy on the whole of the national war-effort. At one time he had been unwilling to afford support to the King's Electorate at Hanover. Now, however, he realized that Britain could not win the peace that would terminate the war unless Hanover remained in allied possession. If the French succeeded in occupying that Electorate, they would be in a position to demand the restoration of such colonies as were wrested from them by the operation of British sea-power. Therefore it was essential for Pitt to devise the survival of his only strong continental ally, Frederick of Prussia. That monarch was beset by the armies of France, Austria, and Russia, and for Pitt to find a solution, which would not entail a vast expenditure of British blood on the Continent, might not have appeared to such Ministers as Newcastle the easiest thing in the world. But, at Pitt's magic touch, the fog of war was dissipated to reveal the clear-cut combinations of the chess-board.

While the naval blockade of France protected England, swept up French shipping, allowed British trade to sail in comparative safety, prevented French army reinforcements from going out to the colonies, and left the British free to concentrate overwhelming forces against any troublesome stronghold, Pitt perceived how sea-power could be used to assist the allied armies on the continent of Europe. Without removing the Western Squadron from the usual area of its operations, yet under the cover of that fleet, he could strike at any important place on the Atlantic coast of France. The destruction achieved might well be considerable; but, above all, one such raid, if carried out by 10,000 troops, would compel the French to protect their shores with several times that number of soldiers. Road transport was so slow that nothing short of strong garrisons could adequately protect their ports, for the British troops would, owing to the Navy, have incomparably superior mobility. Therefore, from the point of view of Frederick or the Duke of Cumberland, one raid would remove from the vital German theatre as many troops as a first-class victory in a land battle — and yet cost hardly any British lives.

If, on the other hand, military affairs took their obvious course on the Continent, and the French were left without opposition there, it was always possible that, with their larger population and potential strength, they might turn their attention exclusively to the sea and overwhelm the British fleet. It was bearing such considerations in mind that Pitt would see to it that Canada was won on the plains of Germany.

In July an effective British intervention was urgently required. Frederick, suffering the onslaught of three major adversaries, was in a desperate plight. On his western flank, Cumberland, in danger of being separated from the sea, was in imminent danger of defeat. Pitt therefore cast about for ideas on how best to provide an effective diversion.[218]

After discussion in the Cabinet Pitt settled on a proposal put forward by General Ligonier that the object of the attack should be the naval port and arsenal of Rochefort. The source of this idea was an army engineer, Lieutenant Robert Clerk, who had examined the fortifications of the place entirely on his own initiative in 1754. This Clerk 'was a very singular man, of a very ingenious and active intellect' and contentious disposition, who rose eventually to Lieutenant-General. (To bring out his reflective qualities, it is worthwhile to notice a closely reasoned letter which he sent in 1766 to Lord Shelburne, suggesting that

[218] Corbett gives a full appreciation of the merits of Pitt's strategy, cf. esp. i, 188-9. Tunstall, pp. 193-4. Whitworth, pp. 219-20.

the solution to the problem of the American Colonies would be to grant them a status resembling that of a twentieth-century Dominion.) Once the decision had been taken, in July 1757, to attack Rochefort, Clerk, who was than aged about 33, was promoted to Lieutenant-Colonel and appointed Chief Engineer of the expedition.[219]

There appears to have been no doubt about the suitability of Hawke — an Admiral of the Blue since February — to command the naval side of the enterprise. Seeing that the raid would be a combined operation it was to come directly under Pitt's control, and when Hawke received his letter of appointment, dated 5 August, he found that it was signed by the Secretary of State.

However, from the point of view of the expedition, it was perhaps even more important to select a first-rate general than a first-rate admiral. It is therefore of particular interest to discover that Pitt's first choice for the army command was Lord George Sackville and his second the Honourable Henry Conway. In view of Sackville's extreme disgrace at the Battle of Minden, two years later, and of Conway's indecisive nature, one is relieved to find that the King overruled his Minister on the matter — relieved until reminded that the monarch's choice fell on General Sir John Mordaunt. Mordaunt certainly proved to be no good at all; but he would be a bold man who could assert that Sackville and Conway would have been much better. The trouble was that Britain was living true to her traditions — good generals were, as usual, approximately as scarce as good admirals were abundant.[220]

---

[219] Cathcart Papers, A67: Papers of R. Clerk. *The Autobiography of Dr. Alexander Carlyle*, 1910, pp. 473-4.
[220] I.L., 5 Aug. 1757. Tunstall, p. 195.

On 7 August Hawke's flag was hoisted aboard the *Ramillies*. James Hobbs was again the Captain. Amongst the business of the day was an acknowledgement of Pitt's letter of the 5th. 'I beg you will do me the justice to believe that I shall exert my utmost abilities for [the King's] honour and the service of my country.'

The subject of the relations existing between Hawke and Pitt requires examination. Typical of the opinion of reputable historians is the statement by Sir John K. Laughton that Anson, in June 1757, 'wished Hawke to join the board, but this was prevented, owing, it was supposed, to a want of cordiality between him and the great minister. There are many indications of Pitt's personal dislike of Hawke.' Both Laughton and Corbett seem to have been content to follow Burrows in propagating this kind of view.[221] There does not appear to be much surviving direct evidence on the subject, but what there is lends little support to the idea that, at this time, Pitt harboured any active dislike of Hawke. After Temple West's death on 9 August, Pitt's feelings on the question of replacing him were reported by Lady Anson thus:

> Lord Anson, with his respectful compliments to Lord Hardwicke, begs pardon for employing a secretary to inform his Lordship of an incident which happened and which embarrasses him a good deal. The occasion of it is the appointment of a successor at the Admiralty in the room of Admiral West who died last night at Tonbridge. Lord Anson waited on the Duke of Newcastle this morning to acquaint him with it, and to express his *strong desire* that as this created a vacancy in the Admiralty, it might be filled up with Sir

[221] O.L., 7 Aug. 1757 (2). For mistaken view of H.'s relations with Pitt: Burrows, pp. 275-8; J. K. Laughton, *From Howard to Nelson*, p. 220-1, and D.N.B.; Corbett, ii, 159.

> Edward Hawke. His Grace insisting very warmly upon his engagement to Mr. Stanley, Lord Anson begged him at least to defer filling it up a little (as he said he must have a vacancy for Mr. Stanley), to try if he could not accommodate both. The Duke declared at the end of the conversation that he would go into the Closet and settle it for Mr. Stanley directly; or he would never go into the Treasury again. Whether he has settled it accordingly is not yet known to Lord Anson, who thinks that if he had gone at first where his Grace said he was going, he should have found it no difficult point to have carried it for Sir Edward Hawke. Mr. Pitt very civilly and reasonably says, as he did upon the subject when this Board was appointed, that as there was nobody of it whom Lord Anson had chosen, he thought it very proper he should recommend one now; and if Sir Edward Hawke was agreeable to him he thought it very right he should succeed.[222]

Seeing that this is the only reliable evidence on the subject, it is fair to conclude that Pitt did not dislike Hawke at this time. It will be seen that, after the failure of the Rochefort expedition, Pitt did harbour resentment against Hawke as well as against the generals. But it will also be seen that he eventually offered Hawke the post of First Lord of the Admiralty, that Hawke accepted, and that, to the end of his days, the Admiral held Pitt in the highest regard as a war leader. Pitt was always ready to fulminate against individuals where he thought that they had failed to carry out his measures, but he was hardly interested in them purely as people. There was probably no personal antipathy between Pitt and Hawke.

After reading his daughter's above-quoted letter of 10 August, Hardwicke took up Hawke's case with Newcastle. On

---

[222] Add.MSS. 35359, f. 399.

the 11th he wrote to his Grace that the promise to Hans Stanley 'is particularly unfortunate now, as Sir Edward Hawke is just setting out upon this important expedition, and it may be of ill consequence to discontent him… Permit me to give it as my advice to suspend any determination at present. Surely this change of circumstances makes it reasonable for Mr. Stanley to wait for another vacancy, especially as this is a seaman's vacancy.'

But the Duke had already been as good as his word in settling it for Mr. Stanley. The King was decidedly unhappy about the appointment and specifically mentioned that he had wanted Hawke to succeed 'to the first sea vacancy'. However, this fundamentally German sovereign, who lacked assurance in dealing with British politics, gave way to the persistence of his parliamentary manager. After reading Hardwicke's letter, Newcastle's enthusiasm for Stanley was transformed into apprehension on the subject of Hawke. He did not at all like the look of the former Chancellor's words about the Admiral's discontent. Would Hawke wreck the whole expedition out of pique? The Duke now busied himself with suppressing the news of Stanley's appointment until the expedition had carried the Admiral to a safe distance.

Meanwhile, Hans Stanley saw no reason to question the wisdom of his appointment. He had already written to thank Newcastle for seating him on the 'Admiraltree' — to use Boscawen's expression. Stanley's words provide an inspiring example of the spirit of true patriotism: 'I… can most sincerely assure you that those marks of your regard to me shall not be lost upon me. I have been since our first connection a steady friend of your Grace's honour and real intentions, nor have I since that period any other views than those of serving you, without paying even the second attentions anywhere else.'[223]

At Portsmouth, Hawke was busy with the inevitable manning problem. The records show that during the Seven Years' War only 1,512 seamen were killed in action, while as many as 133,708 were lost to the Service through desertion or disease. Seeing that the total number of men raised was 184,899, the likelihood of a man pressed in 1756 being still found in the Navy in 1762 was not very-great; and, as Hawke was well aware, the task of manning any new squadron was bound to be something of a losing battle.

In view of the subsequent history of the expedition, including accusations that Hawke was unenterprising in planning how to land the troops and that he was at best lukewarm towards General Mordaunt, his first letter to the army commander, dated 8 August, is now given:

> I have the favour of your letter of this day's date, and have communicated it to Admiral Knowles. We would with great pleasure do ourselves the honour of waiting upon you at the camp; but the service is so pressing that it is out of our power to stir from thence. Yet I hope we shall soon have an opportunity of meeting to consult the properest manner of embarking the troops. The moment the baggage and horse ships arrive I shall order them to proceed to Southampton.
>
> I shall be obliged to you if you will direct a list of the troops to be embarked, distinguished by Battalions, according to their seniority, particularly specifying the number of commission and non-commission officers of each class, to be sent to me, that I may be the better able to form the three divisions of the transports.
>
> Admiral Knowles desires me to make his compliments with mine to yourself and Major General Conway…

---

[223] Add.MSS. 32873, f. 26, 60, 147.

> P.S. I have given directions to my Captain to receive your things on board the *Ramillies*, and to order them to be put into my apartments.[224]

In any case, Hawke can hardly be suspected of a seaman's prejudice against the land service, seeing that he placed two of his three sons, namely Edward and Chaloner, in the Army — and sent none to sea.

This was certainly a period of experiment in more than one direction. Not least important was the introduction of new kinds of preserved food. The Portsmouth Office for Sick and Wounded Seamen, with Admiralty approval, issued 'portable soup' to the fleet for the benefit of the sick, and sent a letter to Hawke saying that the said Office 'had the success of it very much at heart'. It was advised that the caked material should be 'examined often, wiped dry when necessary'. Hawke was energetic in issuing the necessary instructions about the care and use of the cakes. It was some time before any reports on the efficacy of the broth found their way to the Admiralty, but in January 1759 the Sick and Hurt Board heard from the Surgeon of the *Barfleur*. During her last cruise a feature of life had been 'an obstinate malignant fever on board that ceased not till it had gone through above three parts of the complement'. He thought that many lives had been saved by the restorative effect of the broth.

Another new food which was given a trial aboard Hawke's squadron of 1757 was dried apple. This presumably had a slight anti-scorbutic effect — though even Lind, who was working towards the right solution in the struggle against scurvy, was some way from discovering the vitamin-deficiency underlying the disease.[225]

---

[224] Lloyd and Coulter, p. 121. O.L., 8 Aug. 1757.

Among the army officers being assembled for the expedition was a young Colonel by the name of James Wolfe. Seeing that his subsequent criticisms of his superiors have been much quoted and have coloured many interpretations of what happened in the Basque Road, and having regard to the fact that Hawke came in for accusation of lack of forethought and comprehension of the Admiral's role in such an operation, it would be well to consider now what Wolfe had to say. After his return to England, he wrote to a friend:

> I have found out that an Admiral should endeavour to run into an enemy's port immediately he appears before it; that he should anchor the transports and frigates as close as he can to the land; that he should reconnoitre and observe it as quickly as possible, and lose no time in getting the troops ashore; that previous directions should be given in respect of landing the troops and a proper disposition for the boats of all sorts, appointing leaders and fit persons for conducting the different divisions.

It would appear that from seasickness or some other cause, Wolfe was poorly informed as to what was going on. Before the expedition sailed, Hawke had already decided

> To consider with the flag and general officers which will be the properest place to attempt; to settle this in going along; and to fix upon the ships and troops that are to make the attack, which, if done at all, must absolutely be done upon the first going in, or otherwise they will be prepared to make head against you; no time must be lost upon these occasions... To endeavour to cover the landing of the men by sending in two, three, or more small frigates inshore, to fire grape and

---

[225] I.L., 6, 10 Aug. 1757. O.B., 12, 13 Aug. 1757. Adm/F/19, 24 Jan. 1759. cf. Lloyd and Coulter, pp. 4, 87, etc.

partridge; to scour the country while the men are disembarking; to be particularly careful to do this upon their embarking.[226]

The impression that Hawke was determined that the army should be afforded every prospect of success is confirmed further by his entering into a warm dispute with the Admiralty, rather than let the 10,000 troops embark in what appeared to be an inadequate number of transports. The Admiralty's view was that an allowance of 1 ton per man was sufficient and 'that no inconvenience whatsoever will attend the present allowance, but on the contrary the Service will be attended with less accidents and delays by having fewer ships'. To a generation uncomfortably aware of the tightening coils of bureaucracy, this argument is rather refreshing. But Hawke presented a warmly argued case.

> It can not be imagined that a ship of 400 tons burthen could be capable of receiving 400 men. Let there be deducted from her tonnage the room necessary for her proper crew, ballast, water, provisions, cables, and other stores, room for the soldiers' provisions, water, tent-poles, baggage, and arms, and what will remain can only be allowed for the reception of men, who must have room to lie under cover too. My principal motive in directing Mr. Thames to remonstrate on this subject to the Navy Board was to remove any difficulties before it was too late. For from the first I was determined, and still am so, to embark the troops in the best manner I can, as soon as the transports shall arrive. Neither shall I take any blame to myself for the directions I gave to Mr. Thames. It was my duty.[227]

---

[226] Corbett, i, 221-2. Wright, p. 396. Burrows, pp. 299-300, for H.'s notes.
[227] I.L., 11, 19, 20 Aug. 1757. Ad. 1/89, 19 Aug. 1757. O.L., 20, 21,

On 22 August it probably seemed to Clevland that the affair had reached an amicable termination when he wrote: 'The Comptroller of the Navy being arrived at Portsmouth, the Lords hope everything relating to the transports will be done to your satisfaction.' It is conceivable that these words were intended to convey a dig at Hawke. Howbeit, the Admiral was a sensitive man; and he may have had at the back of his mind such incidents as the second rejection of his recommendation of Locker for a commission and his own recent exclusion from the Admiralty Board in favour of that high-minded, self-sacrificing patriot, Hans Stanley. On 24 August, he did not dictate an answer to Clevland's letter; nor did he leave it to Hay. He snatched up the pen and wrote:

> An expression at the end of your letter, I own, greatly astonishes me. 'Their Lordships hope everything relating to the transports will be done to *your* satisfaction.' I never was dissatisfied with any number appointed, and only thought it my duty, for the public credit, as well as the private reputation of the Boards concerned, to give my opinion in a matter wherein some difficulty might have arisen when too late to be remedied. I meant it well… The Comptroller has thought fit to make so great an addition to the first tonnage… I can not think it would have been done in complaisance to any private person's opinion. Besides I beg it to be considered that the difficulty arose from a quarter where I had no immediate concern of my own.

This explosion illustrates Hawke's occasional touchiness, but equally his independence of character, the strength of his moral fibre and the genuineness of his devotion to the public good; also his ability to express himself well on paper when roused.

---

22 Aug. 1757.

But such characteristics do not necessarily endear an Admiral to his superiors, and it will be seen that the following May, when he stood on less firm ground, he suffered a serious humiliation at the hands of their Lordships. For the present, Clevland replied mildly enough that the Lords 'do not doubt of your entire satisfaction in everything that contributes to His Majesty's Service, which is the sense of what they meant to convey to you, and are concerned you should take it [in] any other light than was intended.'[228]

In the middle of this dispute with the Admiralty Hawke received a letter from the Duke of Newcastle, dated 24 August. The Duke assured Hawke that he entertained the loftiest opinion of him and his 'great abilities'. 'But', his Grace explained, 'I always own the Truth, and must trust the goodness of my friends to excuse me, when previous engagements may make it impossible for me to do so, what I should otherwise desire.' He would join with his political colleagues in recommending Hawke to the next vacancy at the Board, and promote his 'interest and service on all occasions' — a truly comforting thought!

Hawke responded with elaborate politeness on the 27th. Only in a single sentence did his disappointment and frustration at so flagrant an injustice break through. 'I beg your Grace will pardon my freedom in telling you that I think it too late to come to that Board at all.' Recovering his composure, he continued. 'It will always make me extremely happy to have the honour of your Grace's good opinion, which I shall endeavour to preserve by a faithful and upright discharge of the duty I owe to my King and Country.'[229]

---

[228] I.L., 22, 23, 25 Aug. 1757. Ad. 1/89, 24 Aug. 1757.
[229] Add.MSS. 32873, f. 263, 309.

Hawke's efforts on behalf of the army were by no means lost upon Sir John Mordaunt, who wrote from his camp at Newport, Isle of Wight, to thank the Admiral for all he had done 'to get the soldiers a little more room in the transports. It was quite necessary', Mordaunt affirmed, 'and I shall ever declare it.' The General's lack of enthusiasm for the expedition is perhaps suggested in his final sentence, 'Since seeing you, I have heard nothing from above.' Nor was he a solitary pessimist. Newcastle confided his fears to Hardwicke. 'Many sensible people begin to be uneasy about our Expedition. The season advances, we shall want our ships home, or they will be wanted to intercept the French fleet from America. It is now the 3rd September; they were to be home by the end of this month. Lord Anson also told us that Dr. Hay and Mr. Elliot [both Lords of the Admiralty], who had been at Portsmouth, said that both land and sea officers *talked down* the Expedition. But Pitt is deaf and... I don't know who dares take upon him *to stop its going.*'

Certainly, by modern standards, the planning of the enterprise was casual. The Admiralty possessed no detailed charts of the anchorage outside the Charente, nor of the shoals off the beaches, nor of the coastline in general. Before leaving London Hawke had been called to a meeting at Lord Holderness's house at which the form of the operation was decided. The date of the meeting was 4 August. Pitt presided. Anson, Ligonier, Mordaunt, Conwav, Vice-Admiral Knowles, and Robert Clerk were in attendance. Reliance was placed on the unsupported evidence of Joseph Thierry, a Huguenot pilot. He stated that the troops could land not far north of Fort Fouras which covered the channel of approach to the Charente. The ships of the line could cover the landing with long-range fire. The fort on the Island of Aix, which commanded the landing place, could soon be reduced by a single ship of the line.

Thierry proved accurate in some particulars; but it was of some significance that, in the event, it was found that even the transports, with their comparatively shallow draught, could not approach within one and a half miles of the beach without going aground, and that no warship could come within two miles. This meant that if the wind proved contrary boats might not be able to complete the journey from the transports to the shore; and certainly no covering fire whatsoever could be given by the warships.

However, overborne by Pitt's powerful and somewhat obsessive personality, the meeting of 4 August produced no definite objections to the expedition. As far as the port of Rochefort was concerned, the generals said that, even if an escalade proved impracticable, they would find a way of penetrating the apparently incomplete defences.[230]

The process of assembling the troops afforded Mordaunt, Conway, and Cornwallis (the third General) an opportunity for further reflection. They spent more and more time in suggesting difficulties to one another. Finally, they seem to have been unanimous in the opinion that success was completely impossible. Clerk, on the other hand, was never shaken in his conviction that the unprepared French, without any units of good, professional troops in the town, were bound to be overcome by a determined assault. Wolfe does not seem to have helped him to overcome the irresolution of the generals. With regard to his efforts in this direction, Clerk later

---

[230] H.P.P., Mordaunt to H., 25 Aug. 1757. Add.MSS. 32873, £. 433. P.R.O. 30/8/78, 21 Oct. 1757 for damaged original. Perfect copy at N.M.M. *Report of the General Officers appointed to inquire into the Cause of the Failure of the late Expedition*, 1758. pp. 68-9; 40, 102.

testified: 'I could not well have driven it harder, consistent with military discipline and my subordinate situation, having everybody against me.'[231]

Hawke may have had his doubts about the expedition's prospects, but his determination to do his best cannot be doubted. He did his best to hurry the transports to Cowes where the troops were to embark, but Pitt was soon impatient and expressed his feelings to Hawke in a communication dated 5 September. A characteristic postscript read:

> 'The Messenger that carries this has my orders to stay to bring an Account of the Fleet's sailing.' But Hawke was not to be intimidated. On the 6th he replied that his correspondence with the Secretary to the Admiralty seemed to have satisfied the King 'that I needed no spur in the Execution of his Orders'! Meanwhile, Sir John Mordaunt, who had received a similar 'spur' from the Secretary of State, wrote to protest his enthusiasm for the enterprise.[232]

A final delay was imposed by capricious winds. At last, on 10 September, an onlooker would have been rewarded with the uplifting sight of sixteen ships of the line, nine frigates or sloops, a cluster of minor warships, and fifty transports standing out for the Channel. Out of the captains of ships of the line, eleven were destined to rise to the rank of Vice-Admiral or higher. They were the Honourable Richard Howe, Samuel Graves, the Honourable Augustus Keppel, Peter Denis, the Honourable Samuel Barrington, Matthew Buckle, James Young, Robert Digby, George Brydges Rodney, James Douglas, and the Honourable John Byron. Charles Knowles,

---

[231] Add.MSS. 32873, f. 433. *Report*, op. cit., pp. 49-58 for Clerk; 46-8 for Wolfe. Wright, p. 396. Cathcart Papers, A67.

[232] O.L., 4 Sept. 1757. *Report*, op. cit., pp. 94-7.

Vice-Admiral of the Red, commanded the van, and Thomas Brodrick, Rear-Admiral of the White, had charge of the rear division.[233]

On 15 September, when still some days from the end of the voyage, Hawke ordered Knowles and Brodrick, with such pilots and officers as they required, to be ready to sound the waters round the Island of Aix and to survey the nearby shore as soon as the fleet had anchored in the Basque Road. Knowles was told, 'You are to make a report to me as soon as possible, in writing, signed by you and the Rear-Admiral.' On the same day, Hawke distributed an order that the troops borne as supernumeraries aboard the warships were to go ashore immediately after the soldiers from the transports. It did not occur to him that there would be no landing![234]

Throughout the voyage the winds were light and, as often as not, contrary. At last, on the morning of the 20th, the convoy was approaching the northern entry into the Basque Road. By noon the Islands of Rhé and Oléron could be discerned. Hawke issued a memorandum to all warships, instructing their captains to see that the soldiers and marines under their command were in every way ready to land. Attention was directed to each man's musket and firelock and to his ammunition. Captains were to ensure 'that each soldier and marine have but one shirt and one pair of stockings and one pair of shoes in his knapsack'; also 'to direct the lieutenants commanding the boats for the disembarkation to be very careful to range the boats in divisions, and in such manner that every regiment may be together'.[235]

---

[233] O.L., 8, 10 Sept. 1757. O.B., 8 Sept. 1757.
[234] O.B., 15 Sept. 1757.
[235] O.L., 29 Sept. 1757. O.B., 20 Sept. 1757.

All in all, it is difficult to discover the substance in Wolfe's implication that no previous directions were given for landing the troops, organizing the boats, and 'appointing leaders and fit persons for conducting the different divisions'. However, as writers have seen fit to quote Wolfe and then proceed to criticize Hawke for inattention to his side of the affair, the final paragraphs of the Admiral's memorandum of 20 September may help to dissipate any lingering doubt on the subject.

> As it is more than probable that the disembarkation will only be opposed by Militia which may be easily dispersed, it is earnestly recommended to all the Marines and soldiers, when directed to attack, to march up vigorously, preserving their fire till they come very near, so as to do certain execution, and, whenever the General orders, that they run in with their bayonets.
>
> As soon as the troops shall be possessed of a post on shore and the Chief Engineer [Clerk] marked out an entrenchment to secure the provisions, heavy artillery, powder, and other necessaries for the army, that then all the tents, blankets, watchcoats, knapsacks, remainder of the entrenching tools, spare ammunition, provisions, scaling ladders, and petards, be immediately brought on shore. Also the fascines and gabions from the *Fyloe* tender.
>
> Six days' allowance of provisions, consisting only of bread, cheese, beef, and pork, to be sent on shore after the troops are landed.
>
> And as the duty of the disembarkation will be hard upon the boats' crews, it is recommended that they may be relieved as often as possible.
>
> No marines to be landed that have been in the French service.[236]

---

[236] cf. Corbett, 210-12. O.B., 20 Sept. 1757.

As for Wolfe's much-quoted advice, directed to the army's role in such operations, Ligonier had already conveyed the same principles in a memorandum addressed to Mordaunt before the departure of the expedition. The only item in Wolfe's celebrated paragraph that might have raised Ligonier's eyebrows was a remark to the effect that, 'in particular circumstances and times, the loss of 1,000 men is rather an advantage to a nation than otherwise, seeing that gallant attempts raise its reputation and make it respectable'. Hawke, certainly, was wanting in enthusiasm for such attitudes.[237]

Hawke and Mordaunt agreed that the Island of Aix must be taken from the French before any move was made towards the beaches. As the fleet approached Oléron on the 20th Hawke instructed Knowles to watch for a red flag at the *Ramillies*' fore topgallant masthead. Then: 'You are… without loss of time to stand in as near to the said Isle of Aix as the pilots will carry you, with all or as many ships of your division as you shall think sufficient for that service, and batter it.' After taking the fort, he was to see that demolitions were carried out.

However, wind and tide made it impossible to enter the Road that evening. A French warship was observed making for the sea, and Hawke made a mistake, possibly of some importance, in signalling to the *Magnanime*, the nearest ship to the enemy, to chase her. The error resided in the fact that Thierry, the chief pilot of the fleet, was aboard the *Magnanime*. However, Hawke believed that pilots aboard some of the other ships had an adequate knowledge of the Road, and did not discover their severe limitations until later.[238]

---

237 O.B., loc. cit. *Report*, op. cit. pp. 20-2. cf. Whitworth, p. 221. Wright, p. 396.

238 P.R.O. 30/8/78;see n. 18 above. O.B., 20 Sept. 1757. O.L., 29 Sept. 1757.

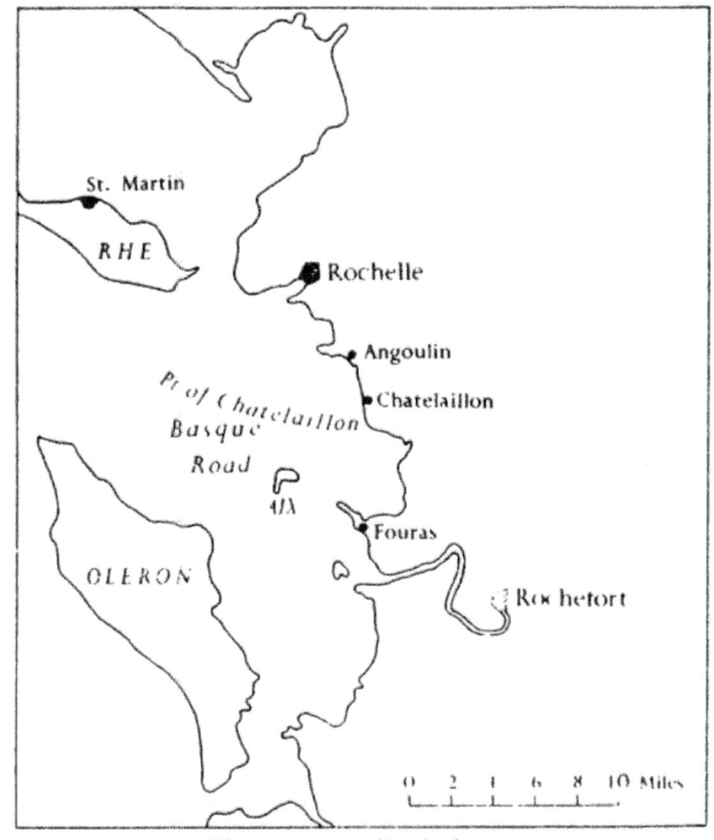

The coast near Rochefort.

Meanwhile, on the 20th, the people of Rochefort learnt of the arrival of the expedition and were greatly alarmed. The defences had not been strengthened since Clerk had inspected them three years earlier. The inhabitants took it for granted that the town would shortly be surrendered to the British.

On 21 September, at 7 a.m., Hawke signalled for the van division (Admiral Knowles) to move into Basque Road.

However, Knowles's pilot, and the other pilots in the division, refused to take the ships in, because of hazy weather. This is where Thierry might, or might not, have made a difference. The *Magnanime* rejoined the fleet before noon. However, Knowles took till 3 p.m. to reform his division and by then the wind was blowing straight out of the Road with an ebb tide, so there was nothing for it but to anchor and wait.

The 22nd also brought unhelpful weather. Hawke had foreseen the possibility of such delay. Still, considering his complete appreciation of the importance of swift action, his extreme frustration can easily be imagined. It was not till 9.30 p.m. on the 22nd that the fleet struggled into Basque Road.[239]

With the tide flooding at 10 a.m. on the 23rd, Knowles stood towards the Island of Aix. As prescribed in Hawke's line of battle, the ships were led by the *Magnanime* (74), and after her came the *Barfleur* (Rowley's old flagship at the Battle of Toulon, now commanded by Graves), *Neptune* (90) (Knowles's flagship), *Torbay* (74) (Augustus Keppel), and *Royal William* (84) (Witteronge Taylor). Owing, no doubt, to the shortcomings of the pilots aboard the other ships, the attack was carried out almost entirely by the *Magnanime*. Howe's personal conduct made a profound impression on friend and foe alike, as was well brought out by an eyewitness in the following account:

> Before the attack began, Captain Howe received the fire of the garrison with great intrepidity, ordered all his men to lay down upon the decks, turned all his live cattle, fowls, and unnecessaries overboard; himself only with his speaking trumpet in hand, the pilot and the man at the helm appearing upon deck, till he came within sixty yards of the bastions of the garrison, when he began so furious a fire that the

[239] Lacour-Gayet, pp. 304, 307. Pajol, vi, 316-17. O.L., 29 Sept. 1757. *Report*, op. cit., p. 86 — H. saw that delay was possible.

> Monsicurs said that something more than a man must be on board that ship; the men in the garrison were so much terrified that most of them clapped themselves down under the works of the garrison and in the ditches, nor could be prevailed on to stand to their guns, which obliged the governor to strike the colours, and was no sooner done than they all jumped up, taking snuff, dancing and rejoicing, as if they had gained a victory.

It was between noon and 1.10 that the *Magnanime* made her silent approach into the fire of the fort. According to Hawke, she then anchored within forty yards of her target, and 'kept an incessant fire for about thirty-five minutes'. The enemy surrendered at 1.45. The ship's damage was mostly sustained aloft. She lost two men killed and eleven wounded; and out of the French garrison of 500, the number of the dead was one!

Still, it would be a mistake to assume that Howe's task was necessarily a simple one, or that the psychological effect of his own conduct was unconnected with the result. Clerk afterwards recorded some interesting observations on the episode.

> In the Island of Aix, there were five or six twelve-inch mortars with proper parapets... They fired cannon and mortars from the fort when the ship was bearing down, but Lord Howe did not fire till he came to an anchor, and when he opened his broadside upon the fort they fired no more from it. It is not clear how many hours Lord Howe would have taken to make a breach, but it is clear that if the Governor of the fort had done his duty he could have destroyed not only Lord Howe's ship, but the other four ships of the line, if they had bore down and come to an anchor in as proper a manner as Lord Howe; and that might have been done without the least danger to anybody in the fort... However, five Governors out of six in such places, and with

> the same circumstances, will surrender in the same manner. Distant places and places upon the coast have not commonly the best Governors or the best artillery officers and engineers.

In order to expedite a landing on the mainland, Hawke decided not to wait for the surrender before getting under way the work of taking soundings. Cancelling his earlier order to Knowles, he instructed Rear-Admiral Brodrick and Captains Douglas, Denis, and Buckle to carry on with the survey.[240]

As Clerk recalled:

> They went out the 23rd September when it was almost dark, lay all the night in the cutter, and the next day, the 24th, in about six or seven hours' time reconnoitred the whole, beginning by the point of land which runs out from Fort Fouras and the Grand Battery, and then going all the way to the South Point of the entrance of Rochelle… Captain Buckle says that as they found the two bays, the one from Angoulin to Chatelaillon, and the other round the Point of Chatelaillon about half a mile to the eastward, very proper places for landing, they gave themselves less trouble in examining what might have been done in other places, which were muddy… There is seldom finer or more moderate weather in the Bay at any time of the year than the ten days we were upon the French coast. The wind blew off shore, so we had no swell. At night, it commonly freshened up a little, but never so much, not even the 28th, as to prevent us going ashore in boats.[241]

Brodrick presented his report to Hawke on the 24th in the afternoon. It followed the same lines as Clerk's account quoted

---

[240] O.L., 29 Sept. 1757. 'The Secret Expedition,' 1757, by a commissioned officer with the Fleet. Cathcart Papers, A67: Papers of R. Clerk. O.B., 23 Sept. 1757; cf. 24 Sept. N.M.M. has H.'s notes for giving evidence at the c.m.

[241] Cathcart Papers, A67.

above. The transports could be run aground, at low tide, about one and a half miles from the beaches. After some deliberation, Hawke came to what he expected to be a final decision. A landing was practicable and he would therefore give the necessary orders as soon as Mordaunt wished. Then came a great shock for the Admiral. Mordaunt, in a nervy, 'peevish' state of mind, refused to agree on the time and place of landing. Instead, he demanded that fatal refuge of irresolute commanders, a council of war. Hawke was particularly averse to the idea, because Anson had warned him of the dangers involved. But Mordaunt was firm in his insistence and had only to refer to Article 5 of his Instructions, corresponding to Article 4 of those issued to the Admiral, to confirm his right to have a council assembled. Because the officers concerned were scattered through the fleet, it was impracticable to collect them and leave time for them to deliberate that day.[242]

The next day certainly left an impression on Hawke's memory. 'The debates of the Council of War on the 25th ulto.', he afterwards wrote to Clevland, 'were so various, tedious and uncorrected that it was impossible to take Minutes.' He had already ordered the transports to move in towards the shore in anticipation of the council's decision to land. But no such decision emerged. The only point on which the generals were unmistakably agreed was that, the enemy having received five days' warning, Rochefort could not be taken by escalade. The four naval members of the council, namely Hawke, Knowles, Brodrick, and Rodney, appear to have been brought to complete exhaustion by the army's flexibility in producing objections against any plan of action. A resolution was at last formulated. This was simply to the effect that Rochefort could

---

[242] O.L., 29 Sept. 1757. Smith, i, 223. Add.MSS. 15956, f. 48. P.R.O. 30/8/78; see n. 18 above.

not be captured by scaling the walls. Hawke, followed by the other naval officers, decided to sign this resolution, because they could not refuse to credit the army officers with 'judgement and knowledge of their own profession'. Undoubtedly, he made a mistake in signing, not because he thereby signified agreement that Rochefort could not be taken by 'assault or escalade merely', but because the document embodied no positive plan of action. Hawke — whose view was independently borne out by Rodney — understood from what had been said that the soldiers, having ruled out escalade, would find some other means of entering Rochefort. But the fact remained that he had put his name to a resolution which was simply negative in intent.[243]

For the next three days Hawke waited fretfully for the generals to decide on a plan of action. Mordaunt, who had in fact abandoned any idea of attacking Rochefort, had numbers of witnesses interrogated with an ostensible view to attacking Fort Fouras or landing on the Island of Oléron. Hawke confined his advice to an insistence that the army should attempt some kind of operation. As if this idea had suddenly struck him as possessing originality, Mordaunt asked for a council at which it could be discussed. Hawke had no option but to agree.

At this juncture Rochefort was still weakly defended. Between the 25th and the 28th, there had been repeated alarms in the town, livery movement of the British vessels was taken to herald a landing. Thus, although the tactical achievements of the expedition had not been great, in terms of grand strategy it was proving a powerful lever. Large numbers of French troops

---

[243] O.L., 29 Sept., 6 Oct. 1757. P.R.O. 30/8/78; sec n. 18 above. *Report*, op. cit., p. 106. Add.MSS. 35359, f. 401 — H. blamed. Smith, i, 219 — Rodney's impression.

were by now on the march with their backs turned on the battlefields of Germany. It was sufficient for the British armada of 1757 simply to appear off Rochefort, and, through its diversionary effect, it showed how Pitt's system would ultimately defeat France at a minimum of cost in British lives.

However, to achieve complete success with this policy, it was essential that the army should actually perpetrate some violent acts on the French mainland.[244]

Hawke certainly never imagined that it would be sufficient for the expedition to show itself and then depart, without carrying out at least a sizeable raid. Before the council was held on the morning of the 28th he again ordered the transports to be moved in.

At the council it was apparently understood that no minutes would be taken, but the generals, whose preference for a lack of a record was stronger than that of the naval officers, had not reckoned with John Hay. He surreptitiously made notes which, to the consternation of the generals, eventually found their way to the court of inquiry. (Hay was given a thorough dressing-down for his pains by Lord George Sackville who sat as a member of that court.)

The deliberations revolved round Fort Fouras and the question whether it could be taken by troops alone. Hawke had already tried to bombard it from the sea, but Thierry's assertion that it could be done had been followed by the *Barfleur*'s going aground about four miles away from the target! Evidence in favour of an assault by the troops was taken from Wolfe and Clerk.

During the discussions, which seem to have resembled those of the 25th, Hawke gave vent to his heartfelt exasperation. He said that, from the time of receiving Brodrick's report, he had

---

[244] Lacour-Gayet, p. 304, 308. Williams, i, 343. Corbett, i, 227-8.

been sure that a landing was possible and should be made. He remained of the opinion that the troops should attempt something. It was the General's business to decide what operation to carry out. He would 'readily assent to any resolution they should come to, and assist them to the utmost of his power'. Finally, after a French prisoner had given an encouraging account of the weakness of the Fort and its garrison, Mordaunt and Conway, with the concurrence of the Admirals, concluded that the place should be attacked. Cornwallis, the most defeatist of a thoroughly unimpressive trio of generals, announced his dissent.

It remained to fix the time at which the operation was to be carried out. Hawke favoured landing 'in the day to prevent mistakes and surprise, while at the same time it would strike more terror'; but the generals, being less concerned with striking terror into the enemy than with the contemplation of their own emotions, determined to go ashore at night. Hawke was, as ever, ready to co-operate with the wishes of the military, and promptly detailed off the several captains and thirty lieutenants required to conduct the landing.[245]

At one o'clock on the morning of the 29th, the long-awaited moment was at hand when the boats, now laden with the soldiery of England, would begin to nose their way towards the shore. But Mordaunt and Conway had found other work to do. They were busily pumping Brodrick and his officers in order to discover some reason for cancelling the operation. At last, they got it clear. It would take the rest of the night to convey the first half of the army ashore because there was an offshore breeze. Then the tide would ebb, and altogether it would take another six hours to bring the second wave of troops ashore.

---

[245] *Report*, op. cit., pp. 9, 10, 18, 19, 29, 38-9, 44-5, 111-13. P.R.O. 30/8/78; see n. 18 above. Walpole, *Memoirs of George II*, iii, 77.

Seeing that the operation was to have been very limited, there is every indication that the first force would have been sufficient for the task and would have run no risk. But the generals, doubtless finding it hard to conceal their self-satisfaction, were not to be denied. Not a single cursing British soldier splashed his way onto the sand that night.[246]

The generals' demand for cancellation of the landing brought Hawke to the end of his patience. The only obstacle to a landing at any time had been the fortifications on Aix. These the Navy had taken and destroyed. Now, seeing that the Army refused to go ashore and that his orders were to take the fleet back to England as soon as operations permitted, the Admiral decided to clarify the situation with Mordaunt. 'Should the General officers of the troops have no further military operation to propose, considerable enough to authorize my detaining the squadron under my command longer here, I beg leave to acquaint you that I intend to proceed with it for England without loss of time.'[247]

After a show of vacillation, Mordaunt, Conway, Cornwallis, and Colonel Howard agreed 'in returning directly to England'.

Even in the depths of vexation and disappointment, Hawke did not fail to report to Anson that he had noticed possibilities for future strategy. The Basque Road would afford safe anchorage to 'the whole fleet of England… Now that we are acquainted with it, it is in our power, with a superior force, to prevent the enemy from making up their fleets here, which will lay them under infinite difficulties, and subject them to great hazard, it being always in our power, now that we know the

[246] *Report*, op. cit., pp. 19, 23, 33. P.R.O. 30/8/78, Mordaunt to Pitt, 4 Oct. 1757. Lacour-Gayet, pp. 308-9.
[247] O.L., 29, 30 Sept. 1757. *Report*, op. cit., pp. 38-9, 109.

place, to prevent any squadron fitted at this port to join that at Brest.'

Moreover, the French had fourteen disarmed ships of the line at Rochefort at that very time. These would normally have been armed and provisioned while lying under the guns of Aix. The chance of catching them there, now that the fortifications had been demolished, was duly taken the following April, as will be related.[248]

Shortly before sailing for England Hawke learnt that a homebound French convoy was shortly expected at Rochefort or Bordeaux. As if to underline the zeal of the Navy and the contrasting passivity of the Army, he forthwith ordered Keppel to cruise for a fortnight 'in the direct tract of these two ports' with four of the line and three frigates.

Then, without very cheerful expectations of the reception likely to be accorded by the British public in general or by Pitt in particular, the expedition withdrew from Basque Road.

There could hardly have been a more disappointed man with the fleet than Lieutenant-Colonel Clerk. In the later part of the war, he served in Portugal under Count Lippe-Buckeburg and rose to the rank of Major-General. When hostilities ceased he lost no time in going to France to discover from enemy sources the likelihood of the expedition's success. When writing to Pitt in 1766 he referred to his visit. 'As to Rochefort, I suppose that you are informed of it as well as myself. Mr. Barre has been there since the peace. It appears to me without doubt that we might have been masters of this place, if we had landed even seven or eight days after we were in Basque Road, and destroyed the great naval magazines there with a great part of the French navy, without perhaps the loss of a single man.'[249]

---

[248] *Report*, op. cit., p. 108. Add.MSS. 15956, f. 48. Corbett, i, 211, 228 n.

At home, Pitt was by no means alone in preparing to lavish denunciation on generals and admirals alike. On 6 October Anson communicated his thoughts to his father-in-law, Lord Hardwicke, and made it clear that Hawke had not risen in his estimation. 'I wish I could send your Lordship any agreeable news, but there seems to be a fatality in everything we undertake and that nothing succeeds. I shall not reason upon the enclosed papers. The Fleet having done well and all in their power gives me satisfaction, but why Hawke put his name to any council of war, when I warned him so strongly against it, astonishes and hurts me.'

By 8 October, the fleet had anchored at Spithead and Hawke was just setting out for Swaythling when he received a summons from Anson to go straight up to London. At the same time a letter from Clevland arrived, instructing the Admiral to prepare a squadron for the next cruise. La Motte had managed to convey to Louisbourg a further reinforcement earlier in the year, and was expected to return to France that autumn. It was thought that the French would try to contest command of the Bay of Biscay and the Channel.

On his arrival in London, Hawke saw no reason to conceal the fact that he had made everything ready for landing the troops. The King, notwithstanding his responsibility for Mordaunt's appointment as army-commander, had not entertained the possibility that his Admiral had contributed to the failure to land. 'I hear', wrote Charles Jenkinson to George Grenville, 'that the King gave Sir Edward Hawke a good reception and Sir John Mordaunt an indifferent one.'[250]

The Government finally decided to establish a court of inquiry — a more cautious procedure than that adopted in the

---

[249] O.B., 1 Oct. 1757. Cathcart Papers, A67.

[250] Add.MSS. 35359, f. 401. O.L., 8 Oct. 1757 (2). Smith, i, 213.

case of Admiral Byng — which was to investigate the causes of 'the Failure of the late Expedition to the Coasts of France'. The diversionary merits of the expedition were little appreciated by the public. Meanwhile, it was thought that Hawke would be better employed at sea than waiting about to give evidence in the Judge Advocate's office (where the court was finally assembled on 12 November).

On 17 October orders were delivered at George Street for the Admiral to resume command of the Western Squadron and to put to sea with all possible dispatch.

Late on the 18th he arrived back at Portsmouth. On account of the forthcoming inquiry, the Admiralty decided to keep back Knowles and Brodrick to give evidence for the naval side, and Boscawen went down to serve as second-in-command. No third Admiral was appointed. These arrangements drew sour remarks from Rodney who wrote to George Grenville on the 21st that 'it seems to bear the appearance of reproach, and points out as delinquents the junior admirals that served on the late expedition'. This notion appears to have been quite groundless. Rodney continued:

> Yesterday they received orders to remain at Spithead to make room for Vice-Admiral B-s-n to command in the second post. We cannot refrain from thinking that avarice has in great measure been the motive for these alterations... The hope of prize money and the unwillingness to have others partake with them seems to have banished true honour from the breast of those who ought to prefer it to every other circumstance... The present fleet is composed of thirty sail, but neither has the Admiral applied or the Board thought fit to appoint a First Captain. The motive you can guess when I tell you the First Captain ranks and shares as a Rear-Admiral.

Rodney sought to clinch his argument by referring to Byng's having been refused a 1st Captain because he had only sixteen of the line, whereas it had been officially stated at that time that 'admirals commanding twenty sail of the line should always have two captains'. Seeing that Hawke soon afterwards sailed from Portsmouth with ten of the line and made his total up to only eleven of the line, a 50, two frigates, and a sloop by a reinforcement from Plymouth, Rodney's reasoning does not exactly support his case. But his letter to Grenville, who then held the office of Treasurer of the Navy, serves to illustrate an unattractive side of its author's character and to bring out the kind of aspersions to which Hawke, as a leading Admiral in a Navy remunerated with prize money, was constantly subject. Nor is the fact that Rodney, a serving Captain, was writing in this way to one of the political heads of the Navy less worthy of remark. Admittedly, such practice was not at all uncommon at that time, but there is no sign that Hawke ever stooped to follow it.[251]

On 21 October Hawke was at the centre of the rush to get a squadron of ships to sea, but he could not put it out of his mind that the inquiry into 'the causes of failure' of the expedition was to be held in his absence. Having witnessed the Government's perversion of justice with regard to Byng, when that Admiral was condemned before he was given a chance to defend himself, Hawke sensibly decided to put a statement of his own view of the affair into the hands of Pitt, the Minister primarily interested in the expedition. He must have known that Pitt had formed a poor opinion of his contribution to the outcome of the expedition, and he doubtless anticipated that the Secretary would furnish evidence to the court. Hawke's letter of the 21st, written in his own hand, contained a straightforward account of his part in the enterprise, which is

---

[251] *Report*, op. cit., p. 5. Ad. 2/79, 17 Oct. 1757. O.L., 19 Oct. 1757. H.P.P., Clevland to H., 19 Oct. 1757. Smith, i, 221-2.

sufficiently corroborated by the other, abundant evidence. The main statements of fact have been embodied in the account of the expedition which has been given above. Otherwise, the Admiral wrote with sincerity: 'The King my master's commands were to me ever sacred… Thus, Sir, have I taken the liberty to lay my own conduct and this unfortunate affair before you, and I submit it to your examination, and, if you think fit, to the World. All through the whole I am certain of the integrity of my heart, and the strong desire I had to serve my King and Country.'

But Pitt did not see fit to publish the letter, or to include it with the documents which he placed before the court of inquiry. It will be seen in due course that he nursed bitter memories of the expedition, and this is understandable; but it will also be seen that, in the face of all evidence and, indeed, the dictates of common sense, he continued to hold Hawke partly responsible for the decision not to land.[252]

It was on 20 October, the day before he wrote his letter to Pitt, that Hawke's thinking on a completely different subject reached final fruition. The subject was naval tactics. As was related above, Hawke had for long been dissatisfied with the defensive tendency inherent in the General Printed Fighting Instructions which had been issued to commanders-in-chief by the Admiralty in the same form since the days of Rooke.

To recapitulate briefly, in cases where the enemy did not flee at the approach of the British squadron, these Instructions called for adherence to a line of battle, with all ships remaining in their prescribed order in the line. The crucial Articles read as follows:

---

[252] O.L., 19, 20 Oct. 1757. P.R.O. 30/8/78; see n. 18 above. Add.MSS. 32913, f. 326 ff.

> XIII. As soon as the Admiral shall hoist a Red Flag on the Flag Staff at the Fore Topmasthead, and fire a gun, every ship in the fleet is to use their utmost endeavour to engage the enemy in the Order the Admiral has prescribed unto them.
> XXI. None of the ships in the fleet shall pursue any small number of the enemy's ships till the main body shall be disabled or run.

Hawke was satisfied with Article XXI. It would be evident to the Admiral when the 'main body' of the enemy had been 'disabled', if such an unlikely contingency ever occurred. The Admiral could also observe the fact that the enemy's 'main body' was on the run. Then he would hoist the chase. The Instructions were entirely adequate for such a case. What caused Hawke concern was the very probable situation where, in a stand-up battle, odd enemy ships sheered away from the fire of British adversaries while most enemy ships stood firm. At the Battle of Toulon, although temporarily baffled, Hawke had found a way out of a problem of this type, by squeezing out of Article XIII every drop of fiery blood contained in it. But the fact that no other captain in Mathews's fleet had followed his example is sufficient proof that no admiral could count on all his captains acting aggressively in that kind of situation. That Hawke had for long been aware of the need for tactical guidance from the admiral if the Instructions were to be aggressively interpreted, is suggested by his address to his captains in the Mediterranean in 1756 — so scathingly and uncomprehendingly recorded by Hervey. Now, in October 1757, Hawke decided to make the letter of the law conform with his intentions. In his view the really cramping phrase was contained in Article XIII. The offending words were 'in the Order which the Admiral has prescribed unto them'. Therefore, on 20 October he issued to his captains copies of the General Printed Sailing and Fighting Instructions, in which

Article XIII of the Fighting Instructions by Day appeared with an unambiguous handwritten alteration. The words 'in the Order which the Admiral has prescribed unto them' were firmly crossed out, but left decipherable, doubtless so that everyone would be aware of what had disappeared from current tactical doctrine. The Article, with an addition which has been italicized by the present writer, now read: 'As soon as the Admiral shall hoist a Red Flag on the Flag Staff at the Fore Topmasthead, and fire a gun, every ship in the fleet is to use their utmost endeavour to engage the enemy *as close as possible, and therefore on no account to fire until they shall be within pistol shot.*'

This put the situation beyond the possibility of doubt. If Hawke had encountered a French squadron bold enough to stand up to him, every captain in the British squadron would have pressed in towards his adversary, silently and inflexibly, until within point-blank range. He would then have fought it out *à outrance.* Hawke therefore brought into effect what may be regarded as the most essential feature of Nelson's tactical method about a year before the latter Admiral was born. The fact that Hawke has been consistently undervalued in the history of naval tactics is due, firstly, to the failure of any French admiral to stand up to him in an unambiguous fashion; secondly, to his own avoidance of any form of publicity.

Finally, something should be said here about the standard interpretation of naval tactics between 1700 and 1782. This interpretation stems mainly from Corbett's volume entitled *Fighting Instructions 1530-1816.* Corbett found so few instances of alterations made by admirals to the General Printed Fighting Instructions (which were just a section of the General Printed Sailing and Fighting Instructions, though this is not well brought out by Corbett) that he classed these alterations as trifling exceptions to the general rule. He thus formed his concept of 'The Permanent Instructions'. This has succeeded in standardizing the erroneous notion that fleet-commanders and their captains were absolutely shackled by the identical Printed Instructions sent out from the Admiralty between 1703 and 1783. Corbett was led into error simply by his not seeing enough copies of the Instructions in the form in which they reached the captains, after passing through the hands of their commanding admiral. Two collections at the National Maritime Museum, the Duff Papers and the Papers of Captain Michael Clements, contain sufficient instances of Instructions altered by admirals to make the concept of 'The Permanent Instructions' untenable. To summarize, the extent to which an admiral was enslaved by the Printed Instructions issued to him depended on the calibre of that admiral. The first admiral to transform an Article of fundamental importance was Hawke. Two years later, Boscawen followed suit.

It is therefore of special interest that, on 20 October, Boscawen was with Hawke as his second-in-command. It is inconceivable that Hawke would, when a Lord of the Admiralty was serving with him, have drastically altered the vital Article XIII, if such a move was likely to be regarded as insubordinate or heretical. On the contrary, Boscawen appears to have taken the alteration very much to heart and enjoined something very similar on his Mediterranean fleet of 1759, when he issued an Additional Instruction. This read: 'XVIII. Notwithstanding the general printed Fighting Instructions, if at any time, when engaged with an equal number of the enemy's ships, and the ship opposed to any of His Majesty's ships is forced out of the line, you are hereby required and directed to pursue her, and endeavour to take and destroy her.'

Hawke's alteration of Article XIII of the General Fighting Instructions is neater than Boscawen's Additional Instruction, in so far as the latter's reference to 'an equal number of the enemy's ships' could have led to difficulty. On the other hand, any captain worried about the limitations imposed by General Article XXI might have found Boscawen's Instruction more helpful. In any case, it is clear that the two greatest fighting admirals of the day were agreed on the sort of aggressive twist which needed to be given to the General Printed Fighting Instructions, if the possibility of paralysis was to be avoided.[253]

On 22 October Hawke and his squadron of ten of the line cleared the Isle of Wight and the next day they were off Plymouth Sound. The Admiral's old friend Henry Harrison was in command there with the rank of Vice-Admiral, and he had one ship of the line and four other sail ready to join Hawke. The latter left orders for other ships, still refitting at the port, to come out to his rendezvous as soon as possible.

Over the next month the weather in the Bay was extremely rough. Hawke received reinforcements which brought news of seven or eight French warships having slipped down from Brest to Basque Road. 'If the weather had been in the least encouraging', he wrote to Clevland on 16 November, 'I had a strong inclination to have followed them. But it has been so very stormy since, that it is as much as we can do to take care of ourselves, lying to under a mainsail and mizen.' In any case, the enemy ships must either have sailed from Basque Road or else been laid up at Rochefort for the winter by the time that he had received the news on 9 November. He was expecting the frigates *Unicorn* and *Hussar* to join him at any moment. As soon as they did so he would shift his rendezvous from latitude

---

[253] N.M.M., Duff Papers; Papers of Capt. Michael Clements. N.R.S., *Fighting Instructions*, pp. 190 n, 195-7, 224. cf. Marcus, p. 31. See p. 58 n. 12.

46° N. to 48° 30, '100 leagues to the westward of Cape Finisterre, in order to look for the Louisbourg squadron'. It had not been feasible to write earlier because, for a whole week, it had been impossible to send a boat to the sloop which would carry the letter.[254]

Once again Hawke was foiled in his sustained efforts to achieve interception. Tempestuous weather from the S.W. swept the squadron to the northward of its station. Between 17 and 23 November, which proved to have been the critical period, signals of distress were both commonplace and superfluous — to keep one's own ship afloat was the limit of the practicable. Between those dates five vessels of various sizes were lost to view, and, for the time being, Hawke heard no more of them. He was informed that Douglas's *Alcide* and Rodney's *Dublin* were damaged, so he sent them into port. By 1 December, the *Burford* (70) had disappeared. On the 6th, because of sickness on board, Hawke decided to send in the *Prince of Orange* (60). But still, with his usual determination, he clung to his station. At last he wrote, 'the weather was so bad and the squadron so much diminished that I thought it most advisable to come into port, leaving the *Medway* and *Southampton* to cruise on my rendezvous'.

Strained and battered, the *Ramillies*, *Royal George*, *Namur*, *Barfleur*, *Princess Amelia*, and *Neptune* came into Spithead on 14 December.[255]

It turned out that the elderly but elusive Dubois de la Motte had reached Brest on 23 November. But it was probably just as well for Hawke that he did not capture the enemy on this occasion. Before la Motte had left Louisbourg typhus was rife in that stronghold, and at the date when Hawke was driven off

[254] O.L., 16 Nov. 1757.
[255] O.L., 14 Dec. 1757.

station by storms the French admiral had 1,000 gravely ill men aboard his ships. So virulent was the fever that, soon after the squadron's arrival at Brest, an epidemic spread throughout Brittany and thousands of people died. A French surgeon wrote of conditions at Brest: 'The stench was intolerable. No person could enter the hospitals without being immediately seized with headaches; and every kind of indisposition quickly turned to fatal fever, as in the old days of the plague.'

After disembarking, Hawke went straight up to London on leave. He found that the court of inquiry had focussed attention on two features of the Rochefort expedition, namely the failure to take Fort Fouras and the decisions of the council of war of 25 September. Mordaunt's court martial had been ordered. Proceedings had begun on 14 December and Hawke was able to attend on the 20th, the final day. Meanwhile, the Admiral must have gathered that he was still out of favour with Pitt. The Secretary of State's pronouncements on Rochefort, as well as the unsuccessful attempt to take Louisbourg, are mentioned in a letter of 16 December, written by the army agent John Calcraft to Lord Loudon (who commanded the army in the Louisbourg expedition). 'The army was voted yesterday and a short debate upon it was brought on by Mr. Beckford, in which Mr. Pitt made a very long speech and abused both land and sea officers exceedingly.'[256]

At Mordaunt's court martial, Hawke confirmed that support by naval guns of an assault on Fort Fouras had proved impracticable. After the *Barfleur* had gone aground four miles or more from the Fort, Thierry had proved unable to carry a bomb ketch within random shot of the target. In general, Thierry had shown that he had a good knowledge of the Road,

[256] Lacour-Gayet, p. 360. Lloyd and Coulter, p. 115. *Report*, op. cit., p. 61. I.L., 16 Dec. 1757. Add.MSS. 17493, f. 127

but his ignorance of the shore, which had been rather obvious from the start, had been fully confirmed in the event.

Hawke said that he had never thought it necessary, from the point of view of taking Rochefort, to attack either Aix or Fouras, and that it was only to comply with the wishes of the generals that he had been involved in such projects. Fort Fouras did not command the beach at Chatelaillon, which had been recommended by Brodrick's survey-party as a suitable place for landing. Hawke's information was that there was a good road from Chatelaillon to Rochefort.

On 28 September he had sent the transports as close in to the shore as possible, and that night he had departed from custom by handing out his orders personally to the Agent of Transports and other officers concerned, thus bringing home the need for efficiency and dispatch.

After hearing Hawke's evidence, the court had to decide whether Mordaunt had failed in his duty. Its judgement was that the General did not appear to be guilty of any specific charge. The King was furious. For several days he kept the court's report and privately he inveighed against its signatories, placing them on a level with Mordaunt himself. With bitter reluctance, he at length complied with his obligations as a constitutional ruler and announced his approval of Mordaunt's acquittal.[257]

---

[257] *The Proceedings of a General Court Martial of Sir John Mordaunt*, 1758, pp. 109-13. H.'s notes — see n. 28 above. W. S. Lewis, Vol. 21, pp. 164-5.

CHAPTER 12: THE BASQUE ROADS AND A RASH STEP

FOR Britain, 1757 had been a year of despondency but the first months of 1758 brought a revival of hope. Though still smarting from recent disappointments, Pitt was at least firmly in control, and his confident leadership together with better news from the Continent made it possible for the nation to believe in ultimate victory. Frederick of Prussia, seemingly on the brink of irretrievable disaster, had roused the world with his victories at Rossbach and Leuthen; and on the Hanoverian front the position had also improved now that one of Frederick's generals, Ferdinand of Brunswick, was in command. France could no longer see a prospect of early success in Germany. Believing that the Rochefort expedition foreshadowed further attacks on her own coast, and hoping desperately to sustain her position in North America, she had made an effort to free herself from her unaccustomed alliance with Austria. But the Austrians succeeded in keeping the bond intact. Subsequently the Duc de Choiseul wrote to his King: 'This new alliance brought with it neglect of the war at sea and in America, which was the real war. All the powers in the state cast themselves enthusiastically and without reflexion into a land war, of which the underlying object was to exalt the House of Austria.'[258]

Meanwhile, Pitt had no doubt as to his first major objective for 1758. This was the capture of Louisbourg, the fortified port commanding the entrance to the St. Lawrence. Even after

[258] Corbett, i, Ch. 10. W. S. Lewis, Vol. 21, p. 181. Calmettes, p. 383.

Dubois de la Motte's success in carrying reinforcements to the stronghold, the garrison numbered no more than 3,000. Provided that the blockade of France could be tightened and no further reliefs reached Louisbourg, it would be comparatively simple to mass overwhelming strength against the port. On 19 February a powerful fleet of twenty of the line sailed from Spithead under Boscawen. With them went Jeffrey Amherst, the military commander of the expedition. By May a force of 12,000 troops had been assembled at Halifax. Meanwhile, it had sufficed merely to prepare Boscawen's fleet for the sea and alarm spread along the coasts of France. The Rochefort venture, despite its 'failure', was proving a sound investment.[259]

Information had reached the Admiralty that convoys for the relief of Louisbourg or Canada were being prepared at Brest, Rochefort, and Bordeaux, so Hawke was again required to hurry to Portsmouth and get together a squadron for the Bay of Biscay.

In January the Admiral's health had been poor, and an incident involving a new appointment for James Hobbs did little to improve matters. Hobbs had apparently asked for a spell in a ship other than a flagship, so Hawke, not being well enough to go to the Admiralty, wrote requesting Clevland to remind Anson about an exchange of appointments between Hobbs and Witteronge Taylor of the *Royal William*. Hawke, perhaps privately prompted by Hobbs, was concerned 'lest the *Royal William* should be under sailing orders' and that the opportunity for the exchange might be missed. The *Royal William* was of 84 guns and would certainly have been an attractive prospect for Hobbs. But their Lordships, while sending Taylor to his ill-fated post in the *Ramillies*, placed

[259] Lacour-Gayet, p. 361. Corbett, i, 254, 320.

James Hobbs in the *Eagle* (60) and do not seem to have favoured Hawke with any comment on this move. The Admiral can hardly have felt very flattered by the transaction. His protégé sailed off in the old 60-gunner to the limbo of the West Indies, while one Captain Thomas Evans in the *Royal William* shared in the glories of the capture of Louisbourg.

On 26 February a presumably disgruntled Hobbs went ashore from the *Ramillies*, leaving Taylor in command. Hawke came aboard on the 28th.

Although under the stress of another hurried departure, Hawke was, as usual, prepared to devote time to a case of avoidable hardship. A seaman called James Graham had been sent from the *Devonshire* to the *Blenheim* hospital ship. From thence he was put aboard the *Royal Ann* to be discharged as unfit for further service. He was given no pay in respect of his time aboard the *Devonshire*, not even a pay ticket. 'The poor man can have nothing to subsist him on his way home', wrote Hawke. 'Numbers have been and many still are in the same situation, whose cases I hope their Lordships will take into consideration.' Nor was he content to leave it at that. He quickly sent off a second letter to the Admiralty, saying: 'The case of Graham, as well as that of many others before, being discharged without ticket or wages, besides their being reduced to beg through all parts of the kingdom, which deters men from entering the service, has induced me seriously to consider of a remedy.'

His suggestions as to the necessary clerical machinery stimulated the Admiralty to issue some new instructions, improving the situation.[260]

---

[260] Ad. 1/89, 'Friday evening' (late Jan.), 3, 5 March 1758; 2/1331, 5 March. I.L., 6 Mar. 1758. Charnock, vi, 169.

When Hawke's Secret Instructions of 5 March reached him, he found that he had been given the command in 'the Channel, Soundings or wherever the services shall require'. This implied that he was, in fact, Commander-in-Chief of the Channel Fleet — the greatest seagoing appointment ever previously bestowed in that century, which had been in abeyance since the Austrian Succession War. But no Commander-in-Chief's commission had been sent with the orders. Hawke therefore wrote privately to Anson, asking him to rectify the position. Without a commission, he would shoulder great responsibilities without a claim to much of the prize-money gained by ships in his area, because most captures would probably be made by cruisers rather than the ships of his own battle-squadron. Only a properly worded commission would avoid confusion and dispute. 'I shall not have it unless your Lordship will be so good as to order it to be done in time for me, and to see that it is right… As a Flag Officer, I have only myself to plead my cause to your Lordship.'

Considering that all officers regarded prize-money as the most attractive part of their normal remuneration, this was a fair plea. But towards the end of the letter comes a point of special interest. This is one of Hawke's exceedingly rare, brief expressions of bitterness at the too-frequent exploitation of his patriotism and capability on the one hand and, on the other, disregard for him personally as a man of no political consequence. 'I am convinced it is the intentions of many of the captains to dispute everything with the commanding officer, as this will always be the case with a person like myself, who has it not in his power to do them favours.'[261]

Hawke obviously believed that Anson would get him the commission if he could. He can not have felt that the First

---

[261] H.P.P., 'Hawke MSS., 1702-1800', f. 84-6.

Lord harboured any serious reservations with regard to his conduct at Rochefort. But, for whatever reason, no commission was forthcoming on this occasion. This slight came on top of the contemptuous treatment of Hobbs; and, in view of the Admiral's explosion of temper the following May, it is likely that, during March and April, he was becoming increasingly oppressed with a sense of grievance.

Meanwhile, headlong effort had produced six ships of the line ready for the sea: *Ramillies* (90), *Torbay* (74), *Union* (90), *Newark* (80), *Alcide* (64), and *Intrepid* (60). By 6 a.m. on 12 March, Hawke was writing to report that he was under way. He had hoped to take some frigates and sloops with him, but none at all were available, so he left orders for some of them, as well as six more ships of the line, to join him in the Bay as soon as possible. On the 13th he was off Plymouth Sound and made the signal for ships to emerge and join him. None came. This pleased him not at all, because as early as the 3rd he had sent urgent orders to Henry Harrison to get ready as many ships as possible. He was particularly disconcerted by the complete lack of frigates. Therefore, he sent a somewhat abrupt letter to his old friend. 'I am extremely surprised to find neither the *Medway*, *Windsor*, nor a single frigate are ready to join me. Herewith I send you orders for them to follow me, which I beg you will distribute and hasten them away with the utmost dispatch, for much depends on it.'

The explanation of Harrison's lack of activity may have been failing health. Having served his country with outstanding merit and devotion for upwards of 62 years, he died on 13 March 1759, having attained the rank of Vice-Admiral of the Red.[262]

[262] O.L., 7, 12, 13 Mar. 1758. Charnock, v, 31. 'Commissioned Officers of the R.N.' See p. 139 n. 57.

With his ill-composed squadron, Hawke cruised down the wintry Bay; but on 19 March, no frigates having appeared, he detached the *Alcide* to skirt the coast between Belle Isle and Groix. If she found no enemy shipping there she was to look into Basque Road and rejoin the squadron at a rendezvous. But before she had time to complete her reconnaissance Hawke gave chase to some ships sighted to the westward. After giving up this attempt he accepted the probability that the *Alcide* would miss him, and decided to trust intelligence indicating that a convoy was being prepared in the Basque Road. As, for the second time in six months, he headed in towards Rochefort, he was at last joined by a frigate, the *Coventry* (28), and he sent her ahead to investigate. She was frustrated by 'flattering winds'. However, on 1 April a substantial reinforcement found the squadron.

The *Chichester* (70), the *Medway* (60), the *Vestal* (32), under the command of the 34-year-old Samuel Hood (of whom Hawke formed a good opinion, amply justified by the Admiral Hood of two future wars), the *Hussar* (28), captained by the gallant Robert Carkett (later celebrated for misunderstanding and spoiling Rodney's plan at the Battle of Martinique), and the *Actaeon* (28) brought the strength of the squadron up to seven of the line and three frigates. On the night of 3 April they brought to near the Isle of Rhé, with the wind at N.E., and prepared for action.

Early on the 4th a large convoy could be discerned a few leagues to windward and Hawke hoisted the signal for the chase. The British ships did their utmost to beat up against the wind, but they could not prevent the enemy from getting into St. Martin on the north coast of Rhé.

At noon Hawke decided to bear away for the Basque Road 'in a line ahead, at two cables' length asunder, with a moderate gale at N.N.W.'. With the ships settling into their positions about two hundred yards apart, and carrying a crowd of sail — as did the frigates on their flank — the line of battle sped before the wind to the S.E. Meanwhile, an assembly of French vessels lay near the Isle of Aix, unsuspectingly preparing to sail to the relief of Louisbourg. The methodical business of loading and arming was soon transformed into general excitement and confusion as Keppel's *Torbay*, at the head of Hawke's line, swept into view. The French had five ships of the line, one being of 74, three of 64, and one of 60 guns; two frigates; and about forty merchantmen. There was no question of fighting it out. Surprise was complete. Amid a frenzy of shouting and cutting of cables, the shallow-draught merchantmen sought safety on the mud-banks round the Isle Madame in the entrance to the Charente. The warships, using the main channel, tried to get up to Rochefort; but evening found them stranded by the ebb-tide near Fort Fouras. The French Commodore waited till last and Hawke's ships made for him, but he managed to escape beyond gunshot.

Owing to the energy and initiative of Langeron, the general in command at Rochefort, the French merchant crews worked feverishly through the night to lighten their vessels for the next flood tide. At dawn, Hawke, spy-glass in hand, made an appraisal of the situation.

Most of the enemy were still aground about five miles away. Many of them, including some of the warships, were heeling right over on their broadsides and Hawke yearned for fireships and bomb vessels.

At last the tide began to make. As soon as the flood attained some proportions, Hawke sent in the *Medway* and *Intrepid*, his two smallest ships of the line, with the best pilots. Meantime his attention was taken up by a swarm of small boats which had emerged from Charente and were soon engaged in the heroic task of warping the French ships forward over the mud. From the *Ramillies*' quarter-deck, Hawke and Taylor watched guns, stores, and ballast being shoved overboard by the enemy. Gushes of water appeared from portholes as the bilges were pumped or baled out. One by one, the enemy vessels were painfully hauled up the *Charente*; but by the time of the ebb the *Florissante* (74) was still only level with Fouras, and several merchantmen were still on the mud round the Isle Madame. It did not escape notice that the French were laying buoys to mark where guns, stores, and anchors had been dropped into the shallows, and boats from Hawke's frigates were soon pulling in the appropriate direction. Eighty or more buoys were cut adrift. However, as the tide fell the British ships were forced to retreat into the Road; and thus the operation known as 'the Basque Roads' came to an end.

That morning (5 April), the Admiral had sent a party of marines to destroy the renascent fortifications on Aix; and the Road was restored to its defenceless state of the previous autumn.

Hawke was, of course, disappointed that no enemy vessels had been actually taken or sunk, but the strategic effect of his incursion was sufficiently great. It was now out of the question for the important convoy, with its 3,000 troops, to reach North America that year. Amherst would be able to conduct his operations against an enemy of known (and inadequate) strength. The fate of Louisbourg had been sealed on the coast of France.

These consequences were more clearly appreciated by Hawke as, on the 7th, he withdrew his squadron from the Basque Road. He learnt from a neutral vessel that the convoy at St. Martin, together with fifteen other merchantmen still at

Bordeaux, was intended to take stores or provisions to America or the West Indies, and that the dismantled warships which had just scrambled up to Rochefort had been designated as escort to the whole array. Hawke therefore reported to the Admiralty: 'As they may not have other King's ships ready, and the present circumstances of their settlements may oblige them to sail without convoy, I have left out the *Torbay*, *Medway*, *Coventry*, *Vestal*, *Hussar*, and *Actaeon* to cruise upon them, which I hope their Lordships will approve of.'

The result was that Keppel did indeed intercept and capture several of the vessels from Bordeaux. The French received the impression that Hawke himself, with his whole squadron, was continuing to sweep the Bay from Ushant to Cape Ortegal.[263]

Hawke reached Portsmouth on 20 April. Immediately he had to set on foot refitting and provisioning for the next cruise. On the 23rd he issued an order which serves as a reminder of an ever-recurrent difficulty. The Captain of the *Royal Sovereign was* to get his ship into the inner harbour. 'You are... to clean, fit and grave for Channel Service, taking the utmost care your men do not desert.'[264]

On the following day the Admiral issued orders which are interesting for quite a different reason. They foreshadowed the method adopted the next year in his great blockade of Brest. Captain Pratten of the *Intrepid* was to cruise with seven of the line, two frigates, two cutters, and a fireship in the offing of l'Orient, la Rochelle, St. Martin, Rochefort, and Bordeaux. 'You are... to curb and annoy the enemy..., keeping the frigates and cutters close in with these ports, that you may have

---

[263] Ad. 1/89, 11, 26 Apr. 1758. Admiral's Journal, Ramillies, with H.'s official L.B. Lacour-Gayet, pp. 310-11. Keppel, i, 265.

[264] Ad. 2/80, 19, 21 Apr. 1758, O.L., 20 Apr. 1758. L.B., 22 Apr. 1758. O.B., 23 Apr. 1758.

constant intelligence of the motions and proceedings of the enemy.'

In the background, Pitt was busy with plans for diversionary raids on the French coast. Frederick of Prussia was assured that a powerful blow would be struck. It was agreed between Pitt, the members of the Cabinet's Secret Committee, and the Generals Marlborough and Sackville, that the landing should take place within a short distance of the English coast. The generals suggested that St. Malo should be taken; it could then be held for some weeks, being a port and in a defensible situation.

But Hawke, despite the wide terms of reference of his Channel command, was given no information about what was intended. Instead, he merely received intimations, which could only have struck him as mysterious, that something was in the wind. He received an Admiralty directive, dated 27 April, that all those ships of the Western Squadron cruising in the Bay of Biscay were to be back at Spithead by 15 May. On the 28th he was directed to facilitate the movement of sixteen battalions of infantry to the Isle of Wight. However, seeing that his friend Francis Holburne had for some months been installed as Admiral in command of the port, Hawke saw no reason against his asking, on 30 April, for three or four days' leave to deal with private affairs. This request was rejected on the ground that 'not only the ships at Spithead, but those cruising' came under his command. Remembering that he had been virtually refused his commander-in-chief's commission, and that he had equally been kept ignorant of the real reason for his retention at Portsmouth, it is difficult to imagine a more unfortunate reply to a man already aggrieved by his exclusion from the Board, by Pitt's groundless censure of his conduct at Rochefort, and by the Admiralty's scant regard for his modest requests for officers' appointments. If Hawke was becoming unduly sensitive to the possibility of further affronts it is not altogether surprising.[265]

The equipping of the fleet continued; so did the inevitable struggle against the desertion of ratings. In order to deter those planning to flee, massive floggings were customary for men unfortunate enough to be recaptured. Once the offender had been condemned by court martial and the Admiralty had approved the sentence, the Admiral on the spot would have to arrange for the punishment to be carried out. Thus, it fell to Hawke to issue the orders which, on 2 May, resulted in one Daniel O'Brien receiving 200 lashes for desertion.

Today, a recipient of such a punishment would hardly be expected to survive. He would be regarded as sentenced to death by torture. The instrument of infliction was a cat-o'-nine-tails, swung by a man of ample muscular development, and the average sailor's hatred of the Service is well illustrated by the common willingness to risk so terrifying a retribution. Indeed, it was sufficient for England to go to war for the normally empty wastes of Dartmoor to become alive with deserters. But Daniel O'Brien had been caught and had to face the penalty.

At 7 a.m. on 2 May, the *Neptune* (flying Hawke's flag while the *Ramillies* underwent repairs) hoisted a signal; and, after the assembled ship's company had been harangued as to the inadvisability of desertion, its members watched O'Brien, spreadeagled in a boat alongside and bound to its thwarts, enduring twenty-five lashes on his bare back. Seven other ships of the line awaited the boat's arrival. Each of their companies witnessed the administration of twenty-five strokes to the increasingly lacerated, sanguinary back. The captain's clerk

---

[265] O.B., 24 Apr. 1758. L.B., 27, 28 Apr. 1758. Tunstall, p. 207. Corbett, i, 265, 271. I.L. 1 May 1758.

aboard the *Newark* did not even pay the victim the compliment of getting his name right — he recorded it as 'George Wallace'; while aboard the *Royal Ann* and *Portland* so commonplace a spectacle was deemed unworthy of remark. But Daniel O'Brien, like most other recipients of such floggings, appears to have lived to strike another blow for the honour of King George II.[266]

In view of Hawke's amply proven humanity it must always have distressed him to have to order these punishments. He doubtless perceived that poor pay and conditions on board, combined with impressment, were the root of the trouble, but he never attempted to bring about a change in the manning system, as did Admiral Vernon and his own friend of later years, Robert Tomlinson. With his grasp of practical possibility, he doubtless saw that the only proper solution, a voluntary system of recruitment and the abolition of impressment, was beyond the country's economic capability. He was interested in administrative improvements, especially where they would diminish human suffering, but preferred to direct his energies to cases where there was some likelihood of success — for example, the plight of sick men discharged from the Navy without pay to which they were entitled.

Meanwhile, events were taking shape which would lead Hawke to make a decision bitterly to be regretted. Pitt had adopted the plan for attacking St. Malo and was discussing with Anson the question of the naval command and organization. Anson suggested that Howe might be made commodore of the transports and their close escort, while the covering battlefleet remained under Hawke. By the 8th, Howe's commission had been written. Meanwhile, Hawke had

---

[266] O.B., 1 May 1758. Ad. 51/632; 51/633; 51/3985; 51/77; 51/3895; 51/810; 51/3941.

been asked for a draught of the Basque Road, and on the 7th he sent to the Admiralty a return of soundings while an officer was compiling a draught from a variety of evidence. The Admiral concluded — fatally, from his own point of view — that the new expedition was going to Rochefort, which, ironically enough, had been seriously considered as a possible objective.

Towards 4 p.m. on 10 May, Howe suddenly appeared and confronted Hawke with his orders, showing that he was to command the naval side of the new expedition. Hawke was simply enjoined to afford him every assistance. The Admiral, believing that the destination was Rochefort, was severely shaken by what appeared to be an announcement of the Admiralty's lack of confidence in his ability to conduct a landing at that place, which he now knew so well. Then anger took possession of him. Pitt has sometimes been blamed for insisting that Howe should take up his appointment with undue haste. But surely it was Anson's responsibility to see that Hawke was given some kind of warning of what was about to happen.[267]

After three hours of tortured reflection Hawke determined to make a decisive gesture. At 7 p.m. he took up the pen and, in the following terms, placed his professional career in the hands of the Lords Commissioners of the Admiralty:

> About 4 o'clock arrived here Captain Howe, and delivered me their Lordships' order of the 9th. In last September I was sent out to command an expedition under all the disadvantages one could possibly labour under, arising chiefly from my being under the influence of land-officers in Councils of War at sea. Last cruise, I went out on a particular service almost

[267] Tunstall, p. 208. Corbett, i, 267-8. O.L., 7, 10 May 1758. Ad. 1/4122, 9 May 1758.

> without the least means of performing it. Now, every means to success is assured; another is to reap the credit; while it is probable I, with the capital ships, might be ordered to cruise in such a manner as to prevent his failing in this attempt. To fit out his ships for this service I have been kept here, and even now have their Lordships' directions, at least in terms, to obey him. He is to judge of what he wants for his expedition; he is to make his demands, and I am to comply with them. I have therefore directed my flag immediately to be struck, and left their Lordships' orders with Vice-Admiral Holburne. For no consequence that can attend my striking it without orders shall ever outbalance with me wearing it one moment with discredit.

The case was nobly stated; but it was based on incomplete knowledge of the facts. In Hawke's view it was the selection of Rochefort as the scene of Howe's landing that was intolerable.

However, even at the moment of making his impetuous and potentially disastrous gesture, Hawke wrote a brief letter to Howe which, in its restraint and attention to the public good, provided a fitting memorial to the qualities of its author — for are not self-control in the face of provocation, refusal to succumb to personal spite, and a continuing care for operations implying an aspersion on his professional reputation, fair indications of greatness in his character? 'Enclosed I send the orders from the Lords Commissioners of the Admiralty that you may distribute them to such as are here as soon as possible, and to [the] rest as they arrive, that no time may be lost in the execution of their orders to you. And as I have ordered my Flag to be struck immediately, you will apply to the Senior Officer for any assistance you want.'[268]

---

[268] Ad. 1/89, 10 May 1758. O.L., 10 May 1758.

But the Admiral's experience of true misery was yet to come. On going up to London, he was told — presumably by Anson — that the expedition was not going to Rochefort. That Hawke's tense indignation ebbed away into a deathly chill of his whole being, may readily be imagined. For a man so sensitive and high-principled, the humiliation could not have been more profound. He had sacrificed his reputation, poisoned the morale of the fleet and withheld his own much-needed abilities in the name of his personal honour, when that honour had not been affronted in the manner which he had supposed.

Within the Board Room at the Admiralty the excitement and perturbation were considerable; but the affair was kept secret and not a whisper of it reached the public. Even the miraculously receptive ears of Horace Walpole were denied a hint of it.

On 12 May, Hawke, in the lowest of spirits, attended at the Admiralty. His career might well have ended in dishonour that day. The proceedings are adequately described in the Board's minutes.

> Sir Edward Hawke attending was called in and told that the Board looked upon his proceeding in striking his Flag (of which he had informed them by his letter received yesterday) to be a very extraordinary step, and desired to hear what he had to say in excuse of it.
>
> Sir Edward said he thought Captain Howe to be intended to proceed with the troops and conduct an expedition to the place where he had lately been; and that it appeared so to him from a draught being desired, two days before, of the parts about Rochefort; that if it was so, he thought he must have been misrepresented to the King and therefore that his honour required his doing as he had done; but he since, upon reflection, finds himself mistaken, and that he proceeded too

much in a hurry, and acknowledges he has done an irregular thing; but he did not do it with any view of disregard or disrespect to the Board, but merely from thinking it would appear a slur upon him to the World, and that they would say that he, a Flag Officer, though he had been twice to those parts, was not thought fit to be entrusted with 16,000 of the King's troops, or to carry on a service of consequence, and he thought he had better not serve at all, if he could not serve with honour.

The above minute being read to Sir Edward, he acknowledged the same to be the purport of what he had said, and then withdrew.

The Lords then proceeded to take the said letter and minute into consideration, and came to the following resolution:

'That Sir Edward Hawke's striking his flag without order is a high breach of discipline; therefore notwithstanding the acknowledgement contained in the said minute, the Lords do not think proper to restore him to the command of the ships in the Channel, although in consideration of his past services, they have not proceeded to any further censure.' Whereupon, as the most proper measure upon this occasion, the Lords have ordered Lord Anson to take upon himself that command.[269]

Anson, at 61 years of age, was far from jubilant at having to take up this command. Only the King, amongst the few who knew what had occurred, was inclined to sympathize with Hawke. 'As I am convinced', wrote Anson to Hardwicke, 'this step of Sir Edward Hawke has spread a very improper spirit of discontent in the fleet at Spithead, which in its effects could be very prejudicial to the public service, I could not avoid offering my service, which the King has accepted, though not very willingly agreeing to the necessity of it.' Hardwicke

[269] Ad. 3/66. 12 May 1758. See also n. 13 below.

commiserated with his son-in-law. 'I was struck with astonishment and concern at the unexpected rash step taken by Sir Edward Hawke; with the former, from the opinion which I had entertained of his prudence; with the latter, from the danger of the public losing the benefit of his service, at least for some time.' Moreover, it meant unwelcome disturbance for Anson personally. By 15 May Lady Anson was deploring 'the hurry and confusion of a departure so hurried and unexpected… Sir Edward Hawke, who is most sincerely concerned at what is past, has earnestly desired to serve under him.' Hardwicke commented to Newcastle: 'Surely this will be very right, and the only way to retrieve, as far as may be, the rash step he so strangely took.'

The impression that Anson was very upset by the whole affair and unlikely to forget it easily, is confirmed by a letter of the 20th in which Lord Royston wrote to Hardwicke (his father): 'I dined last Thursday at the Admiralty and took my leave of Lord Anson who expected then to be setting out… tomorrow… Lord A. did not appear to me so well as I could wish him, and his spirits in a flutter, but I hope this will go off when he gets down to Portsmouth.'[270]

Meanwhile, a profoundly dispirited Hawke had already returned to Portsmouth and rehoisted his flag aboard the *Ramillies* on 16 May. His dejection is signified by the minimal wording of his letters to the Admiralty and to Anson. After the latter's arrival on the 21st this correspondence naturally dried up, and nothing important came from Hawke's pen until 18 June when he reported to Anson that he was sick.

By then the fleet had been at sea for a fortnight, covering the somewhat abortive landing which took place near St. Malo. Shortly after sailing from Portsmouth Hawke had developed

---

[270] Add.MSS. 35352, f. 8; 35359, f. 393, 403, 405; 32880, f. 118.

one of his prostrating feverish colds — a rare event for him when at sea — and he had to ask Anson to let him go back to Spithead. Having disembarked on the 20th, he reported to the Admiralty that he was 'altogether incapable of duty'. 'I hope their Lordships will indulge me with leave to go into the country for the re-establishment of my health, which I would fain hope will not take up a great while.'[271]

Anson commented in a letter to Hardwicke: 'Sir Edward Hawke was certainly very ill when he left me, a good deal occasioned by the uneasiness of his mind from his own late conduct, which, with the assistance of Holburne and a very bad man, his Secretary, has done much mischief in the Fleet.' Anson and Augustus Hervey may have been completely antipathetic towards one another, but they were certainly at one in their assessment of John Hay![272]

Finally, before leaving the cruises of 1758, it is necessary to consider Corbett's opinion that Anson was disturbed to find that Hawke (and Boscawen) had neglected the tactical training of the fleet. There is, in fact, no substance in such an interpretation of what Anson wrote about this training. Anson had put to sea with as many as twenty-five ships of the line — a much larger squadron than any that had sailed under Hawke. Of these ships, eight had been with Hawke during the Basque Roads cruise and ten on the Rochefort expedition. Of the latter ten, four were at the Basque Roads; so only fourteen of Anson's twenty-five ships had been to sea with Hawke during the past eighteen months. If allowance is made for changes of captains and other personnel, Anson's remarks that he 'never saw such an awkwardness in going through the common

[271] O.L., 16, 18 May 1758. Corbett, i, 275 ff. Ad. 1/89, 20 June; 1/90, 13 June 1758. Add.MSS. 35359, f. 410.
[272] ibid., loc. cit. cf. 35376, f. 150; Erskine, pp. 217, 225, 253, 301.

manoeuvres necessary to make an attack upon an enemy's fleet', and that many captains 'declared they had never seen a line of battle', come as no surprise and can hardly have been directed against Hawke. If they had been, they would in any case have been quite inappropriate. On every cruise undertaken by him since 1755, Hawke had formed lines of battle, and, where circumstances warranted, had carried out all the usual evolutions. Corbett seems to have wondered how he could square Hawke's neglect of manoeuvres in 1757-8 with his zeal for them in 1756 — which Corbett himself had (without full investigation) already criticized as excessive! In the present writer's opinion, Anson intended no aspersion on Hawke or Boscawen.[273]

[273] Add.MSS. 35759, f. 410, 413. Corbett, i, 131, 274-5. Ad. 8/32; 51/834; 51/3950; cf. 51/633. Admiral's Journal, Ramillies — see n. 6 above. Erskine, pp. 217, 219. Fighting Instructions: a Postscript. Mr. Brian Tunstall has drawn my attention to the Barrington Papers, i, 231-2, which show that, on 30 August 1758, Anson issued an Additional Instruction like that given out by Boscawen in 1759. R.F.M.

CHAPTER 13: THE STORM-TOSSED SHIPS

BY the beginning of 1759 the war was conforming with Pitt's intentions. Louisbourg had been captured and, provided always that the stranglehold was maintained on the coasts of France, Quebec was likely to succumb. In France, merchants were already complaining 'of the entire destruction of their trade', as Captain Lendrick reported to the Admiralty in February.

Pitt, however, having received intelligence of vigorous naval preparations 'at Toulon, Brest, Rochefort, and other ports of France', realized that the French, in desperation, were resolved to strike at England itself, the nerve centre of the widespread maritime tentacles which were sucking the life-blood out of the French Empire. The Secretary of State therefore urged the Admiralty, in forceful terms, to look to the Fleet. 'All serviceable ships of the line are to be completed and got ready for the sea with the utmost expedition.'[274]

Hawke, though physically recovered, must have wondered whether he would ever be employed at sea again. Osborn had come home from the Mediterranean in bad health, but, in due course, Boscawen went to this station. Saunders was too junior to command the all-important Channel Squadron (i.e. Western Squadron); but, Boscawen having refused the chief naval post on the Quebec expedition, Saunders was given it. As far as the Channel Squadron was concerned, it was always possible that Anson would again take it out — and, in fact, he gave Hawke to understand that he probably would.

---

[274] P.R.O. 30/8/78, 11, 22 Feb. 1759.

However, on 9 May, Hawke was put in command of fourteen sail at Spithead and eleven at Plymouth. He was to proceed with the Spithead ships to Torbay as soon as possible and there await further orders.[275]

As his coach jolted once more down the road from London to Portsmouth, Hawke was uncertain of his responsibilities, and the hope of rehabilitating his reputation with Anson and the Admiralty was probably uppermost in his mind.

On boarding the *Ramillies* on 13 May, he found that several ships were ready, except for completion of complement. He therefore had 1,600 men transferred from frigates and sloops to the ships of the line.

On 14 May he issued to all his captains copies of the General Printed Sailing and Fighting Instructions. These contained the vitally important alteration to Article XIII of the Fighting Instructions by Day which he had promulgated in 1757. This ensured that any stand-up engagement with a French fleet would become a hard-fought mêlée. There was every reason to expect that such a fight would produce decisive results. It should also be remarked that Hawke issued his Instructions although he still thought it possible that Anson would assume the chief command. Therefore, it can hardly be doubted that the amended form of Article XIII had been approved at the Admiralty.

By the 17th Hawke was under way. Clevland minuted his dispatch: 'Let him know that I have communicated his letter to the Lords, who very much approve what he has done.' Hawke was grateful for this reassuring message and replied on the

[275] Erskine, p. 301. Whitworth, p. 287. L.B., 9 May 1759. Ad. 2/82, 9 May 1759. H.P.P., H. to Anson (draft) n.d., but written on 19 or 20 May 1759.

27th: 'It gives me the greatest pleasure to find that I have done my duty to their Lordships' satisfaction.'[276]

Meanwhile, on reaching Torbay on the 18th, Hawke found Sir Charles Hardy, Vice-Admiral of the Blue, awaiting him with six ships from Plymouth, including the *Monmouth*, now commanded by Augustus Hervey. 'We lay here fitting', the latter wrote in his *Journal*. 'Sir Edward Hawke, Sir Charles Hardy, Edgecumbe, Denis, Geary, and Storr dined on board of me, and Denis threw out as if Lord Anson would come and command, but the 20th cleared all that up by Sir Edward Hawke making the signal to unmoor, and soon after to weigh.'

It was not until that day that Hawke received the Lords' instructions. These marked the beginning of one of the most important campaigns in the history of the world.[277]

> Whereas we have received undoubted intelligence that the French are pressing their armaments at Brest, l'Orient, Rochefort, and the other ports on the coast of France; that, on the 7th instant, there were nine sail of ships of war in the Inner Road of Brest, five of them of the line that others were to proceed out of the Harbour, and that four of the line were expected there from l'Orient; that provisions and stores are collected to Brest from several parts of the Bay; and it's given out that the enemy propose to attempt an invasion, either upon Great Britain or Ireland: And whereas it is of the greatest consequence to prevent any such design of the enemy taking effect, you are hereby required and directed, so soon as you shall be joined by Sir Charles Hardy with the ships from Plymouth, to proceed with the Squadron under your command off Ushant, and cause as accurate an observation as possible to be immediately made of the enemy's force in Brest

---

[276] O.L., 13 May 1759. P.R.O. 30/8/78, 11 May 1759. N.M.M.: Duff Papers. Ad. 1/92, 14, 17, 27 May 1759. I.L., 21 May 1759.

[277] Erskine, p. 301. Ad. 1/92, 20 May 1759.

Road, and forthwith send us an account thereof; and you are to continue cruising with the Squadron near Ushant or Brest (taking all possible care not to be drove to the westward) and to use your utmost endeavours to defeat any designs the enemy may have conceived of invading these Kingdoms, and to protect the trade of His Majesty's subjects, and also to annoy and distress the enemy by every means in your power.

And you are to return with the Squadron to Torbay, so as to be there by the expiration of fourteen days from the time of your sailing thence, unless the attempts or operations of the enemy against these Kingdoms should make it necessary, for the defence and security thereof, to prolong your cruise, or take any other station near the coast of Great Britain, in which case you are to send us an immediate account thereof; and on your return to Torbay, you are to cause the provisions and water of the ships to be forthwith completed, and to hold them in constant readiness for putting again to sea, taking care that none of the ships have ever less than two months' provisions on board.

And whereas the intercepting the convoys which convey provisions and stores to Brest and Rochefort must tend greatly to disconcert the enemy's measures, you are to appoint such of the smaller ships of the line and frigates as you shall think sufficient to cruise on the most likely stations for intercepting the convoys, ordering their commanders, in case they shall observe any number of ships of war and transports to sail from the French ports and proceed to the westward, and they shall be too weak to attack them, to send one of the frigates immediately to give you notice of it, either off Ushant or in Torbay, and another frigate to follow and observe their course till her commander shall be able to form a judgement whether they shall be bound to Ireland or not, and then to return and acquaint you therewith, that you may detach such force after them as you shall judge necessary, in case it shall appear to you, from their course and other circumstances, that they are intended for Ireland. And you are immediately to forward to us, by express, an account of any information you receive relating thereto, and of what you shall do thereupon.

How fierce a thrill of inspiration must Hawke have experienced on reading down the column of signatures on this document when, having noted the names of Anson, George Hay, and (Admiral) Forbes, his eye rested on that of Hans Stanley! That politician was usually too much occupied with other interests to put in an appearance at the Admiralty.[278]

As Hawke's fleet moved out of Torbay on the 20th, it must have presented a glorious spectacle. This was the most powerful battle-squadron in the world; twenty-five ships of the line, thirteen frigates (including some 50s), and two fireships spread their sails at the Admiral's command. On Hawke and his squadron depended the destiny of North America and India.

In charge of the van division was Sir Charles Hardy who had been second-in-command of the Navy at the taking of Louisbourg and now smarted with resentment at Saunders's nomination for the Quebec expedition. To command the rear, Hawke had selected Captain Geary and the latter's promotion to Rear-Admiral would soon follow. Only two Admirals had originally been appointed to this mighty squadron because of Anson's uncertainty about reassuming the chief command.

Captains who had served under Hawke previously in that war were Storr, Hervey, Digby, Denis, Keppel, Howe, Barrington, Byron, Edgecumbe, and Taylor of the *Ramillies.* Somewhat curiously, the *Royal George* (100), which was the largest ship in the squadron, had never been fitted as a flagship. After her in size and power came the *Ramillies* (90) and Hardy's

---

[278] L.B., 18 May 1759.

Union, also of 90 guns. There were seven 74s, four 70s, four 64s, and seven 60s in the line of battle.[279]

The winds proved light and, at times, faded away altogether. It was not until 24 May that the squadron was squarely in position off Brest. Hawke must have been cheered by a letter which he had received from Captain John Lockhart who had been cruising off Ushant in the *Chatham* (50). This was the officer whom Hawke had strongly but unsuccessfully recommended to the Board's favour after the Second Battle of Cape Finisterre. (Cornelius Smelt, who had been refused promotion at the same time, was made a Regulating Captain at Hull at the beginning of the war but does not seem ever to have gone back to sea after that.) Lockhart had achieved Post Rank at sea in 1756, and as Captain of the frigate *Tartar* (28) he had acquired a brilliant reputation. After being severely wounded in 1757 he had returned to the fray and capped a long list of successes by the splendid capture of the *Mélampe* (700 tons and 36 guns). He eventually succeeded to a baronetcy, taking the name of Lockhart Ross and rose to be a Vice-Admiral of the Blue.

In his letter of 21 May Lockhart reported to Hawke that there were four ships ready to sail from Port Louis (outside l'Orient) to Brest. As the French would probably try to avoid the blockading British by using the Passage du Raz, Lockhart suggested that an intercepting squadron in Audierne Bay might be appropriate. He was himself on his way back to Plymouth. '[I] hope soon to have the honour to be under your command', he ended, 'and, heartily wishing you success, I am' etc. In fact, he was shortly placed under the command of Rear-Admiral Rodney for operations against the flat-bottomed boats at le Havre; but he returned to Hawke's command in time to share

[279] Ad. 1/92, 20 May 1759. O.B., 20 May 1759. Erskine, p. 301.

that Admiral's greatest day. Lockhart enclosed with his letter intelligence which showed that 'there was great want of seamen in France. The Commissaries all along the coast have orders to send to Brest every person that has been to sea.' At the end of April there were seven of the line in Brest Road, 'ten more docked and all the Carpenters' work finished, and the Slaves employed rigging them with the utmost expedition'. There was also great activity at Dunkirk, Calais, and the other ports, where shallow-draught vessels were being built. 'It was reported that they intended to invade England so soon as their fleet at Brest was ready.'[280]

On first reaching his station Hawke sent three frigates to watch Port Louis, and ordered the frigate *Minerva*, commanded by the youthful Alexander Hood (later Admiral Lord Bridport) to look into Brest. 'They saw very distinctly eleven sail in the Road', Hawke told the Admiralty, 'all of which they judged to be large ships of war, with their colours hoisted, yards and topmasts up, and topgallant yards across.' At this stage Hawke guessed, quite incorrectly, that the real object of all these preparations was the relief of the French West Indies.

However, the Admiral was in any case anxious to prevent any concentration of French naval strength at Brest and, following Lockhart's advice, he detached the *Torbay*, *Magnanime*, *Fame*, *Monmouth*, and the frigate *Southampton* to cruise in Audierne Bay. The four ships of the line were commanded by an *elite* consisting of Keppel, Howe, Byron, and Hervey. At no time did Hawke manifest the slightest trace of resentment towards Howe, whose appointment of the previous year had been the occasion of the Admiral's humiliation. There was no room for malice in Hawke's nature.[281]

---

[280] Ad. 1/92, 27 May 1759. I.L., 6 May 1755 (for Capt. Smelt); 21 May 1759. Clowes, iii, 21511, 293, 567.

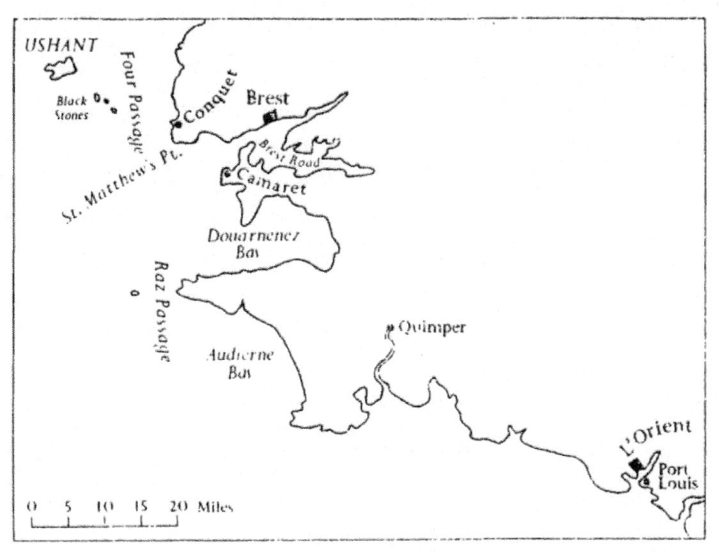

The coast near Brest.

Heading for Audierne Bay, Augustus Hervey was even more pleased with himself than usual, for he discovered that he could outsail Keppel, Howe, and Byron. Any of his achievements, whether professional or amatory, filled him with immense self-satisfaction; and if the testimony of his *Journal* is to be believed, his performance under the second head was very prodigious. 'About 6 o'clock in the morning' [of the 26th], wrote this versatile officer, 'we brought to in the Bay of Hodierne, between Penmark Point and that of Bee du Raz, which appeared a very fine country with many villages dispersed about it, but I thought this as good a bay for the fleet of Brest to come out to and join any force from Rochefort as where they lay.'[282]

[281] Ad. 1/92, 27 May 1759. I.L., 25 May 1759.
[282] Erskine, p. 302, etc.

By 27 May Hawke had begun to envisage a new method of applying sea-power — a close blockade. 'Upon the whole', he wrote, referring to the main French squadron, 'I do not think it prudent, as they may soon be joined by more from Brest harbour, to leave them at liberty to come out by returning to Torbay, till I shall receive further instructions from their Lordships, or the wind shall appear to be set in strong westerly.' He had already established a system whereby Robert Duff in the *Rochester* (50), together with Lockhart's prize, the *Mélampe* (36), commanded by William Hotham, closely observed the activity at Brest, while the *Prince Edward* cutter ran constantly to and from the *Ramillies*, carrying messages.

Meantime, in England the changing attitude towards the possibility of invasion was reflected in letters written by John Calcraft, the army agent. 'We talk much of the French invading Ireland, of which, though, I am an unbeliever.' 'The French threaten mightily to invade us, but with the fleet we have I don't fear them.' 'Our fright about invasion decreases.'

Hawke soon found that the four French ships reported as being at Port Louis had already reached Brest before his own squadron arrived. He therefore kept all his ships of the line off Brest and blockaded coastwise traffic by leaving the *Colchester* (50) and two frigates off Port Louis, while Duff with the *Rochester*, *Minerva*, and *Mélampe* sealed off the Passage du Raz.

At Brest the work of preparation went ahead.[283]

During the early days of June the British fleet's vigil was rudely harassed by 'very fresh winds with a great sea'. By the 5th, the S.W. wind was still increasing and thick fog descended. Seeing that the French could not move out into the teeth of this wind, Hawke bore away for Torbay to repair gale-damage, but he left the *Rochester*, *Mélampe*, *Minerva*, and *Prince Edward* to

[283] Ad. 1/92, 27 May, 4 June 1759. Add.MSS. 17494, f. 95, 97, 100.

watch for enemy ships which might slip quickly out of Brest on a change of wind. It had to be recognized that the French, if they were patient and fully prepared, could evade Hawke under such circumstances, but all would be far from lost if their subsequent movements were efficiently reported. Of course, it was possible for small ships to find shelter on the coast where big ones could not, and where they were few in number they could tack in fog and darkness without great likelihood of collision.

It is time to examine the strategy of the French. If their leaders had applied more logic to their invasion plan, they would not have committed the egregious error of assembling their army at one port and their fleet at another. Oblivious of the lesson provided by the failure of the Spanish Armada — which could have landed an army in England if one had been completely embarked in Spain — they set up the military camps not at Brest, but on the shores of Quiberon Bay. This Bay is situated about 100 miles S.E. of Brest. Thus was the army deliberately separated from its escorting fleet — an absurdity to be explained by fear of interservice quarrels. Had the army been ready to embark at Brest, the French needed only to wait for Hawke to be forced off station by a westerly gale. Then, by sailing at once on a change of the wind to E., they would have reached the Irish Sea before the British squadron began its pursuit.

Given sufficient realism in its execution, Marshal Belleisle's plan was a formidable one. Escorted by the Brest fleet, an army of 20,000 troops was to land near Glasgow; and, as Conflans was to prove by his escape from Brest, this might have been accomplished before Hawke could interfere. The French general, the Due d'Aiguillon, was to march on Edinburgh as quickly as possible. This alarming thrust was not, however, to be the main attack: it was to be a diversion which could not be ignored in England. A further distraction from the culminating operation was to be provided by the famous privateer Thurot, who was to break out from Dunkirk with 800 troops aboard five frigates and make for Northern Ireland. But it was a second army of 20,000, under the distinguished command of Chevert, which was to deliver the *coup de grâce.* Having disembarked d'Aiguillon's force, Conflans was to sail round Scotland into the North Sea, head for Ostend, and convey Chevert across to Maldon in Essex. The latter would then march swiftly over flat ground and take possession of the weakly defended capital.

However, the main attack was entirely contingent on the prior success of Conflans and d'Aiguillon. It therefore rested with Hawke to frustrate the enemy's grand design at the initial stage.

By 14 June Newcastle's intelligence service had placed full details of the French plan in his hands; and the Minister found little reassurance in the fact that at the time Hawke was still windbound in Torbay.[284]

The Admiral had hardly anticipated such a long delay. On 6 June, the day of his arrival in Torbay, he wrote: 'I shall sail again with any moderate wind, as, from the last accounts of the enemy, it appears to me of the greatest consequence that we should be on our station again before they can get a fair wind to bring them out.'

Seeing that the Admiralty had settled on Torbay as the squadron's watering and revictualling base, and that his appearance there was to be expected at any time, Hawke was

---

[284] Ad. 1/92, 6 June 1759. cf. Marcus, pp. 53-4. Corbett, ii, 17-19. Nicolas, pp. 229-30. Lacour-Gayet, pp. 319-22; 348-51. Add.MSS. 32892, f. 27.

displeased to find no supply vessels awaiting the squadron. An urgent message was dispatched to Mr. Cross, butcher of Exeter, who had contracted to supply the fleet, for 46,926 lbs. of fresh beef to be sent to Torbay 'with the utmost expedition'; and a horseman galloped across South Devon with instructions for Commissioner Rogers at Plymouth. Because the Admiral hoped to sail very soon, victuallers were to come round to Torbay at once. Beer was the first requirement. A supply of topmasts, if not immediately ready, was to go out to the fleet at its operational rendezvous.[285]

As Hawke was now evolving a strategy of close blockade, a moment's attention should be paid to the problems of supply which were bound to result from it. The development of this new strategy was a typically British proceeding, in that very little heed was paid to the details of supply until requirements actually arose. Burrows and other writers have warmed to the task of meting out castigation to the unfortunate supply services. Their argument runs somewhat as follows: if the gallant men of the battle-squadron went short of food or beer, this was an absolute disgrace and utterly inexcusable. But Hawke — praise be — struggled manfully to wake up those slack, irresponsible fellows in the victualling offices and by sheer willpower drove them to the performance of their duty.

While sluggishness in a government department is not unknown, it is not entirely reasonable to shower condemnation on supply services subjected to the unprecedented demands of a novel kind of operation. Hawke was, of course, correct to denounce any sign of slackness; but it should be recognized that the difficulty of continuously supplying a large squadron at sea was not imaginary. For example, the Navy, in June 1759, possessed no victuallers to carry out the supplies, and had to

---

[285] Ad. 1/92, 6 June 1759. O.L., 6 June 1759 (2).

hire vessels on the open market. Their owners could withdraw their services whenever they felt inclined. It was, after all, on Hawke's suggestion and not that of the supply services that the new situation, with its attendant problems, came into existence.[286]

Soon after the squadron anchored in Torbay, Hawke, engrossed in the business of revictualling, was advised that Prince Edward, a 20 year-old grandson of George II, was going to join the fleet. 'It is the King's pleasure', wrote Clevland, 'immediate preparation should be made for His Royal Highness's reception on board your ship.' The Prince appears to have been a singularly worthless young man, and Hawke might have been forgiven by posterity if he had exploded with wrath at the news. But his devotion to the Monarch was very real and he was content to respond: 'I shall be greatly honoured in having His Highness, Prince Edward, on board the *Ramillies*, and can only regret that I have not had an opportunity of being better provided for his reception than I am at present.'

By 11 June Hawke was at sea again and at 8 a.m. the next day he was writing to Clevland from a position near the Lizard. He had hoped by then to be nearer to Ushant than to Cornwall, but on the previous morning had been 'surprised by a violent storm', in which the *Hero* (74) had lost all her masts. He had detached the *Nottingham* to tow her into Plymouth. A cutter from the tenacious Duff, who had ridden out the storm, had come in with a report that eighteen two-deckers were visible at Brest and seemed ready to sail. Hawke therefore reaffirmed his intention — already approved by the Admiralty — to maintain a continuous blockade of Brest. 'I shall send from time to time to Plymouth for what may be wanting in the squadron and,

[286] Burrows, pp. 373-4, 376-7, 382. O.L., 8, 12 June 1759. I.L., 15 June 1759.

except I shall be drove off by winds and weather, keep them constantly in view, so as either to prevent their coming out, or doing my utmost, in case they should, to take or destroy them.'

However, the wind sprang up again in its full fury and the fleet had to run back to Torbay. After the *Ramillies* had rounded Start Point, Hawke perceived the mastless *Hero* which had broken away from the *Nottingham* before she made Plymouth and had then been borne up-Channel. He at once detached the *Montague* which succeeded in getting the *Hero* into Torbay.[287]

The Admiral did not fail to report the conduct during the storm of Mr. Snape Hammond, acting Lieutenant in command of the sloop *Albany*. 'He behaved remarkably well in the gale of wind by preserving the topmasts for the Squadron at the utmost risk, notwithstanding the remonstrances of the whole company for cutting them away. He prudently considered, when the *Hero*'s masts went, that she might want them. Lord Howe, who wants a Lieutenant in place of one who never appeared, would be very well pleased to have him in the *Magnanime*.'

Hamond's commission as 5th Lieutenant of the *Magnanime* was sent enclosed with Clevland's letter of 19 June — fee £1 1s. 6d.

Now Hervey may be permitted to resume his tale.

> I went Saturday morning the 16th to breakfast with Sir Edward, who expressed great concern at being drove in, and told me that he had destined me for a very honourable employment, for I should command his vanguard in at Brest water to watch the fleet's motions, and that on my diligence and skill much must depend, but he was pleased to say he did

---

[287] Ad. 1/92, 8, 12, 13 June 1759. I.L., 2, 7 June 1759. L.B., 1 June 1759.

> not doubt of success in my hands... The morning of the 19th the wind was moderate to the North West and we all sailed again to return off Brest. Sir Edward Hawke had lent me a book called *The Prince of Abissinia*, which I read at leisure hours, but could only find it was a very good moral simple tale.

The book, by Samuel Johnson, is better known under the title of *Rasselas*.[288]

Hawke's selection of Hervey for the important inshore command exemplifies the Admiral's flair for assessing an officer's capability. Hawke had little in common personally with this cocksure, buoyantly-lecherous member of the aristocracy; but it cannot be denied that the latter was a supremely bold and effective commander of a ship of war and that Hawke succeeded in getting the best out of him.

On 21 June Hawke, to his heartfelt relief, found Duff still on station off Brest. No French ships had escaped from the port. As to whether troops were being collected there or not, the reports were conflicting. Hawke, following Admiralty instructions, posted the *Minerva* in the Four Passage (between Ushant and the mainland), in order to prevent enemy ships slipping round from the Bay of Biscay to the invasion ports of le Havre and Dunkirk. The *Rochester* and *Pallas*, maintaining the close watch on Brest, were also to 'have an eye' on the Four channel.[289]

Besides the French invasion plan which has already been summarized, indications reached the British Government that the French might try to rush troops suddenly across the Channel under comparatively light escort. Newcastle confided to Hardwicke that he was every day becoming 'more

---

[288] Ad. 1/92, 13 June 1759. Erskine, p. 303. I.L., 19 June 1759.
[289] O.L., 21, 22 June 1759. I.L., 15 June 1759.

apprehensive of this design of the French… My chief dependence still is that our little light squadron in the Downs and at Spithead will prevent or harass them extremely in their landings.' If the French landed 30,000 men, he lamented, the British army would muster less than half that number, unless Pitt's 'famous militia' were used to guard the prisoners of war.

The First Lord of the Treasury was not alone in his fears. 'I really believe the French will try', John Calcraft was now writing. 'They don't mean to trust to the fleet, but to slip over from Dunkirk, and make several attempts at once to land. They have already built as many flat-bottomed boats as cost £170,000 and are building more. They talk of being ready near the middle of July and of having by that time 45,000 men encamped near Dunkirk. Our troops are collecting so as to guard the coast, and be encamped in different places within reach of the Capital.'[290]

Before sending Hervey in the 64-gun *Monmouth* to take charge of the inshore squadron, Hawke was waiting for signs that some of the heavier French ships might try to get out. He did not wish to risk a ship of the line near the potentially dangerous lee shore until it was necessary. Meanwhile Hervey wrote: 'We kept forming different lines of battle every day when the weather admitted, and nothing extraordinary till the 28th when the *Belliqueux* and *Windsor* joined us with bread and beer which was taken out of them by the different ships close to Ushant. I had a very large quantity sent to me, as the Admiral sent for me next morning and gave me orders to take the *Pallas*, Captain Clements, and two cutters, and to go to cruise close in with Brest and to look in on the fleet as frequently as I could, and to send the Admiral frequent accounts of their situation, and he would soon reinforce me

[290] Add.MSS. 17494, f. 104, 109; 32892, f. 27.

properly to keep that service on which, he repeated, much depended on my activity and judgement.'

Hawke's written order to Hervey was dated 3 July. That day the Admiral wrote to Clevland: 'The operations of the enemy indicate a long cruise for the squadron. In order to preserve it in a condition to keep the sea, I purpose to send in two ships of the line to clean at Plymouth every spring. I have begun with the *Fame*, who has got malignant fever on board, and the *Bienfaisant*, whose rudder is not to be depended on. They are above six months foul.'

At the same time he wrote to Captain Edgecumbe who was in charge at Plymouth while his ship, the *Hero*, was being repaired, and to Commissioner Rogers, to acquaint them with his plans and to convey to them the need for expedition, both in refitting and cleaning the ships sent into that port, and in organizing the supply convoys which were to go out to the fleet.

The Board of Admiralty fully exerted itself to see that Hawke was given the supplies required by his system of blockade. If the fleet was to stay at sea for more than three months, health would become a factor of decisive importance. It has been suggested that Anson was impressed by the views of James Lind, Senior Physician at Haslar, on the role of green vegetables, and especially citrus fruit, in preventing scurvy; but doubt is cast on the extent of Lind's influence at this date by the dominance of beer, bread, and fresh meat in the correspondence between Hawke and the authorities. Fresh vegetables were accorded some emphasis but they were of various kinds — not primarily greens. With regard to fruit there is no particular mention of lemons and oranges; but apples, which were not specially advocated by Lind (and were subsequently shown to have quite a low content of the crucial vitamin C), were supplied in quantity. However, it can not be disputed that the diet actually furnished was good enough to eliminate scurvy as a serious threat to the endurance of the fleet. As to typhus, while its real cause remained unknown, Hawke's own enthusiasm for cleanliness contributed to the fact that it was kept within bounds.[291]

Hervey wasted no time in closing right in to observe Brest. On 3 and 5 July the *Monmouth* and *Pallas* approached to within four miles of the French fleet, and sightseers crowded down to the shore to watch the British ships. There were twenty two-deckers in the port, with colours flying. 'Though I could discern men in boats alongside of them', Hervey reported, 'I could not see any number about the ships sufficient to think them anything like manned, as they would have appeared on the decks upon our standing in, as they did everywhere on shore.' On the night of the 5th, there being little wind, he anchored close in and his cutter succeeded in seizing a fishing vessel with a crew of five. These men were interrogated separately. According to the owner-skipper, when he had last been in Brest a week before, none of the warships had more than 150 men aboard. He said that 'they were taking on board all the fishermen from Ushant and along the coast, and all the country people from the plough that could be got to put on board their ships, but that it was generally thought they could not get them manned, having no seamen in France'. Nor could all the ships be supplied with guns until a consignment arrived from Rochefort and Bordeaux.

---

[291] Erskine, p. 304. References to beer, water and meat are scattered through O.L. and I.L. for 1759. Vegetables and fruit: O.L., 14 Aug., 25 Sept.; I.L., 10 Sept. Lloyd and Coulter, pp. 42, 115-16, 302. Marcus, pp. 186, 188; also his article, 'Hawke's Blockade of Brest', in the Royal United Service Institution's *Journal*, Nov. 1759, pp. 479-81, 487. O.L., 3 July 1759 (3). O.B., 3 July 1759.

In a postscript Hervey remarked: 'I write no letters home now, nor suffer any person from my ship, that whatever use you please to make of the intelligence we can get and send you may solely go from yourself first.'

Hawke was delighted with this performance. 'With the greatest satisfaction', he replied, 'I received your letter of the 6th, as it so fully answered my purpose in sending the *Monmouth* on the service in which she is at present employed, more especially by your taking of the boat; tho' we must not absolutely depend upon intelligence received from an enemy. Yet, as part of what you sent carries the marks of truth, it will quiet minds in England, which have lately been greatly alarmed.'

As if to illustrate the point, 8 July found John Calcraft writing: 'We are here in the utmost expectation of invasion. I, who could never believe it before, am convinced the French will attempt coming, and sometime next month.' He was scarcely more optimistic on the 11th — 'There is dreadful preparation making in France.'[292]

By now Hawke had reinforced Hervey with the 60-gun *Montague*, Captain Lendrick, and sent instructions to watch the Raz Passage as well as Brest. It would be a considerable blow to the French if the guns for the squadron at Brest had to be carried overland. Hawke therefore made doubly sure of blocking the approach from the S. by posting Duff with the *Rochester* (50) and *Windsor* (60) off Audierne Bay. The frigate *Thames*, Captain Colby, and the sloop *Swallow* were given the Four Passage but, as Colby soon pointed out, a chain of rocks, screening shallow, inshore channels, made it impossible to intercept all the small craft coming round from St. Malo.

---

[292] I.L., 4, 5, 6 July 1759. O.L., 4, 7 July 1759. Add.MSS. 17494, E 128, 232.

Hervey's character shows through his report of the 8th, compounded of robust humour and a rather sinister contempt for things held sacred by other men:

> I can assure you now of M. de Conflans being arrived. The fisherman I sent ashore yesterday returned for one of his people and his son, which I kept on board till he carried my message to a little battery that had fired upon me in working in, and which lays close to a great convent,[293] to whom I sent word, if they fired another I would level the Church. The Commandant there sent word that they must make their signal guns, but *that he would take care not to let another ball come out of them*, and indeed in the afternoon I tried him by sending my boats and cutter to bring down a Dutch dogger that was coming through the Passage du Four, which they did without being molested.

Hervey would have been quickly at home in the ruthless atmosphere of twentieth-century warfare.

On the 10th Hawke encouraged Hervey to persist with his observations of the port. 'For according to what we see, not what we hear, we must regulate ourselves. As the port of Brest is actually blocked up, I desire you will not let any neutral vessel, of whatever nation soever, to enter it, and direct them to stand off the coast.'[294]

Reflecting on the patiently-awaited day of battle, Hawke took action to prevent confusion over flags. The French would fly white flags. Because Geary was a Rear-Admiral of the White, he would normally fly a plain white flag at his mizen topmasthead and a white ensign (like the modern type) at the stern. The captains in his division would all fly white ensigns.

[293] Near St. Matthew's Point.

[294] O.L., 7, 9, 10 July, 2 Aug. 1759. I.L., 7, 10 July 1759. ff., for Capt. Colby. Ad. 1/92, 9 July 1759 and enclosure of 8th.

In a mêlée, these flags might well be confused with those of the French. Hawke, as an Admiral of the Blue, flew a plain blue flag at his main topmasthead, and Hardy, as a Vice-Admiral of the Blue, wore a similar flag at his fore topmasthead, while they and all the captains in their divisions flew blue ensigns at the stern. For Hawke's and Hardy's divisions, therefore, no change was required. But Geary was ordered, in the event of action, to hoist a red flag and ensign, and to direct his captains to wear red ensigns.

For the time being there was little for the main body of the fleet to do, other than condemn provisions, which were now beginning to go bad, practise manoeuvres and await news from Hervey. For a few days in mid-July the latter was unable to look into Brest because of the swell. 'The tides are now very strong, as well as the swell very great, between the Island of Ushant and the Raz.' However, 20 July found him in a jubilant mood.

Seeking intelligence, he had sent a party in boats to the Island of Benequet, near Conquet, 'in order to intercept some boats which are generally there'. The officer in charge of the British party had brought three Frenchmen back with him, and they confirmed what had previously been supposed about the state of Conflans's fleet. Hervey also discovered that there were twenty-one head of cattle on the little island, and, wind and weather being favourable, it was not long before a band of jolly Jacks was rushing about and rounding them up. 'I take the liberty of sending you one, Sir', wrote Hervey in a covering letter, 'as well as the other admirals, and have divided the others to the Montague's people and our own for a day's fresh meat for them tomorrow.'[295]

---

[295] O.B., 13, 16 July 1759. cf. W. G. Perrin, *British Flags*, 1922, pp. 96-7, 117-18. I.L., 12, 20 July 1759.

Hervey then bottled-up an inward-bound convoy of store ships in the small, but fortified, port of Conquet; and, early on 22 July, four French ships of the line moved out to drive away the troublesome British force — then consisting of two of the line and a frigate. Here was an occasion! Hervey rose to it at once. His immediate reaction was to counter-attack. Seeing the *Colchester* (50) and a frigate in the offing, he signalled to them to close up. He intended to pit them against one of the French ships of the line, while the *Monmouth*, *Montague*, and *Pallas* frigate took on the other three. He was already off St. Matthew's Point. Pressing in towards the enemy, he hoisted a Commodore's 'Broad Pendant' — a long red pennant with a Union Flag at its head. It certainly had the desired effect. Apparently believing that superior force was being conjured up, the French ships fled. Hervey fired at them from long range and claimed a few hits.

Hawke, forewarned that some attempt by the enemy was possible, had begun to move up reinforcements during the night, but the wind had held them up. During the morning, Hawke, with the whole squadron, moved right in towards St. Mathew's Point and was in time to see the latter part of Hervey's pursuit. 'Never did officer show greater conduct and resolution than did Captain Hervey', the Admiral reported, 'and was bravely seconded by Captain Lendrick.'

In the Road there was a flurry of loosening sails, and it looked for a while as if there might be a battle royal between the two fleets in the narrow waters near the entrance. 'I had', Hawke wrote, 'full in their view and close to the entrance of the Road, the squadron formed and lying to for their reception. On the enemy's furling their topsails, I came to an anchor a few miles without, where I purpose staying while the winds and weather will permit.'[296]

At this stage of the campaign, the likely cause of a British defeat was not the violence of the enemy but a failure of supplies. On 23 July, Hawke dispatched to Mr. Ommanney, Victualling Agent at Plymouth, notice that some of the squadron's captains were complaining of 'great delays and neglect' suffered at the hands of his office. These 'have greatly obstructed the Service and, if continued, will oblige me to break up the squadron'. Empty casks must be quickly carried ashore, and fresh water, beer, and provisions as speedily placed aboard. Cheese was short in the squadron. The ships' companies were suffering from the bad Plymouth beer.

No sooner had this communication been sent off than a fleet of victuallers arrived. But, to Hawke's mortification, the consignment of beer was found to be already undrinkable. He therefore informed Mr. Ommanney:

> The beer brewed at your port is so excessively bad that it employs the whole time of the squadron surveying it and throwing it overboard, so it is my direction that no more of it be sent, as I have dispatched an express to the Lords of the Admiralty to supply the squadron from the Eastward.
>
> I likewise desire that the utmost dispatch may be used in sending out all the live bullocks and sheep ordered by the Board.
>
> A quantity of bread from the *Ramillies* will be returned to you by the *Elizabeth*. Tho' not altogether unfit for use, yet so full of weevils and maggots, it would have infected all the bread come on board this day. We had not time to pick it.

These strictures were justified by the facts and it was essential to make them. The close blockade had to be maintained somehow. But, to appreciate the abnormal strain

---

[296] I.L., 21, 22 July 1759 (2). O.L., 23 July 1759.

put upon Ommanney's department, it is instructive to glance over his flustered reply, dated 27 July, to Hawke's first letter.

> I have this minute received your commands of the 23rd instant and am greatly concerned that some of the commanders of the ships that came here to refit should complain of the detention of their ship by neglects of any duties under my direction. I flatter myself, Sir, if you knew the duty that have been done here, loading out twenty-two sail of victuallers here with stores and provisions, unlading them of their empty casks, staves, hoops, etc., and the unlading a number of victuallers here with stores and provisions for the Office, and victualling the sundry men of war that have been lately here, and with the interruption of winds and weather sometimes, you would think the complaint groundless. I beg leave to say that no part of duty was ever knowingly omitted by me, and I hope… the state of the demands and the time of their being complied with, with the considerations above, would acquit me of the charge.[297]

The reverse inflicted on the French on the 22nd had not been without its moral effect. On the 24th the inshore squadron intercepted an outward bound Dutch dogger, and her Master said 'that the soldiers and people are much dispirited and cry out great shame on their fleet for being drove in again… He told me', Hervey reported to Hawke, 'it was surprising the price of everything, and no white bread scarce to be had.' Hawke learnt from another Dutchman that the French ship at which Hervey had fired on the 22nd 'had about twenty men killed and wounded'.

According to John Calcraft, the good citizens of Plymouth were at this time furnished with topics of conversation other than matters connected with the docking and replenishment of

[297] O.L., 23, 24 July 1759. I.L., 27 July 1759.

Hawke's squadron. 'General Onslow', he wrote, 'is ordered to Plymouth to command there, and our preparations against invasion go on most vigorously, as, we are told, those of the enemy do for it.'[298]

But Hawke was more concerned with the fact that his scheme for sending pairs of ships into Plymouth, to go into dry dock with each spring tide, was not working. Instead of coming promptly back to the squadron in time to replace the next ones to go in, ships were accumulating in port. He therefore changed the scheme. On 29 July Reynolds of the *Firm* (60) received the first of a new series of orders. He was simply to clean the ship in Plymouth, 'continuing in port for only ten days for the refreshment of your ship's company'. As the Admiral put it on 4 August:

> Their Lordships will give me leave to observe that the relief of the Squadron depends more on the refreshment of the ships' companies than in cleaning the ships. By the hurry the latter must be performed in (unless the ship continues a month or five weeks in port, which the present exigency will by no means admit of) the men would be so harassed and fatigued that they would return to me in a worse condition than they left me. This made me prefer ordering some of them to heel and boot hose top only, remaining at rest for ten days in port, and at their departure bringing such a quantity of fresh meat as would keep sweet at this season, two or three live bullocks and twenty live sheep.

He implied that it was not practicable to send in five ships at a time as the Admiralty had desired. 'However', he stated, 'I shall endeavour to comply with all their Lordships' directions in such a manner as, to the best of my judgement, will answer

---

[298] I.L., 25 July 1759. O.L., 29 July 1759. Add.MSS. 17494, f. 140.

their intentions of employing me here. For as to myself, it is a matter of indifference whether I fight the enemy, if they should come out, with an equal number or one less.' He had twenty-one of the line at the time; Conflans apparently had twenty-two. Hawke told the Admiralty that his outstanding needs were of beer 'from the eastward' and of frigates.

What with Rodney's and other operations in the Channel, and the requirements of convoys and of other stations, the general shortage of frigates was acute.[299]

On 1 August, however, Hawke had received a reinforcement in the shape of Prince Edward, complete with very considerable paraphernalia.

It was not until about this time that the French government gave any definite instructions, following the lines of the master-plan, to the principal commanders of the expedition, the Comte de Conflans and the Due d'Aiguillon. Conflans had a good record behind him, having captured two British ships of the line in the previous war. (One of them was the *Severn*, retaken by Hawke's squadron of October 1747.) It should be explained that in the French Navy the flag appointments comprised one admiral, two vice-admirals, nine lieutenant-generals, and twenty-two *chefs d'escadre*. Thus, l'Etanduère, the *Chef d'Escadre* of 1747, had really been the equivalent of a British rear-admiral, although sometimes referred to by his opponents as 'the French Commodore'. It can now be understood how, in 1756, Conflans could be promoted from lieutenant-general to vice-admiral (*es mers du Levant*), a position carrying equivalent distinction to that of the Rear-Admiral of Great Britain. While continuing to hold his naval rank, he was, in 1758, awarded in addition the baton of a Marshal of France.

299 O.L., 27, 29 July, 4 Aug. 1759. O.B., 29 July, 2 Aug. 1759. I.L., 23 July 1759.

D'Aiguillon was chosen to command the French invasion-army because of the sharp reverse he had inflicted on the inefficiently led British force at St. Cas, near St. Malo, in September 1758.[300]

Reports had come in to Hawke, especially from the indefatigable Duff, which, though conflicting, allowed him to form a picture of the complex activities of the French. At Port Louis there were at least two dozen transports and seven frigates. They were supposed to pick up 6,000 troops who were waiting at Nantes. But Quiberon Bay was obviously focus of the general activity. About thirty vessels and a couple of frigates were lying in the recesses of the Bay. Off shore, numerous transports or supply-vessels were at anchor or sailing about — 100 of them, according to one source. These latter vessels were said to be laden with supplies for Brest.

No sooner had Duff received news of the enemy ships in Quiberon Bay than he led his force of five sail down to attack. The merchantmen, together with four frigates, flung themselves into the landlocked bay called the Morbihan (or Morbian). Its narrow entrance was easily defensible and there was a broad anchorage inside. It was on the northern side of the Morbihan that the expeditionary force was assembling. Duff also transmitted a report that some warships were expected to break out of Brest in order to escort 100 sail from Bordeaux to Quiberon Bay.

Considering the mounting difficulties involved in the refitting and supply of the fleet, as well as his developing operational commitments, Hawke did not regard as helpful an Admiralty order brought out to him by the *Fame*. This was dated 30 July and was handed to him on 7 August. It ordered

---

[300] O.L., 2 Aug. 1759. Lacour-Gavet, pp. 316-17, 322-3, 325, 499, 517, 521. Cathcart Papers, A67, for criticism of army-command.

the return to Spithead of Duff in the *Rochester.* Hawke maintained the imperturbability which marked his conduct of this supremely successful campaign, but remarked: 'Their Lordships will see by the copy of Captain Duff's letter how importantly he is employed.' He went on to refer to a consignment of Guernsey wine, which was being sent in lieu of the disastrous Plymouth beer. 'Wine, in proportion to the allowed quantity [of beer], is not a bad article; but, as stinking water must be drunk with it, it will not support a squadron. For a continuance, I therefore beg leave to repeat my entreaties for beer.'[301]

While 1758 had seen Hawke tormented, first by a sense of grievance and subsequently by some temporary loss of self-respect, 1759 found him equal to his monumental responsibilities. His resolution gathered strength from the difficulties which he had to face, and he handled his many-sided problems with an unruffled and dignified mastery.[302]

With reluctance Hawke duly called Duff back from his station and sent him in to Spithead. Meantime, by 22 August the Admiralty had received Hawke's dispatch of the 12th, together with 'repeated information' that troops had actually been embarked at Port Louis, Vannes, and Auray (both the last-named places being in the Morbihan). Their Lordships now wanted Duff to stay on his station 'as long as possible', but, of course, their hasty cancellation of their previous order was too late. Hawke had replaced Duff with Roddam of the *Colchester* (50), who had under his command the *Windsor* (60), *Sapphire* (32), *Mélampe* (36), and *Actaeon* (28). In the event, Duff's recall did no harm. After his crew had had a badly needed rest, he returned to Hawke on 17 September.[303]

---

301 O.L., 4, 12 Aug. 1759. I.L., 6 Aug. 1759.

302 cf. monument — see p. 13 n. 17.

In case it should be wondered what the 60-gun *Windsor* was doing under the command of first one captain of a 50-gun cruiser and then another, the answer is that the *Windsor*'s Captain was Archibald Clevland. To elucidate a little further, this young man had risen to the rank of Post Captain at the age of 18 or thereabouts, not because inborn genius justified a breach of the normal rules, but because his father happened to be the Secretary of the Admiralty. When in June 1759, the said Archibald had come out to Hawke in the *Windsor*, he was still only 21. Hawke had him in his own division for long enough to gauge his professional competence, and appears to have concluded that he would not be an outstanding asset in the line of battle. He therefore sent him off to the detached squadron where he could more easily be employed at discretion. Archibald's luck failed to carry him higher in the ranks of the Service. Firstly, his father died in 1763. Thereupon, in the words of Charnock: 'Being ordered to the coast of Guinea, he, on his return from thence, died at the island of St. Thomas, in the course of the year 1766.'[304]

The squadron was experiencing an exceptionally hot summer. The weather was blamed by the Victualling Commissioners as the cause of the Plymouth beer going bad. However, Hervey's inshore force, which was passing the time by taking bearings and soundings and preparing a detailed chart of Douarnenez Bay (just to the S. of Brest), enjoyed pleasant conditions of work. For the fleet as a whole, the monotony was punctuated on 27 August in honour of Prince Ferdinand's important victory at Minden on the 1st of the month. Hanover, so often on the point of being finally swallowed up, was saved by Ferdinand's sudden counterstroke

---

[303] O.B., 15, 17 Aug. 1759. O.L., 28 Aug. 1759. I.L., 22 Aug. 1759.
[304] Charnock, vi, 158. Aspinall-Oglander, p. 209. Namier, pp. 40-1.

against Marshal Contades. Thereby a fair chance was preserved that the gains of the maritime war would not have to be traded at the peace against restoration of Hanover to the English King, so there was every reason why Hawke and his fleet should enjoy celebrating with '*a Feu de Joie* before the harbour of Brest'. At 3 p.m. on the 27th, the whole squadron formed up near St. Matthew's Point and thundered its appreciation of Prince Ferdinand's military qualities.[305]

The Admiralty was pressing Hawke to launch an attack on the transports in the Morbihan, and also drew his attention to M. Bompart's expected return to France from the West Indies with seven or eight ships of the line. It was again reported that four ships of the line were to break out of Brest in order to escort transports 'on a particular service', but now the transports in question were those at Quiberon. Hawke was able to assure the Board that no large ship had yet 'slipped past' his fleet. But he undertook to see whether an attempt could be made on the shipping at Port Louis, Vannes, or Nantes, and had sent Reynolds in the *Firm* (60) to take over from Roddam the command of the detached squadron. Reynolds had two 60s, one 50, and five frigates, and was to examine the possibility of an attack with bomb (i.e. mortar) vessels and fireships. As for Bompart, if he tried to get into Brest, Hawke would deal with him. But if he headed for Rochefort there was nothing to be done. Adequate strength had to be maintained off Brest. By the beginning of September, seven ships of the line were cleaning and two more were with Reynolds, leaving Hawke with twenty-one.

Impatiently, the Admiral awaited Reynolds's report. Then, on 7 September a dramatic message arrived from Lord Bristol, elder brother of Augustus Hervey and British Ambassador in

---

[305] I.L., 13, 16, 22 Aug. 1759. O.L., 28 Aug. 1759. Corbett, ii, 30-1.

Madrid. 'I have just been informed from authority that twelve French ships of the line and three frigates from Toulon, under the command of M. de la Clue, passed through the Strait of Gibraltar in the night between the 16th and 17th of this month, August, that five ships of the line as well as three frigates have put into the Bay of Cadiz, and it is not known what course the other seven large ships have steered.'

Bristol had been told that Boscawen was in pursuit of the latter.[306]

Clearly the French invasion plan would be advanced a step if these seven ships could reach Rochefort. Before the requisite countermeasures could be devised, it was essential to learn whether they had in fact arrived there, so, on 8 September, Hawke rushed off instructions to Reynolds. 'I desire that immediately on receipt of this you will send one or two of your cleanest sailing frigates to look in there, and immediately on their return dispatch the *Success* to me with an account of your proceedings and an account of the state and condition of the ships under your orders.'

Meanwhile Reynolds had not been inactive, and he had sent off his report on the 7th — the day before the *Success* left Hawke with his latest instructions. At Port Louis, there were five frigates and eighteen small vessels ready to sail. There were two dozen or so other small craft there, moored inshore. As for Nantes, there were apparently about thirty transports, many soldiers, and a very few escort vessels in the estuary. The wind had not permitted close visual inspection, but intelligence from a Dutchman had helped to complete the picture. The Morbihan was reported by William Hotham of the *Mélampe* to contain only a dozen vessels — a surprisingly small number.

[306] I.L., 13, 18, 22 Aug. 1759. O.L., 28 Aug., 8 Sept. 1759. H.P.P., Bristol to H., 24 Aug. 1759.

Reynolds, who had been further reinforced by the *Falkland* (50) and *Pluto* fireship, gathered his nine captains together for a deliberation. They agreed 'unanimously' that the shipping in Port Louis could be attacked with the assistance of bomb-vessels and fireships, but that Nantes Road and the Morbihan presented too many difficulties.

Hawke was satisfied with Reynolds's reports. He did not order an attack on Port Louis with existing forces. Instead he told Reynolds to blockade that harbour with most of his squadron, and to station 'two frigates off Nantes, which in bad weather may come to an anchor just within the Cardinals in the entrance of Quiberon Bay' — a part of the coast with which Hawke would attain a certain familiarity. Reynolds himself was to cruise in the *Firm* off the N. end of Belle Isle, with a 50-gun ship and the *Pluto* in company. From this central position he was to keep constantly in touch with his two outlying forces, each of which was to have a frigate 'constantly running' to him.[307]

As far back as 23 July Hawke had drawn the Admiralty's attention to the possibility that he might have to go on a lengthy pursuit of the enemy at a time when his provisions were low. 'I cannot help', he then remarked, 'regretting the want of a Commanding Officer at Plymouth to see all orders executed with the dispatch and punctuality necessary'.

It certainly seems rather extraordinary that no admiral had been appointed to replace Harrison on that officer's death the previous March. Hawke had himself held the post as a rear-admiral and he had been succeeded by a flag officer on going to sea in 1747. Harrison had latterly commanded the port with the rank of Vice-Admiral of the Red. Now, when the responsibility of the post was exceptionally great, there was no-one in it at all! On 7 August Clevland had replied to Hawke

[307] O.L., 8, 11 Sept. 1759. I.L., 7 Sept. 1759.

that the Lords had 'thoughts of appointing a Commanding Officer at Plymouth to quicken the dispatch'. The outcome of these musings was the appointment of — a captain! However, this turned out to be Thomas Hanway who had commanded the *Windsor* at the Second Battle of Cape Finisterre and had taken Hawke out to his squadron in August 1747. On hearing of Hanway's appointment, Hawke, who was still waiting to hear news of la Clue's ships, wrote to his old friend in an informal manner which permits insight into the Admiral's state of mind. The letter was dated 8 September.

> By the *Hercules* [74], *Juno* [36], and cutter, which joined me this morning, I have the favour of your letters of the 2nd and 4th inst. Our objects here increase every day and occasions my repeating my desire of an extraordinary dispatch in sending out the *Dunkirk* [60] and *Chichester* [70] and the vessels with beer. The constant condemning of the beer from Plymouth in the refitted ships has proved a dreadful stroke upon the Squadron, as they, as well as such as have been long out, have been supplied from the pittance sent from the Eastward. If the Commissioner and Agent Victualler will answer for its keeping but six weeks or one month, I should be glad of a large supply from thence at once. For, lying to so often for the few victuallers which come at a time is a great obstruction to that narrow watch we are obliged to keep over the enemy. Beside, the weather in all probability will soon prove too bad for sending out victuallers, and if we should not be supplied before that shall happen, what will be the consequence for the nation?
>
> Except one or two ships, the squadron is very healthy, and for the sake of our Country at this critical juncture, I hope will continue. The *Foudroyant* is the worst, and I must desire you will, from your late supply, send me by the first ship, fifty or sixty able seamen for her...

> I have several neutrals on board the *Ramillies* who all behave well and are good and useful men.
>
> I hope there will be no occasion to dock the *Belliqueux* [which was 'getting the main piece of the knee of the head properly secured']. If there should, I rely on your diligence and activity, of which, without a compliment, I entertain the highest opinion.[308]

In this case, as in his handling of Hervey, the Admiral's first-rate capacity for communicating with subordinates has been demonstrated. He allowed them, by giving them full information, to appreciate the importance of their activities, whether administrative or operational. Also, he was aware of the effectiveness of a word of praise.

The next problem requiring solution appeared in the shape of the *Windsor*, which reached Hawke in a leaky condition on 10 September. She had been damaged in a gale off Belle Isle on the 5th. Hawke wasted no time in sending her into port, to the relief, one may guess, of her not over-seasoned commanding officer.

One of Hawke's major preoccupations was happily cleared away when, at noon on 12 September, the *Resolution*, Captain Speke, rejoined the squadron. Enclosed with a letter from Clevland *père*, dated the 6th, was one from Boscawen to Hawke, written on 20 August. Two days earlier, Boscawen had engaged la Clue's seven ships of the line near the Portuguese port of Lagos. He took three of them and forced the enemy to destroy two. Of the two which escaped, one was badly damaged.

Hawke was quick to send off an appreciative reply. The rough draft, written in the Admiral's own hand and still preserved with his private papers, is interesting for two

[308] O.L., 23 July, 8 Sept. 1759. I.L., 7 Aug. 1759.

reasons. Firstly, it brings out his agreeable characteristics of open generosity and freedom from jealousy. Secondly, it provides sure evidence of the influence of 'that very bad man', John Hay, on the writing of his dispatches.

'I was in great pain', wrote Hawke, 'lest the enemy should have escaped you.' He most heartily congratulated his brother admiral. His success was 'as fortunate an event as could have happened for our Country, as it has entirely overset the schemes of the French'. Now for the editing. Hawke's continuation was phrased: 'Allow me to add that no man in England can be more pleased with your good fortune, nor that will be gladder to see you reap those advantages from it, which you are so truly deserving of.' Hay the *littérateur* soon perceived that this was clumsily put, crossed through Hawke's version from the first comma onwards, and wrote instead: 'nor more rejoiced to see you reap those advantages from it which you so truly merit'.

Other alterations in Hay's hand are more trifling. The matter of the letter remained Hawke's, and much of the manner, too; but the polish was John Hay's.

At a distant date, Hay would remind Hawke of his secretarial services in such a manner as to ruffle the Admiral considerably. But Hawke hardly suspected such a possibility as he handed his written draft to Hay on 14 September 1759.[309]

A continuing headache of the campaign of 1759 was provided, not only for Hawke but for the naval authorities generally, by the fact that the victuallers serving the Fleet did not come under naval discipline. They operated for private profit; and, even before autumn came, they were complaining

---

[309] O.B., 10 Sept. 1759. O.L., 10, 12 Sept. 1759. Burrows, pp. 378-9. H.P.P., draft of H. to Boscawen, 14 Sept. 1759; Hay to H., 17 Feb. 1777.

that the damage entailed by unloading provisions into warships at sea was diminishing their profit-margin. The Victualling Commissioner at Plymouth therefore asked Hawke if he would see that certificates of damage were issued so that compensation could be paid by the Crown. Hawke accordingly issued an order which suggests the passage of warm words between the victuallers and the Navy during the process of trans-shipment. 'In case any of the victualling vessels shall sustain any particular damage alongside your ship, not arising from the neglect or obstinacy of the Masters, you are to give the Master of the said vessel a certificate setting out the said particular damages, in order that he may be paid for the same.' At the same time, Hawke ordered the captains not to impress protected seamen — which implies a grievance of the victuallers against the Service.

Meanwhile, the exuberant Hervey had found ways of amusing himself. On 17 September he reported to Hawke that an outward bound Spaniard had confirmed that there were altogether about thirty warships at Brest, and their crews were 'much dejected at Mr. Boscawen's success'. He continued: 'I yesterday had so very fine a day, and consequently so fine an opportunity that I could not help stripping the small island of Molines of all their cattle, and I laid the Great Island of Molines under contribution for cattle, which was quickly complied with.' Hence supervened two cows, sent to Hawke as a present.

On the 18th Hawke was delighted by the return of Duff in the *Rochester* and he at once sent him off to resume command of the detached squadron. Altogether, the position was easier. Supplies had come out and there was no immediate likelihood of important developments at Rochefort, the only major port in the Bay which he could not cover.[310]

However, on the following day an unexpected and vexatious affair blew up. Hawke had to suspend Alexander Hood from the command of the *Minerva* because his 1st Lieutenant demanded a court martial on him. This officer, one Samuel Swinton, alleged that Hood had not pressed home his attack on five French vessels in the Four Passage on the 17th (although one of them was destroyed and two forced ashore, while the *Minerva* was hit by six 12-lb. shot from the covering French forts). Hood expressed the most acute impatience to get his trial over. He was regarded as one of the best of the Navy's younger officers and Hawke found time to write sympathetically to him on 21 September: 'Being as impatient as you can be to release you from your disagreeable situation, I gave orders for your trial coming on yesterday. Three of the Brest squadron being out occasioned putting it off. As the enemy is in motion I am afraid it must be delayed while the wind continues easterly, as I must prefer watching them to all other business.'

Hood was moved by his Admiral's consideration. He replied on the 22nd: 'I think myself much obliged for your very friendly and feeling letter on my present situation. Since I had the honour to receive it, I have reconsidered the matter of desiring the ship might proceed to England with me, and upon reflection I think I had better remain here till my trial can be brought on.'

Hawke's letter of 21 September was carefully kept by its recipient.

At last, on 24 September it was possible to assemble the court martial aboard Hardy's flagship, and it was held that Hood 'did on that occasion his duty in every respect as an able

---

[310] I.L., 10, 17 Sept. 1759. O.B., 17 Sept. 1759. O.L., 18 Sept. 1759 (2).

and diligent officer'; and he was duly acquitted and restored to his command. The same day, Swinton, his accuser, wrote to Hawke requesting sick leave in England. This was promptly granted.[311]

As indicated in Hawke's above-quoted letter to Hood, the enemy had been attempting to get three ships out of Brest. Between the 17th and the 20th these vessels had moved in and out of the Goulet,[312] and anchored each night in Camaret Bay. The latter manoeuvre presented difficulties for the inshore squadron because the French, safe under the strong forts, were at the same time well placed to make a dash for it under the cover of darkness. However, Hawke had built up Hervey's strength to five of the line and at night he was able to mount guard over both the Four and Raz Passages. Each day Hervey pressed in towards the French ships to force them back into Brest. On the 19th the enemy contingent was backed up by warlike motions on the part of six ships in the Road; but Hervey still advanced and the three ships from Camaret fled in great confusion into the port. Hawke's blockade, together with the shortage of French seamen, had produced a very low standard of seamanship in the enemy fleet, and on this occasion the three retreating ships could negotiate the Goulet only with the assistance of a clutter of towboats. The sparring ceased on the 20th. Somewhat surprisingly, no spectators had come out to watch, but on the 23rd Hervey reported: 'The shore is now again lined with people, especially the Convent and lookouts.'

On 29 September Hervey was again prominent. With five boats, he led in person a night attack on a French schooner

---

[311] Add.MSS. 35193, f. 96, 97. O.L., 19, 21, 22, 23 Sept. 1759. I.L., 18, 19, 21, 22 Sept. 1759. Charnock, vi, 153-4.

[312] I.L., 21, 23, 29 Sept. 1759. O.L., 23, 30 Sept., 1 Oct. 1759.

which had been reporting the movements of the British from its anchorage, 'within half musket shot of the batteries of Camaret'. Despite a great flurry of projectiles from guns, mortars, and small arms, the schooner was carried off, complete with crew of two officers and thirty-six men. The boarding party suffered no casualties. Ten of the enemy were wounded. Subsequent cross-examinations produced the information that, between the 17th and 20th, the *Bizarre* (64), *Sphynx* (64), and *Grette* (32) had been trying 'to join the transports and ships at Nantes and Port Louis. Now they had been ordered to make no further attempt.' In July the *Dauphin Royal* (90), *Glorieux* (74), *Dragon* (64), and *Inflexible* (64) were 'sent only to drive me and the *Montague* off', Hervey reported.[313]

During the last ten days of September there were two developments calling for strategic readjustments by Hawke. Firstly, on the 25th news reached him from Duff and Reynolds that the enemy, to the number of sixty-eight sail, had managed to get up from Nantes into the Morbihan. The thirty-seven larger ships, of 200 to 700 tons, appeared to have gone to Vannes. The others were lying at the mouth of the River Auray. This was undoubtedly a reverse for Hawke who had written to the Admiralty on the 18th: 'In my opinion, Nantes, Vannes, and Port Louis are sufficiently guarded.' On the other hand, it was easier to blockade the enemy ships now that they had succeeded in concentrating. The British ships could also concentrate, eliminating some difficulties of communication and observation. Above all, Quiberon Bay afforded good shelter. In fact the French had obligingly chosen as the port of departure of their expeditionary force one of the few places on the Biscay coast that could be blockaded all the year round. Rochefort and Rochelle could also have been neutralized at

[313] The narrow entrance between Camaret and Brest.

this stage, but this would have strained British communications and supply services more severely on account of the distance from England.[314]

The second development was that Hawke received advice, dispatched from the Admiralty on 21 September, that Bompart had sailed from Martinique to San Domingo, and could be expected to make for home. 'Their Lordships', wrote Milnes, deputizing for Clevland, 'recommend it to you to keep a proper strength down the Bay to intercept them; to enable you to do which the *Sandwich*, *Belliqueux*, and *Torbay* are ordered to join you from Plymouth as soon as possible, and the ships that came home with Mr. Boscawen, which are gone into Portsmouth Harbour to clean, will be sent to you as fast as they are ready.' Bompart was reported to have five 74s, two 64s, a 50, and three frigates.

Rear-Admiral Geary, with the *Sandwich* and *Belliqueux*, rejoined Hawke on 27 September, and the latter lost no time in detaching him to cruise off Rochefort with five of the line and a frigate. Besides reporting this to Clevland, Hawke wrote privately to Anson. He remarked that he thought Geary 'an honest man and a good plain officer', which may be compared with Boscawen's opinion — 'Though my friend Geary is a stupid fellow, he is a good officer and will do his duty without noise, confusion, or puffing himself after it.' 'I hope', Hawke wrote confidently to Anson, 'that my sending Mr. Geary on this service will have your Lordship's approbation.'

Hawke therefore found it sharply disconcerting to receive, on 9 October, a sermon from their Lordships on the subject of keeping the principal objectives, namely the blockading of Brest and the Morbihan, clearly in view. He was to recall Geary and place his ships with the main squadron off Brest. At the

---

[314] O.L., 18, 26 Sept. 1759 (2). Ad. 1/92, 26 Sept. 1759 and enclosure.

same time, wrote Clevland, because the Lords conceded that it would be interesting to know 'what may be coming into the Bay, they recommend it to you to keep small cruisers to the westward for that purpose'.

Seeing that the Admiralty's letter of 21 September had asked for 'a proper strength down the Bay to intercept' Bompart, Corbett's comparison of Anson's strategic clear-headedness with Hawke's robust on-the-spot appraisal of the situation seems quite out of place. The main point was that the Board of Admiralty had performed a complete *volte face* within a period of a fortnight. The attendant dislocation and annoyance in the fleet could be justified only on the ground that the instructions of 21 September represented a dangerous error of judgement, and this was in no way admitted by the Admiralty. For the first time during the campaign, Hawke could not help expressing some irritation in a dispatch, namely that of 10 October. He had promptly complied with their Lordships' latest wishes, but he pointed out that the enemy at Brest had not demonstrated the least inclination to come out and do battle, whatever the strength of the British squadron. The blockade of the port was so tight that, according to French prisoners, the enemy had had to unload forty victuallers at Quimperle and transport their cargoes overland to Brest — obviously no light undertaking. With regard to Conflans's ships, he fairly commented: 'It must be the fault of the weather, not ours, if any of them escape.'[315]

Early October brought with it a recurrence of the beer shortage.

On the 3rd Hawke had to renew his appeals for more frigates.

---

[315] I.L., 21 Sept., 5 Oct. 1759. O.L., 28 Sept., 10 Oct. 1759. H. P.P., H. to Anson (draft holo.), 29 Sept. 1759. Corbett, ii, 43-4.

As he had foreseen, the seasonal deterioration of the weather greatly increased the difficulties of the inshore squadron. Hervey wrote on the 9th that the wind had been 'southerly with constant fogs… If the enemy is so intent on getting out two or three ships, they must at last find an opportunity of a shore wind and thick weather, when our ships have been obliged to stand off… I am thoroughly convinced of the necessity of keeping in here, when it is possible; but I am as thoroughly convinced that this season greatly increases the hazard of it, as you must be sensible. However, Douarnenez must be the resource if catched with any sudden gale westerly.'[316]

Now that there was a large number of enemy vessels in the Morbihan, Hawke had energetically taken up a suggestion by Duff that, should an attack be contemplated, 'some more ships of force, with Bombs, Fireships and armed ships of a small draught of water, and Pilots that are acquainted with the Rivers' would be necessary. By halfway through October, four fireships had been made ready to sail from England and, at the Admiralty's request, Lord Ligonier had lent Captain Stehelin, 'an officer of some consideration in the Train', to go out to assist Duff. As for the problem of finding suitable pilots, Captain Barrington of the *Achilles* (60) claimed that he had two excellent Frenchmen aboard. On the 8th Hawke interrogated them and 'they cheerfully, on promise of a suitable reward, undertook to carry our ships as far up the rivers Vannes and Auray as where the enemy's transports lie'. The Admiral thereupon dispatched the *Achilles* to Quiberon Bay.

The results were hardly inspiring. On 11 October the pilots ran the ship onto a rock in the Teignouze Passage and, seeing that she consequently made twelve feet of water an hour, even at anchor, Duff had to send her straight back to England under

---

316 O.L., 1, 3 Oct. 1759 (2). I. L., 9 Oct. 1759.

the escort of two frigates. However, even if he had lost two frigates and the main squadron was the weaker by a ship of the line, Duff at least had the two pilots. He therefore called his captains together to hear Hawke's orders, which had been delivered by Barrington, to carry out an attack, making use of the pilots 'in whose honesty Captain Barrington can confide'. The pilots were then cross-examined, and it was soon disclosed that if their honesty was impeccable, their knowledge was slight. Duff shelved the question of making an attack, but did not make it very clear to Hawke that he had done so.[317]

However, even if the British could not penetrate the Morbihan, Hawke gleaned from a French source that the situation did not look more cheerful to the enemy within. 'All things are disposing for the embarkation, the troops arriving and joining. But how are they to get out? We see every day, within a league and a half of this, two large English ships with nine frigates of different sizes waiting for us… We see distinctly, and without spectacles, the English walking upon the decks of their ships… The precise day of embarkation is not determined, but every disposition for it is made.'[318]

At this stage one of the expected westerly gales intruded on the scene. It was now more than four months since the squadron had been blown off its station. A gale stiffened from W.S.W. and by the evening of 11 October Hawke's ships were struggling for life against it. In Quiberon Bay Duff's squadron was able to ride quite safely, albeit uncomfortably. Throughout the 12th Hawke refused to surrender to the elements. On the 13th he decided that it was 'better to bear up for Plymouth than run the risk of being scattered and driven farther to the

[317] I.L., 23 Sept., 11, 15, 18 Oct. 1759. O.L., 8, 10, 30 Oct. 1759. O.B., 8 Oct. 1759.
[318] O.L., 10 Oct. 1759,

eastward'. That same day the *Ramillies* and nine other ships of the line flung themselves into the Sound. As long as the westerly gale continued, wrote Hawke, the enemy could not stir. Meanwhile, by day and night, he would have the ships loaded with three months' water and provisions, because the weather might continue too rough for victuallers. 'The instant it shall be moderate, I shall sail again.'[319]

After he had been in the Sound for a day or two the Admiral received a letter from Mr. H. Brown, his banker, with whom he was on very friendly terms. Those who, today, regularly peruse the financial columns of the morning papers might be interested to know that Hawke did not, at the height of the campaign of 1759, forget the potentialities of the stock market. On 2 October he had apparently written to ask Brown, who looked after his investments, to watch for bargains on the Exchange. Hawke's portfolio was restricted to various issues of Government Stock or secured loans to individuals; but the Admiral realized that the invasion scare could bring down security prices to unduly low levels. Completely confident in his squadron's ability to prevent invasion, he was very willing to buy at the prices ruling in October. However Brown replied that he could not advise purchases at a time when his bank expected prices to fall yet further, what with uncertainties about Quebec and continued fears of invasion. In fact, as Hawke had given him discretion, he had already taken an opportunity to sell some of the Admiral's Government Lottery Tickets, 'thinking it best to follow the old maxim, *it is better to sell and repent than keep and repent*'.

In the eighteenth century, which lacked the modern opportunity for investment in equities, this was reasonable advice; but, in this particular case, Hawke's judgement was

[319] O.L., 13 Oct. 1759.

greatly superior to Brown's because it was based on real knowledge of the strategic situation. This was the last chance of buying cheaply before news of victories poured in and bore prices swiftly upwards. Hawke might have coined an adage for Mr. Brown — no repentance exceeds that of a faint heart — but the Admiral was void of malice and the notion of a wounding riposte would scarcely occur to him![320]

By 17 October, despite the severe hindrance of continued bad weather, all the thirteen ships of the line sheltering Plymouth Sound had been 'completed', except for beer. Of the main squadron, three of the line had stayed out with Hervey and three others had ridden out the gale. Seven large ships were with Geary or Duff.

At 4 p.m. on the 18th Hawke was able to weigh anchor; but now the wind dropped away almost completely and ships had to be towed out of the Sound by boats. By noon on the 19th the *Ramillies* was ten leagues S.W. by S. of Ushant. On the next day the Admiral moved in to the Black Rocks and was relieved to find Hervey on guard with the *Monmouth*, *Dunkirk*, and *Bienfaisant*.

Hervey was stricken with the gout in both feet. 'I am far from being well', he wrote to Hawke, 'being only able to be carried from gallery to gallery as I want to look out.' As far as he could judge, the French had made absolutely no move to get out of Brest. 'There appears to be about twenty-two ships of the line, and ten small ships and vessels. All their yards and topmasts down… except the Vice-Admiral.'

On 21 October, seeing that a dispatch had to go off to put minds at rest at the Admiralty, Hawke took the opportunity to send a letter to the Victualling Commissioner at Plymouth,

---

[320] H.P.P., Brown to H., 11 Oct. 1759 — last page missing. 40 O.L., 14, 17, 21 Oct. 1759. I.L., 20 Oct. 1759.

asking for 800 tons of beer and 300 tons of water. These were to be supplied 'with the utmost dispatch', and any victuallers from Portsmouth were to be sent straight out to Ushant. The current spell of tranquil weather was too good an opportunity to be missed.[321]

At home it was now known that Quebec had surrendered. As many as three great victories had been reported in as few months. On 12 August John Calcraft had sent his soldier brother in America tidings of the 'glorious victory' at Minden. On 7 September he was informing Colonel Oughton that 'the Battle of Culloden did not produce more bonfires and illuminations than are at this instant lighted up in every street for Boscawen', the victor of Lagos. By 21 October Horace Walpole was writing to George Montagu about the celebration of the capture of Quebec. 'Our bells are worn threadbare with ringing for victories. I believe it will require ten votes of the House of Commons before people will believe it is the Duke of Newcastle that has done this and not Mr. Pitt. One thing is very fatiguing — all the world is made knights or generals.'[322]

The Royal Navy had won the Battle of Lagos and, through its persistent blockade of France and its operations in the St. Lawrence, had made it possible for Wolfe's aggressive leadership, despite its tactical and strategic shortcomings, to bring off a hazardous eleventh-hour attack at Quebec. Even Prince Ferdinand's victory at Minden would hardly have come about if it had not been for the British Navy's pressure on the coasts of France, and for the diversionary thrusts and threats derived therefrom.

---

[321] Add.MSS. 17494, f. 150, 176. H. Walpole, *Letters to G. Montagu*, 1819, p. 180.

[322] C. Lloyd, *The Capture of Quebec*, 1959, pp. 93-9, 107-9; and for Holmes's opinion of the naval hazards of the final attack, p. 116.

Hawke, as the principal exponent, since 1755, of the blockade of France, had made a fundamental contribution to the establishment of British maritime ascendancy. On top of this he was destined to win the crowning, irreversible victory of the war at sea. Yet two factors were liable to rob him in advance of a measure of the national acclaim to which he would be entitled by the year's end. His unfortunate gesture of May 1758 had jeopardized his position with the Admiralty and, to some extent, with the Government. Secondly, the frequent celebration of victory was exhausting the discrimination of even the educated public.

Meanwhile Conflans had been entertaining some bold thoughts. By the time, in late October, that Hawke reappeared off Brest, the marshal-cum-admiral had submitted to his King a plan, wherein he proposed the logical sequence of a fleet action with the British followed, in case of success, by a voyage to Quiberon Bay, whence he would escort the army into the Irish Sea. Louis XV, in his reply of 14 October, had signified acceptance of the plan. It simply remained for Conflans to carry it out! Lacour-Gayet justly observed: 'As for this unfortunate idea of putting a squadron to sea from Brest to embark an army in the Morbihan, when it was just as easy to assemble that army at Brest itself instead of Vannes, he had accepted it without dissent; perhaps he was content, like d'Aiguillon, that the clashes which might have occurred between the commander-in-chief of the navy and the commander-in-chief of the land forces had thus been avoided.'

The storm which blew Hawke off station provided Conflans with a chance to reach Quiberon Bay without serious fighting. But when it came to the point, he found that the crews were not capable of taking the squadron to sea, because of their long-enforced immobility. One of his *chefs d'escadre*, Guébriant, complained that he had not thirty men aboard the *Orient* 'who deserved the name of seamen'. When the fleet did eventually sail, Guébriant could only negotiate the Goulet by making his officers handle the sails. Apart from the splendid flagship, the *Soleil Royal*, the fighting and sailing qualities of the ships also left much to be desired. In this respect, too, the British blockade had taken its toll, through cutting off the usual supplies of timber and other naval stores.[323]

On 23 October Hawke's squadron was encouraged by the arrival of a consignment of beer and also 'the agreeable news of the surrender of Quebec'.

Rather less welcome, from the Admiral's point of view, was a letter from the Navy Board, dated the 17th. The Commissioners complained that Mr. David Wright, Surgeon of the *Nottingham*, had recently been set on shore because of some offence; and they pointed out, with a fair show of reason, that omission of the normal procedure of trying him made it difficult to judge whether he should be further employed. Hawke decided that the next step was to collect from Wright's commanding officer, Captain Lendrick, some particulars of the case and on 26 October, he received an account which began as follows:

> I am to inform you —
>
> That Mr. George Bowyer, 2nd Lieutenant of the *Nottingham*, having the watch upon deck between 8 and 12 p.m., the 23rd August 1759, and the ship being at sea, and having occasion to tack the ship between 10 and 11, ordered John Harris, Boatswain's Mate, to go down and turn up all the idlers [non-seamen] in about the cockpit to assist in tacking; that whilst said Harris was in the execution of his duty, and, among others, ordering up the Lobb Lolly Man [sick berth attendant],

---

[323] Bamford, pp. 61-5, etc. Lacour-Gayet, pp. 326-7.

> the Surgeon, Mr. David Wright, called out to him from his cabin, 'Get you gone, you rascal! He shan't go for you, and if you don't be gone instantly from this, I'll come out and kick you up the ladder!'

On hearing about this incident from 'said Harris', the Officer of the Watch conceived a wish to interview Mr. Wright. Successive messengers of gradually mounting seniority requested the surgeon's attendance on the quarter-deck, but Mr. Wright signified that no adequate reason for compliance had so far been suggested to him. The equilibrium was disturbed only when the Captain, having heard a recital of these exchanges, sent Wright an order to come to his cabin immediately. The latter appeared but lost no time in stating that he 'would not obey any Lieutenant'. Lendrick thereupon had him locked in his cabin 'for disobedience and mutiny'; and it was at this stage that the Admiral had given permission for him to be sent into port, because the *Nottingham*'s duties in the inshore squadron did not permit a court martial to be held. Finally, Lendrick remarked: 'There are other parts in the Surgeon's character, such as exacting sums of money for the cure of venereal disorders for the common men over and above the Government's allowance in that case provided, which in my opinion would be sufficient to have him discharged from the Service.'

On 29 October Hawke enclosed the above details with a letter to the Navy Board. He said in effect, that he considered the good of the Service more important than the ordinary rules of procedure. 'The *Nottingham* was wanted at a moment's notice to cruise in the Goulet at Brest, a station which required every man in her to be ready at a call.' It was, in the circumstances, not feasible to hold a court martial; and the inconvenience of mounting a guard over 'so worthless a fellow', when the ship expected to go into action at any time, was unacceptable. 'I ordered him to be discharged', the Admiral concluded, 'and his crime noted on his list of pay, for your information.'[324]

Augustus Hervey's long and very distinguished spell in command of the inshore squadron was drawing to a close. The *Monmouth* was leaking badly, and he himself was still unable to put a foot on the ground. Hawke decided to send the ship in and at the same time, in a letter of 3 November, he sent Hervey a handsome acknowledgement of his services. 'I heartily regret your being obliged to go in, and sincerely wish you the re-establishment of your health... Believe me, Sir, I shall cheerfully embrace every opportunity of acknowledging the sense I have of the officer-like manner in which you have performed the duties of your station.'

This promise was abundantly fulfilled in Hawke's dispatch to the Admiralty dated 5 November.[325]

Meanwhile, on the 4th, Lendrick had had to report the poor condition of the *Nottingham*, which like the *Monmouth*, was a veteran of the Second Battle of Cape Finisterre. 'I am excessively sorry', wrote Lendrick, 'this accident should have happened at a time the Service seems to require our greatest attention; but as the ship is old and infirm, I can't think a narrow and strict inspection can be dispensed with.'

Hawke lost no time in sending into port both the ships which had for so long proved a stumbling-block to the enemy; and he marked the occasion by commending to the Admiralty's notice Digby, who now took charge of the inshore force, Barrington, Lendrick, and Balfour, all of whom had given Hervey admirable support.[326]

---

[324] O.L., 24, 29 Oct. 1759. I.L., 17, 26 Oct. 1759.

[325] I.L., 2 Nov. 1759. O.L., 3, 5 Nov. 1759.

On 5 November Digby received an urgent injunction from the Admiral to look into Brest. If the winds made it dangerous for the ships to go in close he was to send a cutter 'at all risks'. But the sharply worsening weather seems to have made any observation quite impossible.[327]

That same day Hawke had received two letters from Clevland. There was strong evidence 'that positive orders [had been] sent to M. Conflans to put to sea directly and at all events to engage His Majesty's ships' under Hawke's command. In view of the strong possibility that Hawke might be blown off his station, he was to leave some frigates 'to the westward of Ushant to observe the motions of the French ships in Brest'. This was a sound idea but Hawke had no frigates just then.[328]

From the 6th to the 9th a great gale, whose fury continually mounted, blew from about N.W. With the spray-laden wind screaming through the shrouds and freezing the hands of the prime seamen as, vertiginously swaying over the foam-streaked waves, they desperately tied new reefs into the wet sails, the squadron repeatedly wore and beat in a grim effort to remain due N. of Ushant. Hawke sought to keep clear of the murderous lee shore without being swept away up-Channel. But, by the 9th, the squadron had been inexorably borne to the E. as far as Start Point. As Hawke had put it in his dispatch of the 5th: 'Single ships may struggle with a hard gale of wind, where a squadron can not. It must always from wearing lose ground in working against a strong westerly wind in the Channel, where it cannot make very long stretches, but more especially if it should blow so as to put it past carrying sail.' On

---

[326] I.L., 4 Nov. 1759. O.L., 5 Nov. 1759.
[327] O.L., 5, 10 Nov. 1759.
[328] I.L., 29, 30 Oct. 1759. O.L., 10 Nov. 1759.

the 9th a brief improvement offered hope of recovering the lost miles to the W., but the gale renewed its onslaught from W. by N. That night, Hawke went with his squadron into Torbay. Thanks to his impeccable judgement of the limits of the possible, no ships were lost.

His dispatch of 10 November was quite unflustered. He referred to the Lords' remark of 30 October about the possibility of Conflans descending suddenly on Duff's force in Quiberon Bay:

> As to Quiberon, I submit it to their Lordships whether or not, considering the season of the year, the *Belliqueux* [64] and the *Firm* [60] should not be called off. If, which is very improbable, the enemy should escape me and make their push there with their whole squadron, these two ships would be of little avail, and without them the five 50-gun ships and nine frigates would be a much more manageable squadron, and therefore better able to preserve itself until my arrival.

With the N.W. gale continuing it was quite possible, he thought, that Bompart would get into Brest; but nothing could emerge from the Biscay ports under these conditions.

In fact Bompart did shoot into Brest within a couple of days of Hawke's being driven off station. The seven ships of the line which he brought with him were welcome to Conflans because they bore crews of recent seagoing experience. These were at once distributed amongst the ships of the main squadron. Perhaps it was only thanks to this reinforcement that the *vice-amiral es mers du Levant* was able to sail at all. Howbeit, those westerly gales which had so often denied Hawke his prey were at last to present him with an awe-inspiring opportunity.[329]

[329] O.L., 10 Nov. 1759. Add.MSS. 32898, f. 292. Corbett, ii, 52.

On the 12th the weather looked better and by 7 a.m. the squadron was weighing anchor. By nightfall, however, it had progressed no farther than Bolt Head. In the autumnal darkness a fresh gale arose from the S.W., and by the 13th Hawke was back in Torbay. It was not until then that Digby and his inshore squadron came into port.

The *Ramillies* had for some time creaked and groaned alarmingly and admitted unwelcome quantities of water when subjected to hard gales. Her carpenter now considered that she was in a dangerous condition, and his brother-carpenters from the *Union*, *Namur*, and *Royal George*, who were ordered by Hawke to survey the ill-fated ship, entirely agreed. The Admiral thereupon shifted his flag (and his secretary) to the *Royal George*, commanded by Captain John Campbell. At 3 p.m. on 14 November the blue flag flew out at the main topgallant masthead of the ship which was to bear him to his tempestuous victory.[330]

Geary had many sick men aboard his flagship, the *Sandwich*, so Hawke ordered him into Plymouth to collect fresh men, whence he was to follow the squadron out to its rendezvous. Meanwhile he instructed Captain James Young of the *Mars* (who had first served under his command off the Genoese coast in 1745) to hoist a commodore's pennant and take charge of the rear division.[331]

During the night of 14 November Hawke and his storm-tossed, weather-stained ships rounded Start Point. Despite all the difficulties, strain, and damage of six months on blockade, ships and men were ready for battle. The level of morale, training, and health represented a hard-earned triumph for the

[330] O.L., 12, 17 Nov. 1759. Ad. 51/811.

[331] Ad. 1/93, 15 Nov. 1759; 1/92, 24 Nov. 1759 and line of battle. Clowes, iii, 218 n.

man who had brought the close blockade into existence. To crown this long endeavour, he would soon have to face the supreme moment of decision for which he had so patiently prepared, and weigh the risk of destroying his fleet against the chance of securing his country's safety and ensuring its imperial destiny. This would call for the highest degree of professional judgement and moral courage. In judgement and character he would prove equal to the occasion, unique in its breath-taking circumstances.[332]

[332] N.M.M.: Longford Papers, Pakenham's Journal. *Westminster Journal*, 15 Dec. 1759 — letter from H.'s fleet.

CHAPTER 14: THE BATTLE OF QUIBERON BAY

ON 14 November, while Hawke was at last getting clear of Torbay, the French fleet was also putting to sea. Assured that all the British ships had been blown off station, Conflans had succeeded, though not without difficulty, in getting his squadron out into the Bay of Biscay. He had a lead of about 200 miles over Hawke and only 120 miles of sea separated him from Quiberon Bay. Yet even this apparently decisive handicap was to prove insufficient! The slowness of the French is to be explained partly by poor seamanship, partly by sheer bad luck with the winds.

Conflans's twenty-one ships of the line were arranged in three divisions. Aboard the *Soleil Royal* (80) from which he commanded the centre division, Conflans had a 1st Captain, borne for flag duties only, as well as the usual two Captains to look after the ship. The prestige of the centre division was further bolstered by the presence, aboard the *Orient* (80), of the equivalent of a British rear-admiral in the person of the Chevalier de Guébriant Budes, *Chef d'Escadre*. The Chevalier de Bauffremont of the *Tonnant* (80), a ship well remembered by Hawke, was the *Chef d'Escadre* of the van. In the rear, the *Chef d'Escadre* was Saint-Andre du Verger, flying his flag in the *Formidable* (80). He was soon to prove his courage in the face of a terrible onslaught. The *Chefs d'Escadre* commanded their own ships. Like the *capitaines de vaisseau*, they had a *commandant en second* — the British equivalent of the latter being the 1st Lieutenant of a ship of the line.[333]

On 16 November, before he had reached Ushant, Hawke sent the *Fortune* sloop to warn Duff that the French fleet might be out. Within a few hours of her departure he received confirmation that this was indeed the case. The master of the homebound victualler, *Love and Unity*, informed him that the French fleet had been sighted on the previous day, only sixty miles or so from Belle Isle, which then bore E. by S. The wind, blowing from a little S. of E., had then been against the enemy.

Hawke passed the weather-scourged outline of Ushant on the 17th, with the squadron carrying 'a pressure of sail' and beat furiously ahead. There was a strong head-wind blowing from S.S.E. which was hardly welcome, seeing that the goal in this vital race was the entrance to Quiberon Bay. On the 18th, however, the wind veered round to N.E., and Hawke was able to reach straight for Belle Isle.

Meanwhile the French had been driven far to the westward by a strong easterly gale. By the 19th the two fleets were almost equidistant from Belle Isle and approaching it on converging courses, the British from the W. and the French from the S.W. Conflans, thanks to a westerly wind springing up during the night, unwittingly re-established a slender lead over Hawke.[334]

Duff meanwhile remained unaware of the approaching danger. On 27 October Hawke had sent him orders to post one cruiser off Belle Isle and another off Basque Road to give him (Duff) 'timely notice of the motions of the enemy'; but the weather had upset his dispositions. After the gales of 6-13 November, Captain John Reynolds of the *Firm* (60) emerged from the shelter of Quiberon Bay to resume his watch over

---

[333] Troude, i, 385. Lacour-Gayet, pp. 494-7.

[334] O.L., 17, 24 Nov. 1759. Ad. 1/93, 17 Nov. 1759; 51/811. Corbett, ii, 57-8, and map facing II, p. 1. Troude, i, 386 et seq. gives Conflans's dispatch in full.

Port Louis, with the frigates *Southampton*, *Pallas*, and *Vengeance* in company. On the 17th he encountered the *Swallow* sloop off the Isle de Groix. The *Swallow* was endeavouring to reach Duff with the news of the French fleet's being sighted on the 15th by the convoy of victuallers (of which the *Love and Unity* was a member). Reynolds at once ordered the *Vengeance* to pass with all possible speed through the Teignouze Passage, and tell Duff that twenty-one French sail of the line and three frigates were 'working for Quiberon Bay'. With the *Firm* and his other two frigates, Reynolds hurried towards Ushant in the hope of finding Hawke but missed him by a few miles.[335]

Frustrated by the contrary winds, the *Vengeance* took two days to reach Quiberon Bay. On the 19th she was still in the Teignouze Passage, making but slow headway against a light south-easterly breeze; but early in the afternoon some of Duff's ships could at last be seen. The *Vengeance* at once began to fire signal guns and flew the pre-arranged warning signal for an enemy fleet.

Most of Duff's ships were anchored and peacefully occupied in shipping provisions. Aboard the *Belliqueux* (64), for example, the crew heard several guns in the distance, but stolidly continued to transfer stores to Hawke's old command, the *Portland* (50). At 3 p.m. the scene was transformed. The *Vengeance*'s signal-flag was recognized aboard the *Rochester* and Duff at once hoisted the signal to cut or slip. He was precipitately obeyed. The *Portland* cut away her anchor and sailed off dragging behind her the *Belliqueux*'s longboat which was still secured to her best bower. At about this time the wind began to swing round from S.E. to S.W., but even so the eighteen or more vessels, including some victuallers, had passed through the Teignouze Passage by 5 p.m. During the

[335] Ad. 51/3834. O.L., 27 Oct., 17 Nov. 1759.

early part of the night they worked round to the N. of Belle Isle. The *Rochester* brought to, while a boat put off from the *Vengeance*. The latter's captain climbed up out of the gloom, mounted the *Rochester*'s quarter-deck, and gave Duff his first details of the enemy. Duff spent the rest of the night feeling his way, in little wind, to the W. side of Belle Isle, presumably in the hope of meeting Hawke.[336]

Meanwhile Hawke, about forty miles away to the W. at midnight on the 19th, did not get the change of wind from S.E. to S.W. till the early hours of 20 November. Having been joined by the frigates *Maidstone* and *Coventry*, he sent them ahead to search for the enemy. If they sighted the French they were to let fly their topgallant sheets.

At 2 a.m. on the 20th the wind began to blow in squalls from the W.S.W. and Hawke put his squadron onto the starboard tack. Aboard the *Royal George* the topmen clambered in the darkness more than a hundred feet up the lurching masts in order to get down the topgallant yards. Then, with the cold wind howling fitfully through the shuddering, ill-defined tackle around them, they set about reefing the topsails.

Before dawn a sounding was taken which showed that the depth of water was down to seven fathoms. At 7 a.m. Hawke ordered Howe in the *Magnanime* to go ahead and make the land. He then signalled to the squadron to bear away directly before the wind and — regardless of the ferocity of the weather — to unreef topsails. As expectation mounted high throughout the fleet, the canvas billowed out powerfully and the ships' bows drove deeply into the water.[337]

---

[336] Ad. 51/792; 51/3784; 51/3941.

[337] Ad. 51/811. O. L., 24 Nov. 1759. N. M.M.: Longford Papers, loc. cit. Troude, loc. cit.

Meanwhile Admiral Conflans was not displeased with the sight revealed to him by break of day. In the background was Belle Isle. In the foreground, Duff's miscellaneous collection, wherein the most powerful ships were the *Belliqueux* (64) and four 50s, was heading directly towards him.

At 7 o'clock, Duff, for his part, ascertained that the large fleet advancing towards him was not Hawke's. Conflans hoisted the chase. Duff's force scattered, the *Rochester*, followed by the *Belliqueux* and two other ships, heading northwards in the direction of Groix, while the rest fled to the S. Conflans and his division rushed off after Duff's group and by 8.30 the *Belliqueux* experienced the unsought distinction of having the French flagship on her tail. But at 9.45, just as he was drawing within gunshot, Conflans abruptly called off the chase.

Aboard the *Soleil Royal*, the lookouts were reporting a number of strange sail in the W. On the flagship's crowded quarter-deck, zest for the pursuit began to give way to anxiety. A battery of telescopes focussed on the distant shapes of many ships, arranged in a line abreast and bearing down before the wind under a great crowd of sail. The main battlefleet of England was racing down to the attack.[338]

As early as 8.30 the *Maidstone* had let her topgallant sheets fly out and a shout, compounded of joy and relief, had rung round Hawke's ships. The Admiral ordered a line abreast; but it was not till 9.45 that the *Magnanime* signalled to confirm that the fleet ahead was indeed the enemy.[339]

It is appropriate that Hawke's order of battle should now be given.

---

[338] ibid. P. R.O. 30/8/79, disposition of ships, 19 Nov. 1759. Ad. 51/792; 51/37845 51/3941. O. L., 24 Nov. 1759.
[339] Ad. 51/811. *Gentleman's Mag.*, Dec. 1759 — chaplain's letter. Longford Papers, loc. cit. O.L., 24 Nov. 1759.

Under command of Sir Charles Hardy, Vice-Admiral of the Blue:
Ship: *Warspite*, Captain: Bentley, Guns: 74, Men: 600
Ship: *Kingston*, Captain: T. Shirley, Guns: 60, Men: 400
Ship: *Swiftsure*, Captain: Stanhope, Guns: 70, Men: 520
Ship: *Duke*, Captain: T. Graves, Guns: 90, Men: 750
Ship: *Union*, Captain: Sir Charles Hardy; Evans, Guns: 90, Men: 770
Ship: *Hercules*, Captain: Fortescue, Guns: 74, Men: 600
Ship: *Intrepid*, Captain: Maplesden, Guns: 60, Men: 420
Ship: *Montague*, Captain: Rowley, Guns: 60, Men: 420

Under command of Sir Edward Hawke, Knight of the Bath, Admiral of the Blue:
Ship: *Revenge*, Captain: Storr, Guns: 64, Men: 480
Ship: *Dorsetshire*, Captain: Denis, Guns: 70, Men: 520
Ship: *Torbay*, Captain: Keppel, Guns: 74, Men: 700
Ship: *Royal George*, Captain: Sir Edward Hawke; Campbell, Guns: 100, Men: 880
Ship: *Magnanime*, Captain: Howe, Guns: 74, Men: 700
Ship: *Burford*, Captain: Gambier, Guns: 70, Men: 520
Ship: *Chichester*, Captain: Willett, Guns: 70, Men: 520

Under command of James Young, Esq., Commodore
Ship: *Dunkirk*, Captain: Digby, Guns: 60, Men: 420
Ship: *Temple*, Captain: W. Shirley, Guns: 70, Men: 520
Ship: *Namur*, Captain: Buckle, Guns: 90, Men: 780
Ship: *Mars*, Captain: James Young, Esq., Guns: 74, Men: 600
Ship: *Resolution*, Captain: Speke, Guns: 74, Men: 600
Ship: *Essex*, Captain: O'Bryen, Guns: 64, Men: 480
Ship: *Defiance*, Captain: Baird, Guns: 60, Men: 420
Ship: *Hero*, Captain: Edgecumbe, Guns: 74, Men: 600

Bentley and Stanhope will be remembered as captains at the Second Battle of Cape Finisterre. They had both been knighted for their services at the Battle of Lagos and now they had rejoined Hawke in time for the greatest naval occasion of their lives.[340]

Seeing that Hawke's squadron was rapidly approaching, Conflans had to decide quickly on his course of action. He began hesitantly to draw his ships into a line of battle. Then reflecting that his strategic object was to unit his fleet with the transports in the Morbihan, and assessing Hawke's superiority of strength, he decided to make for Quiberon Bay. He thought it unlikely that the British would follow him, considering the very high wind (of nearly forty knots) and alarming swell. In any case, there was not room in Quiberon Bay for two large fleets to manoeuvre; and the British could have little knowledge of the abundant rocks and other hazards. Conflans therefore took the decisive step of signalling 'l'ordre de marche sur une ligne', which required him to place the *Soldi Royal* at the head of his squadron and lead it in a line ahead.[341]

This development, according to the General Fighting Instructions, permitted Hawke to hoist the chase, and he immediately did so. A white flag with a red cross ran up to the *Royal George*'s fore topmasthead, and a signal gun sounded three times. In consequence the seven ships nearest the enemy formed line as they chased. The rest of the fleet followed under as much sail as could be carried in those conditions, ready to form a line in their actual order if the enemy stood to fight. The British ships hummed with preparations for action. Partitions were cleared from the gun-decks and longboats hoisted out. Confusion of purpose might have reigned under a Mathews or a John Byng, but under Hawke everyone knew that the attack would be pressed home.[342]

---

[340] Ad. 1/92, 24 Nov. 1759 — enclosure. Clowes, iii, 215.

[341] Troude, loc. cit. Longford Papers, loc. cit. Ad. 51/3941.

[342] O.L., 24 Nov. 1759. Ad. 51/811. N. R.S., *Fighting Instructions*, p.

At the end of his seagoing career Lord St. Vincent remarked, 'Lord Hawke, when he ran out of the line and took the *Poder*, sickened me of tactics.' If the image of Hawke's action at the Battle of Toulon was seen so clearly at the end of the century, there could not have been a man in that fleet, racing forward on the wings of the gale, who was unconscious of his Admiral's resolute qualities. As St. George's flag run up to signal that the chase was on, Hawke 'told his officers he was for the old way of fighting, to make downright work with them'. He was doubtless referring to his own instructions for close action, as well as to the methods of the mêléeists in the Dutch Wars.[343]

At 11 a.m. Duff, with his four 50-gun ships (including 'the brave Captain Lockhart' of the *Chatham*, who had narrowly escaped capture) joined up with Hawke's squadron. The frigates *Minerva*, *Vengeance*, and *Pallas* also came up.[344]

By noon Midshipman Pakenham of the *Dunkirk*, Captain Digby, reckoned that the rear enemy ships were only three miles ahead. Beyond them, about twelve miles distant, loomed the tail of Belle Isle.[345]

Conflans had expected to get the whole of his line safely round the Cardinals — the rocks which marked the W. of the entrance to Quiberon Bay — before any of Hawke's ships could close within effective range. Then, with the gale at about W.S.W., he would head direct for the safety of the Morbihan. It was with surprise and consternation that, at noon, he saw the British leaders gaining rapidly on his straggling rear

---

221. Longford Papers, loc. cit.

[343] N.R.S., *Signals and Instructions*, p. 34. *Gentleman's Mag.*, loc. cit.

[344] ibid. *Whitehall Evening Post*, 1 Dec. 1759 — 'extract of a letter from a Gentleman aboard the *Royal George*'. O. L., 24 Nov. 1759.

[345] Longford Papers, loc. cit.

division. Saint-Andre du Verger was beginning to look fearfully vulnerable.[346]

In this respect, the opening phase of the Second Battle of Cape Finisterre was about to be repeated.

At half-past two, the *Dorsetshire* and *Torbay* opened fire. Hawke thereupon had Campbell order the red flag to be hoisted to the fore topmasthead — 'every ship in the fleet is to use their utmost endeavour to engage the enemy as close as possible'.

The weather had not abated in the least and ships could open their lower gun-ports only at immediate risk of giant waves sweeping catastrophically through them. The hawser attached to the *Dunkirk*'s longboat had already snapped like cotton. Despite their immediate danger of envelopment by the British, in that wind and leaping water the French still did not dare to carry as much sail as their adversaries.[347]

The *Dorsetshire* (Denis) and *Torbay* (Keppel) were quickly followed into the action developing outside the Cardinals by the *Magnanime* (Howe), *Resolution* (Speke), *Swiftsure* (Stanhope), *Warspite* (Bentley), *Montague* (Rowley — son of Hawke's C-in-C of 1745), and *Defiance* (Baird). The French rear struggled desperately against this overwhelming concentration of firepower.[348]

Conflans could see this disastrous action beginning, as he rounded the Cardinals and headed for the Morbihan. At this juncture a decisive event occurred: the wind changed from W.S.W. to W.N.W. The French line was thrown into disorder and the Morbihan was placed out of reach. Conflans seems to

---

[346] ibid., for comments on tactics. For the direction of the wind, the logs have been preferred to the dispatches. Troude, loc. cit.

[347] Ad. 51/811. N. M.M.: Duff Papers and Papers of Capt. M. Clements. O. L., 24 Nov. 1759. Longford Papers, loc. cit.

[348] *Gentleman's Mag.*, loc. cit. Marcus, pp. 149-50.

have sailed on for a time in a northerly direction, doubtless praying for the wind to swing back towards the S.W. Meanwhile Hawke in the *Royal George* was past Belle Isle and chafing to catch up with French rear, which, embattled with the nine British leaders, was still sweeping ahead for the Bay. At about 2.50 p.m. they were in. The *Royal George* rounded the Cardinals at 3 o'clock.[349]

Saint-Andre du Verger's *Formidable* (80) had been the focus of the British onslaught. The *Chef d'Escadre* and his elder brother, who was *Capitaine en Second*, chose to fight to the death. At 3.40, as Speke in the *Resolution* pressed home his attack with great tenacity, the French flagship's fore topmast crashed down. By 3.55, when the senior officers and many others had been killed, the *Formidable*'s survivors decided to surrender.

At the same time Hawke came up and passed rapidly ahead. He was continually urging Captain Campbell to put his ship alongside the *Soleil Royal.* These injunctions, overheard by officers on the quarter-deck, were probably the origin of the legendary remark, supposed to have been addressed by Hawke to the ship's Master: 'You have now done your duty in apprising me of the danger; let us see next how well you can comply with my orders. I say, lay me alongside the French Admiral! '[350]

What was doubtless a simple instruction proved a fertile source of imaginative reporting. An elaborate version can be found in E. H. Locker's *Memoirs of Naval Commanders.* 'As they neared the coast, the Master of the *Royal George* observed, "If

---

[349] Troude, loc. cit. Longford Papers, loc. cit. O.L., 24 Nov. 1759. Ad. 51/811.

[350] Lacour-Gayet, p. 332. Log of Lt. Kerswell of the *Maidstone. Whitehall Evening Post*, 1 Dec. 1759. *Gentleman's Mag.*, loc. cit. Ad. 51/811. *Naval Chronicle*, ii, 558-9.

we run on much longer, Sir, we must inevitably be on shore." "That may be," coolly replied his Admiral, "but they must be on shore first. At all hazards their ships must be destroyed, so lay me alongside the *Soleil Royal*.'"

Locker's father, William, for whom Hawke had twice tried to get a commission, was an acting Lieutenant aboard the frigate *Sapphire* which had been with Duff and was in time to participate in the later part of the battle. William Locker — who, as has been mentioned, was much respected by Nelson — afterwards held that Hawke's attack at Quiberon was 'an achievement which very few men would have had nerve to hazard'.[351]

From 4 p.m. onwards Hawke either witnessed or actively brought about some highly sensational events. The *Thésée* (74), Captain Kersaint, of the French centre division, had borne down to engage Keppel's *Torbay*. In the furious wind and great swell, both ships tried to use their main batteries at imminent risk of being swamped. Keppel justified his reputation as a brilliant seaman by flinging the *Torbay* round into the wind as soon as water began to burst into his gun-ports. Kersaint and his crew were less nimble. Hawke, as he forged past, saw the *Thésée* fill and go down with a horrifying abruptness. Keppel, despite the near-impossible conditions, at once had boats hoisted out to save survivors. One boat's crew demonstrated its skill and courage by retrieving nine Frenchmen and finding its way back to the *Torbay* after dark. Altogether, there were twenty-two survivors out of a complement of 650.[352]

---

[351] Locker, 'Wm. Locker', p. 11 and 'Hawke', p. 10. O.L., 24 Nov. 1759.

[352] Keppel, i, 284-8. Lacour-Gayet, p. 332. Ad. 51/811. Longford Papers, loc. cit.

Meanwhile Conflans wore his ship and headed back towards the entrance. He intended to place himself in the middle of his disordered fleet and get it into a line of battle. As a result the *Soleil Royal*, with white flag at main topmasthead was approaching the *Royal George* almost head on.

The action had become general. At 4.30 the *Magnanime* forced the *Héros* to strike her colours but, because of the dangerous sea running, Howe did not put a prize crew aboard her and she later tried to escape. No sooner had the *Héros* surrendered than Hawke found himself close to the *Soleil Royal*, together with the *Tonnant* (Bauffremont) and twelve other French ships of the line. At the *Royal George*'s headlong approach, they all wore. As they did so they loosed a hail of ill-directed shot at the British flagship. Hawke at once swooped down to take the chance of raking the *Soleil Royale* from aft, but the *Intrépide* — the same ship that had helped to save the *Tonnant* at the Second Battle of Cape Finisterre — swiftly intervened. There was a rapid exchange of broadsides between her and the *Royal George*. Hawke pressed on into the body of French ships as they headed at speed in an easterly direction, straight towards where Dumet Island lay in the thickening murk. The *Superbe* (70) challenged the *Royal George* which swiftly replied with two broadsides. The effect was cataclysmic. At 4.41 the *Superbe* plunged deeply and in an instant she had sunk. There were no survivors.

The *Superbe*'s crew of 630 — like that of the *Thésée* — was entirely composed of Bretons. Many of them were conscripted peasants who had never been to sea before.[353]

---

[353] Troude, loc. cit. *Gentleman's Mag.*, loc. cit. Ad. 51/811. For confirmation of the passage: 'At 35 minutes after 4, we got up with 14 sail of the enemy ships, who all wore and gave us their broadside', see N.M.M.: Log of Lt. R. Williams of the *Royal George*. Lacour-Gayet, p. 333.

Lieutenant Roger Williams of the *Royal George* recorded what happened at the end of the run towards Dumet. 'We were still under sail to get alongside Conflans, who lay on our lee bow, as was the French Vice-Admiral. Soon after, they starboarded their helms and hauled their wind to the northward to get clear of us. We was obliged to haul our wind to the S.W. to prevent being ashore on the island Dumet. '

During the phase of the combat when Hawke was in pursuit of Conflans, it seemed to observers in other ships that the *Royal George* would be destroyed by overwhelming odds; but, as Hawke must have estimated, the French gunnery was sufficiently poor — owing to lack of training and practice — to make the risk acceptable.[354]

Visibility was now very restricted. At 5, as he headed back a mile or so towards the entrance of the Bay, the Admiral hauled down the signal for a close engagement. He afterwards wrote: 'Night was now come, and being on a part of the coast, among islands and shoals, of which we were totally ignorant, without a pilot, as was the greatest part of the squadron, and blowing hard on a lee shore, I made the signal to anchor, and came to in fifteen fathom water, the Island of Dumet bearing E. by N. between two and three miles, the Cardinals W. ½ S., and the steeples of Croisie S.E., as we found next morning.'[355]

Meantime Conflans had at least succeeded in shaking off the *Royal George* but he had entirely lost contact with his scattered, thoroughly routed fleet. He decided to use the cover of darkness and escape from Quiberon Bay. Heading for the entrance which lay somewhere to the S.S.E., he soon discovered that the advantages of invisibility were

[354] N.M.M.: Log of Lt. Williams, op. cit. cf. Troude, loc. cit.; Ad. 51/811. *Gentleman's Mag.*, loc. cit.
[355] Ad. 51/811. O.L., 24 Nov. 1759.

counterbalanced by its drawbacks. No sooner had one his own ships suddenly appeared and bounced off his port side than another emerged from the gloom and crashed into his starboard side. With the gale still blowing hard from the N.W. it is not surprising that he fell away to leeward and found his egress from the Bay blocked by the extensive Four Shoal. Conflans had had his fill of seamanship for one day. He dropped anchor. Such relief as he experienced might well have been modified if he had realized that he was in the middle of the British fleet and not far from the *Royal George*! The *Héros*, having eluded the *Magnanime* in the darkness, also happened to anchor near by.[356]

Several French captains reflected on the desirability of not being in the Bay when dawn broke. With the gale at about N.W., Basque Road offered attractions as a possible refuge and, when Bauffremont in the *Tonnant*, with the severely damaged *Magnifique* in company, approached the Isle of Aix on the following day (the 21st), he found five of Conflans's ships of the line already at anchor there. The *Intrépide* joined them on the 22nd.[357]

Another attempt by an enemy ship to escape from Quiberon was less successful. The *Juste* had received a severe hammering during the action and had lost both her captains, the brothers Saint-Allouarn. The 1st Lieutenant managed to navigate her out of the Bay and tried to reach the Loire estuary; but he went ashore and there were few survivors out of a crew of 630 Bretons.[358]

For their part, the British also suffered losses on this hazardous occasion. When night came the *Resolution*, with the

---

[356] Troude, loc. cit. Chevalier, i, 339.
[357] ibid., loc. cit. Lacour-Gayet, p. 335. O.L., 24 Nov., 1 Dec. 1759.
[358] Lacour-Gayet, p. 339. O.L., 2 Dec. 1759.

surrender of the *Formidable* to her credit, was near the entrance. Speke kept his crew working on the cut rigging till 9.30 p.m. Then he set sail for Hawke's anchorage. The Officer of the Watch afterwards stated: 'We put the ship to stays [i.e. tried to tack, in order to sail in a northerly direction], but, missing stays, we wore, and, in standing to the fleet, the ship struck, in about half an hour, upon a sand we knew nothing of.' The *Resolution* stuck fast, came off at high water, and went firmly aground again on the ebb. Her sides bulged with the strain, which meant that she would not float again.

That night was likely to be remembered, not only by survivors from the *Resolution*. The wind shrieked over the dark, tormented desolation of water and swept away the forlorn boom of distress signals. In any case the firing of such signals was nothing more than an expression of helplessness and terror. No aid could possibly be sent under such conditions.

All but four of Hawke's ships spent the night in Quiberon Bay. Those four, the *Dorsetshire*, *Revenge*, *Defiance*, and *Swiftsure* have been mentioned as participants in the attack on the French rear division. At the end of the day, they, like the *Resolution*, were close to the entrance, and they elected to sail out into the open sea. Although they had all suffered considerable damage in the fighting — except the *Defiance* — they avoided mishap during the hours of darkness.

At daybreak on 21 November Hawke could see the *Resolution* not far away, stranded on the Four Shoal and dismasted. He was at least equally interested to find that the *Soleil Royal* was at hand, trapped between his ships and Croisic. Conflans was also interested, at once had his cable cut, and ran for Croisic. Hawke hoisted the *Essex*'s signal. She made sail in pursuit of the French Admiral, but unfortunately ran onto part of the Four. Like the *Resolution* she became a total loss. When, in the usual way, her loss was investigated at a court martial, it was stated that everyone on board had 'behaved after she struck with great propriety'. Nearly all her crew were saved and even some of her stores.

Aboard the *Resolution*, however, the opening of the ship's sides during her nightmarish ordeal on the Four Shoal had resulted in a partial breakdown of discipline. Although Speke vehemently ordered them to desist, about eighty half-demented sailors, including some prisoners who had been brought aboard from the *Formidable*, pushed off on improvised rafts. In the continuing gale this was a suicidal proceeding. None of these men was ever seen again.

In the course of all this excitement the *Héros* and the *Soleil Royal* tried desperately to enter the little harbour of Croisic. The flagship nearly succeeded — but in such a case 'nearly' was somewhat inadequate. The net result was that both ships lay wrecked on the foreshore.

Now that it was light, the damage received in the battle by the *Royal George* could be ascertained. Despite the boldness with which Hawke had thrust her amongst large numbers of the enemy, the tally amounted to no more than 'a pair of main shrouds shot away, two pair of mizen shrouds, three pair of fore topmast shrouds, and most of our running rigging; our foresail much shattered, unbent it and bent another; one shot through the bowsprit and one through the mizen mast; one lodged in the foremast; part of the main trussel trees shot away, and eight shot in the hull'. Even allowing for the state of the weather, the ineffectiveness of the French gunnery is well illustrated — one of the fruits of the British fleet's long endurance on blockade.[359]

---

[359] Ad. 1/5298, 29 Nov. 1759, 22 Jan. 1760. Ad. 51/811. O.L., 24 Nov., 1 Dec. 1759. Troude, loc. cit.

It remains to describe the last phase of the battle. Seven enemy ships of the line and all four of their frigates were seeking to escape into the River Vilaine — the Morbihan being, of course, out of the question because of the persistent north-westerly gale. At 8 a.m. Hawke signalled the squadron to weigh anchor in the hope of working up towards the French but it proved impossible against that wind.

At 11 o'clock boats heroically went out from the *Royal George* to pick up some survivors from the *Thésée* who were noticed still clinging to pieces of mast. They had been in the water for nineteen hours.

Meanwhile the crews of the enemy ships near the Vilaine were vigorously occupied in what Hawke might have considered a regular feature of French naval life — namely, lightening ship by dropping guns and stores overboard. By nightfall, all of the enemy but two of the line had managed to scrape over the bar on the flood tide.

On the 22nd Hawke with his main body was able to work up towards the Vilaine, but the last two French ships escaped — in a thoroughly disarmed condition — at high water. However, it transpired that the *Inflexible* (64) was wrecked at the entrance to the river.

The losses of French ships at the Battle of Quiberon Bay have not often been accurately stated. The following ships of the line were destroyed or captured:

Thésée (74), sunk N.E. of the Cardinals.
Formidable (80), surrendered near the Cardinals.
Superbe (70), sunk near Dumet Is.
Soleil Royal (80), wrecked near Croisic, and afterwards burnt by her own crew.
Héros (74), wrecked near Croisic, and later burnt by the British.
Juste (70), wrecked at the entrance of the R. Loire.

Inflexible (64), wrecked at the entrance to the R. Vilaine.

One persistent fallacy is that four or so of the ships which escaped into the Vilaine had their backs broken and were thenceforward unserviceable. In fact, only the *Inflexible* was lost. All the other six ships of the line escaped from Quiberon Bay between January 1761 and April 1762. Still, it is true enough that they remained useless for offensive purposes for more than a year.[360]

It only remained for Hawke to complete the paralysis of the remnants of Conflans's fleet by dispatching Keppel with a squadron to the Basque Road. That officer's appearance was the signal for yet another *sauve-qui-peut*, with the usual accompaniment of brisk jettisoning of guns and stores. The seven enemy ships of the line reached the safety of Rochefort but no longer constituted any sort of immediate embarrassment to the Royal Navy.[361]

For an assessment of the strategic significance of the Battle of Quiberon Bay it seems appropriate to turn to the French historians. Lacour-Gayet wrote:

> The Battle of the Cardinals was the grave of the French Navy in the reign of Louis XV... The troops in the Morbihan had

[360] Ad. 51/811. O.L., 24 Nov. 1759. Lacour-Gayet, p. 333, gives number of survivors as: *The see* 22, *Superbe* 0; and, on p. 339, *Juste* 0. Chevalier, i, 339; I.L., 23 Nov. 1759; and Longford Papers, loc. cit. (with Chart) all show that the *Inflexible* was wrecked at the entrance of the Vilaine. For the escape from the Vilaine of the other 6 ships of the line, see Lacour-Gayet, pp. 347-8. He does not name the *Sphinx* among the 'derniers navires' which escaped in April 1762, but he includes her in the list of the French navy on p. 522. cf. Corbett, ii, 69 for a version of the broken-backs fallacy — but see also ii, 3231 I.L., 29 Nov. 1759. Clowes, iii, 313, shows accurately the ships lost by the French.

[361] O.L., 24 Nov., 2 Dec. 1759. Ad. 1/92, 1 Dec. 1759 — enclosure.

> to be dispersed..., all plans for the Channel and the North Sea had to be abandoned. This meant the ruin of all our hopes and of our last chance of salvation. But, painful as it was, it was not perhaps as cruel as the humiliations which we were now to have to suffer on all sides. We possessed no means of opposition. After Lagos and Quiberon, France had no more squadrons either in the Mediterranean or in the Atlantic.
>
> Hawke, whose boldness, combined with methodical calculation, foreshadowed the warlike genius of Nelson, exploited his victory in striking fashion by spreading terror along the whole coast of Biscay.

And the Comte de Germiny, who expressed elsewhere a particular admiration for Hawke, both as an admiral and as a man, had this to say about the Battle of Quiberon: 'It brought on us a bewilderment and a sense of helplessness which can only be compared with the huge disappointment experienced later by Napoleon I on account of the disaster at Trafalgar.'[362]

Yet today Hawke is hardly remembered in England. This is surely a most extraordinary injustice to his character and achievements.

However, it is gratifying to know that an admiral who has, apparently, failed to capture the imaginations of writers — could it be because he did not indulge in dramatic gestures? — did not fail to inspire his men with a zest for battle. In this respect, a letter from someone in his fleet, published in the *Westminster Journal*, is worth citing. Certainly it is couched in terms extravagant enough to satisfy any Victorian patriot! 'I have seen fire; I have seen men behave with courage and resolution; but never till the late engagement had I seen such

---

[362] Lacour-Gayet, p. 342. Germiny, p. 232. See pp. 239-40 for a very substantial tribute to Hawke.

uncommon ardour in all degrees of men! Such a noble emulation who should best do his duty, and serve his King and Country! The crew of every ship, animated with a thirst for glory, that every individual seemed to fight for a kingdom.'[363]

But among all the accounts of the battle which have been written, none surpass in restrained nobility Hawke's own comments on it towards the end of his dispatch of 24 November.

Our loss by the enemy is not considerable. For in the ships which are now with me, I find only one Lieutenant and fifty seamen and marines killed, and about two hundred and twenty wounded.

When I consider the season of the year, the hard gales on the day of action, a flying enemy, the shortness of the day, and the coast they were on, I can boldly affirm that all that could possibly be done has been done. As to the loss we have sustained, let it be placed to the account of the necessity I was under of running all risks to break this strong force of the enemy. Had we had but two hours more daylight, the whole had been totally destroyed or taken; for we were almost up with their van when night overtook us.[364]

---

[363] *Westminster Journal* — see p. 238 n.
[364] O.L., 24 Nov. 1759.

CHAPTER 15: AN EXPLOITATION OF VICTORY

HAWKE was so busily occupied in ensuring the destruction of the *Soleil Royal* and *Héros*, in seeing that stores were saved from the *Resolution* and *Essex*, and in finding out whether the enemy vessels in the Vilaine and Morbihan could be attacked, that it was not until 24 November that he had time to write a dispatch or a private letter. But on that day he did not fail to rush off a letter to Sally Birt with messages for his children. This letter is so thoroughly expressive of Hawke's very simple, homely manner in communicating with his intimates that it is given here in its original form, with spelling, capitals and abbreviations intact.

Dear Sall,

My Express being just agoing away for England, I have only time to tell you, that wee got up with the French fleet off this place, and have beat them, and dispers'd their fleet. Wee have burnt two of their ships of seventy four and eighty four guns; wee sunk two, one of seventy four and another of seventy guns, and have taken the Formidable, a ship of eighty four guns. In the Evening near dark, and blowing fresh and bad Weather, some of them run away, clear out; seven of them with two Frigates, anchor'd so near the shore that wee cou'd not get at them, and the second day, they flung every thing over board (for fear the Wear. shou'd moderate, and that we should get at them) and got into a little harbour near the place they were lying at. There they must remain this Winter at lest without anything in, and can be of no service to the french till we please to permit them.

Thank God. I am very well, tho' almost starved with Cold; I hope to be allow'd to go home soon, for I have had a long and tiresome service of it. Write to My Children, the instant you receive this, and give My Love and blessing to them, and make My Compliments to all My Neighbours, and believe me that I am truly,

Dear Sall,

Your sincere Friend,

E. Hawke.

P.S. Two of our ships had the ill luck to run ashore and was lost; but these accidents can't be help'd on these occasions, for it was next akin to a Miracle that half our ships was not ashore in the pursuite of the Enemy, upon their own coast, which wee were unacquainted with; besides its blowing strong and squally, and having no Pilots.

I am so cold I can scarce write.

Pray write to Mr. Brown, and make My Compliments to him and his sons.[365]

With his official dispatch Hawke sent a private letter to Lord Anson. In it he said that he was sending, with an account of the battle, Captain Campbell, who had proved himself 'an honest, brave and good officer in all respects, and fully answered the good opinion I had ever conceived of him'. Secondly, Hawke interceded with the First Lord on behalf of the widow of Lieutenant Stewart. This officer had, in fact, been rather unintelligent in carrying out his Admiral's orders. It was he who, on the 16th, had been sent ahead in the *Fortune* sloop to warn Duff that the French fleet was out; but he had, both gallantly and stupidly, sought action with a powerful French

[365] O.L., 24 Nov. 1759. I.L., 22, 23 Nov. 1759. O.B., 23 Nov. 1759. H. to Miss Birt, 24 Nov. 1759. The MS. is in the possession of Lord Hawke. (Miss Birt's Christian name was really Sarah, cf. H.P.P., 'Hawke MMS., 1702-1800', f. 156.)

frigate which he saw moving slowly along under jury masts. During the unequal combat Stewart was killed, and it was not until three days after Hawke's battle that the damaged *Fortune* reached Quiberon Bay. However, the Admiral, with his customary solicitude, asked Anson to have Stewart posthumously confirmed as Master and Commander of the sloop, 'in humanity to his widow, who he has left starving with three or four children'. Finally, he pointed out that the loss of both the *Resolution* and *Essex* was due to their not having copies of the *Neptune Francois* on board. He advised Anson to see that this navigational guide was 'correctly printed, on a large scale, and translated, at the King's expense', and issued to all ships, together with comprehensive charts.

Hawke's current relationship with Anson is reflected in the fact that this letter was purely professional, cordial in tone rather than friendly.[366]

At home Hawke's stock had stood by no means high with the public at the time when he was defeating the French fleet. Believing that he had let Conflans get out of the Bay of Biscay, together with a French army which would soon subject England to fire and sword, a mob was expressing 'absolute detestation of this worthy man, by hanging him in effigy, and branding him with every contemptuous epithet that could be thought disgraceful to a man of honour and courage'. These lively tongues no doubt worked more quickly still when a cutter, which Duff had dispatched early on the 20th to seek Hawke off Ushant, arrived at Plymouth without the slightest news of the Admiral's movements.[367]

---

[366] H.P.P., H. to Anson. Draft in clerk's hand, with alterations by the Admiral. No date, but fair copy probably dated 24 Nov. 1759.
[367] Charnock, iv, 285. Marcus, p. 169.

But those with real knowledge of military affairs were not necessarily apprehensive. Lord Ligonier, the Commander-in-Chief of the Army, wrote on that appropriate date, 24 November: 'We expect to hear every moment that Hawke has thoroughly thrashed Conflans.'

On 28 November Campbell duly arrived home in the frigate *Vengeance* and there was a general outburst of exultation. According to the *Whitehall Evening Post*: 'Thursday [the 29th] being the day appointed for a General Thanksgiving for our late Success, the morning was ushered in with ringing of Bells, at noon the Guns were fired from the Park and Tower, and the Churches were everywhere crowded on the Occasion… Dr. Dayreel preached before the Rt. Hon the Speaker and upwards of 200 members of the Hon. House of Commons, from Psalm XCV, 1, 2. "O come, let us sing unto the Lord. Let us make a joyful Noise to the Rock of our Salvation…".' Hawke's official dispatch was printed in *the London Gazette Extraordinary* of the 30th, and subsequently many newspapers reproduced it in full.[368]

Anson rode in a coach with Campbell to present Hawke's tidings to the King. On the journey, Anson is said to have intimated to Campbell that a knighthood was his if he wanted it. Campbell — widely regarded as a very decided Scotch character — replied: 'Throth, my Lord, I ken nae use that will be to me.' Anson murmured that his wife might like it. 'Weel then,' Campbell swiftly replied, 'His Majesty may knight her if he pleases!' George II apparently followed Campbell's mode of reasoning and gave him a reward for his services of £500.

However, signs of impatience with the series of victories can be discerned in some of the newspaper editorials. For example, the *Westminster Journal* of 1 December carried the following

[368] Whitworth, p. 312. Marcus, p. 169. *Whitehall Evening Post*, 1 Dec. 1759.

ironical reflections: 'Happy is the man who lives in these times! Nothing is to be heard but the voice of exultation... But may not Victory itself be purchased too dear? Take out, gentle Reader, thy pencil with a slip of paper, and calculate at 3 per cent what the annual income of 25 millions come to. If I mistake not, it amounts to £750,000 a year. This is money...'

There was no popular cry that Hawke, having won a victory fit to rank with the world's greatest, should be adequately rewarded. In France, however, there was no doubt as to the significance of the event. General Joseph Yorke, Hardwicke's third son and British Minister at the Hague, wrote to his sister, Lady Anson: 'The French are and well may be in a terrible consternation.' And he was soon reporting that the populace of Brittany, bereaved of so many sons at Quiberon, was raising a general outcry against the French navy. On 29 November Hawke himself received similar news from Young, who, with a small squadron, was standing guard over the Morbihan.

> I beg to acquaint you that there is no alteration in the situation of the French ships here since my arrival... Yesterday, our boat, in sounding the passage, spoke with a Dean from Port l'Orient, where there is three frigates and about thirty merchantmen. They say there is seven of their ships destroyed (which seems to have been the true total) and three of ours; but that is all they could get out of them, as they are very silent; but all their shops were shut up and they appeared in very great consternation.[369]

By the end of November Hawke knew that the *Juste* had been wrecked but he had nothing definite about the *Inflexible*. In the course of reconnoitering the mouth of the Vilaine,

---

[369] Charnock, VI, 35-6 n. Clowes, iii, 222. *Westminster Journal*, 1 Dec. 1759. Add.MSS. 35389, f. 188, 190. I.L., 29 Nov. 1759.

Willett and Hood had seen a ship on her beam ends on 23 November but they thought that she was only a frigate.[370]

The Admiral had become involved in negotiations with d'Aiguillon about an exchange of prisoners. The British were prepared to send ashore 120 French soldiers who had been in the *Formidable*. For their part, the French were believed to have a lieutenant and a boatload of men who had been blown ashore at the time of the loss of the *Essex*, and also one seaman of Duff's squadron who had likewise been swept ashore in a boat on an earlier occasion. Out of humanity, Hawke had the 'very great and very nauseous' company of the *Formidable*'s wounded put on shore, without waiting for an agreement to be concluded. He then asked d'Aiguillon to see that Britain was credited, under the cartel (or agreement) concerning the exchange of prisoners, with the number of unwounded men returned to France, and to send out any British prisoners who were being held locally.

On 8 December Hawke informed d'Aiguillon that the exchange was not being properly carried out. The French had sent out boats and vessels to collect their own people and had brought no British in them. Already annoyed, albeit unreasonably, at the French reluctance to hand over the crew of the *Héros* which had surrendered during the battle, he threatened that if the British prisoners and the *Héros*'s men were not produced, the consequences might be 'very fatal'. Eighty British seamen were transported with miraculous speed from prison to Hawke's squadron, whereupon the Admiral released the rest of the French prisoners.[371]

After a meeting of senior officers, the French sent a statement to Hawke to the effect that prisoners, like those of

---

[370] O.L., 1 Dec. 1759. I.L., 23 Nov. 1759.

[371] O.L., 29 Nov., 2, 3, 8, 9 Dec. 1759. Ad 1/92, 16 Feb. 1760.

the *Héros*, who had not given parole, were entitled to try to escape. Surprisingly, Hawke could not agree, and he threatened retaliation if there was any interference when the frigate *Actaeon* went in to pick up the guns of the *Héros*. As might have been expected, Ourry, commanding the said frigate, was duly greeted with gunfire, whereupon he followed Hawke's instructions and levelled part of Croisic. D'Aiguillon sent a protest. Hawke, adhering sincerely but perversely to his original attitude to the *Héros*'s surrender, replied:

> I shall endeavour to recover the *Héros*'s guns, as also those of the *Soleil Royal*, which was deserted and left to our mercy. The delivery of the officers and men is all that depends at present on the honour of your Court; the artillery are within our reach. Our endeavours to take them away being justifiable, I was in hopes would not have been interrupted; but since your Grace and the Marquis de Broc have thought fit to fire on my ships, I shall take as severe a revenge as I can, as soon as I receive supplies from Britain.[372]

This incident, like that of May 1758, provides an example of Hawke's occasional wrongheadedness. In view of his merciful treatment of the *Formidable*'s wounded, he can hardly be charged with ruthlessness.

By 9 December Hawke was recommending to the Admiralty that the blockade should be continued by anchoring strong squadrons in Quiberon Bay and in the Basque Road. These, he said, should be supplemented by frigates cruising at sea. For example, he had already stationed some of them off Groix, Belle Isle, and Bordeaux. As there was now no immediate threat from Brest, he considered that cruisers — frigates, or 50-gun ships — could blockade that port. Installing the two

[372] Lacour-Gayet, p. 343. O.L., 12 Dec. 1759. Burrows, pp. 414-16.

main squadrons in Quiberon Bay and the Basque Road would 'distress the enemy more effectually than keeping the sea, and at the same time be a great saving to the Government in wear and tear of the ships and their furniture'.[373]

Thus, even after his culminating victory, the Admiral kept weariness at bay and settled down to a methodical exploitation of victory. French maritime power was brought close to extinction. Solicitude for the condition of the blockading ships was extremely well advised, as any post-war head of the Admiralty would know only too well.

However, it proved impossible to implement Hawke's suggestions immediately. During December many ships had to be sent home for repairs; and the fortunes of Rear-Admiral Geary affected the whole situation.

As long ago as 17 November, Hawke had sent Geary instructions to cruise off Ushant with such ships as he could collect, until further orders. Geary, who had meanwhile been trying unsuccessfully to work his way to Quiberon against contrary winds, did not receive these instructions until after the date of the battle. The beginning of December found the Rear-Admiral off Brest with seven of the line. Hawke sent him orders, dated 1 and 9 December, to join him with the larger ships, leaving only a 60-gun ship and 'a frigate or two' on the rendezvous. But this, Hawke's best hope of obtaining reinforcements, was frustrated by fierce easterly gales which blew continually from 3 December onwards. By the 14th Geary could no longer pick out a single one of his ships in the surrounding murk. When the weather abated on the 15th, he calculated that he was 480 miles W.N.W. of Ushant! With commendable determination he headed the *Sandwich* back towards Brest. On the 22nd, when he was at last drawing close

[373] O.L., 9 Dec. 1759 (2)

to Ushant, he was beset by a new series of squalls, this time from the S.W. An admixture of rain did little to bolster the general enthusiasm. On the 24th Geary found that he was lying to the E. of Ushant — which could only mean that he was virtually on the rocks! On 26 December he was at Spithead; and he dispatched to the Lords an unassailable case for being there.

> As the upper works, sides and decks of the *Sandwich* are very leaky and the oakam worked out of all the waterways of the seams upon every deck, in so much that the officers and ship's company lay wet, whenever it rains... and having upwards of 120 sick on board, 100 of whom are in fevers, the scurvy, fluxes, and consumptions, that the Surgeon says there is an absolute necessity of their being sent to the Hospital; the beer having been out some days, and having no wine or brandy on board, and in want of sails and stores; I judged it absolutely necessary, as the wind was southerly and I could not recover my station, to bear up for the first port.[374]

Because of the bad weather, supplies to Quiberon were suspended; and, gradually, Hawke was forced to relax his grip on the French coast. Considering his 54 years and latterly uncertain health, he had himself displayed an endurance which he regarded as God-given; but, by 16 December, he found that the physical and mental strain was telling on him. He wrote to the Admiralty: 'I have now been thirty-one weeks on board, without setting my foot on shore, and cannot expect that my health will hold out much longer. I therefore hope to be relieved. Sir Charles Hardy and Rear-Admiral Geary are in the same condition.'[375]

---

[374] Bamford, p. 8. O.L., 17 Nov., 1, 16 Dec. 1759. Ad. 1/93, 26 Nov., 26 Dec. 1759.

John Hay, however, seems to have enjoyed robust health during the campaigns which he shared with his Admiral, and the rough draft of a letter from Hawke to Saunders, dated 21 December, is in the secretary's hand. In November Saunders, after the fatigues of his successful campaign in the St. Lawrence, was on his way home with three of the line, when, near the shores of England, he was informed that Conflans was out. On his own initiative he at once altered course for Quiberon, and only resumed his homeward voyage when he received news of the battle. Seeing that Hawke's letter of appreciation has not hitherto been printed and that it provides an instance where the original draft appears to have been composed by John Hay, it is given in full, with insertions in Hawke's hand italicized.

> The hurry I was in when I had the favour of your obliging letter of the 25th November will, I hope, excuse my not answering it sooner. After your endeavours to serve your country by coming this way, it would have given me the greatest pleasure to have shared the little success we had with you; and I heartily thank you for your kind *and generous* intentions.
>
> Give me leave sincerely to congratulate you on your safe arrival after the critical and fatiguing services you have been employed in, and heartily to rejoice in your *fresh* acquisition of honour, being with great truth, *the sincerest esteem and regard,*
>
> *Dear Sir*, etc.

Of course, it is quite possible that most of the letter was dictated by Hawke. It carries a good deal of the flavour to be expected from him on such an occasion. In any case, the

[375] O.L., 10 Oct., 9, 16 Dec. 1759.

insertions are thoroughly characteristic of the Admiral and emphasize his invariable lack of professional jealousy.[376]

In an attempt to secure a local supply of fresh water, Hawke sent a ship to take possession of the Isle d'Yeu, lying about fifty miles S. of Croisic. But this measure was rewarded with 'very little water, and that very brackish... they have it only in draw wells in their houses'.[377]

By Boxing Day it was clear that, unless a supply convoy was already on its way out, the last ships of the squadron might have to leave Quiberon Bay within about a fortnight. By 2 January Hawke had decided to send in the *Royal George*, amongst others, and he shifted his flag to the *Torbay*. Of the ships of the line, he would keep the *Hero*, *Dunkirk*, *Hercules*, *Chichester*, *Warspite*, *Burford*, *Defiance*, and *Intrepid*. Of these, only the first four shared with Keppel's *Torbay* the distinction of having served throughout the Quiberon Bay campaign.

Just before Hardy, with several of the line, sailed for England on the 7th, the *Anson* and *Monmouth* arrived, bearing some supplies and official acknowledgements of the victory of the previous November. Referring to one of Clevland's letters, the Admiral replied: 'The last has communicated to me the most substantial pleasure that I could enjoy in this world, my Royal Master's most gracious approbation of my conduct.'

After Hardy's departure there were only enough ships to blockade the Morbihan and the Vilaine, but in the former the situation was satisfactory. It seemed that the transports had been emptied and that the troops were marching away from the coast.

On 11 January Hawke sailed for home in the *Torbay*, leaving Sir John Bentley in command with ten of the line.

---

[376] H.P.P., draft of H. to Saunders, 21 Dec. 1759. Clowes, iii, 222.
[377] O.L., 9, 26 Dec. 1759.

In the Channel the wind remained obstinately against the *Torbay* and Hawke abandoned his original intention of heading for Portsmouth. On 16 January 1760 he anchored in Plymouth Sound.[378]

[378] O.L., 26 Dec. 1759, Ad. 1/92, 2, 7, 16 Jan. 1760.

CHAPTER 16: BELLE ISLE AND THE DEATH OF A KING

ON 9 February 1760 Hawke was at his London home answering a letter from Lady Kingston. She was the widow of his old patron, Sir Chaloner Ogle, and had married again. The Admiral told her that he had experienced 'a very long, tiresome, and fatiguing cruise, and as hard a piece of service to go through with as could be put upon any man'. But he gave no sign that he was disappointed with his reward — the thanks of the House of Commons and a pension of £2,000 a year. 'The King was infinitely good and kind to me, which has given me greater satisfaction, if I may be allowed to say so, than the addition he was pleased to make to my fortune, which as times are is no bad thing.' He was happy to have his children round him again — Martin was now 15 years old, Edward 13, Chaloner 9, Catharine 8. 'My little girl is playing her tricks and romping about me, that I hardly know what I write. She had the small pox a little before I came home.' He was glad that he had recently succeeded in getting the late Sir Chaloner's cousin, Lieutenant Chaloner Ogle of the *Ramillies*, promoted to master and commander.[379]

As has been indicated, Hawke's 'rash step' of 1758 had militated against his being awarded the peerage which he had fully earned. Anson before him and Rodney, Jervis, and Nelson after him were all ennobled after winning a single victory — and the First Battle of Cape Finisterre and the Battle of Cape

---

[379] N.M.M.: MS. 108, 9 Feb. 1760. H.P.P., H. to Anson — see p. 256 n. 2.

St. Vincent, at least, were less strategically decisive than Hawke's victory of 1747, let alone that of 1759. That Pitt had been prejudiced against him by the outcome of the Rochefort expedition; that Newcastle would regard as sheer waste of bargaining power an awkward of a peerage which did not assist the cause of parliamentary management; and that the general public was sated with victory — these factors may all have helped to deny Hawke his most obviously appropriate reward. After Hawke, the most distinguished naval commanders of the war — the most triumphant war that England ever fought — were Boscawen and Saunders, yet they, too, were given rewards other than the peerages which they might normally have expected.

Hawke was much shocked when the news was spread about that, on 15 February, his old flagship, the *Ramillies*, with much the same company aboard as during the previous year, had been wrecked on Bolt Head with a loss of over 700 lives. He at once took up the case of four widows of warrant officers. 'They are left destitute of everything', he wrote to Clevland, 'and both they and their children must infallibly starve unless the Board will commiserate their unfortunate situation.' He also sought relief for Captain Taylor's widow.[380]

Young William Locker went down to Bigbury Bay to search for the body of a friend who had been a Lieutenant of the *Ramillies*. In his boat he went from one to another of the multitude of floating corpses, but had to abandon his horrifying quest because the storm had been so violent 'that all distinction of features was lost'.

During the first three months of 1760 Hawke went three or four times to the Admiralty in a determined effort to get Locker's commission confirmed. He would certainly have

[380] Add.MSS. 9338. Ad. 1/92, n.d., but about end of Feb. 1760.

known of Locker's gallantry during a celebrated action of June 1757 between the frigate *Experiment* and the powerful privateer *Télémaque*, because it was he who had appointed the young man an acting Lieutenant of the *Experiment* in 1756 and he had tried to get him a permanent commission in February 1757. Locker was at last promoted in March 1760. He served under Hawke in the *Royal George* later in the year and also during 1762; and his remarks on the Admiral's character will be noticed in due course.[381]

On her last voyage the *Ramillies* was with a squadron going under Boscawen's command to Quiberon Bay in order to continue the blockade. General damage was suffered on 15 February. 'I think', wrote Boscawen, 'it blew stronger than I ever felt it in my life.' It was only after a month's refit in Plymouth that he was able to proceed to his station, where, for the next five months, he implemented the strategy flowing from Hawke's victory and subsequent suggestions. Meanwhile, despite his exhausting service of the preceding year, Hawke was preparing to relieve the man whose abilities and character in some ways closely resembled his own — determination, an aggressive tactical doctrine, fine seamanship, and careful attention to matters of health and supply are prominent in the careers of both men. In accordance with Secret Orders of 8 August, he was to sail in the *Royal George* and, on reaching Quiberon Bay, to control a blockade of the French coast, paying particular attention to the French warships in the Vilaine and at Rochefort. He would have seventeen ships of the line and twelve frigates and sloops at his disposal.[382]

---

[381] Locker, 'Wm. Locker', pp. 8, 12, 13, 32. Ad. 1/89, 30 Oct. 1755; 1/383, 6 Feb. 1757.
[382] Ad. 2/1331, 8 Aug. 1760.

By 18 August Hawke had collected reinforcements from Plymouth and was sailing out into the Channel past Smeeton's Eddystone Lighthouse, completed the previous October. He reached Quiberon Bay on the 26th. This proved to be his last meeting with Boscawen who sailed for home the next day. Still only 49 years of age, Boscawen was already an Admiral of the Blue of two years' standing, a Lord of the Admiralty, a member of the Privy Council and a General of Marines at a salary of £3,000 a year. The atmosphere of his family life was happy and marked by the mutual devotion of its members. His wife, Frances, was a leader of intellectual society in London and had enhanced her husband's career besides bearing him five children. Towards the end of 1760, Boscawen, though living at home, developed a fever which was attributed to his long spells of sea service. He died on 10 January 1761. Like Hawke after him, he was buried in a small country church. His finely-composed epitaph ends with the sentence: 'His once happy wife inscribes this marble — an unequal testimony of his worth and of her affection.'[383]

Hawke found that Boscawen had stationed three of the line and a frigate under Geary off Oléron in order to neutralize Rochefort; five of the line and some smaller vessels to guard the Vilaine and the Morbihan and to provide a corps de réserve; three frigates off Ushant — one close in and two well out to the W.; one frigate stationed 100 leagues W. of Belle Isle; frigates off Bordeaux and Cape Finisterre. Hawke maintained this formidable combination, using as reliefs the ships which had come out with him.[384]

Soon after taking over the command the Admiral discussed with Lord Howe the matter of taking Dumet Island. As Hawke

[383] O.L., 18 Aug., 4 Sept. 1760. Aspinall-Oglander, pp. 283-6.
[384] O.L., 4 Sept. 1760.

had noticed on his last visit to Quiberon Bay, the guns of the fort on this island commanded the best anchorage for ships watching the Vilaine. Howe did not think that a landing party alone would succeed, so Hawke asked him whether he thought that the advantages of possession of the place would outweigh the risk of damage to the bombarding ships. Howe's written reply of 29 August is a fair example of that rock-like officer's ponderous style. The italicized words were inserted in his own handwriting. 'The chief advantage which would arise from the possession of that Isle I suppose to be the gaining of a smoother anchoring for the ships during the winter season than is reported *to be the quality* of the present in bad weather, at the distance from the shore that they are now necessarily placed.'

The outcome of these deliberations was that Howe with three of the line duly executed Hawke's order to take Dumet Island. After a few shots had been fired, the garrison, consisting of a company of the Regiment of Bourbon, capitulated.[385]

The fact that the fifty-four French soldiers, together with a 'servant, woman and boys five', had lived near the middle of a British-commanded Bay for more than a year might suggest that there was a good water-supply on the island. By 7 September Howe was reporting the discovery of a cistern of water and of good gardening ground, both of which Hawke was glad to utilize. For a squadron based about a week's sail from its normal sources of supply, these were important assets.[386]

Information reached the Admiral that some survivors from the *Soleil Royal*, *Héros*, and *Juste* had somehow found their way to the Isle d'Yeu, of which he had taken possession the

[385] O.L., 5, 28, 30 Sept. 1760. H.P.P., Howe to H., 28, 29 Sept. 1760.
[386] O.L., 7 Sept. 1760.

previous December. He sent Hughes in the *Tamar* sloop to collect them, 'assuring them they shall be kindly treated and returned in safety to their habitation'.[387]

While Hawke in Quiberon Bay was effectively directing the blockade, the War Cabinet in Whitehall was entertaining a strategic idea with which the Admiral was soon to become acquainted. By early October the masterful Pitt was intimating that the time had come to send a new expedition to the coast of France. He named Belle Isle — on which he had had an eye for some time — as the objective.

Newcastle was full of complaints. Pitt had 'flung out *in his vague way*' that he wished to divert French troops from Germany. Newcastle was prepared to tolerate a raid on Boulogne, but when Pitt 'flung out Belle Isle' his Grace was aghast. Undeterred, Pitt explained his plan to the King and, to Newcastle's dismay, 'His Majesty was violently for it'. Pitt at once 'sent to the Admiralty to have transports ready for 10,000 men'.

But the First Lord of the Treasury was not so easily to be brushed aside. Fretfully, he marshalled his forces for a counter-attack. He protested to the King that it was too late in the year for such an enterprise. Anson expressed agreement. Ligonier was 'rather against' the project. The King began to shift his ground. But the Secretary did not readily surrender on such occasions.

A meeting of the War Cabinet was held and the formidable personality of the Great Commoner began, as usual, to impose itself. Predictably, Lord Holderness would do nothing to assist Newcastle's resistance. 'I expected', the Duke wrote plaintively afterwards, 'to have been supported by my Admiral and General, but that was not my good fortune.' However,

[387] O.L., 13 Sept. 1760.

Ligonier at first raised Newcastle's spirits by pointing out that it would be three weeks before the army could sail. Just as doubt seemed to be entering Pitt's mind, Ligonier, to the Duke's mortification, spoilt everything by wondering whether the date of embarkation could not be advanced. As if to cap this treachery: 'Anson said that we should probably have good weather till the middle of November, and that the ships would lie very safely at Belle Isle.' The damage was done. The Secretary was 'encouraged greatly'! The Duke, deserted by his henchmen, fought on — but without hope. The proceedings terminated with Pitt asking Ligonier to ascertain the earliest date for embarkation.

'It is a cruel thing to be alone,' Newcastle lamented, 'to be scoffed at by a Lord Holderness, or overrun by the torrent of his Colleague. I can bear a great deal, but there may be an end of my patience.'[388]

Soon afterwards another Cabinet meeting considered the project. Keppel, who had recently examined the coast of Belle Isle, gave evidence that the best place for a landing was on the north-easterly beaches, not very far from the citadel. But he said that these beaches might prove to be too close to the guns of the citadel, and the water not deep enough for ships to give direct support to the troops. After Newcastle had made the most of these two uncertainties, Pitt proposed that Hawke be asked to report on them.[389]

In a letter of 9 October Anson explained the position to Hawke. He put the case as Pitt would have wished, and included no hint that the scheme in general was open to discussion. Belle Isle was the objective. Hawke was asked about the two specific points already mentioned as well as

---

[388] Add.MSS. 32912, f. 323.
[389] Add.MSS. 32913, f. 48.

some others of a purely tactical nature. But Anson seems to have been opposed to the project all the time, although he had not declared his attitude openly to Pitt; and — which does not seem to have been brought out in previous writings on this subject — he adopted the device of getting Clevland to write to Hawke a separate covering letter in which his doubts were implied. Clevland wrote: 'His Lordship depends upon your thoroughly considering what prospect there may be of success, and would be glad to be favoured with your private thoughts in a separate letter on this subject.'[390]

Anson might have been disturbed if he could have foreseen the consequences of this invitation. Hawke took the surprising course of answering the detailed questions and stating his views on the general issue in a single letter. Clearly, it might be difficult for Anson to avoid production of the letter in the War Cabinet and altogether the First Lord was placed in a very awkward position. Writing on 17 October Hawke ran somewhat perfunctorily over the detailed questions about the landing and then settled down to business. Referring to Belle Isle, he continued:

> But suppose it taken, will the possession of a place detached by water from the Continent draw troops from any part of that Continent to retake it, while we are masters of the sea? On the contrary, I think it may prove a great accession of strength to them, as by the cartel settled last year with General Conway, within a few weeks we must deliver up three regiments and two battalions of militia, now useless in a detached isle, to be employed against Hanover.
>
> Your Lordship will readily conclude that I cannot subscribe to Belle Isle's being the properest place for making a diversion.

[390] Add.MSS. 15956, f. 54. H.P.P., Clevland to H., 9 Oct. 1760.

For your Lordship's satisfaction, I send this express by Captain Hotham.

The short stay I made here last winter, together with tempestuous weather, prevented my making the necessary observations on the enemy's coast. But ever since my last arrival, I have not been idle, and employed my officers in sounding and reconnoitring Morbian, the Rivers Auray, Vannes and Vilaine, with an intention to attempt destroying the men of war in the last, and the transports in the two first. For this purpose I have also got what intelligence I could from the crews of several *chasse marées,* who by promises of rewards have been pretty open. From the whole I formed sanguine hopes of success, as, by all accounts, there are not above 1400 regulars to defend the coast from Morbian to Nantes. Croisic, with the Salt Pans, I had also included in my plan. But your Lordship's letter has opened a wider view to me, and induced me to lay aside for the present the execution of my own. The batteries at the mouth of the Vilaine and Morbian may be attacked at the same time, while the boats may push on to fire the ships in the one and the transports in the other. In the meantime, about a thousand Marines and other troops may land and secure the neck of land on which stands St. Jacques, where in the case of disaster our troops from the Morbian and Vilaine may retreat, meet, and defend themselves against all the force of France, in case of succeeding in the first attack. I think there will be little hazard against making a lodgement at Vannes, Auray, and Croisic, or, according to the number of troops, advancing to l'Orient.

From Vilaine to Vannes is twelve miles, from Vannes to Auray nine miles, and from Auray to l'Orient twelve miles. Croisic is about fifteen miles from Vannes, but may be easily defended by itself.

Enclosed are sketches of some part of the coast.

I have some Frenchmen who will serve for pilots for the Rivers Vannes and Auray.

> Whichever plan shall be approved of, I shall have everything in my power ready for the troops to enter on action the instant they arrive. The better to enable me to do this, I hope your Lordship will send by a clean frigate beforehand the number of troops, transports, frigates, bomb vessels, fireships, cutters, and flat bottomed boats.
>
> The transports must have good ground tackling, or they will be liable to be drove on shore, if we should run into bad weather.[391]

Coming from a man who has sometimes been represented as a good sea-commander who lacked a flair for combined operations, this is a respectable military testament. However, a modicum of diplomatic skill is needed to get a strategic idea accepted; and it might be felt that a frontal assault on one of Pitt's cherished ideas was not a favourable beginning. Yet, a curious feature of the situation is that, had Hawke possessed the subtlety of a Talleyrand, he might have acted very much as he actually did. Provided that he was prepared to disregard the formidable wrath of Pitt, there was a chance that his own plan would be adopted in the face of the protests of the Secretary of State. It was reasonable to assume that Newcastle would be opposed to any new expedition of Pitt's and would prefer a suggestion for exploiting an existing commitment. Anson had revealed his doubts. The King loved his Admiral better than his principal Secretary of State. Indeed, it is tempting to speculate as to how deeply John Hay was involved in this affair; but Hawke's *naïveté* in political matters provides a more likely clue.

If some mystery surrounds the composition of Hawke's dispatch, there is no doubt whatever about its effect. Pitt was quite unprepared for such a communication. It had never

[391] Add.MSS. 32913, f. 163.

occurred to him that Hawke would produce a criticism of his strategy. Nor had Newcastle found any reason to hope that Hawke would resist Pitt's policy. Hardwicke had tried to hearten the Duke but not because he expected any kind of bold intervention by the Admiral. The ex-Lord Chancellor argued that Pitt would not, at this advanced season, have lost time in referring technicalities to Hawke, if he had seriously intended the expedition to sail that year. 'In the next place', he wrote, 'I cannot persuade myself that Sir Edward Hawke, whose character I take it is to be diffident and balancing and not of a decisive turn, will take upon himself to give a clear opinion upon these two questions, so as to encourage so hazardous an enterprise at this season of the year, wherein he himself must, I suppose, have some sort of share.' And would he, asked Hardwicke, risk the reputation which he had recently gained through his victory at Quiberon?[392]

No doubt other politicians, having observed Hawke's modest bearing, would have agreed with Hardwicke's assessment. But all speculations were soon to evaporate in a towering conflagration.

By 24 October Hawke's letter of the 17th was in Anson's hands. As soon as he had appreciated its contents Anson decided to act boldly. If he could use it at once to set the King against the Belle Isle scheme, Pitt might be worsted before he could inquire why Hawke had sent so widely ranging a reply. In any case, Hawke's own plan looked very promising. Anson therefore went straight to St. James's Palace to show the letter to the King. He found the assiduous Newcastle already in attendance and, in view of the Duke's consistent opposition to Pitt's scheme, he conveyed the gist of what Hawke had said. Then he entered the royal closet.

---

[392] Add.MSS. 32913, f. 48, 69, 326 ff.

Newcastle was jubilant. Nothing could please him more than to see his terrible colleague discomfited on such an issue. Filled with joyous anticipation, he awaited Pitt's arrival.

In due course the Great Commoner made his majestic entrance. Newcastle hastened to communicate to him what Anson had just divulged. To the Duke's intense satisfaction, the Secretary 'immediately grew angry and complained much'. Why had not Anson first shown him the letter? Instead, he would be giving 'His Majesty impressions upon it'.

Anson came out from his audience. Pitt at once demanded to see Hawke's letter and stated that he would not go into the closet till he had read it. The Duke therefore preceded him. To his pleasure, he found that Anson, with the help of Hawke's letter, had indeed made 'impressions'. The Monarch was now firmly against any landings on Belle Isle and held that Hawke's plan was 'infinitely more practicable'. Newcastle, savouring every detail, afterwards recounted for Hardwicke's benefit:

> I avoided saying much except that Mr. Pitt seemed much displeased. He went in after me and the King immediately saluted him, 'Sir Edward Hawke thinks the scheme impracticable and I will not send my troops *a la boucherie*!' Mr. Pitt replied that he did not understand Sir Edward Hawke's letter; that he had not answered the only question which he was directed to return an answer to, viz: whether there was depth of water sufficient for the ships to come and land the troops; that Sir Edward Hawke's letter was reasoning. But if His Majesty thought the thing impracticable that was sufficient.

The audience came to an end. Pitt and Newcastle found Anson waiting in the vestibule and the Secretary gave full vent to his chagrin. Newcastle happily told Hardwicke:

> He was indeed more disturbed and full of complaints than I had almost ever seen him. He attacked Sir Edward Hawke most bitterly and dissected his letter from one end to the other; that he had not executed the orders sent to him; that his orders were positive, to send an account whether there was depth of water in the Sandy Bay sufficient for landing the troops; that as he had not answered the question, [he] thought there was depth of water enough; that he did not know what Sir Edward meant by saying in one place "that they may approach Point Andro, but not be able to injure the higher batteries that defend it", and in another, "So they may the Sandy Bay" — but there he did not mention the high batteries; that the letter was reasoning which Mr. Pitt did not want; that Sir Edward did not know what use to make of Belle Isle; that Mr. Pitt did; that Sir Edward had proposed another plan — which he had no orders to do — and which he very rightly had intended to execute with his own force; and that now he had put a stop to his own design; that he was a very good sea officer but no minister; *that this seemed to be concerted*; that the whole should come out; that Sir Edward Hawke's letter should be produced in Parliament; that there was sure to be an end of the project of Belle Isle, but in a way very injurious to him (Mr. Pitt,) the author of it.

Seeing that Pitt's accusation of collusion came closer to the mark than the Duke himself knew, it is hardly surprising that Anson 'said little'! Newcastle remarked that he had not read Anson's letter to Hawke and was therefore not in a position to say whether the latter Admiral had exceeded his instructions. In any case, Hawke 'appeared plainly to be of opinion against the thing'.

'Mr. Pitt then declared that he had done with the whole.' As far as he was concerned, Anson and Ligonier could see that Hawke's plan was carried out or the expedition cancelled altogether, as the King wished.

Anson departed. Pitt, with Newcastle pattering at his heels, sought out Lady Yarmouth, the King's mistress, to enlist her support. 'Mr. Pitt renewed his complaints in the strongest manner with great bitterness against Sir Edward Hawke, ripped up his conduct at Rochefort, which, he said, he never could understand.' Now, his plan for Belle Isle had been spoilt. As for Hawke's alternative, he 'would not say one word for it, or against it… he did not understand it.' He thought the only reasonable objection that Hawke could have made against the Belle Isle project was that it was too late in the year; and he had not made this objection.

That night (24-25 October) it certainly appeared that Hawke's 'Counter Project' would be adopted. Newcastle commented that such a rebuff would 'mortify a less passionate man than Mr. Pitt… To be sure, Mr. Pitt is stung to the quick by the ridicule Sir Edward puts upon supposing the attack, or even the taking of Belle Isle, could operate a diversion. I own I always thought so. But Sir Edward puts it in a ridiculous light. From this letter, I date poor Sir Edward's fall and Admiral Boscawen's rise.'[393]

But on the morrow all was changed. On 25 October George II, the veteran of the Battle of Dettingen, the last King of England to lead his troops into battle — 'What do you think I came here for? To be a poltroon?' — the Hanoverian who allowed his English Ministers to rule England for him, was seized after breakfast with an apoplectic fit and fell to the floor, dead. He was 77 years old.

With his passing Hawke lost the unfailing protector, who, even at the time of the *faux pas* of 1758, had stood by his Admiral.[394]

---

[393] Add.MSS. 32913, f. 326-31.

[394] Williams, i, 107, II, 58. Add.MSS. 17495, f. 167; 35359, f. 393.

The old King's grandson, George III, was now sovereign. At once all the leading politicians became engrossed in the question of the Government which would emerge from this new situation. In the event, the former Ministers continued at their posts, but with the significant addition of Lord Bute, the King's private adviser, as a member of the Cabinet.

As far as Belle Isle was concerned, the disturbance caused by the change of monarch allowed Pitt to re-impose his will. When the War Cabinet met at St. James's on 13 November it was resolved that, taking account of the evidence of Captains Keppel and Hotham, a landing on the island was practicable and that 'the expedition… should be ordered to proceed as soon as possible'.[395]

Meanwhile Hawke, unaware of the vicissitudes experienced in London by his Morbihan scheme, had continued to collect information about the depths of water, the beaches, and the disposition of French troops in the neighbourhood of the Rhuys Peninsula. As far as the blockade was concerned, he was handicapped by his old trouble, a lack of fresh beer. His letters of 11, 20, and 31 October complained about it, and eventually he was forced to send home without replacement some of his cruising vessels. By 8 November Bordeaux and Port Louis were left unguarded. The Admiral was also preoccupied with a French attempt to sail a frigate out of the Morbihan under Spanish colours. It was claimed that the ship had been sold to the pro-French but still neutral Spanish; but Hawke ordered her back into harbour until she obtained a pass from the Court of Great Britain.[396]

On 21 November Hawke learnt that his excellent plan for diversionary landings, combined with the destruction of enemy

[395] P.R.O. 30/8/79, 13 Nov. 1760.

[396] O.L., 11, 20, 31 Oct., 8 Nov. 1760. Gambier to H., 4 Nov. 1760.

warships and transports, would not be adopted. The frigate *Unicorn* arrived with an Admiralty letter communicating the Cabinet's decision of the 13th. Hawke was instructed to be ready to put the troops ashore on Belle Isle as soon as they arrived. He lost no time in sending Captains Peyton, Lendrick, Evans, Bennett, and Lee to reconnoitre the N.E. coast of the island: 'in order to find out the most convenient place for landing a body of between eight and nine thousand troops, with a large body of artillery'. His feelings on the subject may be discerned in a letter which he wrote on 1 December to Captain Gambier, who had recently been in charge of the ships guarding the Vilaine and had been intimately involved in planning an attack on the Morbihan and Vilaine. 'It is with much regret that I inform you our plan was not so much as taken notice of in England. Of consequence, Vilaine is not likely to prove the scene of action.'

The Admiral might have been surprised if he had known to what extent the first of these sentences understated the truth![397]

The plan prepared by Hawke foreshadowed the Duke of Wellington's strategy based on the Lines of Torres Vedras. Despite Pitt's argument that Belle Isle was invaluable as a pawn to be traded against Minorca, it is difficult to agree that his plan was superior to Hawke's. Hawke's scheme was much easier to execute and would surely have effected a much greater diversion of French troops. To have seen the British army firmly established on the shores of continental France would have been intolerable to the French government. Nor was the destruction of the transports and of six French ships of the line a negligible secondary objective; for, in the event, after numbers of British ships had been tied down to blockade the latter, under favourable conditions of tide and visibility all six

[397] O.L., 1, 15 Dec. 1760. O.B., 22 Nov. 1760. Ad. 51/146.

of them escaped. Again, it is not clear that Belle Isle provided a better base for the blockading squadrons than the Rhuys Peninsula would have done. As for the concept of the political pawn, Guadeloupe and Martinique were both captured during the course of the war, and at the time of the peace negotiations it was thought that one of those islands was equal in value to the whole of Canada. Could not one of these have been traded for Minorca? (In fact, they were both returned to France gratis.)

The rejection of his Quiberon plan was the last great disappointment of Hawke's seagoing career. However, having once received his new instructions on 21 November, he settled down to a thorough investigation of the coast of Belle Isle and speedily prepared a detailed plan of assault. As early as the 28th the orders were all written and ready for distribution. The troops were to be landed on the beaches at Sauzum Bay, S.E. of Palais, and the places were clearly marked on duplicated maps. The whole sequence of conveying the troops in boats from the transports to the shore was laid down. At this time the enemy had few batteries covering the selected beaches. Hawke provided for these guns to be methodically destroyed by bomb vessels, immediately before the troops landed. His attention to such other details as the depth of water in which the transports would anchor and the nature of the ground beneath them; the room outside the transports for the ships of the line; the scheme of bombardments just before the landings — all these preparations possess a truly modern flavour. Nor was the refinement of a diversionary bombardment of Sauzon, in the N. of the island, forgotten. The fact that Hawke was able to produce so complete and thoroughly professional a scheme in the course of a week was doubtless due to the expertise and organization built up during preparation of the Quiberon project. There is no reason to doubt that, if Hawke had been sent troops destined either for Belle Isle or for the Quiberon area, the landings would have proceeded as methodically and effectively as his monumental blockade of Brest had done.[398]

With regard to the amateurish way in which Pitt determined on his landing operations, it is apposite to notice a paragraph in Hawke's letter to the Secretary of State dated 15 December:

> As I received no plan of operation, nor so much as a hint of the General or Captain Keppel being acquainted with the soundings or proper landing places, I presumed from thence that my first duty was attentively to reconnoitre and sound the accessible side of Belle Isle on the N., from Point Lomaria on the S.E. to Point Daubourg on the N.W. end of the island. For this purpose, I dispatched Captains Peyton, Lendrick, Evans, Bennett, and Lee in a sloop and cutter, to examine that coast with care and attention. They had the advantage of very fine weather and of meeting with no obstruction from the enemy, who either did not perceive them, or did not penetrate their employment. Enclosed is a copy of the report they made to me on their return. After maturely considering it, I formed the enclosed plan of attack, under cover of which the troops are to land immediately on arrival, if the weather will permit.

He went on to report that a Dutch dogger was seen sending a boat towards the S.E. end of Belle Isle on 3 December. Obviously, a message was carried to the French about the British observations because the enemy soon after began to work vigorously on the fortifications. By 15 December Hawke had intelligence of French plans to ferry troops by night from Croisic to Belle Isle.

---

[398] O.B., 22, 28 Nov. 1760 and undated copy of an order to Sir Charles Hardy of about 28 Nov. O.L., 15 Dec. 1760 (2). H.P.P., orders for Keppel, 27 Nov. 1760.

On 27 December news arrived of the postponement of the expedition till the following year.[399]

Altogether, Pitt's direction of the Belle Isle affair is suggestive of the muddle which led to disaster in the vital Gallipoli campaign of 1915. Pitt was certainly superior to Kitchener in so far as he was eager to use sea-power to give the troops a decisive advantage. But to decide to invade Belle Isle without full knowledge of the landing places was inexcusable, seeing that there had been nearly a year in which to make the observations. Also, by rushing matters late in the year, Pitt forced Hawke to make an intensive examination of the coast, thus drawing more attention to his activities than need have been the case if he had been given ample time. The fact that General Hodgson's army of 1761 had to face greatly strengthened defences as a consequence of the enemy's long forewarning, suggests a clear parallel with the disastrous events of 1915. The lack of proper knowledge and maps proved no more of an asset in 1915 than it would have done in 1760; but in 1760 Hawke's activity and organizational ability would probably have ensured the success of the landings.

Pitt was a great war-leader with a flair for grand strategy but he demonstrated no real understanding of operational problems. Typically, he was prepared to override Anson and Ligonier, his chief service advisers, whenever he disagreed with them. What is more, he persisted with his preparations of the autumn of 1760 even though he himself — judging by some of his above-quoted remarks of 24 October — knew that it was really too late in the year.

Christmas Day found Hawke still on his station. At his home at Swaythling, his eldest son, Martin — now a 16-year-old Etonian — was writing to his father.

---

[399] O.L., 15, 30 Dec. 1760.

Dear Pappa,

I hope you have received my letters, you may be assured that nothing hinders me writing to you, so often as my inclination and my filial duty would prompt me, but my school business, which, at the part of the school I am in, is excessively great, if I apply close to it, as I do; which, you having commanded me, I hope you will pardon my writing not so often, as I still fulfil your commands. I have for my Xmas task 160 Latin verses to compose, 450 Greek ditto, and 640 Latin to get by heart.

The people gave from two to five guineas to see the King's funeral go by. The money was given for a place in the street. The present King coming to the playhouse with the Royal Family and Lord Bute, they hissed Lord Bute and mobbed the Princess Dowager, crying out, "No Scotch! No petticoat government!" The King was obliged to nod to Lord Bute to go out, which he did.

P.S. We are all well, as we hope you are. We pray God to preserve you and send you home soon and safe to your loving and dutiful children.[400]

Young Martin Bladen Hawke was developing into a man of parts. He and his brother Edward, having enjoyed their mother's love till they were 12 and 9 years old, held an advantage over the younger Chaloner and Catharine which was manifested in greater stability of character. The children were all handicapped, in addition, by frequent separation from their father, who nevertheless retained their affection.

Thanks to Lieutenant William Locker there exists a satisfying character-portrait of the Admiral at this stage of his career. Locker was struck by his reproof of impiety, his concern for his men's welfare, and his 'mainly decision whenever anything important occurred'; also by his dignity which he thought had a

[400] H.P.P., Martin H. to H., 25 Dec. 1760.

general influence throughout the Fleet. 'He was a strict but temperate disciplinarian — affable rather than familiar with his officers — reproving with all sternness all approaches to ribaldry or impiety in their conduct or conversation. His mind, impressed with a devout regard for the faith in which he had been educated, loved to dwell on the many mercies he had experienced, and to ascribe every success to "the Giver of Victory".'[401]

However, the blockading squadron was to suffer a reverse in the New Year. Berryer, the Minister of the French Navy promised promotion to the rank of captain for any subordinate officer who escaped from the Vilaine to Brest with a ship of the line. Lieutenant the Chevalier de Ternay accepted the challenge. To promote the likelihood of gaining surprise over the watching Gambier, he had all the ships in the Vilaine moved as far upstream as possible and disarmed them completely. Then he awaited favourable weather conditions.[402]

Hawke was alive to the possibility of such an attempt. However, the position was complicated by the fact that Pitt's abortive decision to send troops to Belle Isle had led to the French being alerted, and Hawke had now to prevent nocturnal reinforcements from furtively slipping across to the island from the mainland. For this, as well as watching the Vilaine, he needed many more small vessels, especially cutters. He had been repeatedly asking for these since 11 October. By December the position had not improved, so he requisitioned and manned four victuallers. He was still very dissatisfied with the Belle Isle situation but his sensitivity to the chance of escape from the Vilaine is brought out by a remark of 18

[401] Locker, 'Hawke', p. 15 and 'Locker', p. 14.
[402] Lacour-Gayet, pp. 346-7.

December: 'It would be very imprudent to call off the cutter from the Vilaine at present.'[403]

After New Year's Day 1761 a dense fog settled over Quiberon Bay, and Ternay decided that the spring tides of 7 and 8 January offered a fair opportunity to slip out from the Vilaine. Gambier, owing to the high tides and E. wind, was on the alert, but, as he afterwards reported: 'The weather was so extremely foggy that we could not see our bowsprit end.' He put boats out on patrol, though even this was risky, and had his ships ready to cut or slip at a moment's notice. At 7.30 p.m. on 7 January: 'the fog then excessively thick, we saw a large ship close on board us under all her sails who disappeared in a moment, and immediately after another on the other side, whom I hailed and fired at; and lost sight of directly'. With his pilot protesting against the danger, Gambier headed straight out to sea in the *Burford*, followed by the *Frederick* and *Modeste.* He guessed that the enemy would make for Brest. It appears that he just failed to intercept them, owing to their hugging the coast near Quimper.

The ships which had escaped were the *Dragon* (64), *Brillant* (64) and two frigates. However, one of the frigates, the *Vestale*, was seen by the frigate *Unicorn* (28) at 8 a.m. on 8 January. The *Unicorn* gradually closed and at 10 a.m. brought down the *Vestale*'s main topsail yard. Between 10.30 and 12.30 a close action was fought. Finally the French surrendered. The *Vestale* seems to have been armed with 30 guns and had 240 men aboard. The captains of both frigates were mortally wounded.

Hawke considered that no blame should attach to Gambier's force, because conditions had been completely favourable to the French.[404]

---

403 O.L., 15, 18 Dec. 1760.

404 O.L., 13 Jan. 1761. Ad. 52/818; 51/3996; 1/92, 9 Jan. 1761.

Although French commerce had largely been immobilized, Hawke's ships continued to bring prizes into Quiberon Bay. On 13 February two small French frigates, 'prime sailers and very fit for Channel cruisers', had been taken, after making a break on the previous day to get from Rochefort to the Guinea Coast.

The Admiral was beginning to doubt whether his health could stand further mid-winter service when, on 8 February, the frigate *Stag* arrived. She brought the Lords' Order of 31 January for Hawke to return home with the three deckers and any other ships unfit to keep the sea at that season. With the *Royal George*, *Union*, *Princess Amelia*, a frigate, and a convoy of victuallers and prizes, Hawke sailed from Quiberon Bay on 18 February, leaving the rest of the ships to maintain a looser but still formidable blockade. A fierce westerly gale made Hawke seek shelter; and it is significant that he preferred Quiberon Bay to the lee of Belle Isle.

When the *Royal George* reached Spithead on 11 March, Hawke's seagoing contribution to the triumphant blockade of France was completed.[405]

Yet it was a cheerless homecoming for the Admiral. The talk of the town was that he had been unenterprising and had generally wasted the great resources allocated to him. In fact, he had been short of supplies and small vessels to such an extent that he could barely carry out his original instructions, and the suggestion that he should have 'cut out' the ships in the Vilaine was grounded on ignorance of the situation. In any case there was no lack of achievement. No one was better qualified than Choiseul to describe the condition to which the British blockade and the battles which arose from it, had

---

Lacour-Gayet, pp. 347-8. Clowes, iii, 304.

[405] O.L., 28 Feb. 1761. Ad. 1/92, 11 March 1761.

reduced the French Navy. He later wrote to Louis XV, referring to the Ministry of Marine:

> You charged me with its direction in 1761, in the month of October. You know, Sir, what was the condition of that navy. Few things left in the stores were up for auction; there was nothing with which to repair, or means whereby to furnish with crews, the ships which had escaped from M. de Conflans's action; after M. de la Clue's action, the port of Toulon was no better off than that of Brest. The ships were left to rot, the stores empty. The navy was everywhere in debt and had not a sous of credit. The morale of the fighting and civil officers was at the lowest ebb, and the Minister who ruled the Department was exhausted and beyond caring. The desire to serve you led to my relinquishing a Department of Foreign Affairs, which was doing well, to shoulder the odium and toil of a Department which was in worse case than if it had been destroyed, for it was in a state of degradation.[406]

[406] Corbett, ii, 159. Calmettes, p. 405.

CHAPTER 17: THE COMMANDER-IN-CHIEF

HAWKE lived at George Street until the summer. He was there when newspapers carried reports of General Hodgson's troops going ashore at Belle Isle. After a repulse on 8 April, they achieved a difficult landing on the 22nd; and the French commander, after making a determined resistance, surrendered on 8 June.

In the summer Hawke visited his house at Swaythling. Although he only rented the property it was there that he had lived with his family during his wife's last years; and the broad, gently sloping, tree-lined meadows surrounding the fine parish church where Catharine and the baby William lay buried, must have comprised a part of the Admiral's most intimate and deeply felt experience.[407]

By September he was back at George Street. Up to this time the new King, George III, had not made many important changes in his Government, except that, on 25 March, he had appointed Bute Secretary of State for the Northern Department in place of Holderness. By September Pitt was advocating a preventive war against Spain, but was opposed by Newcastle and Bute. Pitt could not suffer such contradiction. Not uncharacteristically, Hawke happened to choose 28 September — a date at which Newcastle was thoroughly excited by the signs that the Great Commoner would resign — to ask the Duke for a living for one of his kinsmen. The Admiral had apparently gathered that Newcastle had been his

[407] Ad. 1/92, 22 March, 22 July 1761. H.P.P., bill dated 27 May 1761.

only protector during the crisis over Belle Isle during the previous October. 'I… had nobody to espouse my cause heartily but yourself', he wrote.[408]

In fact, the Duke had done little on Hawke's behalf; but the latter had probably learnt that Anson had done even less. Anson, of course, doubtless thought that Hawke had dealt in a foolish manner with his and Clevland's letters of 9 October. The First Lord himself was unhappy from the loss of his still-youthful wife in June 1760. Relations between Anson and Hawke had never been better than cordial, and to all appearances the two men did not see much of each other during the period leading up to Anson's death in June 1762.

Certainly, once Belle Isle had been taken it was by no means universally apparent that the British cause had been greatly advanced thereby. In October Joseph Yorke wrote to Newcastle: 'All Europe wonders at the force we have kept this year at Belle Isle, without a single attempt even to alarm the French coasts, whilst such a reinforcement to Prince Ferdinand would have turned the scale in our favour.'

Pitt resigned the seals of office on 5 October.

On 3 November Parliament reassembled and Hawke was probably in the House of Commons when, on the 13th, Pitt rose to speak on the Address of Thanks. The ex-Secretary of State was the centre of universal expectancy. He deplored the official suggestion that Britain should sign peace without the agreement of Prussia. 'America,' he declared, 'has been conquered in Germany.' In Walpole's words: 'He paid a handsome compliment to Admiral Hawke and the navy; but said, "Ask the French whether they could not engage you hand to hand, if delivered from the war in Germany."'

---

[408] W. S. Lewis, Vol. 21, p. 487 n. 3. Watson, p. 74. Williams, ii, 106-7. Add.MSS. 32928, f. 410.

Pitt had certainly been infuriated by Hawke a twelvemonth earlier but he had not taken long to forgive him; for, as Horace Walpole put it on another occasion: 'Mr. Pitt is not a man of vengeance.' This saying might have been received with scepticism in France: but it was true with regard to individuals.[409]

However, it was no longer the strong, masterful Pitt who directed the national destiny, but a group of bickering Ministers amongst whom Bute predominated. With George III's support he worked for peace. He wished to break free of the Prussian alliance; but his efforts in that direction merely brought him a rebuff from Kaunitz and hostility from Frederick. In the early months of 1762 Bute tried to revive peace negotiations with the sharp-witted Choiseul, and the French Minister found it agreeable to fence with so unequal an adversary. Choiseul, in fact, was far from accepting the defeat of France. Although, on the one hand, Frederick had been reprieved by the death of the Czarina Elizabeth on 5 January 1762, and although, on the other, the weakness of the French navy could not be redressed, Choiseul saw a way of wresting victory over England from a bleak and unpromising situation. By widespread diversionary operations, he would, with the help of Spain, disperse British naval and military strength around the world. He would conceal his ultimate objective, the invasion of England, by concentrating the force designed for this purpose — 50,000 troops — between the Meuse and the Lower Rhine, simulating a reserve for the Westphalian army. Meanwhile, in order to avoid attracting attention, a small number of transports only would be made ready in Calais and

---

[409] Add.MSS. 32929, f. 388. *Journals of the House of Commons*, XXIX, 6. H. Walpole, *Memoirs of the Reign of George III*, ed. G. F. Barker, London, 1894, 4 vols., i, 74-5. W. S. Lewis, Vol. 22, p. 433. Williams, ii, 131.

Dunkirk. When the moment came the army would march swiftly to the coast. The first embarkation would at once secure a foothold on the English coast and, as the transports plied to and fro, waves of reinforcements would follow.

Choiseul considered that a French and Spanish command of the Channel for as long as five weeks was necessary to bring the enterprise to a successful conclusion. This might be done by getting the Spanish to move against Gibraltar and invade Portugal, thus threatening Lisbon, the chief supply-port of the British Mediterranean fleet; by the energetic use of the combined force of thirty or more of the line already in the West Indies; and by persisting with the war in Germany. While Saunders was pinned down at Gibraltar by naval and military activity in the Mediterranean, and Rodney (soon to be superseded by Pocock) was kept busy in the West Indies, Choiseul would concentrate twenty-two ships of the line at Ferrol. Of these, six would come from Brest and eight from Cadiz. Eight were already at Ferrol. If it had not been for the British blockade of Rochefort — a legacy of Hawke's post-Quiberon policy — ten more ships of the line would have been ordered to Ferrol. Ferrol was chosen as the focal point because it was anticipated that the British Government, receiving news of the activity of the Cartagena and Toulon Squadrons, would think that Gibraltar was the objective. From Ferrol the twenty-two ships of the line would sail for the Channel and hold it while the French army brought Britain to a reasonable frame of mind.

The Spanish co-operated to the extent of fomenting war with Portugal, while Choiseul entertained himself by pretending to negotiate with Bute.[410]

---

[410] Watson, pp. 77-81. Corbett, ii, Ch. 10.

By April the British Government became aware of the threat of invasion. On the 9th orders reached Hawke to hoist his flag at Portsmouth. At last, the proper commission for which he had asked in vain in 1758 was given to him. He was appointed as Commander-in-Chief 'in the Channel, Soundings, on the coast of Ireland, and in the Bay of Biscay'. Having been granted leave to settle some private affairs, he took up his command on 27 April. This was to be the Admiral's last spell of active service in wartime. The occasion was also remarkable as being the last on which he enjoyed the services of John Hay as secretary. While Hawke was ashore during 1761, Hay had filled the post of Purser aboard the *Royal George*, and when Hawke finally struck his flag in 1762 the secretary was given a Warrant as Purser of the *Britannia.* At Portsmouth Hawke found his old friend Vice-Admiral Holburne still in command of the port.[411]

Before he left London Hawke discussed with Anson the naval policy to be applied in the Channel. The 65-year-old First Lord was, in fact, mortally ill with a disease of the lungs, and soon after his meeting with Hawke he went to put himself in the care of Dr. Oliver at Bath; but this proved of no avail. However, the last interview between the two admirals found them of one mind. Anson considered that Dunkirk must be closely watched. Hawke proposed a close blockade of that port and Anson agreed.[412]

On 3 May Hawke wrote to the commanding officer in the Downs, Commodore John Moore — his Captain aboard the *Devonshire* at the Second Battle of Cape Finisterre. Hawke asked

---

[411] Ad. 1/92, 9, 27 April 1762; 6/19 f. 248, 458. H.P.P., Clevland to H., 10 April 1762. cf. 'Hawke MSS., 1702-1800', f. 84-6. O.B., 2 May 1762. L.B., H. to Clevland, 30 April 1762.

[412] Ad. 1/92, 26 May 1762. W. S. Lewis, Vol. 22, p. 33 n. 21.

for a report as to whether frigates and sloops could be stationed in the two channels leading into Dunkirk.

In Hawke's command there were altogether three commodores in charge of detached squadrons, and all of them had previously served under him in the Western Squadron. Besides Moore in the Downs, there was Young off le Havre. Denis was off Rochefort, blockading the ten ships of the line there.

Apart from the Channel, Hawke was chiefly preoccupied with Ferrol. In April the Cabinet had decided to send troops to help Portugal. Most of them were to come from Belle Isle and the problem arose of ensuring them a safe passage in face of the enemy ships at Ferrol. Therefore, on 2 May, Hawke ordered the Captain of the *Tartar* frigate to observe 'the number, strength, and motions of the enemy' at Ferrol and Corunna.

On the following day a Spanish army moved across the Portuguese frontier. Nevertheless, it will be clear that Choiseul's plan was developing badly, in that the British were already paying close attention to Ferrol and were on the alert in the Channel.[413]

At this point the Chevalier de Ternay who, in January 1761, had escaped from the Vilaine with the *Dragon* and *Brillant*, was about to require Hawke's further attention. Between the time of his exploit sixteen months before and the month of May 1762, Ternay had not been idle. In January 1762 he brought two more ships of the line safely out of the Vilaine — this time during a violent storm. The following April he once more broke clear, and triumphantly carried into Brest the last two serviceable ships of the line belonging to the force which had

---

[413] L.B., 3 May 1762. Add.MSS. 32936, f. 440. Corbett, ii, 316-17. O.B., 2 May 1762.

barely escaped into the Vilaine in November 1759. Now, in May 1762, Ternay was at Brest in command of two of the line, a frigate, and two transports carrying 570 troops, and ready to make a bold surprise attack on Newfoundland as part of Choiseul's scheme of widespread diversion.

On 5 May Hawke received intelligence from the Admiralty that an expedition was being prepared at Brest; also the Lords' desire that a frigate should be sent to look into the Road. Hawke, who happened to be formulating a protest against Admiralty interference with the disposition of his ships, scanned the intelligence with a somewhat jaundiced eye. Fortunately, although he communicated his scepticism to their Lordships, he did not fail to send the frigate *Shannon* to go 'as close in as possible to Brest water', and bring back her report at once to him, or, if the winds proved easterly, send it direct to the Admiralty from Plymouth by express.[414]

On the 6th a further Admiralty order reached Spithead and Hawke put it into effect by instructing Captain Sayer to make for Ushant with three of the line. There he would be joined by three frigates and he was to send one of them in to make a close observation of Brest. If he concluded that it was desirable he was to blockade the port.

However, unfavourable winds prevented Sayer from sailing till the 11th. On the 8th Ternay had swept out of Brest and the helpless *Shannon* had seen him heading westward.

Ternay achieved complete surprise on his arrival at Newfoundland and captured St. Johns. After destroying nearly 500 craft and doing other damage, he slipped away without the loss of a single vessel.[415]

---

[414] Lacour-Gayet, pp. 348, 364, 513. L.B., Clevland to H., 4 May 1762; H. to Clevland, 5 May. O.B., 5 May 1762.

[415] O.B., 6 May 1762. Ad. 1/92, 12, 13, 14 May 1762. Corbett, ii, 324-

Owing to the comprehensive nature of his command, Hawke was constantly busy with the dispatch of transports, with escort, to Portugal and other parts of the world. In particular, he was anxious to hasten six transports and a sloop to Belle Isle where they were to pick up a large part of the garrison. It would be his own responsibility to cover with the Western Squadron the movement of the convoy from Belle Isle to Lisbon. However, indiscipline among the masters delayed the sailing of the transports from Portsmouth and on 13 May only four of the six left under the escort of the *Druid* sloop.[416]

The 16th found Hawke back on board the *Royal George*. Captain Bennett was in command of the ship (as in 1760). Her team of Lieutenants included John Birt as 2nd.[417]

On 20 May the Admiral had occasion to issue an order to Captain Maurice Suckling, the uncle and eventually the patron of Horatio Nelson (who was then aged three). Suckling was to help the fitting of the squadron for sea by lending from the *Nassau* men 'that can be trusted'.

At the same time Hawke asked the Admiralty to have a set of guns, then at Woolwich, sent round to Spithead for the *Royal George*. They had been cast especially to replace the heavier ones then aboard the flagship. The new guns would 'be of the greatest advantage in case she should come to action, as well as prevent the many accidents of laming men, every time her present unwieldy ones are laid up and down, when there has been occasion to run them out and in'. And on the 23rd he reinforced his request by pointing out that 'beside about twenty men having been lamed last cruise, many fingers in particular have been lost in running them out and in'.[418]

5.

[416] O.B., 11, 22 May 1762. Ad. 1/92, 13 May 1762 (2).

[417] O.B., 16 May Ad. 1/92, 18 May 1762.

Meanwhile, the enemy at Dunkirk, wishing to chase an inquisitive British vessel away from the entry to the port, decided to organize a little pulling practice in their galleys. On 14 May, Lieutenant Stirling, against whom this exertion was ultimately directed, reported the current form. 'There are three small galleys of twenty oars each. They have two men to an oar, but they are raw and a number of them boys. One of the galleys mounts two 12-pounders, the other two, one each. Last Saturday, they came out into the Road to exercise but performed so bad they were immediately ordered in again.'

And on the 20th, Stirling wrote: 'There are four privateers of different sizes, the largest of 12 guns. The townspeople would force them out to take our ship last Thursday night (it being then calm), but they refused go out on such an expedition, for which reason some of their officers were put in prison and remain there still… There are so many Spanish sailors there that a Dutchman dares not walk for them.'

Moore handed this information on to Hawke. The latter remarked to Young that 'as the enemy seem to be in motion at Dunkirk', he should keep a frigate to the E. of le Havre, in order to intercept anything slipping along the coast. Meanwhile, he reinforced Moore with a view to tightening the blockade of Dunkirk. He continually advised Moore on matters of detail but was careful to repeat that he left the Commodore, as man on the spot, with discretion to act as he saw fit.[419]

The dual system of control by the Admiralty on the one hand and the Commander-in-Chief on the other continued to work badly until it was terminated by Hawke's sailing with his squadron. The Lords, with the Earl of Halifax deputizing for

---

[418] O.B., 20 May 1762. L.B., H. to Clevland, 20, 23 May 1762.
[419] L.B., H. to Young, 1 June 1762; H. to Moore, 31 May, 2 June.

Anson, persisted in sending orders direct to some of the ships, thus cutting across Hawke's dispositions. Similarly, Hawke sent on service vessels for which the Admiralty was in the process of preparing different orders. As Hawke put it on 31 May: 'I therefore submit it to their Lordships' reflection whether it would not be more proper that they should signify their directions to me with regard to the King's ships and vessels under my command, and leave me to give the orders in consequence. Was I a person fond of authority, it would not prove a little mortifying to reflect that at present my flag is flying without so much as the shadow of weight.'

The Lords answered, somewhat equivocally, that they 'will signify all their directions through him, whenever it can be done consistent with the Service'.

Any sense of frustration harboured by Hawke can hardly have been soothed by the arrival at Portsmouth of that seasoned officer of 23 years, the Duke of York, in the guise of a Rear-Admiral of the Blue and with the appointment of second-in-command of the squadron. However, the Prince's other interests kept him out of the way until the ships were ready to sail. (After receiving him, Hawke reported to the Admiralty on 31 May: 'He also had my leave to return to Town, which he did early this morning.')[420]

On 6 June an almost permanent feature of Hawke's professional life was removed by Anson's death at Bath. Newcastle (who had himself been edged out of the Cabinet in May) reported to the Duke of Devonshire gossip to the effect that Hawke ought to be appointed in succession to Anson. Now that he was out of power, Newcastle, abandoning his former criteria, was eager to give to merit its proper weight. 'But,' he remarked with unconscious hypocrisy, 'I hardly

---

[420] Ad. 1/92, 31 May 1762 and endorsement.

believe they will do so right a thing.' Needless to say, he was not far off the mark in making this prognostication. Lord Bute found it more convenient to appoint Lord Halifax, who, as Walpole was prompt to observe, was popular with the merchants.[421]

Hawke, still near the height of his powers and vigour, would have been a worthy replacement for Anson. He was not inferior to the latter as a strategist or organizer. However, the post of the First Lord in the eighteenth century was difficult to fill satisfactorily, because it combined the political and professional roles which were subsequently allocated to the separate posts of First Lord (political) and First Sea Lord (professional). From the point of view of obtaining adequate funds for the Navy in peacetime, a politician like Lord Sandwich was better suited to be First Lord, eighteenth-century style, than a naval officer such as Anson or Hawke. This will be treated at greater length in a later chapter. But, with a war still in progress, it was not so difficult to obtain funds and it would have been very appropriate to appoint Hawke.

In the event, Hawke did not receive an invitation to become First Lord, but instead Admiralty Orders dated 12 June. Seven transports were to take troops to Belle Isle under the escort of two of the line, disembark their soldiers and take aboard from the island others destined for Portugal. Meanwhile, Hawke was to proceed with nine of the line and two or three frigates to a rendezvous near Ferrol. As seven Spanish sail of the line had been reported at sea off Ferrol, Hawke, on arrival off the port, was to ascertain whether they were still at sea. If the enemy were in harbour he could simply see the convoy past Cape Finisterre and let it go on to Lisbon without close cover from

[421] Add.MSS. 32939, f. 266. W. S. Lewis, Vol. 22, pp. 42-3.

the squadron. But if the Spanish were still at sea he was to accompany the convoy to Lisbon. He was to finish by cruising off the Spanish coast for a week, then make his way back to Torbay by way of Cape Clear.[422]

The folly of giving Hawke so vast a command and then sending him to cruise with a squadron is well illustrated by his final interchange of letters with Commodore Moore. The latter reported that their Lordships had taken so many ships away from him that he could not properly execute his Commander-in-Chief's orders with regard to Dunkirk. On 20 June Hawke could only reply: 'I have been so hurried in preparing for sea that I have not had time to pay a proper attention to your several letters. I sail on Wednesday next, therefore till I return you will apply immediately to the Board for their directions.'[423]

The Admiral had, of course, to send similar instructions to Commodore Young. His cordial relations with both Commodores are indicated by his typical parting words to Young: 'I heartily wish you health and success.'[424]

Fuss and difficulty arose over the matter of selecting a flagship for his Royal Highness, Prince Edward. The problem was not mitigated by the total lack of communication with him. Immediately before the squadron's departure, the said Prince put in an appearance at Portsmouth and discovered that the taciturn, granitic Howe had been assigned to him as his Flag Captain aboard the *Princess Amelia.*

By 24 June Hawke had moved down to St. Helens with ten of the line, four frigates, and a cutter. Among the captains of large ships were Suckling and an old acquaintance, Samuel Barrington. Hawke informed the Admiralty that his

---

[422] Ad. 2/88, 12 June 1762.

[423] L.B., Moore to H. and H. to Moore, 20 June 1762.

[424] L.B., H. to Young, 20 June 1762.

rendezvous would be ten leagues N.W. from Cape Finisterre, but did not think it necessary to furnish any reasons for selecting this position. Had he realized that considerable perturbation then reigned at the Board on account of the Spanish squadron at Ferrol, and that their Lordships were excitedly discussing the notion of attacking that port, the Admiral would doubtless have communicated his reasons. Unaware that he had become once more the focus of strong emotions at the Admiralty, Hawke reached the latitude of Ushant on 28 June, detached his cutter with orders for the convoy at Belle Isle to make sail for the rendezvous, and, favoured by the wind, completed a swift passage to the meeting place. He then ordered the frigate *Tartar* to ply between the squadron and Cape Finisterre, both to collect intelligence of the enemy from neutral vessels and to watch for any ships that might try to slip away northwards during the night.[425]

Direct observation of Ferrol having proved very difficult, Hotham of the frigate *Aeolus* could not give Hawke a satisfactory account when he returned to him on 6 July. However, intelligence gathered from neutrals indicated that all ten of the Spanish ships were in port. Of these, only six were thought to be ready for sea.

It was at this juncture that Hawke became aware of the malaise troubling the minds of their Lordships. On the 7th the sloop *Senegal* arrived from England with two letters from Clevland, both dated 30 June. The Lords were extremely alarmed because they thought that Hawke was waiting so far away from Ferrol that there was an imminent danger of the Spanish dashing out from port and destroying the convoy,

---

[425] Ad. 1/92, 14 June and endorsement, 20, 24 June, 9 July 1762. O.B., 26 June, 1 July 1762. Corbett, ii, 319.

without Hawke knowing anything of it. The Admiral was to inform them 'by the return of the sloop' of the steps taken by him to remedy this frightening situation. Hawke was past the stage of taking overt exception to communications from their Lordships. He waited for two days before composing a reply. Then he observed that he had 'maturely considered every circumstance, both with regard to the enemy and the transports from Belle Isle'. He had had to fix the rendezvous far enough to the W. to avoid the possibility of westerly winds blowing the convoy into the Bay of Biscay where it might be trapped for some time. As for blockading the enemy, he could not station the squadron closer to Ferrol because the danger of westerly winds was again apparent. But this did not mean that the enemy could easily come out. The British squadron's presence had been well advertised, and it could only be removed by westerly gales; but these would prevent the Spanish from leaving port. If the wind was easterly, it would indeed be physically possible for the Spanish to come out, but the fact that the same wind would prevent them from going in again was unlikely to appeal to them, in view of the proximity of ten British ships of the line.

Needless to say, the Spanish were very content to remain out of harm's way. The fact that the victor of the two most decisive fleet actions of the mid-century was in command of the British Squadron did not enhance the attractions of a possible encounter.

While Hawke was giving his last masterly lesson in the art of blockade, Saunders was applying his initiative and sound judgement to ensure the safe passage of the convoy from Belle Isle; for there existed a potential threat from the S. The French were reinforcing Minorca and at the same time spreading rumours that they would attack Gibraltar. For a time they succeeded in pinning down Saunders's squadron in the Gut. However, when he knew that the convoy was due to sail from Belle Isle for Lisbon, Saunders did not hesitate to leave Gibraltar for the time being and establish a blockade of the fourteen ships of the line then at Cadiz. This morally courageous, highly intelligent initiative made the British troops' safe arrival at Lisbon an absolute certainty — given also the sagacious dispositions of Hawke.[426]

On 13 July the sails of the Belle Isle convoy could be discerned from Hawke's squadron. The Admiral saw his charge past Cape Finisterre and then let it proceed with its own escort. The troops subsequently did good service under the capable command of the German general, Count Lippe-Buckeburg. He recognized the merits of a British Brigadier-General who came under him, namely Robert Clerk, the Chief Engineer of the Rochefort expedition. This active-minded, if over-vehement, officer rose to Major-General before the end of the campaign.[427]

Hawke had received orders to try to intercept the French *Chef d'Escadre* Blénac, who had managed at the beginning of the year to make his way from Brest to the West Indies in conformity with Choiseul's complex plan. Now he was expected to head for home with a squadron including eight of the line.

As in 1747 Hawke tried to narrow down the channel within which interception was most probable, and he concentrated on an area of sea eight to twelve leagues S. of Cape Clear. However, on 6 August, having almost come to the end of the month given him by the Admiralty and having seen nothing, the Admiral sailed back down the Bay of Biscay. Following another stratagem which he had used before, he showed the

[426] Ad. 1/92, 9 July; 2/534, 30 June 1762. Corbett, ii, 321-2.
[427] Ad. 1/92, 15 July 1762. Corbett, ii, 322. Cathcart Papers, A67.

squadron off Cape Ortegal. The winds did not permit sending a ship to look into Ferrol, but the intelligence collected was to the effect that the Spanish squadron had not stirred. One or two prizes were collected; otherwise nothing of note occurred. On 13 August Hawke bore up for Torbay, leaving frigates off Capes Clear and Ortegal.

The *Royal George*, like so many other ships in the Fleet, was suffering from the prolonged wear and tear consequent on the lengthy cruises and arduous blockades of the Seven Years' War. Water was penetrating many parts of the ship and the rudder was making disagreeable noises. No doubt, some contribution was being made towards establishing dry rot in the flagship's great timbers. As a result of this insidious ailment, the frame of the ship abruptly collapsed in 1782 and she went straight to the bottom, with the loss of Admiral Kempenfelt and nearly all her company.

On 23 August Hawke entered Torbay for the last time. He wrote to advise the Admiralty against using that anchorage as a base. 'Ships from a cruise', he observed, 'want to be near an hospital, a victualling office, and a dockyard.' He asked to be allowed to strike his flag and come ashore. Meanwhile, he ordered the *Magnanime*, *Revenge* and *Prince of Orange* to water at 'Brixholm', the *Prince* (90) at Pentland Sands and the ships of the Duke of York's division at 'Torr Abbey' and at 'Torr Quay'.[428]

The Duke of York does not appear to have regretted the proximity of terra firma. On the 26th, he wrote:

> Sir Edward Hawke,
>
> I have this moment received a letter from the Secretary of the Admiralty acquainting me that you are directed to dispense with my absence [*sic*] to go to Town for a few days,

[428] Corbett, ii, 322-3. Ad. 1/92, 23, 24 Aug. 1762. O.B., 24 Aug. 1762.

and I propose setting out this afternoon in consequence of it, provided you have no objection, remaining, Sir Edward,

Your very affectionate friend,

Edward.

Hawke failed to conceive of any objection to dispensing with his presence.[429]

Possibly to the Admiral's mild surprise, no dispute arose from his suggestion that the squadron should go to Spithead. The Lords merely agreed and on 3 September the ships arrived at Spithead. That same afternoon Hawke's blue flag was struck aboard the *Royal George*. It would not be re-hoisted.

Anson had been succeeded as Admiral of the Fleet by Sir William Rowley. On 21 October 1762 Hawke was promoted to Admiral of the White.

Christmas Day found Hawke at Swaythling — doubtless accompanied by his children and Sally Birt — and he deemed the occasion appropriate for assisting those who had served with him at sea. He wrote to the Admiralty on behalf of the Boatswain and Carpenter of the *Royal George*, asking particularly that Mr. Andrew Jeffreys, then at Plymouth with the ship, might be moved into the *Victory* at Chatham which was his home port. 'He has been a long time settled there with his family, and it would put the poor man to great expense to carry them and his goods to a place where he has neither friends nor acquaintance. As he is really a most deserving, good man, and the best of his profession I ever saw, I shall hope their Lordships will be so good as to grant him this favour.'

In spite of the weakness and incompetence of Bute (who became Lord of the Treasury in May 1762), Britain's predominance at sea, and the use which had been made of that predominance, had forced France and Spain to acknowledge

[429] L.B., Prince Edward to H., 26 Aug. 1762.

defeat. Although, to Pitt's indignation, the Peace both left the French with access to the Newfoundland fisheries and returned to them their main West Indian islands — thus restoring the training-grounds for seamen which were essential to Choiseul's secret plans for a war of revenge — even so, the Peace of Paris was exceedingly triumphant. On 10 February 1763 the plenipotentiaries of Britain, France, and Spain signed the treaty. The first Article was couched in grandiloquent language: 'There shall be a Christian, universal, and perpetual peace, as well by sea as by land, and a sincere and constant friendship shall be reestablished between their Britannic, most Christian, Catholic, and Faithful Portuguese Majesties... There shall be a general oblivion of everything that may have been done or committed before, or since, the commencement of the war, which is just ended.'[430]

Among the events which were to be thus happily forgotten were the passing to Great Britain of Canada, Nova Scotia, and all French and Spanish territory E. of the Mississippi; Grenada, St. Vincent, Dominica, and Tobago; Senegal; Minorca; and a dominant position in India. The relatively small population of the British Isles was thus brought to the beginning of a period of long-lasting influence over many people in many lands.

If there have been any real military triumphs in history, here surely was one of them. It was a triumph forged by the use of sea-power; and a leading element of strength in that prolonged exercise of sea-power was derived from the character and ability of the man who, finally, ruled supreme in the Channel, the Soundings, on the Irish coast, and in the Bay of Biscay.

---

[430] Ad. 1/92, 24 Aug. and endorsement, 3 Sept.; 1/578, 25 Dec. 1762. Corbett, ii, 377.

CHAPTER 18: HAWKE AS FIRST LORD

ON 21 October 1762 the last list of promotions of admirals during the Seven Years' War had been issued. It has already been mentioned that Hawke was advanced to Admiral of the White. The impetus of seniority carried Thomas Griffin up to the same rank; and there was a third promotion to Admiral of the White which, despite the physical incapacity of the officer concerned, was much better deserved than Griffin's — namely that of Henry Osborn. However, amongst the three Admirals of the White, Hawke's ascendancy was manifest. Provided that he outlived Sir William Rowley it was certain that he would become the first officer of the Service.

With the exception of this ultimate possibility, Hawke probably considered that his professional career was at an end. But in fact a great charge was yet to be laid upon him.[431]

The Navy had, during the Seven Years' War, firmly impressed its seal on the centuries that were to follow. Yet, within little more than a decade of the triumphant year of 1763, Britain would stand nearer to mortal danger than at any time since 1588. From the time that he took over the Ministry of the Navy in 1761, Choiseul methodically prepared for a war of revenge. Bitterly but patiently he salvaged what he could from the years of French disaster, in order to ensure that France, during the conflict to come, would never again lie helpless in the meshes of a British blockade.[432]

Within two months of the signing of the 'Christian, universal, and perpetual peace' of 1763, Louis XV was ordering

---

[431] Ad. 6/19, f. 445.

[432] Lacour-Gayet, p. 387 *et seq.*

the Count de Broglie to draw up plans for the invasion of England. An officer was sent to make a comprehensive inspection of the English Channel-coast, and this officer's findings were laid before the Council at Fontainbleau during the crisis of 1770.

However, in 1763 Hawke's troubles were of a humbler and more domestic nature. For example, in mid-September he was prostrated by 'a violent fit of the gravel'. The lack of fresh water, combined with a badly balanced diet, predisposed eighteenth-century seamen to suffer from urinary calculi; and it is less remarkable that at the age of 58 Hawke needed treatment for them than that they had not caused him serious discomfort before. The disorder arose from lack of protein compared with carbohydrates, from deficiency of vitamin A (due to insufficient fresh vegetables and fruit), and from lack of fresh water and the imbibing of alcoholic substitutes. Strong wines were probably more harmful than beer or spirits from this point of view. Of course, scurvy and fevers were a far greater threat to the lives of seafarers than were the more slowly developing gout and gravel. Lestock and Augustus Hervey, who both suffered from the gout, lived to the respective ages of 67 and 55. Mathews and Hawke, martyrs to the gravel, lived to be 75 and 76.

The dried apples taken to sea in Hawke's Squadron of 1757, besides helping a little to keep scurvy at bay, tended to protect the seamen against forming the gravel; and the portable soup was useful in a general sort of way.

Hawke was still prey to coughs and colds, and Dr. H. Bowles prescribed remedies in 1762 and 1764. The same physician's prescription of a medicine to act against the gravel, dated 15 September 1764, is interesting for the scientific reasoning on which it was based. Its effect would be to counteract that acidity in the urine which led to the formation of the tissue-rending calculi. However, the operation of the medicine would have been too slow to effect a cure, once the stones had formed; and today surgery is considered the only real remedy. Hawke, lacking such treatment, had to bear intermittent but extreme discomfort for the remaining eighteen years of his life.[433]

In 1763 Hawke became a member of the Board of Longitude. At this time the Board was occupied with the testing of Harrison's chronometer. The trials of 1761 and 1764 proved its remarkable accuracy and by 1765 it was possible to complete tables for finding, by the lunar method, the longitude in which a ship was situated. Thus was solved one of the fundamental problems of marine navigation.[434]

Martin, the Admiral's eldest son, was now 19 years old and his father was already wondering whether he would be able to jockey him into a seat in Parliament. However, the young man matriculated at Oxford University on 11 July 1764 and subsequently followed the example of both his grandfathers by entering Lincoln's Inn on 17 November 1766.[435]

On the whole, the years 1763 to 1765 seem to have been quiet and uneventful as far as Hawke was concerned. With substantial capital and the half-pay of an Admiral of the White, with the devoted Miss Birt to keep house for him, and with the interest of watching his children grow up, he was probably quite content with his life.

---

[433] Pajol, v, 479. H.P.P. Prescription by Dr. Haberden, 15 June 1763; prescriptions by Dr. H. Bowles, 16 May 1762, 3 April, 1, 18 Sept. 1764.

[434] H.P.P., Sandwich to H., 15 July 1763. Clowes, iii, 13, 14, 338.

[435] H.P.P. Hervey to H., 3 Dec. 1763. Martin H.'s certificate of matriculation, July 1764; record of his admission to Lincoln's Inn, 17 Nov. 1766.

Some time during 1762 he had disposed of his house in George Street, Hanover Square, and had moved to Bloomsbury Square. Three years later he purchased a house at Sunbury, apparently with the intention of withdrawing to it for his last years. While he continued to live at Bloomsbury Square he had extensive repairs and improvements carried out at Sunbury.

During 1765 one of the Admiral's sons began to cause him anxiety. Chaloner, then 15 years old, had left school and, though it is not clear what occupation he was following, it is certain that his father already suspected him of irresponsible conduct. On 5 November, Chaloner wrote, in a beautiful regular, open hand, to Miss Birt, who had for nine years done her best to supply the absence of a mother's love: 'I like my breeches and greatcoat very well, and return my father many thanks for it and all other favours.

'I note a hint about Plays, and shall go to no more.

'When you are kind enough to favour me with your advice, I shall always follow and be very thankful for it.'[436]

Within a few days of hearing that Chaloner liked his breeches, Hawke was appointed Vice-Admiral of Great Britain. This post was a sinecure, carrying a salary, which was awarded to meritorious admirals. Junior to it was the appointment of Rear-Admiral of Great Britain which Hawke had held since the beginning of 1763. But he did not advance financially unscathed to the senior post, as may be readily ascertained from the list of fees which he had to pay. Before the Patent could be handed from Dowdeswell, the Chancellor of the Exchequer, to the grateful Admiral, it had to pass through no less than four government offices. In the process of running

[436] H.P.P. Chaloner H. to H., 30 April 1765; Chai, to Miss Birt, 5 Nov. 1765.

this bureaucratic gauntlet, the said Patent incurred fifteen different charges, ranging from £18 5s. 0d. for the 'Warrant Bill and Revocation', through a modest £2 2s. 0d. for 'Gratuity to Clerk', to a humble two shillings for a messenger. The total amounted to £86 6s. 6d.[437]

When New Year's Day of 1766 dawned Hawke had little reason to suppose that Christmas would find him near the heart of the country's political life. Yet such would prove to be the case.

Once the unifying pressures of the Seven Years' War had been removed, ministerial quarrels became a source of instability in the government of the country. The new King unfortunately lacked the practical *savoir-faire* to compose such differences. At the Treasury, the unpopular Bute gave way to George Grenville. Grenville, busy with a number of financial measures, took steps to make the American colonies pay for their own defence; but few people realized that his Stamp Act had raised the dominant issue of the next twenty years. By 1765 the King could no longer endure the importunate Grenville and he turned to Lord Rockingham who led the group vaguely identifiable as 'Newcastle's friends'. Still, as in George II's reign, there was no true Opposition in Parliament. Rockingham, as First Lord of the Treasury, and Newcastle, content in his old age to be Lord Privy Seal, continued to behave as King's Ministers rather than as Ministers responsible to Parliament and people. It was not until the Ministers of the day had been discredited by the calamities of the American War that British governments began to feel themselves responsible to a body of opinion in the Commons and the country at large. Of course, the House of Commons always possessed at least an ultimate veto through its control of the

[437] H.P.P., Patent for V/A of Gr. Br., 14 Nov. 1765.

supply funds. To some extent, therefore, the King's policy, as voiced by his Ministers, had to be acceptable to the lower House; and George III, in due course, learnt the necessary arts of parliamentary management.

Nevertheless, by April 1766, the notable absence of Pitt from government office and his refusal to serve under Rockingham were bringing the latter's administration under strain. Pitt's tremendous speeches of 14 January had powerfully assisted the repeal of the Stamp Act. However, he refused to return to office except on his own terms.

In July the King, faced with the resignations of two leading Ministers, sent for Pitt and allowed him to form a Government. It was perhaps a national tragedy that this invitation was not given earlier, for Pitt was now nearing the limit of good health and strength. Indeed, the manner of forming the Ministry boded ill for its future. Pitt intended to dictate policy, though with more reference to public opinion than had been normal, and the other Ministers were to execute policy rather than help to form it. They would see that their departments realized their leader's wishes. If Pitt had been at the height of his powers and vigour, the plan might conceivably have worked; but in any case such an arrangement was more suited to conditions of war than of peace.

Moreover, instead of asserting his dominance over the House of Commons, Pitt withdrew, as Earl of Chatham, to the House of Lords. He took this exceedingly unpromising step at least partly in order to protect himself against undue stress. Yet, owing to his dictatorial attitude, he was unable to recruit a sufficiently strong team of Ministers in the Commons.

The Chatham Ministry originally included the youthful Duke of Grafton as First Lord of the Treasury, General Conway as Secretary of State for the Northern Department, the Earl

Camden as Lord Chancellor, and the Earl of Northington as Lord President of the Council. These Ministers, together with Chatham who took the office of Lord Privy Seal, comprised the Cabinet. The leadership of the House of Commons thus fell to the inadequate Conway, who, however, remained a member of the Rockingham group and was constantly torn between his obligations to that group on the one hand and to Lord Chatham on the other.

Some other 'Rockinghams' survived as holders of minor offices, among them Admirals Saunders and Keppel, both Lords of the Admiralty. Lord Egmont stayed on as head of that Board but he soon resigned because he could not suffer Chatham's lofty attitude. In an attempt to win the support of the Bedford group, Chatham then offered the Admiralty to Lord Gower. On his refusal Chatham asked Sir Charles Saunders to take the First Lord's post and on 27 August he accepted.[438]

Saunders was still only 46 years old. Four years earlier he had been promoted Vice-Admiral of the White, and he had always demonstrated sagacity as well as courage and professional competence. Hawke, like Anson, had steadily held him in the highest regard. Pocock, the naval commander at the conquest of Havana in 1762, wrote to Chatham on 1 September to protest against Saunders's appointment, which placed 'an indignity… upon fifteen Flag Officers' who were senior to the new First Lord. He went on to remark: 'I don't mean to derogate from the merits of the worthy Admiral who is placed at the head of the Admiralty, for whom I have a great regard, but I apprehend it will occasion discontent and murmuring.'

---

[438] Watson, p. 90 *et seq.*, 106, 109-12, 114, 120-4. cf. Williams, ii, 168, 174, 176, 189-95, 201. 205-18.

Hawke is said to have been delighted that so well qualified a person as Saunders had been appointed, and to have hastened to congratulate him.[439]

There is no doubt that Saunders had been a favourite of Chatham's for some time, especially since the capture of Quebec. However, when assessing Chatham's reasons for preferring Saunders to Hawke on this occasion, one should note that Saunders was already a Lord of the Admiralty as well as a member of the Rockingham group. Part of Chatham's strategy was to weaken the 'parties' by detaching some of their members. Saunders's appointment was well-timed in that Rockingham himself was still smarting from his own dismissal. No such political advantage could have resulted from Hawke's being made First Lord because that Admiral, though an M.P. for Portsmouth since 1747, had consistently remained a non political servant of the Crown and had not linked himself with any group. Even so — according to Horace Walpole — Chatham was 'sorely unwilling to raise Sir Charles Saunders above Sir Edward Hawke and Sir George Pocock', and had been loathe to accept the demands of political expediency. On the other hand, once the Government had been formed, it came to Newcastle's ears that Chatham 'was full of encomiums upon Sir Charles Saunders, his ability, his integrity and his good disposition, and the great service he was of in that station'.[440]

By November Chatham, who was subject to manic depression, was entering a phase of over-excitement and he rashly offended the Rockingham's by bringing about Lord Edgecumbe's dismissal from the post of Treasurer of the

---

[439] P.R.O., 30/8/53, Part I, f. 5. Charnock, iv, 405-6.

[440] Williams, ii, 176. H. Walpole, *Memoirs of George III*, ii, 256. Add.MSS. 32977, f. 41.

Household. This led no less than seven members of the Rockingham group to resign their offices, including the three Lords of the Admiralty, Saunders, Keppel, and Meredith (27-28 November).

'The blow', wrote Walpole, 'was heavy on Lord Chatham.'

With the vacant offices in hand, Chatham made a half-hearted approach to the Bedford group. Inferring that the choicest plum, the post of First Lord of the Admiralty, was on offer with the rest, the Duke of Bedford hurried up to London. He was not overjoyed to find that, immediately after Saunders's resignation, Chatham had written to Hawke and offered him the appointment.

It was six years since Chatham had angrily condemned Hawke as 'no minister'. On 28 November 1766 he saw fit to write to him as follows:

> I am commanded by the King to acquaint you that Sir Charles Saunders and Mr. Keppel having come to a resolution to resign their seats at the Admiralty, His Majesty has been graciously pleased to turn his thoughts to you, Sir, for the Head of that Board. I have the honour, in consequence, to propose to you in His Majesty's name that very important office.
>
> Give me leave to assure you, Sir, that I have particular satisfaction in executing the King's commands to me upon this interesting occasion, and allow me to add my sincere hopes that this letter may find you in as full possession of health as your country wishes you to be.[441]

Horace Walpole was far from being a partisan of Hawke's, but in the course of criticizing this appointment he paid a

---

[441] W. S. Lewis, Vol. 22, pp. 470-2. Tunstall, p. 384. Burrows, pp. 453-4. Brooke, p. 65.

splendid tribute to the Admiral. 'Sir Edward Hawke had as much merit in his profession and to his country as man could have, but no moment of rewarding him could have been more imprudently taken. Though the place might have been destined for him, still the faith of negotiation ought to have been observed till Lord Chatham could have satisfied the Bedfords and agreed with them on the disposition.'[442]

Needless to say, Hawke had been offered the post 'without any solicitation on his part'. This fact, noteworthy in an age of incessant clamour for places and favours, testifies to the integrity both of Chatham and of Hawke. Together, the two men represented much that has been finest in British history. Chatham promoted the ideal of political freedom and asserted the dignity of individual men. Hawke stood for the thoughtful, fearless, humane, and incorruptible service of his country.[443]

Incensed by the recent resignations, Chatham had had Keppel dismissed from the sinecure of Groom of the Bedchamber. Hoping to increase Chatham's difficulties, Keppel, in return, had gone in company with Rear-Admiral Sir Piercy Brett to persuade Hawke to refuse the post of First Lord. Much to the vexation of Newcastle, who was fretting to get back into office, the upshot was that Hawke converted Sir Piercy to his own notions of non-factious service and recruited him as a member of his Board! In his indignation, Newcastle quite forgot that he had once referred to the suggestion of Hawke's appointment as 'so right a thing'.[444]

---

[442] H. Walpole, *Memoirs of George III*, ii, 283.

[443] H.P.P., 'Considerations on the State of the Navy from the End of 1766 to the Commencement of 1771'. Robert Tomlinson probably helped H. to compile this document, but it bears pencilled corrections in the Admiral's hand. See p. 349 n. 21.

[444] Add.MSS. 32978, f. 147.

The Bedfords were not alone in being disconcerted by Chatham's appointing Ministers without reference to their previous political background. Just before the resignations of November, Charles Jenkinson had written to his friend Lowther: 'There are certainly the strongest symptoms that the Government is coming to a conclusion.' Seeing that he had been Bute's private secretary, it had not occurred to Jenkinson that Chatham's Ministry was likely to offer him any kind of political future. Yet, within a few days of Meredith's resignation Jenkinson found himself in the former's seat at the Admiralty.

The survival of Chatham's Government was a matter of vexation to the Bedford group. The coarse-grained, self-seeking Richard Rigby sought to amuse Lord Sandwich — doubtless successfully — with the remark: 'Parts I take to be the last objects looked for by this Ministry or Minister. To prove it, Sir Edward Hawke is made First Lord of the Admiralty.' Although Hawke was far from unintelligent, Rigby's jest was apposite enough in so far as it was aimed at the Admiral's lack of flair for parliamentary manoeuvre and debate.

On 10 December Hawke was sworn a member of the Privy Council. The tale of fees was:

> To the Clerks of the Council: £10 0s.
> To the Under Keepers: £4 0s.
> To the Under Record Keeper: £6 0s.
> To the Council Chamber Keepers: £5 0s.
> To the Under Keeper: £1 0s.
> To the Messenger who summons the Council: £1 1s.
> To the Sergeant Trumpet: £2 2s.
> Total: £29 3s.

Thus there was good reason why the Sergeant Trumpet and

the rest should find in governmental instability an excellent occasion for melodious celebration.[445]

Two days after joining the Privy Council Hawke took his seat at the head of that Board from which he had received all manner of communications, ranging from formal congratulation to querulous complaint and solemn reprimand. Among the other Lords who, to his right and left, sat listening to the Commission of the 11th being read, were the survivors of Saunders's Board, Charles Townshend (cousin to the brilliant but unstable Chancellor of the Exchequer), John Buller (who was still on the Board as late as the calamitous year of 1778), Henry Viscount Palmerston (who stayed at the Board almost as long as Buller), and Sir George Yonge. The new Lords, Brett and Jenkinson, together with the permanent Secretary, Philip Stephens, completed the gathering. Stephens had succeeded Clevland on the latter's death three years earlier. When Hawke became First Lord, the Secretary was still only 38 and he had a long stretch of service ahead of him. In 1795 he was rewarded with a baronetcy and appointed a full member of the Board.[446]

Although Hawke would certainly have chosen, on the grounds of health and vigour, to have gone to the Admiralty some years earlier, he began his task in an energetic manner. As a result of studying the records he came to a clear understanding of the problems confronting his predecessors and the extent to which these had been solved.

Tribute has often enough been paid to Anson's ability as a naval administrator. He introduced many useful reforms and,

---

[445] Add.MSS. 38205, f. T08-9, 112. Sandwich Papers, Box 254. Rigby to Sandwich, 2 Dec. 1766. H.P.P., list of fees paid on being sworn a Member of the Privy Council, 10 Dec. 1766.
[446] Ad. 3/74, 12 Dec. 1766. N.R.S.: Sandwich Papers, i, xvii.

both at the end of the Austrian Succession War and during most of the Seven Years' War, he proved an able director of naval strategy. However, one aspect of the functions of an eighteenth-century First Lord has received insufficient attention — namely, the finance secured for the Navy in time of peace. Before Anson, Hawke, and Sandwich can be compared as heads of the Admiralty, it is necessary to examine this aspect of their work. In his day Sandwich was accused by political enemies of spending too much on the Navy for too small a result; and Anson was criticized at the time because the Navy was far from ready at the beginning of the Seven Years' War. But since then historians have tended to overlook this side of Anson's performance because Britain was, in the event, very successful in the Seven Years' War.

On investigating the records Hawke 'found that, by the economy adopted after the peace of 1748, the supplies assigned to the Navy had been by no means adequate to the necessary repairs; that in 1755 the Admiralty had been so sensible of it that they had increased the number of shipwrights by every means in their power, and had set up in the King's and Merchant Yards as many ships as could be admitted'.[447]

The accounts of eighteenth-century naval expenditure may be found in the records of the Treasury and the Admiralty. In view of the fact that little has been published on the subject, it may be as well to observe that the Estimates printed in the Journals of the House of Commons are of little value unless corrected for changes in the Navy Debt. In many years the increase or decrease in the Navy Debt was sufficient to alter radically the significance of the figure described in the Estimates as 'The Whole Sum Granted for Naval Services'.

[447] H.P.P., 'Considerations' — see p. 301 n. 13.

Therefore it is unprofitable to compare the expenditure made in one year with that of another, unless changes in the Navy Debt have been embodied in the figures. This fact was certainly appreciated at the Treasury and the Admiralty, and, to judge by his papers, Hawke understood the position as well as anyone did.[448]

In so far as actual expenditure exceeded the amount granted according to any year's Estimates, the excess resulted in a parallel increase in the Navy Debt. In the consolidated figures given below, allowance is also made for sums granted from time to time to reduce the Navy Debt. Finally, it must be remembered that in wartime funds were comparatively easy to obtain. The crucial test of a peacetime Administration is the level of expenditure which it achieved. Consideration of the extent to which money might have been well or badly used will follow in due course; but the first step is to examine the true totals of expenditure.

Year: 1745, First Lord: Bedford, Total Expenditure: £3,033,334, Remarks: War of Austrian Succession.

Year: 1746, First Lord: Bedford, Total Expenditure: £3,939,096.

Year: 1747, First Lord: Bedford, Total Expenditure: £3,541,886.

Year: 1748, First Lord: Sandwich (Anson influential), Total Expenditure: £3,430,565, Remarks: End of the war.

Year: 1749, First Lord: Sandwich (Anson influential), Total Expenditure: £1,586,954.

Year: 1750, First Lord: Sandwich (Anson influential), Total Expenditure: £871,693.

448 Binney explains the importance of the Navy Debt. Ad. 2/542, 28 Jan. 1768. H.P.P., 'Considerations' — see p. 301 n. 13. cf. Clowes, iii, 5.

Year: 1751, First Lord: Anson, Total Expenditure: £1,015,429.

Year: 1752, First Lord: Anson, Total Expenditure: £1,063,670.

Year: 1753, First Lord: Anson, Total Expenditure: £997,411.

Year: 1754, First Lord: Anson, Total Expenditure: £1,074,850.

Year: 1755, First Lord: Anson, Total Expenditure: £2,677,569, Remarks: Pre-declaration hostilities.

Year: 1756, First Lord: Anson, Total Expenditure: £3,898,239, Remarks: Seven Years' War began.

Year: 1757, First Lord: Anson; (brief intermission), Total Expenditure: £4,828,896.

Year: 1758, First Lord: Anson, Total Expenditure: £4,986,882.

Year: 1759, First Lord: Anson, Total Expenditure: £6,052,664.

Year: 1760, First Lord: Anson, Total Expenditure: £5,448,534.

Year: 1761, First Lord: Anson, Total Expenditure: £5,973,095.

Year: 1762, First Lord: Anson; Halifax; Grenville, Total Expenditure: £6,276,374.

Year: 1763, First Lord: Egmont; Sandwich; Egmont, Total Expenditure: £4,246,752, Remarks: End of the war.

Year: 1764, First Lord: Egmont, Total Expenditure: £1,974,817.

Year: 1765, First Lord: Egmont, Total Expenditure: £1,503,647.

Year: 1766, First Lord: Egmont; Saunders; Hawke, Total Expenditure: £1,694,612.

Year: 1767, First Lord: Hawke, Total Expenditure: £1,625,470.

Year: 1768, First Lord: Hawke, Total Expenditure: £1,652,442.

Year: 1769, First Lord: Hawke, Total Expenditure: £1,668,356.
Year: 1770, First Lord: Hawke, Total Expenditure: £2,036,675, Remarks: Falklands crisis.
Year: 1771, First Lord: Hawke; Sandwich, Total Expenditure: £2,780,455.
Year: 1772, First Lord: Sandwich, Total Expenditure: £2,410,637.
Year: 1773, First Lord: Sandwich, Total Expenditure: £2,237,050.
Year: 1774, First Lord: Sandwich, Total Expenditure: £2,104,258.
Year: 1775, First Lord: Sandwich, Total Expenditure: £2,496,537, Remarks: Fighting in America.
Year: 1776, First Lord: Sandwich, Total Expenditure: £4,152,896.
Year: 1777, First Lord: Sandwich, Total Expenditure: £4,589,458.
Year: 1778, First Lord: Sandwich, Total Expenditure: £6,173,928, Remarks: War with France.
Year: 1779, First Lord: Sandwich, Total Expenditure: £7,771,339, Remarks: War with Spain.
Year: 1780, First Lord: Sandwich, Total Expenditure: £9,018,034, Remarks: War with Holland.
Year: 1781, First Lord: Sandwich, Total Expenditure: £9,882,099.[449]

Before commenting further on these figures it is necessary to ask two questions. First, did the value of money change significantly during the period covered? Second, was there any discernible change in the degree of corruption in naval administration, including the dockyards?

Between 1755 and 1792 the rise in wholesale prices seems to have been of the order of 30 per cent. This was by no means a

[449] T. 38/638. Ad. 49/38.

rapid inflation, compared with that of the mid-twentieth century. However, the Seven Years' War and the American War did exert an upward pressure on prices, particularly in the shipbuilding and manufacturing industries. On the other hand, prices tended to fall during much of the time (1766 to 1775) which was taken up by the peacetime administrations of Hawke and Sandwich. There were bad harvests in 1767-8 and 1772-5, and, because agriculture was still predominant in the economy as a whole, an initial rise in the prices of farm products was soon followed by widespread depression in most kinds of activity, falling wages, and unemployment. Despite the general shortage of timber the Admiralty's constructional and supply services must have derived some advantage from lower costs under such conditions. Therefore, if, for example, Anson's expenditure in 1754 is compared with that of Sandwich in 1774, the change in the value of money hardly necessitates amendment of the figures. Even if the figures for 1774 are deflated by 10 per cent., they remain about double those for 1754, and therefore argue quite strongly that Sandwich's Navy was better prepared for its approaching war than Anson's was. However, before making a firm affirmation of this kind it is necessary to consider the question of corruption.[450]

This is a matter which it is difficult to assess with certainty, but the available evidence does not appear to justify the inference that corruption was worse under one First Lord than another between 1745 and 1781. Sandwich came under attack on this and other grounds. The disasters of the American War have to some extent, though most unfairly, been treated as confirmation of Sandwich's guilt. For example, so excellent a

[450] T. S. Ashton, *The Industrial Revolution 1760-1830*, 1948, pp. 142, 145, 148.

historian as Basil Williams has written, referring to the year 1775: 'Sandwich was reducing the navy almost to vanishing point.' But the opinion of Charles Middleton, who served with distinction as Comptroller of the Navy under Sandwich and other First Lords, militates against the view that Sandwich was either especially corrupt or inefficient. That penetrating and usually accurate observer, Horace Walpole, had a high regard for Sandwich as a First Lord. It is safe to infer that the dockyards were riddled with corrupt practices, not only during the third Sandwich Administration, but throughout the century. It was very difficult for the Admiralty to obtain reliable information on the subject, because such dockyard employees as were honest could not give evidence openly for fear of reprisals. The present writer is strongly inclined to believe that there was no great change in the degree of corruption between 1745 and 1781.[451]

One is left with the opinion, therefore, that Anson notably failed to make headway against Pelham's peace-policy and maintain a really adequate Navy. His reputation was saved only by the shortcomings of French naval policy. If France, with double the population of Great Britain, had entered the Seven Years' War in the manner that she entered the American War, with a comparatively well-prepared Navy and free of European commitments, she should have been able decisively to win the war at sea, and thus the whole war. For how much would Anson's reforms have counted after that?

It can be seen from the figures that Hawke, under less threatening international circumstances, achieved an annual peacetime expenditure about 50 per cent, greater than Anson's.

---

[451] N.R.S.: Sandwich Papers, i, xiii; Barham Papers, i, 10, 30, 315-18. Ad. 3/75, 30 June 1767. Albion, pp. 47-55. cf. Clowes, v, 2-8, for dishonesty in the dockyards when St. Vincent was First Lord.

The year 1770 was exceptional: naturally, during the Falkland Islands crisis, Hawke was able to spend more on the Navy.

Sandwich was given a good start by this same crisis. He was forced gradually to give ground to 'economy' during 1772-4 because the threat of war seemed less obvious, but he succeeded in maintaining a comparatively high level of expenditure. In view of the unprecedented commitments which he had to face from 1778 onwards, and taking account of the effects on the Navy of domestic disunity, it can be said that, despite the reverses suffered, Sandwich had not made a bad use in time of peace of the money which he had obtained.[452]

During his investigations Hawke was much impressed by the effect on the Navy, since 1762, of the damage done to the ships during the Seven Years' War. Admittedly the Service finished the war with half as many ships again as it had possessed in 1755, but their condition was alarming. 'By a series of constant service in a variety of climates, they had been mostly worn out, or in want of considerable repairs.' But Hawke saw no reason to criticize the efforts of his more immediate predecessors to deal with the situation. 'From the commencement of 1764 to the close of 1766... the buildings and repairs of the Navy had been carried on with great diligence.'[453]

As First Lord of the Admiralty, Hawke attended most meetings of the Cabinet. It has been remarked that he was not attuned to political life; and he incurred additional discomfort in the House of Commons and elsewhere, from the fact that the Government had now lost its leader. Chatham succumbed to gout and severe mental depression at a time when firm

---

[452] For an estimate of Anson as First Lord, cf. Sir Oswyn Murray in *Mariner's Mirror*, *Apr.* 1938, p. 221.

[453] H.P.P., 'Considerations' — see p. 301 n. 13.

control was particularly needed. The colourless, indecisive Conway was quite unable to exert a restraining influence over the irresponsible Charles Townshend, the Chancellor of the Exchequer. Hawke attended 'peevish' Cabinet meetings over which the distressed and ineffective Grafton attempted to preside. Grafton's later recollections of this period are worth quoting.

'Lord Chatham's illness, and indeed his constant bad state of health, which often made it impracticable to talk with him on business, or even to get access to him, brought a weakness on the Ministry which will be easily conceived; and placed us, who wished to forward his views, in the most uncomfortable and perplexing of all situations, scarce knowing what line to adopt; for Lord Chatham never did open to us, or to the Cabinet in general, what was his real and fixed plan. He would have found Lords Northington, Camden, and Shelburne, together with Sir Edward Hawke and myself, full of zeal to support him.'[454]

Matters dragged on like this for some time. Not till 9 October 1768 did the tragically stricken Chatham resign the Privy Seal and the nominal leadership of the Ministry.

Hawke was deeply disappointed by this outcome. There had been every likelihood that Chatham, alive to the threat presented by Choiseul's growing navy, would ensure a sufficient supply of funds to the Admiralty and Navy Board. Hawke had accepted office, believing that he would be able to devote himself almost completely to his executive functions, in furtherance of general policy laid down by Chatham. Instead, the Admiral was embarrassed by having to sit in the Commons as one of the leaderless Government's three senior Ministers in that place, and witness the ineffectiveness of Conway as Leader

[454] Smith, iv, 213 and W. S. Lewis, Vol. 22, p. 494, n. 7, 8, for an example of H.'s *naïveté* in debate. Tunstall, p. 387. Grafton, p. no.

of the House and the wayward, capricious brilliance of Charles Townshend, who spoke as often against the Government as for it.[455]

Hawke's health was poor for a time during the autumn of 1767 but, taking the year as a whole, he gave an energetic lead at the Admiralty. The Board met on 131 occasions, at 118 of which Hawke presided. The average attendance of the other Lords was about 80. A great variety of useful work was performed, including further trials of portable soup and the testing of different inventions, including ships' pumps, blocks, tackles, and catheads, and a composition prepared by a chemist called Jackson for preserving ships' bottoms. The Board does not seem ever to have rejected an invention without trial.

The half-pay of lieutenants, which had been very inadequate, was increased.

The First Lord's common-sense and methodical way of thinking can be seen in the Board's reception of an offer of sago powder from a plantation in Georgia. The prospective supplier, one Mr. Bowen, claimed that he had learnt about the virtues of sago powder while a prisoner of the Chinese — that it was a good food in warm climates and prevented scurvy. The Board asked the College of Physicians to compare the quality of Bowen's commodity with that of the sago imported from the East Indies. After a lapse of two months a favourable report was received. The decision then reached by Hawke, Yonge, Brett, and Jenkinson is recorded in the following minute: 'It appearing to their Lordships that it may be imported from Georgia at a much cheaper rate, resolved, in consideration of saving expense to the public, and of giving encouragement to the commerce of His Majesty's Colonies,

[455] Williams, ii, 220. Brooke, pp. 92-3. H.P.P., Samuel Hood to H., 14 Oct. 1767.

that the Navy Board be directed to contract with Mr. Bowen for a quantity of his powder.'

The powder was to be issued to ships' surgeons who were to report back to the Board, and the Commissioners of the Sick and Hurt were to try it out in the naval hospitals.[456]

During the year Hawke and the Board received a number of requests from James Cook who, as Master in command of the schooner *Grenville*, was conducting a survey of the coast of Newfoundland. Cook asked, for example, for a 'reflecting telescope' which would be of 'great utility for navigation'. All his requests were granted, so it could well be that Hawke was already forming a good opinion of Cook.[457]

However, the Board's outstanding work of the year was an attempt to tighten control over the dockyards. As long as the Navy Board remained separate from the Admiralty, the Lords could only exercise this control through the Navy Board. On 10 June the Lords having received a perfunctory report from the Commissioners on their annual visit to the dockyards: 'resolved that they be directed to send a Report respecting each yard separately, and to be more particular and circumstantial therein, for their Lordships' better information.'

The Commissioners wrote again on the subject on 17 June. Hawke and the other Lords subjected both reports to exhaustive examination, and the result was a forceful and detailed directive to the Navy Board, dated 23 June. The abuse of the 'Privilege of Chips' was vigorously assailed: that is, the practice of selling useful timber for the private profit of workmen was to be eradicated. Seeing that Chatham Dockyard seemed to have been the worst in this respect, and that the

---

[456] Add.MSS. 38205, f. 283. Ad. 3/75, 26 Feb., 23, 26 March, 21 May, 18 June, 16, 23 July, 5, 6 Aug., 29 Oct. 1767.

[457] Ad. 3/75, 12 Feb., 24 March, etc., 1767; cf. Jan. 1768.

Navy Board had detected 'in the workmen of the said Yard a particular degree of sloth and inactivity', a forcible rebuke was to be administered 'to the Master Shipwrights and other Officers of that Yard, to whose negligence this evil must in great measure be imputed'. The Board thought fit, however, to insert a compliment to the Commissioners, which would make ironical reading in 1770: 'It is with pleasure that the Lords observe in the said Report that the ships lying up in the several Ordinaries were found in excellent order, and that the Regulations on that head had been punctually observed.'

Nevertheless, it was clear that irregularities had tended to increase in the dockyards. 'Their Lordships cannot therefore expect that the reformation now attempted will long continue but by a regular and constant exertion of the same zeal and attention which has been shown on the present occasion.'

The Commissioners were to pay a second visit to the Yards that year and they were not to 'fail through mistaken good nature or indulgence to represent by name' any officers who were not doing their duty.

The Commissioners appear either to have resented the Admiralty's directive or else to have relapsed into apathy. The Lords understood that a second visit had been paid to the Dockyards but 15 December arrived without any report having reached Stephens. 'Therefore', wrote the latter, 'their Lordships direct [the Commissioners] forthwith to make such report.'

On 18 December Messrs. Cokburne (Comptroller), Slade (Surveyor), Williams, Mason (Clerk of the Acts), T. Brett (Controller of the Treasurer's Accounts), and Sir Richard Temple (Extra Commissioner) duly signed a report. The Lords found it inadequate. On 25 February 1768 the Commissioners of the Navy were summoned to appear in the Board Room and subjected to an examination. The Lords considered that the latest report had been too general; but the Commissioners insisted that all the dockyards were being run in accordance with orders issued since their first visit of 1767. In the end the Lords accepted the Navy Board's explanation, though not without some misgiving, for they demanded that after future visits to the dockyards the Commissioners should 'report particularly the state of each'.[458]

During his first year at the Admiralty Hawke had been subjected to the stream of applications for appointments inseparable from the life of an eighteenth-century First Lord. For example, when he took three weeks' holiday in the September of 1767, nineteen such requests followed him down to Swaythling. Some people even stooped to importuning the help of Catharine, the Admiral's daughter, who was then only 16 years old.

Hawke was satisfied with the progress of his first and second sons. Edward, though only 20 years old, was a major in the Army. Martin, at 23, had completed his studies at Oxford and had entered Lincoln's Inn. Martin's relations with his father had always been happy and the Admiral seems to have derived increasing pleasure and satisfaction from his son's well-balanced and cultivated personality. Now that the Hawke family was involved in it, the political scene had become quite fascinating to Martin, as appears from a letter which he wrote to his father on 19 September, when the latter was at Swaythling.

> [Gossip has it] that the Dukes of Newcastle, Bedford, Northumberland, and Richmond, the Marquess of Rockingham, the Earls of Sandwich, Halifax, Gower, and Shelburne, Messrs. Dowdeswell, Conway, Barre, and Burke

---

[458] Ad. 3/75, 10, 23 June, 15 Dec. 1767, 25 Feb. 1768.

> are to be included in the new Ministry, and that Mr. Grenville will be appointed Chancellor of the Exchequer. Not to mention the clash of interest, sentiment, and family connexion, which will undoubtedly prevent this expected union, I humbly conceive the conjunctive introduction of these worthy patriots will require a second miracle of loaves and fishes.
>
> I am informed, from very good authority, that Lord Chatham having sold sufficient estate to raise £25,000 is perfectly easy in mind, and sleeps well, and is freed from those complaints on which the worthy Junto abovementioned founded their claims and expectations.[459]

The end of 1767 found the Chatham Ministry still continuing its bickering, uncoordinated existence.

On the first day of 1768 Sir William Rowley, the Admiral of the Fleet, died; and it was for the Admiralty to select his successor. Of the Admirals of the White, Griffin had never been employed since his court martial in 1750. Osborn, who had for long been senior to Hawke on the list of admirals, might have been considered for the ultimate promotion, but he was in poor health and, in 1765, he had resigned the post of Vice-Admiral of Great Britain in exchange for an Irish pension of £1,200 a year. Therefore, whether on formal grounds or with regard to the claims of merit, the Board Meeting of 15 January could do no other than resolve 'that Sir Edward Hawke be appointed Admiral and Commander-in-Chief of His Majesty's Fleet'. Thus, in rank as in achievement, Hawke became the first seaman of England.[460]

---

[459] H.P.P. Bundle of letters received at Swaythling, Sept. 1767; Martin H. to H., 19 Sept.

[460] Ad. 3/75, 15 Jan. 1768.

Soon afterwards Hawke was made responsible for organizing what turned out to be one of the most important voyages in British history. Earlier in the century, the famous astronomer, Edmund Halley, had predicted that the planet Venus would pass between the earth and the sun in 1769. After an accurate observation of the event, it would be possible to calculate the earth's distance from the sun. On 29 February 1768 the Royal Society recommended to the King that a ship should be sent to Tahiti with the astronomers who were to make the observation. The project was approved; and on 2 March Lord Shelburne asked the Admiralty to provide a suitable vessel to sail for 'a southern latitude' early in the spring.

The Royal Society tried to persuade Hawke to appoint one of its Fellows, a not-very-agreeable person by the name of Alexander Dalrymple, to command the expedition. The Board, in rejecting this proposition, made it clear that a naval officer would be in charge. A story was circulated that, in an interview with the President of the Royal Society, Hawke had thumped the table and declared that he would lose his right hand before permitting a civilian to command one of His Majesty's ships. The most recent example of a civilian commanding such an expedition had been provided by Halley himself; and here the upshot had been a mutiny! Therefore, when Dalrymple's unattractive character is taken into account, it is understandable that Hawke might have expressed himself forcibly on the subject. It was established that the astronomers and botanists were to travel simply as passengers.

The ship which was destined to do so much more than carry the astronomers to Tahiti was 'a cat-built vessel' of 370 tons called the *Earl of Pembroke*. In compliance with the Admiralty's order of 21 March, the Navy Board chose and bought this vessel and renamed her the *Endeavour*. By April she was being sheathed, fitted, and provided with a light armament of '6 carriage guns of 4-pounders, and 8 swivel guns' — adequate enough to deal with hostile natives. It remained for their Lordships to select a naval lieutenant to command her.[461]

At the end of 1767, having done excellent work on the survey of the Newfoundland coast, James Cook had returned to England on leave. The Board asked Pallisser, who was now Commodore in charge of the Newfoundland station, to report on Cook's suitability for command, and received a favourable reply. Cook was promoted to Lieutenant, but the Lords seem to hesitated before appointing a commander for the *Endeavour*. She was to carry two lieutenants, one of whom would act as captain; but Cook was in the first instance appointed as 2nd Lieutenant. However, the matter was settled on 25 May. Hawke, Townshend, Yonge, and Lord Charles Spencer (who had recently replaced Jenkinson) 'resolved that Mr. James Cook, 2nd, be appointed 1st Lieutenant of the *Endeavour* Bark'; and this proved to be an excellent decision. At the same time, the Board sent out orders for the vessel to be fitted for foreign service, and for food for twelve months to be put on board.[462]

Credit for the victualling should be shared by the Admiralty, the Victualling Board, and the Sick and Hurt Board. In general, no ship had ever been so well provided for, although there was too great a bias towards salty and starchy foods to satisfy a modern dietician. The Board was as open-minded towards suggested cures or preventatives of scurvy as it was towards inventions. On 10 June the Lords ordered a trial to be given to sauerkraut, of which the Victualling Board had a supply, and to

---

[461] S.P.Dom. 44/232, f. 25-7. Lloyd, pp. 31, 88. Ad. 3/76, 5 Apr. 1768.

[462] Ad. 2/94, 25 May; 3/76, 12 Apr., 25 May 1768; 6/20 f. 203. Lloyd, pp. 19, 34.

'robs from the juice of lemons and oranges', which could be supplied from Haslar Hospital (where Lind was still Senior Physician). The juice was, in fact, a good preventative; but sauerkraut is known to contain a little ascorbic acid and therefore represented a move in the right direction. It was not until 30 July that the Lords — with Hawke presiding, as on 10 June — decided also to order a trial of 'malt made into wort', which was recommended by Dr MacBride and others. Therefore, while admitting that MacBride's suggestion is now known to be worthless as an anti-scorbutic, it is difficult to accept the statement in *Medicine and the Navy* that 'the Admiralty was interested, not in Lind's methods, but in those of David MacBride'. If so, why were the orders for a trial of Lind's method issued in such good time, and those relating to MacBride's suggestion at the very last minute? (On 30 July the *Endeavour* sailed from Deptford for Plymouth.) In any case, at a time when Lind himself could not have given the true reasons why citrus juice was superior to sauerkraut or 'wort', surely the fact that the Lords decided to give a further trial to the much-publicized wort illustrates very well their lack of prejudice.

From the point of view of improving knowledge about how to combat scurvy, the results of the voyage were disappointing. Owing partly to the surgeons' lack of skill in controlling the experiments, and partly to the frequency with which fresh food was obtained from on shore, no definite findings of any value emerged.[463]

Hawke should more especially be remembered in connexion with the two sets of Secret Instructions dated 30 July. The first set contained Cook's orders for the astronomical side of the expedition, and the second, called Additional Instructions,

[463] Ad. 3/76, 9 June, 30 July; 2/94, 10 June, 30 July 1768. Lloyd and Coulter, pp. 302-12. cf. Lloyd, pp. 38-42.

related to a search for the much-talked-of southern Pacific continent. (The French were known to be active in the area, doubtless seeking compensation for the loss of their Empire in North America.) As soon as the observation of Venus had been completed Cook was to sail due S. from Tahiti. Assuming that he found no continent en route, he was to continue to the southward until he reached latitude 40°, then head due W. till he reached New Zealand. (At this date French charts showed much of the west coast of New Zealand but nothing more.) Cook was to make charts, record magnetic variations of the compass, bring home specimens of vegetation and minerals, and write accounts of the manners and customs of native peoples. Not least in importance, he was to take possession in the King's name of any place, if he thought fit. He could judge for himself whether he should return home round the Cape of Good Hope or Cape Horn. Finally: 'You will also observe with accuracy the situation of such islands as you may discover in the course of your voyage that have not been discovered by any Europeans, and take possession for His Majesty and make surveys and draughts of such of them as may appear to be of consequence, without suffering yourself, however, to be thereby diverted from the object which you are always to have in view, the discovery of the Continent so often mentioned.'

Cook proved himself admirably suited to command such an expedition. On 31 January 1770 he hoisted the Union Flag on the shore of New Zealand as a mark of British sovereignty. During his examination of the western coastline of the North Island, he named a fine, sweeping bay 'Hawke's Bay' after the man who had sent him on the voyage. The surrounding province, now one of the loveliest and most productive in New Zealand, took the same name and is a fitting memorial to the Admiral.[464]

While the Admiralty was playing a part in the establishment of a new empire in Australasia, it was made to contribute towards the destruction of the old. Doubtless to the satisfaction of the King, Charles Townshend, 'the brilliant artificer of ruin', had passed his provocative duties on imports into America — notably tea — and in September he had died, leaving his ministerial colleagues to reap the rising whirlwind. During 1768 smuggling and rioting became prevalent in the American ports, and in August the Admiralty was instructed by King's Letters Patent to set up four Courts of Vice-Admiralty instead of the existing one. The four Judges were to sit at Halifax, Boston, Philadelphia, and Charleston.[465]

However, a more pressing problem for Hawke arose from the lack of oak timber for the construction and repair of ships. A letter dated 9 August 1768 was received from the Navy Board. The latter stated that it had become very difficult to obtain supplies of English oak, which 'exceeds all other in quality', because of the great quantity cut down during the Seven Years' War and also the ever-increasing requirements of the East India Company. The Commissioners therefore asked the Admiralty to approach the Treasury in order that the felling of all oak trees in the King's forests should be placed under their control. The Lords appear to have made investigations into the position. Then, on 19 November, Hawke, Townshend, and Palmerston resolved to send a copy of the Navy Board's letter to the Treasury, and to ask that the said Board's recommendations be accepted.[466]

---

[464] Ad. 2/1332, f. 160-9. Lloyd, pp. 22-33, 60-1.
[465] Tunstall, pp. 393-6. Williams, ii, 235-40. Ad. 3/76, 21 Sept. 1768.
[466] N.M.M.: Navy Board to Stephens, 9 Aug. 1768. Ad. 3/76, 19 Nov. 1768.

As Hawke realized, an additional source of difficulty was the increase in the sheer size both of the ships of the line and of the East Indiamen. Not only did each ship use up more oak; a stage had been reached where the East India ships required the scarce great-timbers out of which the keels, stern-posts, and knees of large warships had to be fashioned.

It became clear to the Admiralty that it was faced with a difficult, long-term problem, to which there would be no easy solution.[467]

During the winter of 1768-9 Hawke received a somewhat fantastic petition from an old acquaintance, Lieutenant Robert Tomlinson. The latter recalled that he had originally been recommended 'to a most amiable lady, once inexpressibly dear to the Admiral', by a Miss Brooke — doubtless a relative of Catharine. He thanked Hawke for his 'kindness' to him in the past, for showing 'great anxiety' for his welfare, and for 'appointing' him a Lieutenant in 1757. (He did not mention that he had commanded the cutter *Success* during Hawke's campaign of 1759.) More latterly, he had been 1st Lieutenant of the *Lynn* (44) from 1760 to 1762, 'all of which time', he asserted, 'I had not a Captain of any interest, or should undoubtedly have been promoted for my extraordinary services in that ship'. On three occasions he had saved the *Lynn* from shipwreck. Hawke had often said that he would help him 'to the utmost of his power'.

> I appeal to Him who sees in secret how very often my heart has been poured out in fervent intercessions for every spiritual and temporal blessing being showered abundantly upon Sir Edward Hawke. Which is a demonstrable proof that I looked upon him as a faithful patron, for it is not in our

[467] H.P.P., 'Considerations' — see p. 301 n. 13.

> Nature to retain such an extraordinary esteem for any but those whom we suppose to be our most valuable friends.
>
> I earnestly beseech Sir Edward Hawke to reflect that if I am not made a Master and Commander whilst he presides at the Admiralty, it will be an unsurmountable obstacle to my preferment. I most earnestly entreat Sir Edward Hawke would be pleased to consider the number of noblemen's sons, etc., which are in the Navy, *who must have promotion.* And also the growing power and interest of the Scots Officers in the Service…
>
> Finally, I humbly entreat that Sir Edward Hawke would be pleased to recollect that I am the only one of his old standers left, which is not a Captain, that was wholly brought up in the Service under the Admiral.[468]

All the indications are that Tomlinson was a valuable, if rather eccentric, officer; and, being still a Lieutenant at the age of 35, on half-pay at that, and being married with three young children, he had reason for desiring an improvement in his fortunes. It appears that the best Hawke could do for him was to have him appointed Lieutenant in command of the cutter *Boscawen* on 21 February 1769.

During the 1770's Tomlinson (who remained a Lieutenant on full pay until 1774) emerged as an authority on the problem of manning the Fleet, wrote a treatise on timber, and gave much time to assisting Hawke's protagonists in their battle with Sandwich at the end of the decade. Hawke told his son Martin that he hoped to see Tomlinson promoted to Post-Captain, but the expression of this sentiment presumably dated from some time after the Admiral's retirement from the Admiralty. Tomlinson eventually became a Master and

---

[468] H.P.P., petition of Robert Tomlinson, *circa* Jan. 1769. O.B., 12 Sept. 1759.

Commander in 1782; and in 1809, at the age of 76, he was promoted to Captain on half-pay.[469]

At the beginning of 1769 Hawke, together with Parliament as a whole, was distracted by the affair of John Wilkes, M.P. The latter had been convicted in 1764 of libelling the Crown in the famous No. 45 of the *North Briton*, which contained a free attack on government policy. His claim of parliamentary privilege having been rejected, Wilkes had fled abroad before this conviction. In 1768, however, he had returned to England and was ordered to serve his sentence; but as the result of a disorderly and drunken autumn election, he was chosen as Member by the borough of Middlesex. When the Cabinet discussed the matter in January 1769, Conway, Hawke, and Granby opposed Grafton's determination to have Wilkes expelled from the Commons; and, according to Walpole: 'Had Conway, Sir Edward Hawke, and Lord Granby been firm to their first resolution, the Court would not have ventured on such obnoxious and alarming precedents.' It therefore appears that Hawke's attitude on this issue was far from reactionary.[470]

On 1 May Hawke would have had another opportunity to express his liberal inclinations when the Cabinet discussed the repeal of Townshend's vexatious duties on the American colonies' imports, but, most unfortunately, he was not well enough to attend. By five votes to four it was agreed to remove all the duties except the tax on tea. On this question, Grafton (into whose weak hands Chatham had resigned leadership of the Ministry) afterwards wrote that the deplorable exclusion of tea from the repeal was 'contrary to the declared opinions of

---

[469] Ad. 3/76, 21 Feb. 1769. N.R.S., *Tomlinson Papers*, pp. vii-xii, etc.

[470] Watson, pp. 99-101, 131-6. cf. *The Correspondence of George III, 1760-83*, ed. J. Fortescue, London, 1927-8, 6 vols., ii, 73. H. Walpole, *Memoirs of George III*, iii, 237. Grafton, p. 198.

Lord Camden, Lord Granby, General Conway, and myself. Sir Edward Hawke was absent through illness. Otherwise, I think that he would have agreed with those who voted for including the teas in the repeal.' Hawke was unable to attend at the Admiralty from 2 to 15 May, and again missed Board Meetings on the 19th and 20th.[471]

Meanwhile, that Board was preoccupied not only with the supply of timber for the Navy, but also with the problem of seasoning wood in order to avoid subsequent rotting. Trials were ordered of the various preservatives suggested. Also, although earlier experiments with copper sheathing had failed, its potential value was realized and the Navy Board was encouraged to persist with its investigations. On 20 July 1768, Hawke, Brett, and three of the landsmen-Lords took account of 'the ill effects of copper sheathing in corroding and destroying the rudder irons, bolts, and other iron works under water', and resolved that, as proposed by the Navy Board, 'an experiment be made on board the new sloop to be set up at Deptford, by the bolts in her works under water being wrought out of forged copper, instead of iron'. This did indeed prove helpful and became standard practice over the next ten years. During Middleton's time as Comptroller, it was eventually found that iron bolts could be treated to prevent corrosion and they came back into use. However, Hawke's administration received scant credit for its valuable preparatory work, largely because Sandwich, driven onto the defensive by the parliamentary inquiries of 1782, denigrated the efforts of his predecessor. In any case, it should be recognized that the coppering of most of the Fleet, achieved under Sandwich,

---

[471] ibid., p. 229. Watson, pp. 143-4. Ad. 3/76, 2-19 May 1769. H.P.P., H. to Martin H., 27 Aug., 26 Sept. 1776, for H.'s liberal attitude towards the American colonies.

helped considerably to save Britain from utter defeat during the American War. The ships' sailing qualities and endurance were enormously enhanced.

In 1769 Hawke's Board ordered the frigate *Stag* and the sloop *Hawke* to be sheathed with copper, and issued like instructions for the sloops *Dolphin* and *Swallow* in 1770.[472]

The continuing seriousness of the shortage of oak was again emphasized in a letter from the Navy Board dated 30 May 1769. The Commissioners were especially concerned about the depletion of the Forest of Dean. This forest had been protected in the time of Charles II but had latterly suffered severely from the depredations of 'colliers in that neighbourhood', who 'annually cut down great numbers of oak trees under a right they claim to timber for the use of their coal pits'. Plymouth Yard had largely depended on this source of supply for the previous sixteen to eighteen years. The Commissioners therefore strongly urged that the powers which had been granted to them for controlling activity in the New Forest should be extended to include the Forest of Dean. The Admiralty recommended to the Treasury that this suggestion should be adopted as far as was practicable.[473]

On the general timber situation, which was so important a determinant of potential strength at sea, Hawke noted: 'By the intelligence received, it appeared that there was not a sufficiency of timber in England to be purchased at any price.' The large timber which was near enough to the coast to keep carriage-costs within reasonable bounds 'was nearly exhausted'.

---

[472] Ad. 3/75, 26 March 1767, 22 Jan. 1768, 17 Feb., 1 March, 8, 12 April 1769, for testing preservatives. Ad. 3/74, 15 Aug. 1766; 3/75, 18 June 1767; 3/76, 20 July 1768, 15, 19 July 1769. *6* April, 3 Oct. 1770 — for copper sheathing. N.R.S.: Sandwich Papers, iv, 285.

[473] N.M.M.: Navy Board to Stephens, 30 May 1769. Ad. 3/76, 7 July 1769.

Troubles in Poland cut off supplies from that source; yet the demand, in respect both of naval and East India ships, continued to increase. Hawke tried every suggested expedient for which money could be found; and, during 1767-9, he managed to lay in the yard considerably more loads of British timber than had his predecessors of 1764-6. Moreover, it was in consequence of his initiative that measures restricting the size of East Indiamen became effective in Sandwich's time. If it had not been for the war-scare of 1770, he would himself have seen the matter through. Finally, representations made by the Board in his time resulted in the planting of 2,000 acres in the Forest of Dean and 1,000 in the New Forest.

In default of Polish supplies, Hawke took Stettin plank; also timber from Hanover, Prussia, and the Rhineland, and, in 1769, from Quebec. He obtained mahogany and cedar from the 'Mosquito shores'. Therefore he is not open to the accusation of undue conservatism, in the sense of stupid insistence on English oak only, which has been levelled against eighteenth-century naval administrations.[474]

Early in 1770 the friendly relations then subsisting between Britain and Russia led to the arrival of a Russian squadron for repairs in His Majesty's dockyards. The Russians made the curious demand that one of their three-decked ships should be reduced to two and a half decks. This idea aroused little enthusiasm at the Navy Board and Hawke settled in favour of a less eccentric scheme suggested by the said Board.

Our recently acquired allies gave other occasions for perplexity. One such example of Russian awkwardness appears to have been satisfactorily dealt with by their Lordships on 26 February. The relevant minute reads: 'The Commander of the

---

[474] H.P.P., 'Considerations' — see p. 301 n. 13. Cf. Albion, p. 134; and, for criticism of undue conservatism, see pp. 23-5, 37-8.

Russian frigate at Sheerness having taken upon him to fire the evening and morning gun; resolved that the Secretary of State be made acquainted therewith, and desired to move the Russian Ambassador that effectual orders may be immediately given to prevent the like irregular proceedings for the future.'[475]

Meanwhile, the final collapse of Grafton's political leadership brought about a situation disquieting to Hawke.

On the death of Charles Townshend (1767), the King had installed the capable but easy-going Lord North as Chancellor of the Exchequer, and had further strengthened the Government by securing the adherence of the Bedford group. Gower, Weymouth, Hillsborough, and Sandwich accepted the sweets of office.

On 6 July 1769, Chatham, apparently quite recovered from his illness, waited on the King at Court. He declared his opposition to all the most notable acts of government which had occurred since his involuntary retirement two and a half years before. To his way of thinking, these acts were: the coercion of Parliament in the matter of Wilkes; the policy of repression in America; and the failure to redress the Indian grievances against the East India Company. This forthright pronouncement occasioned no comment from the King; but never again was there personal contact between the two men.[476]

In the House of Lords Chatham now proceeded to attack the Government in the name of freedom. On 9 January 1770 the House was roused by forceful words on the related subjects of America and of British political liberties: 'I love liberty wherever it is seated, it is a plant that ought to be cherished; and that country was settled upon ideas of liberty... Tyranny, my Lords, is detestable in every shape... This

[475] Ad. 3/76, 30 Jan., 26 Feb. 1770.

[476] Watson, pp. 128-9. Williams, ii, 248-53. Tunstall, p. 396.

Middlesex case is laying the axe to the tree of liberty... Let slavery exist nowhere amongst us.'

Thus spake the 'scarecrow of violence to the gentle warblers of the grove', and not without effect. 'For the honour of Lord Chatham and their country's quiet', Lord Coventry and the Duke of Beaufort resigned from their Household posts; and, disturbingly for Hawke, Sir Piercy Brett and Sir George Yonge gave up their seats at the Admiralty. Lord Granby, after hesitating between his sense of professional duty and his liberal instincts, succumbed to Chatham's continued persuasions and resigned the command of the Army. Lord Camden, who rallied to Lord Chatham but would not resign as Lord Chancellor, was dismissed by the King. On 27 January many people must have concluded the Government was at an end when they heard that Grafton, the First Lord of the Treasury, had tendered his resignation.

By the debate of 2 February, the vacillating Conway had also joined the ranks of the opposition in the Commons, where an onslaught was made on the Government's handling of the Middlesex elections. However, the King placed North in the post of First Lord of the Treasury; and thus — surprisingly — he ushered in a long period of ministerial stability.[477]

Hawke found himself placed in a position where his conscience was troubled. It was Chatham who had appointed him to the Admiralty; he had himself persuaded Brett to join the Board and serve the Chatham administration; and in the Cabinet, he had tended to share the views particularly of Granby and Conway, and to some extent those of Camden and Grafton. Now his former master together with his friends had taken their stand against the Government, in defence of

---

[477] Williams, ii, 255-9, 261-4, 266. Watson, pp. 146-7. Tunstall, pp. 414, 416.

political liberty and American freedom, causes with which he sympathized. On the other hand, he had always placed loyalty to the Crown before any duties, other than religious ones. On balance, he felt that it was incumbent on him to continue to do what he could for the Royal Navy. But the conflict of duties was severe and it is significant that from about this time his health rapidly declined. He was a man who could not harden himself to weaknesses in his moral position, as he had already demonstrated through his illness after the 'rash step' of 1758. Likewise, during 1770 he became progressively more overburdened with the ailment which he had hitherto borne more successfully, namely the gravel.[478]

On 5 March Letters Patent for a new Board of Admiralty were read. Besides Hawke, Buller, Palmerston, and Spencer, all members of the old Board, there were 'Wilmot, Viscount Lisburne of the Kingdom of Ireland, Francis Holburne, Esq., and Charles James Fox, Esq.'. Thus, at a very late hour, Holburne came to a seaman's seat at the Admiralty in place of Brett. Since 1748, when he was Hawke's Captain aboard the *Kent*, he had maintained good relations with that Admiral; but he himself had remained a controversial figure since he and Loudon had failed to take Louisbourg in 1757. He was a year older than Hawke and, at the time of his appointment to the Board, he had only sixteen months to live.[479]

During 1770 Britain had to face a threat of war. Choiseul had made remarkable headway in building up the French Navy, and he had also made improvements in the army. Planning and surveying in preparation for the invasion of England went on continuously. Not to be outdone, the Spanish communicated

---

[478] Add.MSS. 38208, f. 243. Grafton, p. 256. Grafton MSS., 615, Bradshaw to G., 24 July 1770. N.R.S.: Sandwich Papers, i, 7, 8, 13.
[479] Ad. 3/77, 5 March 1770.

to the British naval commander in the Mediterranean 'pretensions to part of the Bay of Gibraltar'; and in the Falkland Islands, the Captain of the sloop *Tamar* was invited to evacuate the British settlement. The officer in question, Captain Hunt, declined. He left another naval captain in charge and sailed for England in the *Tamar*. On 6 June his news was considered by Hawke, Palmerston, and Fox. They decided that copies of the letters exchanged by Hunt and the Spanish officers should 'be sent to the Secretary of State for His Majesty's information'. On the same day, a report was read that French naval reinforcements had arrived in the West Indies. What with this and other news, an appraisal by the Government of the real dangers could not be avoided.[480]

At this time, Thomas Bradshaw, who had stayed on as Secretary to the Treasury, continued to supply information to his erstwhile chief, the Duke of Grafton, and a letter of 4 March gives a fair impression of North's reaction to the earlier alarums. Bradshaw had sounded the Minister as to the readiness of the Royal Navy, but the latter did 'not seem alarmed at the situation in France and Spain'. However, North said that he would call a Cabinet meeting to discuss the intelligence from abroad and the state of the Fleet. He wished to avoid causing alarm and, if it was found that the Navy needed extra money, it would be best to get a grant 'for discharging the debt of the Navy'. This money could then, in fact, be spent on strengthening the Navy instead of on reduction of the debt! Judging by his behaviour during the Falklands crisis, North hardly seems a man to sound clarion calls in hours of danger, but it would be a mistake merely to dismiss him as uninterested in foreign affairs and heedless of

[480] Tunstall, p. 377. cf. Pajol, v, 479. Ad. 3/77, 6 June 1770. Keppel, i, 407.

naval requirements. During the summer Hawke himself paid a visit to France and took keen note of any signs of war-preparations. His assessment, which both agreed with North's and proved to be correct, was that France was far from ready to fight.[481]

Meanwhile, a whispering campaign against Hawke had been set in motion by Captain Augustus Hervey. True to his usual form, he had referred during a Commons debate of July 1767 to 'that great and brave Admiral, whom His Majesty has placed at the head of that Service'; but by October 1768 he was insinuating to George Grenville: 'I hear… that Sir Edward Hawke must soon give way to the Earl of Sandwich.' Sandwich was indeed discontented with his post of joint Postmaster. 'The Admiralty, in which he had formerly served with credit', wrote Hervey's friend Horace Walpole, 'was the favourite object of Lord Sandwich's ambition.' And to rise to the Board through Sandwich's favour was the present ambition of Augustus Hervey.[482]

Grafton also had an eye on Hawke's place. Bradshaw therefore fed that Duke with information which he might wish to read.

I find your Grace's coming to the Head of the Admiralty is now universally talked of by everybody, and I am told that Lord Bristol mentioned it at Court as a thing that was certain — Sir Edward Hawke is most certainly dying, and his death can not be a distant event. Lord North has not said a word to me upon the report, and tho' I have talked seriously to him upon the wretched and dangerous state of the Navy, I have never touched upon the report, tho' in stating what ought to

[481] Grafton, p. 256. Cobbett, Vol. 16, 13 Nov. 1770.
[482] Cobbett, loc. cit. Smith, iv, 383. N.R.S.: Sandwich Papers, i, xii, xiii.

be the character and situation of the First Lord of the Admiralty, I have pretty exactly described your Grace.[483]

Hawke must indeed have been showing signs of worsening health. Yet, during the year, despite enforced absences in April, November, and December, he drove himself to attend at the Admiralty even more frequently than before, on account of the international situation. During his term of office, the number of meetings at which he presided, year by year, was 1767 — 118; 1768 — 126; 1769 — 118; 1770 — 156. The figures for meetings held in his absence were: 1767 — 13; 1768 — 18; 1769 — 28; 1770 — 30. His record of attendance for 1770, in particular, testifies to his devotion to duty and strength of will.[484]

Late in July, dismaying news reached the Admiralty of a conflagration at Portsmouth dockyard. Pallisser, whose work on the Newfoundland station had won him the Board's commendation, was made Comptroller of the Navy a few days after the disaster, and even twelve years later he saw it as a major misfortune. 'All the furniture and stores for twenty-five capital ships of the line were destroyed; every mast, yard, sail, cable, cordage, etc., appropriated to those ships were destroyed, consequently those ships were for a time useless.'[485]

However, there was one naval person who was delighted by the reports of the fire, and that was Augustus Hervey. He had never been slow to adapt himself to circumstances. Whereas on 8 July 1759 he had informed his Admiral that 'Sir Edward Hawke's praise might at any time justify' his happiness, towards the beginning of August 1770 he was writing to Sandwich:

---

[483] Grafton MSS., 615, Bradshaw to G., 24 July 1770.
[484] Ad. 3/75-8.
[485] Ad. 3/76, 14 Feb. 1769; 3/77, 1 Aug. 1770. N.R.S.: Sandwich Papers, iv, 308-9.

> Sir Edward will not now resign unless a peerage is given him. This is refused absolutely; and as he can raise himself out of his bed, he thinks he can last for ever, and there are reasons why they will not dismiss him. How far this unlucky accident [i.e. the fire] may operate, I know not; for to be sure, if it has resulted from any want of care, it will be a good excuse for doing as they please with him; and there will not want prompters for it, who can only point out such an able person as yourself…

There is no reason to doubt that this communication was well received by Lord Sandwich; but had that nobleman been afforded a glimpse of his situation on 23 April 1779, he might have experienced a degree of disenchantment. He would have observed himself in the House of Lords, listening to Hervey (who had by then succeeded his brother as Earl of Bristol) moving the dismissal of the Earl of Sandwich from the post of First Lord of the Admiralty![486]

Yet, even as late as August 1770, the news received by Sandwich on the likelihood of Hawke's resignation or dismissal was not necessarily encouraging. Richard Rigby wrote on the 11th: 'What is worse than all the rest, Sir Edward Hawke is in better health than he has been for some time past, at his house in the country, and I know has been offended at the idea of his being disposed to quit his employment.'

Nor did Rigby think that the King had 'imagined a vacancy at the Admiralty Board so near as ever to have thought of a successor to Sir Edward'.[487]

It was certainly not true, as Hervey had suggested, that the King had 'refused absolutely' to give Hawke a peerage. According to Grafton, the King had said in 1768 'that when

---

[486] Ad. 1/92, 8 July 1759. N.R.S.: Sandwich Papers, i, 7; ii, 255.
[487] ibid., i, 8-9, 14.

any peers should be made, [he] would consider Sir Edward Hawke and Sir Jeffrey Amherst'. And such evidence as exists on the subject indicates that Hawke never solicited a peerage. This most unusual dignity and restraint did not apply to Amherst who, unlike the Admiral, stooped to follow the universal habit of importunity.[488]

However, Sandwich had been effectively encouraged by Hervey, and on 30 July he had written to North asking for the Admiralty outright. North replied briefly in the negative on 21 August and wrote at greater length on the 24th as follows:

> It is true that Sir Edward Hawke's health grows every day more precarious, and it may be equally so that there are persons who look towards the Admiralty in the case of his death. No person, however, except your Lordship, has yet applied to me; and you may depend upon it that my good offices are not and shall not be engaged to any other. I am too sensible of the importance of the situation of a First Lord of the Admiralty, and too well acquainted with your Lordship's abilities, not to be desirous of seeing you at the head of that department. I ought at the same time to tell you that there was not, when I was in town, the least appearance of any inclination in Sir Edward Hawke to resign, and that his office will not in all probability be vacated before his death, which notwithstanding the weak state of his health may still be at a great distance.[489]

Yet despite the brave face which he presented to the world, the Admiral was in fact gravely concerned at the way in which his ailment was preventing him from discharging all his duties. He had been enduring the torments to be expected when

---

[488] H. Walpole, *Memoirs of George III*, ii, 163. cf. N.R.S.: Barrington Papers, i, 409.
[489] N.R.S.: Sandwich Papers, i, 9-14.

passing stones with the urine — a process known as a strangury. On 5 August he referred to this when writing to Jenkinson (now a Lord of the Treasury) who had inquired after his health.

> It is very true that I have been under the necessity of keeping away from the House of Commons, owing to a very troublesome disorder which I have unfortunately been plagued with, called the strangury, and which has given me little or no respite for a considerable time past, in so much that I am often obliged to remain within doors for several days together — much against my inclinations; and I am so heated when in the House that I am not able to stand it on any account whatever. Thank God you did not want me. Nothing less than this should have made me kept away.[490]

During September the Falklands affair became more critical. News reached England that the Spaniards had gone as far as to make the British settlers leave Port Egmont. Consequently, on the 7th Lord Weymouth, one of the Secretaries of State, sent directions to the Admiralty to make a squadron ready for immediate service.[491]

The Board forthwith ordered the sixteen guardships to be fully manned and victualled for three months. But it soon became evident that the squadron, which comprised six frigates as well as the sixteen of the line, could not be manned by volunteers; and therefore Hawke, with Lisburne and Holburne, decided to ask for 'an Order in Council empowering this Board to issue Press Warrants, as usual'.[492]

---

[490] Add.MSS. 38208, f. 243.

[491] Ad. 3/77, 11 Sept. 1770. Williams, ii, 271-2.

[492] Ad. 3/77, 11, 14 Sept. 1770.

By 20 September Hawke was signing orders for twenty-two more ships of the line to be made ready — a measure which soon put to the test the Navy Board's earlier assurances about the condition of the ships in ordinary. On the 24th the peacetime establishment of seamen was raised from 16,000 (which was already an improvement on Anson's 12,000 of 1755) to 25,000. On the 25th it was decided to use merchant yards for naval purposes. During the intensely active months of September and October, Hawke presided at every meeting of the Board except one. The other Lords averaged only a 50 per cent, attendance.[493]

Many years afterwards, the Duke of Grafton saw fit to include in his memoirs criticism based on a letter from Bradshaw, dated 15 September, in which the latter asserted that the Admiralty had 'most miserably bungled', through lack of secrecy amongst other things. In fact, the news of these preparations produced a most salutary effect in the country on which the issue of peace or war depended, namely France. The aging Louis XV, without whose support Spain would do nothing decisive, took fright at the prospect of a re-enactment of the tragedies of the Seven Years' War. Moreover, he feared that Russia might patch up its current quarrel with Turkey and involve France in a new series of campaigns by land. Therefore although Choiseul, who was now back at the Foreign Ministry, was ready to fight, the King was more inclined to listen to Madame du Barry and other opponents of the redoubtable Minister.[494]

On 30 September and 3 October Hawke set down some notes for his own guidance in view of the possibility of war.

---

[493] ibid., 20, 24, 25 Sept. 1770.

[494] Grafton MSS., 617, Bradshaw to G., 15 Sept. 1770. Grafton, p. 258. Tunstall, p. 423. Pajol, v, 507.

These show that he fully retained his old strategic grasp and ability to clarify essentials. Adequate concentrations of force had to be ensured and great pains taken over the selection of the operational commanders. Arising from these reflections was a promotion of admirals on 18 and 24 October. Keppel went up to Vice-Admiral of the Blue, and Richard, Viscount Howe, who was now aged 44, was given his first flag.[495]

By 10 November, when the mobilization of the Navy was well under way, Hawke found that he could hardly carry on at the Admiralty any longer. However, he appeared in the House of Commons after the opening of Parliament on the 13th and, together with the other Ministers, faced the lively attacks of the opposition. 'France is now arming in all her ports,' Beckford asserted. 'England is indeed the only power in Europe which is not in a condition to go to war.' Hawke replied to this: 'I shall only observe that I was in France last summer and that I know certainly by the observations I made that they are not in a condition to go to war.' The formidable Colonel Barre accused Hawke of evasion. He pointed to the Treasury bench and snapped: 'I call upon that wretched row of no-ministers for a more explicit answer.' Lord North, who was never at a loss in debate, was quickly on his feet and retorted: 'If we are no-ministers, why does the honourable gentleman call upon us for an answer?' He then deployed a smooth and skilful refutation of the charges levelled by the opposition; but it may be inferred that Hawke, ill as he was, suffered much more from these attacks than did the easy-tempered First Lord of the Treasury.

Hawke struggled to the Admiralty on 16 November. Then he appears to have been prostrated by pain and exhaustion. He did not reappear at the Board until 12 December. While away, he was doubtless distressed to learn of the purely factious and

---

[495] H.P.P., notes dated 30 Sept, and 3 Oct. 1770. Clowes, iii, 565-6.

even abusive onslaught aimed by Chatham at the Admiralty and at the Government in general. This speech of 22 November was described by Dr. Samuel Johnson as a 'feudal gabble'.[496]

However, during his absence from the Board, Hawke was responsible for the decision of 26 November to appoint Lord Howe 'Commander-in-Chief of His Majesty's ships and vessels in the Mediterranean'. This was surely one of the boldest and most brilliantly imaginative naval appointments of the century. Howe had just risen to the most junior of flag ranks, that of Rear-Admiral of the Blue, yet Hawke did not hesitate, in allocating this very important command, to set aside the claims of seniority in favour of those of professional capacity. Predictably, there was some murmuring against this dramatic and utterly unconventional step. Hawke is reported to have rebuked the malcontents with the admirably just remark: 'I have tried my Lord Howe on many occasions; he never asked me how he was to execute any service entrusted to his charge, but always went straight forward and performed it.'

The whole Service knew that this was no more than the truth and Howe's appointment soon received general acceptance.[497]

But during Hawke's illness the reputation of the Board suffered a severe set-back. Orders from Lord Weymouth had caused five ships of the line to be made ready to carry two regiments of infantry to Gibraltar, in case the Spanish should attack that fortress. Late in November they sailed but met foul weather. The result was sharply disillusioning, in the light of the Navy Board's assurances about the condition of the ships.

---

[496] Ad. 3/78, 10, 16 Nov.-12 Dec 1770. Cobbett, Vol. 16, 13 Nov. 1770. Tunstall, pp. 422-4. Williams, ii, 273.
[497] Ad. 3/78, 26 Nov. 1770. J. Barrow, *The Life of Richard, Earl Howe*, 1830, pp. 79-80.

The *Arrogant* and *Achilles*, 'having received great damage', fell back on Spithead. No sooner had the Admiralty ordered the *Centaur* and *Yarmouth* to sail in their stead than a report was received from Captain Allen of the *Achilles* that 'his rigging was found to be rotten, that none of the spare sails fitted, and that there had been a great want of attention in fitting the ship for sea'. Understandably, the Lords communicated their indignation to the Navy Board. Then they were informed that the *Yarmouth* was unfit to sail at all. Their Lordships' anger and frustration may be inferred from the somewhat desperate wording of a minute of 3 December, that the *Yarmouth* 'having been found unfit to proceed at present with troops to Gibraltar, resolved that the *Belle Isle* or any other ship at Spithead (if she should be found unfit) be ordered to be got away'. It was soon reported that the *Belle Isle* was 'unfit to proceed'.[498]

On 12 December Hawke reappeared at the Board and also went to the House of Commons. At the Board the Lords decided to suggest to the Commissioners of the Navy that the defects of the *Yarmouth* and *Belle Isle* 'must have been owing to some very great neglect or inattention at the time they were fitted as guardships, or when they were lately refitted for Channel service'. The Navy Board was to report 'to whose neglect it was owing that the said ships were allowed to go out of dock in so very bad a condition'.

In the Commons Hawke stated that the Navy was in much better shape than in 1755; and, despite the mishaps just recounted, he must have been correct in making this assertion. It will be remembered how low naval expenditure was allowed to fall in Anson's time, and that, as one of the consequences, the number of guardships — the ships which it was the duty of

[498] Ad. 3/77-8, 12 Oct., 26, 30 Nov., 1, 3, 10 Dec. 1770.

the Navy Board to have immediately ready for sea — was reduced at Portsmouth, the Navy's principal base, from eight to one. Even before the Falklands crisis Hawke maintained a total of sixteen guardships. Addressing the House of Commons on 12 December, Hawke said that twenty ships of the line were already manned and fit for action. Another twenty were in commission, had 3,000 men towards their complement, and would soon be fit for service. Of the 40,000 seamen recently voted by Parliament, 33,000 had already been collected. Keppel and Saunders, as chief spokesmen for the Rockinghams, questioned the accuracy of Hawke's statement. Why, if the Navy was so strong, had no squadron been sent to the West Indies? Hawke, who was not unaware of Choiseul's efforts on behalf of the French Navy, very reasonably replied that he was determined to ensure British superiority in European waters.[499]

The upshot of the whole affair was a little-recognized triumph for the Government. War was averted without the loss of national honour or interest. On 23 December Louis XV wrote urging the King of Spain to reach an accommodation with Great Britain; and on the next day the French King concluded the matter by dismissing Choiseul from office and exiling him to his estates. Such was the Minister's reward for preparing so patiently and methodically to reassert the warlike greatness of France.[500]

Though only at the cost of great physical distress, Hawke was once again attending all the meetings of the Board. But now that the threat of war had definitely receded he decided that he must lay down his charge. The pathos of the moment is

---

[499] Ad. 3/78, 12 Dec. 1770. J. Almon, *Debates and Proceedings of the British House of Commons, 1743-74*, 1766-75, Vol. 9, pp. 84-5.
[500] Pajol, v, 479.

conveyed in a paragraph written by Bradshaw to Grafton on 5 January 1771. Even the interested Secretary of the Treasury could not help being moved by the Admiral's plight.

> I enquired of his Lordship [North] how Sir Edward Hawke was. He told me he did not know. But I know that he is very ill, and that Lord North now has a letter from him to Lord Rochford in his possession, in which the poor man tells him that he Ends himself unable to attend Cabinets, or St. James's; and that, if he does not very soon find an alteration of his health for the better, he shall endeavour to creep once more to St. James's and there, thanking the King for all his kindnesses to him, lay his office at his feet.[501]

On 10 January Hawke wrote again to Lord Rochford to confirm that he wished his resignation to be laid before the King. The King had always — and with good reason — been well disposed towards the Admiral and, if he had not been so tied up in political engagements as a result of his having undertaken the direct management of Parliament, he would surely have conferred on Hawke the peerage which he had so amply deserved. However, Lord Rochford replied on the 11th:

> I was favoured with your letter last night, and was extremely unhappy to have a letter of that sort from you to lay before the King, for no one can have a higher opinion than I have of the able and disinterested manner in which you have served the King for so many years. When I had the honour this day to acquaint the King with your intentions, His Majesty was pleased to express in the strongest terms how sensible he was of the loss of so able and gallant an officer, and regretted very much the bad state of your health which obliged you to come to this resolution.[502]

---

[501] Grafton, p. 260.

Horace Walpole — perhaps influenced by sympathy with the aspirations of Augustus Hervey — treated the matter more light-heartedly. On 15 January he wrote to Mann: 'There seems to be a pestilence amongst our politicians. They go off by wholesale. The Duke of Bedford died last night… Sir Edward Hawke is only dead politically, having resigned from age and infirmities. The new Secretary of State, Lord Sandwich, succeeds him, and no man is fitter for the office.'[503]

Perhaps the most substantial appreciation which Hawke received for his work at the Admiralty came from Lord Palmerston, who had been at the Board with him from the time of his appointment as First Lord. 'I did intend waiting on you this morning to have assured you in person how very sincere a regret I feel on hearing that your present state of health had made you determine to quit the laborious office you have held with so much advantage to the public credit and to yourself, and satisfaction to those who had the honour of sitting with you at the Board.'[504]

---

502 Burrows, p. 472. Fortescue, op. cit., ii, 204.
503 H. Walpole, *Letters to Sir Horace Mann*, *London*, 1843-4, 8 vols., ii, 125.
504 Burrows, p. 464.

CHAPTER 19: ASPECTS OF RETIREMENT

HAWKE was certainly very ill when he left the Admiralty; yet he still had a good ten years of life before him. Thanks to the fact that more family letters relating to this period have survived than is the case with regard to the Admiral's earlier years, it is possible to appreciate how simply and warmly he was attached to his children.

After he left the Board Hawke seems to have taken up permanent residence at Sunbury, although he continued to own the house in Bloomsbury Square. By now he had given up the property at Swaythling.

Martin, who turned 26 during 1770, lived at Bloomsbury Square, and at that time the interest which he had previously devoted to politics and the law was to a large extent transferred to Cassandra, the youngest daughter of Sir Edward Turner, 2nd Baronet, of Ambrosden. Hawke's Catharine had found it difficult to express herself fully in matters of the heart, but Martin's future wife suffered from no such impediment. For example, when staying at Sunbury in the summer, she took up the pen on 13 July and conveyed to her beloved, who was presumably at Bloomsbury Square, the state of her sentiments as follows: 'I, unexampled by the trivial past of my sex; I, steering carefully from splitting on that rock, which shipwrecks the happiness of too many married pairs, shall differ from the unamiable character of a modern wife. My sole happiness will be centred in the domestic scene.'

It may not come as a surprise to learn that Cassandra, while living up to her promises of devotion, also found it possible in due course to write a novel which was published in 1788 under the title of *Julia de Gramont.*

On 28 August the Admiral — on the eve of the Falklands crisis — gave careful thought to the matter of a wedding present and wrote the following specification for a coachbuilder named John Wright: 'To make a handsome large coach of the best materials, with two glasses in front, to be lined with superfine light-coloured cloth… The springs to be gilt. The mouldings to be very neate and to be gilt… All the brass work to be very handsome. To be painted and varnished in the best and newest manner of the Devonshire colour, as it is call'd, and the Arms to be done very neately.'

Wright, who kept within his estimate of £135, seems to have delivered the coach to the Admiral on 5 February 1771. On the next day Martin married his Cassandra and they made their home at Bloomsbury Square.[505]

Later in the year Hawke wrote from Sunbury to give Martin news of his brother, Major Edward. 'Ned is come home, fat, jolly, and good looking. I thank God he appears to be what I would wish him. We were able to see his regiment reviewed on Hounslow Heath. It made a fine appearance, being a very fine body of men… Sir Jeffrey [Amherst?] was very pleased with all that Ned had done for the regiment.

'I suppose you know that poor Holburne is dead.'

After a month at the Admiralty, Sandwich had removed Holburne from the Board by the tactful device of making him Governor of Greenwich Hospital, and his seat was swiftly taken by the Honourable Augustus Hervey.

Meanwhile Hawke was well cared for by Miss Birt and had his daughter Kitty living with him, but he had been occasioned

---

[505] H.P.P. Receipts and bills; Cassandra Turner to Martin H., 13 July 1770.

further concern by Chaloner, as is sufficiently indicated by a letter from the said Chaloner to Hawke's banker, Mr. Henton Brown. 'Enclosed is an exact list of my debts — the Sum is large, but I hope my future behaviour will convince my father and friends I am not unworthy of their favour.

'I have deserted my old companions, attending my business, and am taking and will take every step in my power to retrieve the follies I have been guilty of.'[506]

After due reflection, Hawke put Chaloner into a regiment as a Cornet and by 1774 he was in Madras, to all appearances fully occupied in serving British interests in that place.

Meanwhile, on 2 October 1773 a tragic hunting accident had caused the death of the Admiral's second son, Edward, who at the age of 26 had risen to the rank of Lieutenant-Colonel. This was a bitter affliction for Hawke. Fortunately he was able to derive consolation from the fact that he now had a grandchild. Cassandra had brought forth a daughter, named Cassandra Julia, on 16 January 1772; and on 3 May 1774 she presented Martin with a son and heir, who was very suitably named Edward. Hawke had now made over to Martin a family estate at Scarthingwell in Yorkshire, and, after visiting the young family there, the Admiral wrote on 21 December to Martin: 'I suppose little Cass will have forgot her grandpapa by the time she sees him again, for she had almost forgot me the last time she saw me. I hope little Brother will have a better memory, if I should live to see him so old.'[507]

The time was at last approaching when political commitments would allow the award of one or two peerages to

---

[506] H.P.P., H. to Martin, 3 Aug. 1771; bills; Chaloner to H. Brown, about 9 Nov. 1768. N.R.S.: Sandwich Papers, i, xv. Charnock, v, 41.
[507] *Burke's Peerage*, 1959 and A. Collins, *Peerage of England*, 1812. H.P.P., H. to Martin, 21 Dec. 1774.

faithful and distinguished servants of the state, although this was not apparent to George Selwyn while he wrote on 11 October 1775 to the Earl of Carlisle. He referred to George III's promises of peerages, made as political inducements, and went on:

> I suppose if he fulfilled all his engagements on that score, there would be an addition to the House of Lords equal to the present number.
>
> Ergo, if I was King, I should expunge the whole debt and begin *nouveaux frais*. I think that I should have an answer ready to make my Minister against these promises. I should tell him if my affairs required a Sir G. Hawke or whom you please to be made a peer, it should be, *sur le champ*, but I would not be hampered by engagements.

Perhaps similar desires occurred from time to time to the mind of the King. Although he could not have seen the slightest political advantage in so doing, he made Hawke a Baron on 20 May 1776.

It was for Hawke to select the place to be attached to his title. He chose to be Baron of Towton, in memory of his wife — for he had ascertained that Catharine's forebears, the Hammonds, had for long been recognized as lords of the manor of Towton, Yorkshire. Before the end of May, four brass coronets were affixed to the roof of his town carriage, and on each side two coronets were painted 'with pearls'. The body and wheels of the carriage were given a fresh coat of green paint and the edges and corner pieces of the body were gilded.[508]

---

[508] Roscoe and Clergue, p. 99. H.P.P. 'Hawke MSS., 1702-1800', f. 122; bills, 25 May 1776.

Hawke wrote to Martin on 29 August 1776 commending him for his improvements to the Scarthingwell property. He himself had not been well. 'I have been so much teazed with my disorder that I have scarce been able to sit down to write.' He referred to the American War which was now in full swing, with the brothers Howe commanding the British Army and Navy respectively. 'I must own', wrote Hawke, 'I had some charity for the Americans before they attacked the private property of the people of this country, but now they have had the assurance to do that, I think every man in Great Britain should be against them.'

Although the Navy had been his university and he never made any display of his intellectual interests, the Admiral did in fact read a very fair number of books on serious subjects. When at the Admiralty he bought several volumes on such matters as discoveries, political history, and astronomy. During 1768-9, he acquired numerous dictionaries, atlases, and charts (including such unfashionable coastlines as those of Africa and 'Russia in Asia'). In 1769, he purchased a copy of *Discoveries in the South Seas*; and altogether it is reasonable to conclude that his interest in Cook's voyage, in particular, was active and informed. After 1771 Hawke's interest in reading was much stimulated through conversation and correspondence with Martin.

The year 1776 was not free of domestic tribulations. The Admiral was anxious because Kitty showed marked signs of illness, but no satisfactory diagnosis was ever achieved of what appears to have been basically a mental disorder. Thus in his letter to Martin of 29 August he mentioned that Kitty, who had been away from home, was now back with him at Sunbury and continued: 'I think upon the whole she mends, and by the blessing of God I hope in time she will come properly to herself.' Seeing that Chaloner had returned from India at the beginning of the year, it will come as no surprise to learn that he was also making demands on the Admiral's earnest attention. There is every indication that, basing his operations on Bloomsbury Square, 'the Cornet' was again delighting in the activities of a young man about town; and as a logical step towards a general enhancement of life, he sounded his father's willingness to buy him a lieutenant's commission. He aspired, as he hopefully informed the Admiral, to 'be loved and respected in the Corps... and should you hereafter be able to promote me, I will continue to do honour to every favour you confer on me'.[509]

On 10 July Hawke doubtless hoped that this subject was closed when he wrote to the effect that he had already been put to sufficient expense in settling the gallant Cornet's debts.

Chaloner, however, was a resilient tactician, and on 18 July he was writing from Manchester, to which place he had gone with his regiment. Before returning to the attack, he sought to restore a completely peaceful atmosphere. He therefore professed entire acceptance of his father's attitude. What could possibly be more reasonable than what his good parent had said? 'In regard to unnecessary things', he continued, 'I have only a servant and my horses are going to grass.' For all he knew, others might assert the contrary; but he maintained that he had nothing else to finance, 'either *male* or *female*'. He concluded, no doubt sincerely enough, 'My love attends Miss Birt'.

The softening-up stage having been completed, 7 August marked the resumption of the offensive. Chaloner wrote that he was staying with Lord Adam Gordon at Preston Hall, near

[509] H.P.P., H. to Martin, 29 Aug. 1776; bills; H. to Martin, 27 Jan. 1776; Chaloner to H., n.d. (1776).

Edinburgh, and passed on to the Admiral the said Lord Gordon's opinion that the Cornet should consult his father about a lieutenancy in the Guards. 'I know', Chaloner tactfully remarked, 'your Lordship has objections to the Guards.' However, he hoped that Lord Gordon's advice would commend itself to his father.

But Chaloner appears to have overlooked that he was dealing with a formidable strategist who also possessed the highest tactical qualities. His new advance was immediately repulsed. Even then, he seems to have clung to a lingering recurrence of hope, and on 14 September he edified his father with evidence of his interest in Scottish society. 'The women… are very open and artless. The freedom of their manners resembles much of the French, and I think they have an ease which I think our own Beauties on this side Tweed generally want.' This sally having produced no very enthusiastic response from the direction of Sunbury, Chaloner wrote on 10 October, asking if he could go out to America to serve under General Howe. He said that was very sorry to hear that his father had been suffering from his disorder. He added pathetically: 'But perhaps, my Lord, the same unfortunate fatality that has hitherto thrown a gloom over all my actions may still represent me as insincere.'[510]

Hawke never lacked an underlying affection for Chaloner, as was shown by his reaction to his son's death when it occurred during the following year. However, he rightly resisted all Chaloner's attempts to impose upon him; and apparently he did not approve of the Cornet's wish to go to America. That the Admiral had been closely following the campaigns in that country is indicated by the fact that in September he had bought for £6 7s. 6d. 'an American Atlas, with additions and

[510] H.P.P., Chaloner to H., 18 July, 7 Aug., 14 Sept., 10 Oct. 1776.

sundry other plans'; and on the 26th he wrote to Martin at some length on the subject:

> Everybody is full of expectation to hear from the Howes now they are joined; it appears to me very extraordinary that we have not had some express from them before now. I wish to God they may be able to bring those stubborn people to a just way of thinking, without fighting. If we must come to that work, we have certainly 25,000 effective men at Staten Island, which are as good troops as any in the world, so that I should think there can be no fear but we shall beat them, yet it will be far happier for us if fighting can be avoided.
>
> Your observations in regard to our rights are very clear and just. Happy would it have been for this country if we had let them alone. Indeed an infinite deal might be said on this subject, which is as well let alone, as we can't make things otherwise than as they are, and we have now (as good subjects) only to hope for the best. It appears singular to me, as well as you, that the Ministry don't grant Letters of Marque, and reprisal, to all our merchants, for the Americans have taken several of our merchantmen, for which in my opinion they are very great fools.

At this date, Hawke was on quite friendly terms with both North and Sandwich, and recently he had paid a call on the latter.[511]

In January 1777 Miss Birt wrote to tell Chaloner that his father was displeased with him because of some new debt which had come to light. On 3 February Chaloner penned an eloquent but unconvincing explanation of the unavoidable nature of the expenditure in question. Hawke, who was refusing to communicate directly with his son, drafted on the

---

[511] H.P.P. Bills; H. to Martin, 26 Sept. 1776; A. Chorley to H., 7 Aug. 1776.

back of Chaloner's letter the answer to be sent by Miss Birt. This was to the effect that 'your father… is always desirous of living upon a footing of love and friendship with you'. But Chaloner, for his part, must have 'the honour and sincerity' to adhere to his professions of good intent. The Admiral had 'wrote to Mr. Brown to pay your draft for £36'. Chaloner was to let Brown know the amount of his other debt and his father would settle it. His father, wrote Miss Birt, 'only hopes you will reflect that it is much easier to contract debts than to pay them. He never wishes to distress you but wishes you would recollect you are a single man.'[512]

Martin and his family had spent New Year's Day 1777 with the Admiral at Sunbury, and had gone on to stay at Bloomsbury Square for a few months. It was at this time that a forgotten figure suddenly rose up from the Admiral's past. On the morning of 18 February he opened a bulky-looking letter which had been delivered at the house. The address was written in a familiar hand, though one that Hawke had not seen for more than ten years. He spread out the enclosed letter and read:

Senegal Coffee House,
St. Michaels Alley,
Cornhill.
17th Feby. 1777

My Lord,

Your Lordship's years increase apace. So do mine. 'Tis therefore time that I should, agreeable to my promise in a letter to you some years ago, lay the saddle on the proper horse and give the public an *éclaircissement*, after the dark shades you threw on my character, when you was placed at the head of the marine department, as unmerited as

[512] H.P.P., Chaloner to H., 20 Jan., 3 Feb. 1777.

mysterious. For, if ever one man served another with attentive integrity, fidelity and disinterestedness, I did you; and had anyone questioned my conduct, I should never have looked for other means of justification than an appeal to your Lordship. However, since a continued neglect renders it now (having the world to begin again at near 70 years of age) absolutely necessary that I should publish a comparative view of your Lordship's conduct and mine, from the year 1747 to 1762, as I abhor strangling as a mute, I scorn stabbing in the dark like an assassin, I shall send your Lordship from time to time copies of a series of letters, which I shall begin to publish, signed with the name J. Hay, sometime next week. As these letters will contain facts, the style will be simple and unembellished.

To this is subjoined a sketch of one from,

Your Lordship's most devoted, faithful servant, as ever,

J. Hay.

Enclosure.

In the year 1758, when your Lordship was detached with six sail of the line and three frigates to scour the French coast in the bottom of the bay and prevent any succor sailing for Louisbourg, then intended to be beseiged, you will remember that after getting as far as the mouth of the Charente in the evening, about three o'clock next morning, the squadron lying to, the report of two or three guns was heard to leeward. Your Lordship was immediately acquainted by the proper officer; but, not getting up or giving any orders, I rose and came down to the side of your cott and beged you to come on deck, for it was probable the guns had been fired from the very ships we were in quest of. In consequence you came up, gave orders to prepare for clearing ship and coming to action. Being very dark and day break at some hours distance, amongst various subjects of conversation you at last addressed me to this effect, 'You know the world say, you are admiral;[513] now I beg, as there is a probability of coming to action, that you would leave me to myself today.' I readily answered, 'With all my heart. In the mean time let us have some coffee.' During breakfast the different manners of attack, either in the offing or at anchor before the isle of Aix, were fully discussed, in so much that I thought no risque would be run in leaving you to yourself. In consequence, after chasing the convoy with the transports destined to carry about 3,000 troops to Louisbourg with no other success than one of the latter being burnt by one of our frigates, when you hauled up to enter the Charente in order to attack the five French ships of the line, I asked the surgeon to retire to backgammon with me, till there should be occasion for us in the Cockpit. He complyed, and we went down. During the flood, the wind veered and proved bafling. It no sooner began to ebb than a fair and strong breeze came in from sea. Upon this auspicious change you retired below with the Captain, Taylor, of infamous memory. In a little time, Williamson, the master, came down to me growling that all would be ruined if I should not immediately come up. For there was not sail upon the ship half sufficient to carry the squadron as far as the enemy before night. Him I huffed and bid him mind his own duty, or apply to the Captain. After him came down Lieut. Johnston with a like tale and was sent away in the same manner. At last, as he has told me an hundred times, Capt. Bennet, for I was then so confounded that I minded neither persons nor other things, and told all would be entirely lost if I did not repair on deck. On this I flung down box and dice, and ran up and enquired first for the admiral and then for the captain. Being answered, 'They are below', I ran down to the great cabin, where I found your Lordship in the starboard quarter gallery looking at the enemy through a spy-glass and Capt. Taylor in its door way with an albow on each post, as if

---

[513] 'In another letter will be assigned the reasons of my requiring the title of admiral and unanswerable proof given of its being owing to neither word or deed of mine, but solely to your own conduct.'

intentionally keeping you in. I rudely passed him [and] passionately asked you why more sail had not been set on the ship. The then situation sufficiently apologizes for the abruptness of the question. You answered that you had ordered it! I replyed, 'To whom gave you these orders?' 'To the captain.' 'Then they have not been complyed with.' Up you went and found true what I had said. You ordered immediately, tho' too late, more sail and a general chace, and particularly threw out the signals for the two sternmost ships to chase. As the general signal happened to be fixed abaft, Mr. Keppel in the *Torbay*, the leading ship, could not possibly see it, and therefore could not comply with it, and so jog'd on easily as before. But when the *Chichester* and *Medway*, in obedience to it, came abreast of the *Ramilies*, your heart shrunk and you asked me if it was not too dangerous to let these two weakest ships go in first and if it would not be better to haul in their signals. I beged, prayed, conjured you to suffer them go on. In spite of all I could say, you hauled in their signals, and then, trembling with passion, I left the deck. In consequence of these delays you got not in till dusk, when the flood was made, which carryed the enemy to the mud by isle Madame, where they lay safe during the night, and in the morning got up to Rochefort.

At night there happened a pretty smart altercation between your Lordship, Capt. Taylor and me concerning the infamous manoeuvres of the day. Next morning, you both fairly owned that you were in the wrong, and beg'd no more might be said on the subject. I acquiesced; but as I was sensible the lookers on would not be silent, to prevent their clamors having any effect at home, and in consequence your being brought before a court-martial — luckily for you, I recollected, or found in your orders, that a fire-ship had been included in the squadron, but had been left behind to come out with Capt. Campbell. So I boldly wrote to the Board[514] that the ships of

> the enemy had been drove on the mud, but escaped on the flood next morning, when if you had had with you the fireship, some of them at least might have been destroyed. In your register of letters you will find Lord Anson's answer, in his own hand writing, expressing his sorrow and regret that the fireship had been detained, since she might have been of so essential utility.
>
> To be continued to the third day, when the *Chichester* stranded on a bank owing to your etc.

This skilfully compiled travesty of the Basque Roads attack testifies to Hay's literary and other qualities. However, the Admiral, if annoyed, was not to any great extent disconcerted. On 19 February he wrote to Martin:

> I send you enclosed a most infamous, impudent letter, as likewise a villainous charge which I received with it, yesterday morning, from that wicked fellow Hay, wherein he accuses me of a number of bare falsities of doing and saying things which I give you my faith and honour I never did, nor even ever thought of doing anything like it, to the truth of which I can safely take my oath. I send them for your perusal, and beg you will turn this affair in your thoughts, in order to advise me what will be the proper steps to take upon it. If you shall think right, Tomlinson, I dare say, would come to you; as he has heard a good deal of these kinds of affairs, perhaps his advice may be of some use…
>
> I have now a bond of that wicked fellow's for £500 which 1 have had this twelve years, which is in the custody of Mr. Chorley [Hawke's solicitor]…

---

[514] 'Your Lordship never dictated a single sentence of a public letter while I was with you, except at the request of Admiral Harrison and Sir John Moore, making me spoil the letter of the 14 Oct. 1747.'

P.S. This fellow is drove to his last shifts by his wicked course of life, and wants to get a good sum of money if possible.

Tomlinson had maintained a connexion with Martin for some years before this. Martin himself, of course, had been trained in the law. However, there is no evidence to show whether or not Hay was brought before the courts. At this point, the ex-secretary sinks back into the obscurity from which Hawke had so mistakenly raised him in 1747.[515]

Even at this date Hawke maintained contact with the local politics of Portsmouth, which had of late become much more lively than before. Although the borough had for long remained in the Admiralty's pocket, a vigorous opposition arose in the Corporation during the 1770's, and Hawke had friends amongst the independents. The Admiral had continued to be one of the constituency's M.P.s until he was raised to the peerage. He was then made an honorary member of the Corporation. From 1774 onwards, the Government, incensed at the Corporation's attempts to free itself from ministerial control, found pretexts for getting rid of the leading independents. Sir John Carter, member of a family well-known to Hawke, was elected Mayor in 1772; but in 1774 his right to call himself a Burgess was challenged by the Government faction. The courts ruled against Carter on the ground that the Aldermen of the Corporation could elect only those who were 'fit and necessary' as Burgesses, and that Carter did not meet this requirement because at the time of his election he had been aged 5 years and 10 months! The independents — who, incidentally, opposed the Government's policy in America —

515 H.P.P., H. to Martin, 19 Feb., enclosing Hay to H., 17 Feb. 1777. N.R.S., *Tomlinson Papers*, pp. 85-6.

were quick to respond in kind. Soon, they succeeded in ousting a number of Burgesses belonging to the Ministerial faction; and, before long, there was a formidable casualty list on either side. By 1775, only four Aldermen were left in the Corporation, namely Messrs. William Carter and White (independent) and Linzee and Varlo (Government). At the beginning of 1777 a friend wrote to Hawke with news of a case, presumably concerning an election of Burgesses, where Lord Mansfield had passed judgement in favour of Carter and White with whom Hawke was in sympathy. But the Mayor had to be elected by the Aldermen and the deadlock between the latter, who were two against two, was not resolved until 1782. By then Linzee and Varlo had been removed from the scene by death, and in any case Lord North's Government had been replaced by Lord Rockingham's.[516]

On 17 September the Admiral's hopes of an eventual reformation in Chaloner's character were abruptly shattered. As the *Gentleman's Magazine* put it, on that day 'the Hon. Mr. Hawke, son of Lord Hawke, was most unfortunately killed by his horse running him against the shafts of a chaise, one of which penetrated his body, so that he died on the spot'. Chaloner, like his brother Edward, had died at the age of 27. The fact that he had found it difficult to live with Chaloner 'upon a footing of love and friendship' did nothing to lessen Hawke's distress. It was said that the Admiral's health never recovered from this shock and that 'his paternal feelings were so deeply affected by that unhappy event that it was some time before he could prevail upon himself to see company'.[517]

---

[516] Lake Allen, *The History of Portsmouth*, 1817, pp. 104-8. Murrell and East, pp. 409-10. H.P.P., G. Goodenough to H., 25 Jan. 1777.

[517] *Gentleman's Mag.*, 1777, p. 458. *St. James's Chrontcle*, 20 Oct. 1781.

Chaloner's death caused concern not only to his family but also to his creditors, who soon made themselves known to the Admiral. On 25 April 1778 Hawke wrote to Martin:

> I think it is a long time since I writ to you, which has not been owing to any neglect of mine, but from my not having been able to do it from my late illness, and from the pains that I have felt ever since, which has tormented me continually, in so much that I am scarce able to sitt down quietly for a quarter of an hour at a time to do anything. Indeed, I have been very ill, having had a great cold and cough which, added to my other pains, made me very miserable and lasted a long while. I was obliged to send for Dr. Addington [Chatham's physician] who ordered me to bed immediately, tho' I had been bled twice before he came down; however, his prescription relieved me, and at length I got rid of my cough, so that I am picking up a little strength and getting better, but I cannot shake off my old disorder, which is really very troublesome to me.
>
> I have now paid all the debts that I can hear of at present of poor Chaloner's, which I do assure you has been no small trouble, both to Miss Birt and myself, for we have been the whole winter about it, by people sending in their bills at different times. I have paid upwards of £3,000, besides the money he left, poor young man. I beg you will get your mason to lay a handsome stone over his grave; it is the last thing I can do for him. I will pay for it.

The Admiral went on to refer to the attempts of the Rockinghams in the Lords to induce the King to abandon the American War, especially in view of the imminent intervention of France. (The outstanding incident during these debates had been Chatham's speech of 7 April, opposing such a surrender — 'My Lords, any state is better than despair; if we must fall, let us fall like men.' But the clarion had rung out for the last time. Chatham was taken seriously ill in the House and on 11 May he died.) Regarding these debates, Hawke commented:

> The disputes which were kept up so long in the House of Lords with so much acrimony and ill-nature has quite made me sick of Politicks, a subject I will have done with for the future while I live, as I am truly sensible it is a very difficult thing to know who is in the right, or who is wrong.
>
> I expect a visit from my poor Kitty every day, as I am told she has a mind to come. And she must come whenever the fancy strikes here, and I am glad of that opportunity to see her, tho' she says very little…
>
> I am very glad to hear that my little Martin [born on 1 April] took his weaning so well, and that the poor nurse is recovered of her fever. You will excuse me, but I think you would do well not to hurry my dear Cassandra [aged 6] too much about her French, her good sense will induce her to take it by degrees…
>
> My heart is with you. I think it an age since I saw you, and I cannot express to you the joy it will give me should I find myself any ways enabled to pay you a visit.
>
> Pray give my kind love to your wife, and to my dear babies. Kiss them all for me, and tell them how much I love them.[518]

Although Hawke found the political situation difficult and depressing, as Admiral of the Fleet he saw fit to communicate to the King his good opinion of the state of the Navy. The King mentioned this in a letter to Sandwich dated 14 April 1778.

> I have received a message from Lord Hawke to express his sorrow that his health disables him from offering his service, or of coming at this time to Court and of attending in

[518] H.P.P., H. to Martin, 25 April 1777; packet labelled 'Debts of Chaloner Hawke'.

> Parliament; but that he thought it his duty to assure me that, whatever others might from private views declare, that he is convinced a finer or better officered and equipped fleet never was seen in this kingdom than the present. I thought the testimony of so brilliant an officer must afford pleasure unto Lord Sandwich, and therefore have sent him this account.[519]

On 27 July the main British battle-squadron, consisting of thirty ships of the line, met thirty-two French ships of the line at the Battle of Ushant; and the substance behind Hawke's assessment of the British officers is at once indicated by the list of admirals and captains involved. Several names quickly catch the eye of anyone acquainted with the two previous wars. The Commander-in-Chief was Augustus Keppel, Admiral of the Blue. There was also Vice-Admiral Sir Robert Harland — Captain of the *Tilbury* at the Second Battle of Cape Finisterre; Vice-Admiral Sir Hugh Pallisser — of proven capacity in a number of respects; Rear-Admiral John Campbell, who had distinguished himself as Captain of the *Royal George* at the Battle of Quiberon Bay; and Captains Alexander Hood and Michael Clements — both prominent frigate-captains of the previous war. Other outstanding officers were Captains John Jervis and Sir Charles Douglas. Moreover, the Fleet had been in the care of the ablest peacetime First Lord of the century, and Keppel made no complaint about the state of the ships before his battle was fought. Indeed, even after it, in August 1778, Keppel wrote to Hawke and expressed agreement with Hawke's judgement that his senior officers were very good and the ships 'fine'. Yet the result of the action was a costly draw. Not until the end of the war — long after the irretrievable loss of the American colonies — was Britain able to assert any

[519] Williams, ii, 328-331. N.R.S.: Sandwich Papers, ii, 24.

degree of sea-supremacy over the comparatively strong fleets of France and Spain. It has been said that the British officers and men were 'rusty'. Surely this applied even more to the French who had not, like the British, been involved in a colonial war during the two previous years. Why should it be forgotten that Choiseul and Praslin had built up a new French Navy which was good enough to win a strategic victory at Ushant?[520]

If people have at any time been inclined to deny that d'Orvilliers commanded a squadron worthy of respect, Hawke, despite his high opinion of the British Fleet, was not to be numbered among them. His estimate of the situation is clearly put in a note which he wrote to Martin two days before the Battle of Ushant. 'No news arrived yet to be depended on. The fleets must fight if they come in sight of each other… Both fleets are strong and the action must be bloody.'

That the Admiral's judgement remained so unprejudiced and sound, despite his poor health and considerable age, as well as his lengthening years of retirement, is a fact deserving of respect.[521]

On 29 July Keppel wrote to Sandwich: 'That I have beat the French there cannot be a doubt'; but a different picture emerges from Hawke's letter of 8 September to Martin.

> I think this poor Country is going down hill very fast… The Ministry I believe see the errors they have committed, and don't well know at present what to do. It has all proceeded from a want of a proper spirit at first… They should have

[520] Clowes, iii, 415. N.R.S.: Sandwich Papers, ii, 12 ff., for Keppel's opinion of his ships, cf. pp. 266-7. Also, Keppel to H., 11 Aug. 1778 (Burrows, p. 479).
[521] H.P.P., H. to Martin, 25 July 1778.

> relieved Generals formerly, when they relieved Admirals… Lord Chatham would not have borne such mismanagement.
>
> I received two letters from Edwards after he came into Plymouth, giving me an account of the action with the French fleet, which was pretty severe while it lasted. Our ships suffered a good deal in their 'masts, yards, sails and rigging, and had a great many shott between wind and water… Edwards' ship suffered considerably in the above articles… Many of our ships were so ruffly handled in the action, if truth were known, Keppel could not get them together (they were so much dispersed in the afternoon) to attack the French again that evening, and therefore we could not prevent them getting off… [Keppel] is now gone after the French again with two and thirty sail of the line of battle, the finest ships that ever went from England.

Turning to family matters, Hawke went on to say that he had received a letter addressed to Chaloner by a Captain Robert Kirby, stationed at Madras, who wished to thank Chaloner for looking after his natural son, 'Bobb'. Deeply touched by this revelation of Chaloner's kindness of heart, the Admiral had located the boy. He decided that he would himself look after the little fellow and would place him in a school near Sunbury. 'I don't chuse to have him too far from me', he commented.[522]

The disastrous quarrel between Keppel and Pallisser broke out during November 1778; and on 9 December Pallisser — who was in the anomalous but quite common position of being both a Lord of the Admiralty and ranking below other admirals in the squadron — demanded a court martial on Keppel for misconduct and neglect at the Battle of Ushant. Hawke, as Admiral of the Fleet, would in the ordinary way

---

[522] N.R.S.: Sandwich Papers, ii, 128. H.P.P., H. to Martin, 8 Sept. 1778.

have been asked to preside at this court martial, but on 10 December the King wrote to Sandwich: 'On the present very unpleasant business, the public must have approved of Lord Hawke's presiding; I am sorry his health gives him so fair a plea to decline.' Indeed, on that very day the Admiral was suffering acutely from the gravel, as he told Martin in a letter. 'Notwithstanding this', he added, 'I am desirous you should hear from myself rather than from anybody else, if I can possibly make shift to do it.'[523]

Hawke was in any case shocked to hear that a court martial was to be held on Keppel, and his name appeared first among the signatures on a memorial asking the King to stop the proceedings. It was submitted that public order and naval discipline could only suffer where subordinate officers were allowed to make 'recriminating accusations' against commanders-in-chief, and emphasized 'particularly the mischief and scandal of permitting men who are at once in high office and subordinate military command, previous to their making such accusations, to attempt to corrupt the public judgement by the publication of libels on their officers in a common newspaper'. Besides Hawke, the signatories were Admirals Francis Geary, the Duke of Bolton ('Captain Sternpost'), James Young, Sir John Moore, and Samuel Graves; Vice-Admirals Clark Gayton, Sir Robert Har-land, Hugh Pigot, Lord Shuldham, and the Earl of Bristol (Augustus Hervey!); and Rear-Admiral Matthew Barton.[524]

Nevertheless, Keppel was court-martialed in January 1779 but, amid tumultuous expressions of enthusiasm, he was acquitted.

---

[523] N.R.S.: Sandwich Papers, ii, 191-3, 210. H.P.P., H. to Martin, 10 Dec. 1778.
[524] Burrows, pp. 482-3.

In Parliament, the opposition attacked the Government with renewed vigour and the wheel of Bristol's political affiliations completed a full revolution. After sitting with Sandwich at the Board of Admiralty for five years, he had succeeded his brother as Earl of Bristol in 1775. He left the Board. In due course it seems to have occurred to him that, if Sandwich had been admirably suited to the post of First Lord, it was none the less evident that a better man was to hand — himself. But Sandwich proved difficult to unseat. Therefore one might suspect that patriotism was not the sole motive behind a motion put before the House of Lords on 23 April 1779 for the removal of Lord Sandwich from the Admiralty, for the mover was the ennobled Augustus Hervey.

Hungry for information with which to discredit Sandwich, Hervey had been in touch with Tomlinson, who probably helped Hawke to compile his 'Considerations of the State of the Navy from the End of 1766 to the Commencement of 1771' at about this time. On 17 April Hervey thanked Tomlinson for his notes and declared: 'No man can value, no man has done more Justice than I do, to Lord Hawke, and only lament that his successor in that office would never follow that great Admiral's precepts.'

And during the debate in the House of Lords he had the effrontery to extol the list of ships bequeathed to Sandwich by 'that excellent officer, that great and good man, Sir Edward Hawke (now Lord Hawke)'.

But Sandwich, though afflicted by the recent loss of his mistress, was fully a match for Augustus Hervey, and dealt with his assertion about Hawke's ships in the following manner: 'In answer to the number of line of battle ships Lord Hawke left when he quitted the Admiralty, it was not necessary to contradict the noble Earl, or minutely inquire into the state of each respective ship; it was enough to say that they only cut a figure upon paper.'[525]

Although immobilized by gout, Hervey on 26 April sent Hawke a lively account of the outcome of the debate.

> I [wish to let] you know particularly how happy I have been again in the opportunity of doing justice to your Lordship's most valuable name in every respect, when I thought Lord Sandwich threw out insinuations on the state he found the Fleet in, which I forced him to explain and contradicted every word.
>
> We divided 38 to 64 — but *four* of our young and sprightly ones were locked out by having just gone to dinner, and Lord Besborough and Lord Beaulieu did not vote — and Lord Monson came too late — or we should have been 45 — and they had 16 bishops out of their 64.[526]

At this time Martin was in London, propagating justifications of his father's work as First Lord; and three years later, with Tomlinson's help, he produced a small book entitled *A Seaman's Remarks on the British Ships of the Line, from the 1st of January 1756 to the 1st of January 1782*. This was largely based on the earlier 'Considerations on the State of the Navy from the end of 1766 to the Commencement of 1771' which, to judge by alterations to the manuscript in Hawke's hand, was compiled by the Admiral and Tomlinson — probably in 1779.[527]

---

[525] N.R.S.: Sandwich Papers, ii, 255 *et seq*. Erskine, p. xxvi. Cobbett, Vol. 20, pp. 437, 447. N.R.S.: *Tomlinson Papers*, pp. xiii, 40-1.
[526] H.P.P., Bristol to H., 26 April 1779.
[527] H.P.P., cutting from *London Chronicle*, 6 May 1779, about no. of H.'s ships still in service, with note in Martin's handwriting. The copy of 'A Seaman's Remarks' now in the Admiralty Library is inscribed, as a gift to Lord St. Vincent, in Martin's handwriting (29 Aug. 1801). M. also wrote: 'By Martin Lord Hawke, assisted by Captain Tomlinson Senior'.

Despite his natural desire to see that his own work as First Lord was justified, and despite a politically-motivated communication from Rockingham at the end of Keppel's trial early in the year, Hawke remained quite uncommitted to any faction. What is more remarkable is the fact that no personal bitterness arose between him and Sandwich. Thus it was possible in August — only four months after Hervey's motion in the Lord's and six after Keppel's court martial — for Pallisser to suggest to Sandwich that he might seek Hawke's advice on how to meet the immediate threat of invasion. In December Hawke wrote to Sandwich asking whether one Robert Boles could be appointed as a Boatswain, and Sandwich amiably replied that it had been done at once.

The likelihood of invasion was indeed imminent. In June Spain had entered the war on France's side. By 16 August a mighty combined expedition was off Plymouth. Sir Charles Hardy, with a markedly inferior squadron, showed about as much eagerness to fight as an average French admiral of the previous war. However, to the mystification of the British public, the threat was withdrawn by the enemy for no obvious reason. On 21 August Martin wrote to his father: 'The arrival of the French fleet with the Spanish at Plymouth has made much noise, but this day's paper informs us that they are again sailed.'

England's escape from an unaccustomed and disagreeable experience was largely due to the inept direction of the French government. Pestilence and scurvy ran through the enemy ships and the good folk of Plymouth, observing the large number of putrid bodies floating off-shore, declined to eat fish for a month.[528]

---

[528] Burrows, pp. 485-7. N.R.S.: Sandwich Papers, iii, 64. H.P.P., Sandwich to H., 9 Dec. 1779 (bolo.); Martin to H., 21 Aug. 1779.

In the same month of August Hawke made over to Martin more than £11,000 in order to enable him to pay off debts contracted by him with the family bankers. The latter had advanced the money so that Martin could improve the house and farming property at Scarthingwell. Shortly afterwards, the Admiral was offended when it appeared that Martin had deliberately failed to reveal the full extent of his debts; but he soon accepted his son's assurance that there had been no intentional concealment. Martin, having written at length on the subject on 10 October, terminated: 'I hope you will consider this letter as written to explain matters for your peace of mind. I honour, respect, and love you too much to think of giving you offence in any word, action, or letter of mine.'[529]

Although undoubtedly generous with money, Hawke always watched carefully over it and it annoyed him if people did not take their financial obligations seriously. Records survive of some of his charitable subscriptions to such causes as 'educating the Sons of Lieutenants of the Navy' and to the Marine Society. He also lent money to individuals at low rates of interest, for example to Robert Tomlinson and to a kinsman in Yorkshire, Thomas Mosley. On 10 September 1780, the last-named wrote a contrite letter to the Admiral. He had heard from Martin that he had 'given great offence' by being late in paying interest on the loan which Hawke had 'so kindly and readily advanced… at a very low rate of interest'. He admitted that he was completely in the wrong and undertook to be punctual in future. As far as Tomlinson was concerned, Hawke ultimately refused to take any interest.[530]

Lloyd and Coulter, p. 125. Clowes, iii, 443-6.

[529] H.P.P., T. Collinson to H., 6 Aug. 1779; Martin to H., 10 Oct.; Collinson to H., 16 Oct. 1779.

[530] H.P.P., Collinson to H., 30 Nov. 1776; receipt from Marine Soc., 1 March 1779; T. Mosley to H., 10 Sept. 1780. N.R.S.: *Tomlinson Papers*,

Before this date Martin had suffered a domestic tragedy. On 10 December 1779 his wife had given birth to a daughter who had been named Catharine. The baby died on 3 March 1780. Martin wrote despairingly to his father. On the 30th the Admiral urged his son to accept the event as a Christian should.

> For God's sake, reassume your spirits like a man, and submit to the will of God, like a man and a Christian, and repine no longer for the loss of your pretty baby, who is gone to Heaven and to peace and rest, which the world cannot give... To say true, the dear baby had made a great impression on me. I had taken a particular liking to her by Miss Birt's bringing her into my room to me so often, and singing and playing with her, which made me regret her very much, and to shed several tears for her; but God's will must be done.

A further letter to Martin dated 30 April contains a reference to the Admiral's mother. 'I am glad', wrote Hawke, 'you found out where my poor dear Mother was buried. Consider the tombstone and examine it.' He would pay for a new one if the present stone was not 'quite decent and respectable enough'. He owed much to his mother 'for taking so much care' of him. Kitty, he remarked, was still the same. She 'appears to be perfectly easy'.[531]

Although he was now for the most part confined to his house, Hawke maintained contact with a number of the leading officers now serving at sea. The seamanlike if uninspired Geary succeeded, on the death of Sir Charles Hardy, to the command of the Channel Squadron. Less than two years before (in 1778) Hawke had commiserated with Geary on the loss of his wife

---

pp. 87-90.

[531] H.P.P., H. to Martin, 30 March, 30 April 1780.

and had remarked to Martin: 'He won't now know well what to do with himself, having nobody to keep him in order.' However, on succeeding in May 1780 to the chief seagoing command, Geary wrote cheerfully enough to his old Commander-in-Chief: 'I shall be made happy by having so many of my old sea friends with me that I sailed with last war.'

Two of Hawke's letters to Geary were fortunately printed by Charnock before being lost. On 6 June 1780, he exhorted Geary to get onto the 'old station off Brest… When you are there, watch those fellows as close as a cat watches a mouse; and if you once have the fortune to get up with them make much of them, and don't part with them easily.' And on 26 August:

> My good friend, I have always wished you well, and have ever talked freely and openly to you upon every subject relative to the service. Recollect some of these passages; and for God's sake, if you should be so lucky as to get sight of the enemy, get as close to them as possible. Do not let them shuffle with you by engaging at a distance, but get within musket-shot if you can; that will be the best way to gain great honour, and will be the means to make the action decisive.

These remarks are of particular interest in that they comprise the only confirmation from Hawke's own pen of the basic tactical principles which, from the use of other sources, have been ascribed to him in this book. Here is the confirmation, also, of the Admiral's habit of constant discussion of tactical and other matters with his subordinate officers. That there remains so little in the way of comment by the Admiral on his own methods is the measure of his own unfailing modesty. It was this combination of sound tactical theory and effective communication of that theory to his officers that made Hawke, like Nelson after him, so formidable a commander of a battle-squadron. The naval historian must place these qualities in the context of Hawke's outstanding grasp of strategy and his relentless application of a strategic scheme, his attention to detail without detriment to his sense of proportion, and his inspired readiness at the right moment to take a breath-taking risk. When the historian has considered the whole, he must surely wonder whether he has not under his scrutiny the greatest of British naval commanders.[532]

A letter of some interest to reach Hawke from the Fleet was written on 26 August by Samuel Barrington, in his usual sour style. Of Geary, he remarked: 'He is so good as to place confidence in me; and he shall never want an honest, disinterested opinion. He has not lived much in the *wicked world*; and has so little art himself as not to suspect others. He has done well hitherto, and yet should anything happen they mean to lay all on him.'[533]

Ever since Keppel's court martial, the Navy had been torn by faction to a near-disastrous degree. Barrington had refused to take the first command on any station. Keppel and Howe would not serve at all. But it was not merely the court martial, which was interpreted as a matter of the Government against the Rockinghams, that underlay the trouble. Fortified by the growth of popular discontent with the course and cost of the war, the Parliamentary Opposition was now ready to seize on any pretext useful for the destruction of the Ministry.

As late as November 1780 Hawke's interest in books was well maintained. A large number of purchases included Bolingbroke's *Patriot King*, Hurd's *Sermons* and Goldsmith's

---

532 H.P.P., H. to Martin, 8 Sept. 1778; Geary to H., 29 May 1780. Charnock, iv, 186-7 n.

533 H.P.P., Barrington to H., 26 Aug. 1780.

England. On this occasion there was no comment — as in 1759 — on the Admiral's taste in reading, for Augustus Hervey, Earl of Bristol, had died the previous year of 'gout' in the stomach at the age of 55. Hawke's own time was also drawing near.[534]

In the summer of 1781, he had little Cassandra, now aged 9, to stay with him at Sunbury; and on 7 June he reported to her parents the success of the visit. He described her as 'engaging' and said that she had 'behaved as a good girl'. On the morrow she would depart to her school. Cassandra enclosed a carefully written note with her grandfather's letter, including the following passage: 'I am very much obliged to my Brother Edward [aged 4] for inquiring so much after me. I hope he will find me much improved when he sees me again.'

On 2 October Hawke sat down to write what was probably his last letter to the son who, with his family, had been for so long the principal solace of his life. Cassandra had again been staying with him. To judge by one of her later letters, she was deeply attached to her 'Grand Papa'. 'As to Politicks', wrote Hawke, 'I give myself no concern about them, as I look upon myself in a great measure to be out of this wicked world… I am always thinking of you and your family, and am desirous of doing everything for you, to the utmost of my poor power and abilities.'[535]

On 17 October 1781 the Admiral's life came to an end.

The next day, having occasion to pass comment on the recent Battle of the Chesapeake — which sealed the loss of the American Colonies — Horace Walpole found space for a

---

[534] Watson, pp. 213, 227, 229. H.P.P., bookseller's bill, 16 Nov. 1780, labelled by H. Erskine, p. xi.

[535] H.P.P., H. to Martin, 7 June and enclosure; 2 Oct. 1780. Hawke MSS. 1702-1800 f. 152-4.

tribute to Hawke which, though fleeting, was not lacking in splendour.

> The Admirals Graves and Hood have attacked a superior French fleet at the mouth of the Chesapeake, and have not beaten it… Lord Hawke is dead and does not seem to have bequeathed his mantle to anybody.[536]

It was not until 31 October 1781 that Hawke's remains were interred in the Church of St. Nicolas at North Stoneham, near Swaythling. As he would have wished, they have since rested there undisturbed, near those of his wife and the infant William.

Untroubled by the din of change, the broad fields and great trees still surround the church. One enters by the North Door. The confrontation with the Hawke Monument opposite is immediate and abrupt. The motto STRIKE stands boldly out from the coat of arms.

Of the interior as a whole, the impression is of cleanness, simplicity, and light.

The inscription on the Monument resulted, no doubt, from the mature reflections of the Admiral's son, the second Lord Hawke. One notes the sentences: 'The bravery of his soul was equal to the dangers he encountered; the cautious intrepidity of his deliberations superior even to the conquests he obtained. The annals of his life compose a period of naval glory unparalleled in later times: for wherever he sailed victory attended him. A prince unsolicited conferred on him dignities which he disdained to ask.'

What defects should be weighed against these merits? His personal sensitivity amounted occasionally to touchiness; his

---

[536] H. Walpole, *Letters to Mann*, 1843-4, iii, 325-6.

blindness to the motives of tricky or complex characters was sometimes obvious — even remarkable; and he lacked the slightest flair for parliamentary manoeuvre or debate. This is all the known debit.

Here, then, rests a man who won great victories — and who stood for something more. Modesty, integrity, Christian compassion, and the higher forms of courage were marks of his character. On such a count — if he so wished — he could face comparison with any of the great commanders.

LIST OF SOURCES

MANUSCRIPTS:
A. PRIVATE COLLECTIONS

The Hawke Papers:

Lord Rosse's important collection consists of (1) official letters contained in books, and (2) of private correspondence, thus:

(1) Hawke's out-letters, in-letters, letter-books, and order-books.

(2) Hawke's private papers and correspondence; also correspondence of other members of the Hawke family.

The Cathcart Papers:

Lord Cathcart's collection includes the papers of General Robert Clerk — Section A67.

B. INSTITUTIONAL COLLECTIONS

Public Record Office:

The Admiralty documents were by far the most important for this book. Other sources were: the State Papers, Domestic, Naval; the Chatham Papers; and the Treasury archives.

Many items in the Hawke Papers (1) above have their counterparts among the Admiralty documents, and vice versa.

National Maritime Museum:

Microfilms of the Hawke Papers (1) — see above.

Photostats of some of the Hawke Papers (2); and a few original letters to or from Hawke.

Navy Board correspondence.

Lieutenants' logs.
The Duff Papers.
The Papers of Captain Michael Clements.
The Longford Papers.

British Museum:
Additional Manuscripts, including:
The Anson, Calcraft, Hardwicke, Liverpool, and Newcastle collections; also the Bridport Papers, the letters of George Jackson, and the P. A. Taylor MSS.
The Stowe MS.

East Suffolk Record Office:
Grafton MSS.

Bodleian Library:
Montagu MSS.

PUBLISHED ORIGINAL SOURCES:

CALMETTES, F. (ed.), *Memoires du duc de Choiseul*, Paris, 1904.
ERSKINE, D. (ed.), *Augustus Hervey*'s *Journal*, London, 1953.
GRAFTON, 3rd Duke of, *Autobiography and Political Correspondence* (ed. W. R. Anson), London, 1898.
LEWIS, W. S. (ed.), *Horace Walpoles Correspondence*, Vols. 20-22, London, 1960.
MURRELL, R. J. and EAST, R., *Extracts from the Records of the Borough of Portsmouth*, Portsmouth, 1884.
Navy Records Society:
Barham Papers: *Letters and Papers of Charles, Lord Barham* (ed. J. K. Laughton), 1907-11, 3 vols.
Barrington Papers: *Letters and Papers of Admiral the Hon, Samuel Barrington* (ed. D. Bonnor-Smith), 1937-41, 2 vols.

Fighting Instructions, 1550-1816 (ed. J. S. Corbett), 1905.
The Loss of Minorca: *Papers relating to the Loss of Minorca in* 1756 (ed. H. W. Richmond), 1913.
The Naval Miscellany, Vol. 4 (ed. C. C. Lloyd), 1952.
Sandwich Papers: *The Private Papers of John, Earl of Sandwich* (ed. G. R. Barnes and J. H. Owen), 1932-8, 4 vols.
Signals and Instructions, 1776-94 (ed. J. S. Corbett), 1908.
The Tomlinson Papers (ed. J. G. Bullocke), 1935.
SMITH, WILLIAM JAMES (ed.), *The Grenville Papers*, London, 1852, 4 vols.

SECONDARY WORKS:

ALBION, R. G. *Forests and Sea Power, 1652-1862*, Cambridge, Mass.,
1926.
ANSON, W. V., *The Life of Admiral Lord Anson*, London, 1912.
ASPINALL-OGLANDER, C., *Admiral's Wife* (Mrs. Edward Boscawen), London, 1940.
BAMFORD, P. W., *Forests and French Sea-Power*, Toronto, 1956.
BARROW, J., *The Life of Lord Anson*, London, 1839.
BINNEY, J. E. D., *British Public Finance 1774-92*, Oxford, 1958.
BROOKE, J., *The Chatham Administration*, London, 1956.
BURROWS, M., *Life of Edward, Lord Hawke*, 1st ed., London, 1883. Revised, abridged editions followed in 1896 and 1904.
BUTTERFIELD, H., *George III and the Historians*, London, 1957.
CHARNOCK, J., *Biographia Navalis*, London, 1794-8, 6 vols.
CHEVALIER, L. E., *Histoire de la marine francaise depuis les débuts de la monarchic jusqu'au traité de paix de 1763*, Paris, 1902.
CLOWES, W. L., *The Royal Navy*, London, 1897-1903,7 vols.
COBBETT, W., *Parliamentary History*, London, 1806-20, 36 vols.
CORBETT, J. S., *England in the Seven Years War*, 1st ed., London, 1907, 2 vols. Second ed. of 1918 is identical.

Dictionary of National Biography (D.N.B), London, 1908-9.

GERMINY, MARC DE, *Les Brigandages maritimes de l'Angleterre*, Paris, 1924.

HUTCHINSON, J. R., *The Press Gang Afloat and Ashore*, London, 1913.

KEPPEL, T., *The Life of Augustus, Viscount Keppel*, London, 1842, 2 vols.

LACOUR-GAYET, G., *La Marine militaire sous Louis XV*, Paris, 1902.

LAUGHTON, J. K. (ed.), *From Howard to Nelson*, London, 1907.

LEWIS, MICHAEL, *The Navy of Britain*, London, 1948.

LLOYD, C., *Captain Cook*, London, 1952.

LLOYD, C., and COULTER, J. L. S., *Medicine and the Navy*, Vol. 3, Edinburgh and London, 1961.

LOCKER, E. H., *The Naval Gallery of Greenwich Hospital*, London, 1831. Published in 1830 as *Memoirs of Celebrated Naval Commanders.*

MAHAN, A. T., *The Influence of Sea Power upon History, 1660-1783*, 1st ed., Boston, 1890.

MARCUS, G. J., *Quiberon Bay*, London, 1960.

NAMIER, L. B., *The Structure of Politics at the Accession of George III*, 2nd ed., London, 1957.

NICOLAS, L., *La Puissance navale dans l'histoire*, Vol. 1, Paris, 1958.

PAJOL, C. P. V., *Les Guerres sous Louis XV*, Paris, 1881-91, 7 vols.

PARES, R., *King George III and the Politicians*, Oxford, 1953.

RICHMOND, H. W., *The Navy in the War of 1739-48*, Cambridge, 1920, 3 vols.

ROSCOE, E. S., and CLERGUE, H., *George Selwyn: his Life and Letters*, London, 1899.

SALMON, E., *Life of Admiral Sir Charles Saunders*, London, 1914.

TROUDE, O., *Batailles navales de la France*, Paris, 1867, 4 vols.
TUNSTALL, B., *William Pitt, Earl of Chatham*, London, 1938.
WATSON, J. S., *The Reign of George III*, Oxford, 1960.
WHITWORTH, R., *Field-Marshal Lord Ligonier*, Oxford, 1958.
WILLIAMS, BASIL, *The Life of William Pitt, Earl of Chatham*, London, 1913, 2 vols.
The Whig Supremacy, 2nd ed., rev. by C. H. Stuart, Oxford, 1962.
WILLSON, B., *The Life and Letters of James Wolfe*, London, 1909.
WRIGHT, R., *The Life of Major-General Wolfe*, London, 1864.
YORKE, P. C., *The Life and Correspondence of Philip Yorke*, Earl of Hardwicke, Cambridge, 1913, 3 vols.

ACKNOWLEDGEMENTS

I wish to express thanks especially to my friend Neville Williams for his advice and frequent assistance, and to the Earl of Rosse for making the Hawke Papers freely available and taking so sympathetic an interest in the writing of this book.

My grateful acknowledgement is due to the following institutions and their staffs:

The Public Record Office, the National Maritime Museum, the British Museum, the National Register of Archives, the Admiralty Library, the East Suffolk Record Office, the Bodleian Library, Messrs. Coutts & Co., and the R.N. Colleges, Greenwich and Dartmouth. Unpublished Crown-copyright material in the Public Record Office has been reproduced by permission of the Controller of H.M. Stationery Office.

Among the many persons who were kind enough to help me, I wish to mention the Hon. David Erskine, Professors M. A. Lewis, C. C. Lloyd, and J. G. Bullocke, and Messrs. J. D. Spinney and O. Warner. Surgeon-Captain F. B. B. Weston, R.N., and Surgeon-Lieutenant M. T. Inman, R.N., gave valued advice concerning the gout and the 'gravel'. The criticism of Mr. C. H. Stuart led to the correction of a number of errors. I am very grateful to him; also to the present Lord Hawke and to Colonel the Earl Cathcart, who made documents available to me.

Finally, I wish to thank the following publishers for allowing me to quote from the copyright material mentioned:

William Kimber & Co., Ltd. — *Augustus Hervey*'s *Journal*, edited by D. Erskine.

E. & S. Livingstone, Ltd. — *Medicine and the Navy*, Vol. 3, by C. Lloyd and C. J. S. Coulter.

The Navy Records Society has kindly granted me a like permission.

R.F.M.

A NOTE TO THE READER

If you have enjoyed this book enough to leave a review on **Amazon** and **Goodreads**, then we would be truly grateful.

The Estate of Ruddock F. Mackay

SAPERE
BOOKS